DEVELOPMENT AMONG THE TRIBAL AND MINORITY SOCIETIES

Edited by
Sudip Bhui
Mita Sarkar (Das)
Palash Chandra Coomar

GYAN

First Published, 2018

Published by

Gyan Publishing House
5, Ansari Road
Daryaganj, New Delhi-110002
Phone: 9811692060
E-mail: books@gyanbooks.com

Printed at: G. Print Process, Delhi.

Cataloging in Publication Data—DK
Courtesy: D.K. Agencies (P) Ltd. <docinfo@dkagencies.com>

Development among the tribal and minority societies / Palash Chandra Coomar.
pages cm
"This volume is an outcome of selected papers presented in the International Seminar on "Globalisation and Tribal" by learned speakers"—Preface.
Includes bibliographical references.
ISBN 9789351282426

1. Globalization—Social aspects—India—Congresses. 2. Tribes—India—Social life and customs—Congresses. 3. Tribes—India—Social conditions—Congresses. 4. Tribes—India—Economic conditions—Congresses. I. Coomar, Palash Chandra, 1956- editor.

GN635.I4C66 2017 DDC 305.800954 23

Dedicated

In Honour of

DR. MANIS KUMAR RAHA

An Anthropologist, Philanthropist,
Guide, Well-wisher and Sympathizer

Contents

Preface

India within its landmass, has given shelter to a large number of castes and religious groups with varied cultures sects, economy, political ideologies and religious faiths. All these have made Indian society a highly stratified and complex one. Along with these the biological variations are also highly significant. The critical and detailed analysis of all these will certainly provide adequate knowledge and idea about how these are functioning, and for the deep and detailed analysis, what is essential is first hand detailed data direct from the field. The results achieved from the analysis of the first hand data will help the planners to plan development programmes properly and also help the administrators to implement these programmes correctly. In a similar way academicians and the scholars will get clue from these analytical studies to judge whether country's progress is in the right direction or not.

With this idea in mind we have incorporated a good number of articles with varied themes written by the academicians and scholars. The articles we have included in this book, cover indigenous people of India and the problems faced by them, human resource development, anthropometry and health and vulnerable and essential of our population. These are the major themes and under each theme come articles of varied nature related to that particular theme. Ecology, food, nutrition and health, human development, demography, socio-cultural life of the minorities, indigenous population and marginal communities and their role in the development of the country are some of the aspects highlighted in some of the articles.

In this concern interpretation in village and regional levels in different articles of this book, has added a flavour to grasp the actual situations and usher an emerging aspect of development and other issues. Some of the studies also reflect some suggestive measures in nourishing human resources.

This little mission, we believe will enrich the knowledge of the academicians, scholars and the students to understand the real situation at the grass root level and also help the planers and bureaucrats in realising the real problems and also help in implementing proper development programmes.

DR. MANIS KUMAR RAHA (b. 1937) was graduated with Honours from the University of Calcutta and obtained his M.Sc. (1960) and Ph.D. (1971) degrees in Anthropology from the same University. He also completed a certificate course, Management Development Programme for Educational Administrators from Indian Institute of Management, Joka, Kolkata in 1981. Before joining Cultural Research Institute, Govt. of West Bengal in May 1962, he undertook research work in different research projects under Professor K.P. Chattopadhyay, the then Head of the Department of Anthropology, University of Calcutta. In the Cultural Research Institute he served as the Research Assistant and Cultural Research Officer and undertook research work in different research projects like ethnographic study, village study, culture change study etc. in different districts of West Bengal. In 1970 he joined North Western Regional Office of Anthropological Survey of India, Govt. of India in Dehra Dun and undertook research works in different areas of Jammu and Kashmir, Himachal Pradesh and U.P. Hill districts (now Uttarakhand). He also served Andaman and Nicobar Regional Office, Port Blair, Central India Regional Office, Nagpur Eastern Regional office, Kolkata and finally Head Quarters of Anthropological Survey of India in Kolkata. He entered Anthropological Survey of India as Anthropologist in March, 1970 and retired as Joint Director in January 1995. During his stay in different Regional Offices of Anthropological Survey of India, he was involved in different research projects. After retirement he was also involved in different research programmes under Institute of Psychiatry, Govt. of West Bengal and also Netaji Institute for Asian Studies, Govt of West Bengal. Dr. Raha was examiner, paper setter and moderator of Postgraduate examinations and also paper setter and examiner of M.Phil examination of different Universities of India. He was also Ph.D. guide and examiner of different Universities. He was a member of Undergraduate Board of Studies, Calcutta University, Ph.D. Committee and Post-graduate Board of Studies, Vidyasagar University and Member, Research Advisory Committee, Cultural Research Institute, Backward Classes Welfare Department, Govt. of West Bengal. He became President,

Anthropology and Archaeology Section, Indian Science Congress (83rd Session 1996) held in Patiala, Punjab. He was Visiting Fellow of the Department of Anthropology, Arunachal University (now Rajib Gandhi University, Itanagar) and also Dibrugarh University, Dibrugarh, Assam. He is the Life Member of different Anthropological Academic and Research Organisations and also of Asiatic Society and Indian Science Congress. He was editor of two scientific journals and also in editorial board of different other journals of India and U.S.A.

Dr. Raha has published 30 books, 192 articles and 167 book reviews. His three more books are awaiting release and two more are in the process of finalization.

Editors

Acknowledgement

Health, Economy and Development are important parameter in flourishing human resources. Scholars from different disciplines have to make endeavor through harmonizing works in this end. This mission was possible to achieve with a University Grant Commission sponsored National Level Seminar, held in Mahishadal Girls' College, Purba Medinipur of West Bengal on February 2-7, 2012. We express our deep sense of gratitude to the authority of University Grant Commission and also to the authority of Mahishadal Girls' College for their help and co-operation to make this endeavor a success.

Professor Gopal Krishna Chakraborty provide his valuable suggestions to make it more enriched. Academicans and Scholars from different disciplines have made their unique and important contribution to take this mission to a path of success. We are indebted to all of them.

We are also immensely grateful to Gyan Publication House, New Delhi for publishing this book.

Editors

Introduction

I

India is a vast country and inhabited by a very large number of population (1,21,05,69,573 according to 2011 Census). Even with the burden of such a huge population India has made marked progress in different fields. The Government, Civil societies and other organizations are responsible for building modern India with strong infrastructure in health care sector, education, industry, energy harnessing and other concerning fields with the help of the common people.

This country of ours with a tradition of golden heritage, is a developing one. The people here live in different ecological settings like the hilly terrains, vast Gangetic plain, Deccan plateau, islands as well as long coastal settings. These are adorned with rich bio-diversity located in countless ecological niches with valuable biota. A large numbers of communities with distinct physical structure and unique cultures are found to live in these variable settings. A sense of Indianness has made these people of India to stand united expressing their faith on their age-old tradition and at the same time, accepting the modern way of life. Here both tradition and modernity are symbiotically existing.

For better existence, for getting more comfort in life and also for achieving secured future, the mankind makes continuous effort to improve the quality of life. The indigenous population of India are also keen to improve their economic condition and educational status, and so they need sustainable input in this regard. Individual as also community activities in different levels of human development such as access to education, health care and various other development programmes, and also the well being of vulnerable population like children, mother and aged person are essential. Different States and Union Territories are progressing fast, though of course, these indicators of course, vary from region to region of the Indian sub-continent.

Anthropology the science of mankind, helps us to understand about human adaptation, variation and evolution. At the same time, other major areas of application of anthropological knowledge are to understand human society and culture, genetic and environmental components of physical and biological attributes, health, sanitation and nutrition etc. All these attract the attention of the academicians, scholars, scientists, policy makers, planners and bureaucrats. The inter disciplinary approach to understand human resources development, makes any discourse highly enriched with scientific knowledge and wisdom of all thinkers of Human Resources Development. In this book a humble attempt has been made to examine some of these issues.

II

In this book, we have included thirty articles of different themes, Contributors have made their contribution on different topics and view points. Therefore, we have broadly categorised these for proper understanding of the multifaceted problems and issues. We have spread over the articles in four parts, each part having one particular theme though in some articles overlapping of more than one theme is seen.

Part-One (Indigenous and Minority Population)

The tribal people of India have been receiving special attention since the days of British Government. After Independence, Government of India has taken many welfare measures for the overall development of these people. Dr. Mita Sarkar (Das) and Dr. Palash Chandra Coomar have critically examined the role of the British Government in the development of the tribal people, and also to assess the steps taken by the Government of India in the field of tribal development since independence. An attempt has been made to find out whether these approaches are very much justified or there is still possibility of rethinking.

To bring the tribal people at par with the general population of India several developmental schemes have been implemented. Academicians, social scientists and bureaucrats have their own views, which differ from the others regarding the concept for the overall development of our tribal brethren. Dr. Mita Sarkar (Das) captures the diversity of views and approaches prevalent for implementing tribal development. She has emphasized the need for separate administrative structures appropriate for tribal development and suggests the government agencies should work in tandem with voluntary organizations.

Forest plays a very important role in the development of human civilization. From the very inception of their life human being were nurtured in the forest and developed with its resources. Even many communities in the age of globalization and space live in the forest and depend on the forest for all the life support commodities. Non-timber Forest Products (NTFP) are very much important forest resources for the forest dwellers as well as for other communities. At present rapid deforestation, ecological degradation, mining, quarries and industrialization, etc. have induced difficulties in the life of those people. Dr. Swapan Kumar Kolay has conducted intensive field work on the problems and prospects of NTFPs and stakeholders among the Sahariya tribe in some selected villages of Sherpur district in Madhya Pradesh. He has also given valuable suggestions for the improvement and development of NTFPs and other forest products. Side by side he has also mentioned about market reforms, more people's attachment, and alternative programs etc. which are thought to be essential for the Sahariya to reach a satisfactory level of economic development.

The indigenous populations throughout the globe have come to limelight as many members of them are now involved in human resource development, management and also in academic activities. Main problems of these people are identity crisis, ascription of their status for administrative purposes, misinterpretation or less exposure of their age old traditions etc. Dr. Prabhat K Singh and Mr. Jagdeep Oraon have thoroughly examined the status of some of the marginal or less discussed communities in the perspectives of indigenous identities. They have emphasized on the indigenous people of Jharkhand, as they are relevant and heuristic in Indian scenario.

Social scientific approach in the welfare of the tribal people is well discussed and an urgent agenda of research. Population studies, demographic data, land-space analysis etc. are effective to understand these situations. Mr. Brajaraja Mishra has analysed a large amount of data to get the real picture of the tribal welfare. Impacts of Forest Rights are also crucial for the deprived tribal people as also the land reforms act. The mega projects of development are the major causes for the displacement of these innocent tribal people. Especially, hydro-electric projects, industrial projects, mining, sanctuary etc. are in the major focus of the social scientists and planners. Mr. Mishra has advocated for the development of social relations between the administrators and the beneficiaries for the sake of a sustainable tribal welfare.

The tribal development in this era is the outcome of integrated activities of social scientists, policy makers, planners and administrators. Globalization, newly emerging politico-economic force, ecological degradation and some such factors have critical effects on tribal development. Dr. Samar Kumar Biswas through his heuristic vision, has evaluated the perspectives of changing life of two tribes of North Bengal like the Toto and the Drukpa. The Toto are well discussed but the Drukpas are little known. Here the author has made a comparative account relating to problems and prospects of these two tribes. Developmental impetuses to these tribes do not make infrastructure in their persisting development. He has also gone through history of human right movements of these two tribes and examined present scenarios. Community identities and transformation due to various rational or irrational purposes are also kept for consideration.

Our history and tradition have made a prolonged contribution in making of heritage. These are the fuel of future progress and life support for survival. Religion and belief systems regulate our socio-cultural life. The Muslim of India are leading a conservative life style with fully devoted in their golden tradition of religion. Through many interdisciplinary studies we have come to know that they are for maintaining a peaceful social life as well as environmental sustainability. Mr. Hasibul Rahaman has given emphasis on the positive effects of the religious ritual and beliefs in preservation of sacredness of Hussain Dighi in North Dinajpur of West Bengal. These customs and practices keep live a bio-sphere which acts as the lungs of the region.

Empirical and grassroot level research among the Muslim community are not in good number in India. In the perspective of Qurran and evolutionary trends this community is egalitarian in nature. But because of this they are distributed throughout the country, and live in the midst of diverse ecological and economic set up. So gradual changes are noticed in this status. Social, reformatory and other movements, money, polity and globalization, etc. introduce some changes in their age old social structures. Different types of social strata like stratification, social classes, occupation, power structure and authority have also emerged among them. Dr. Rajib Chatterjee has made an analysis of these perspectives in his article. In his another article, Dr. Chatterjee has probed the major problems of development from the angle of their conservative religious perspective and dependence on fate. He examines the situations of North Bengal.

Ecology has had a lot of effects on socio-cultural life of the tribal population of Purulia district. Isolated, dispersed and undulated habitats have created a problem to bring them in an integrated development. Hard labour for forest collection in the lean sessions has made feeble health condition of these people with severe energy deficiency. Dr. Srikrishna Mondal in his empirical study among the Hill Kharia of three villages of Purulia district, has observed that the transformation of their economic life is ardent and helpful to initiate developmental programs to lift these downtrodden people in a standard level. The author has also collected and interpretted to the age old tradition of indigenous treatment system for their survival.

The Lodha, a primitive tribe (now as PTG) of West Bengal achieved have an importance in social science researches due to the outstanding research work of Late Prof. P.K. Bhowmick. These people show marked changes on their dependence on forest due to ecological degradation and stringent forest protection laws. Mr. Santanu Panda has evaluated the development programs like Rashtriya Sama Vikash Yojana (RSVY) for development of the Lodha tribe, inhabitant of some villages in Binpur-II, C.D. Block of Paschim Medinipur. He has given special focus on the lack of co-ordination of these programs between the implementers and target population. People also could not utilize these programs due to the lack of infrastructure. Proper land distribution, more people orientation programs and systematic assessments are helpful for their development.

Part-Two (Dimensions of Human Resource Development)

Teachers of the discipline of Anthropology have multidimensional goals as their subject has been diversified into research and study areas. They should not only spent their effort in class room but also create innovativeness among their students in observing real phenomenon, express the problems in mass media in ushering human resource development. Dr. Abhijit Guha in his article, has added a new flavour and described vividly his twenty five years experiences in university level research and teaching. He makes his movements and contributions through popular articles, news report and has glorified traditions of the discipline.

Agriculture is the main pillar of economy of Indian continent even in the era of advance technology. Introduction of modern technology has created drastic change in the agricultural sector of West Bengal. These techniques are not applied in sustainable or scientific manner and for this reason some anomalies are also found in irrigation and application of pesticides. In their article Dr. Arun Makal, Dr. Abhradip Banerjee, Mr. Avik Roy, Mr. Suman Hazra and Dr. Krishnendu Polley have examined the problems with irrigation, soil erosion, marketing of products etc. Agriculture has become unprofitable against the industrial products, and the globalised market has adversely affected the social life of farmers. They need a series of beneficiary support from government and other voluntary organizations.

Human resources in industrial sector help in growing an economically strong nation; it is the main means to produce ultimate development. Dr. Salil Kumar Dutta, Dr. Dibyendu Maiti and Mr. Avijit Halder have explored the recruitment processes and status of the workers in Gujarat and West Bengal. Workers of West Bengal belong to and are swiftly influenced by trade unions, whereas in Gujarat workers are recruited through the kinship networks. The form and function of the related institutions vary with socio-political conditions in both the states.

Rural society is gradually changing into urban society throughout the world and also in India. Inner features because of the influence of urbanization forces, take urban nature even to the distant places from urban centres. In this concern, urban research is also popularized with its institutionalized nature. Urban administrations (i.e. Municipality) are not ready to mitigate the problems of urban population. Problems like sewerage, sanitation, garbage cleaning, and drinking water are major problems which have come into major focus. Here Ms. Sonali Giri and Mr. Suman Kalyan Samanta have made an attempt to assess the quality and availability of drinking water in the various wards of Midnapore town. They have given emphasis on processing and supply of drinking water to different wards. To prevent water born diseases isolation of bacteria through identification, and also screening of the bacteria are done here. They make analysis of the contents of drinking water and effects of these on peoples' health.

Gandhian Philosophy spread over the entire Indian sub continent with its economic condition, social welfare policy and political ideology. This trend also pervades Manbhum region (i.e. Purulia district) of West Bengal. In the hay day of nationalist movements the people of Purulia district played a pivotal role. These were expressed in socio-economic life of the inhabitants especially those who are influenced. They established Loka Sevak Sangha. Dr. Pradip Kumar Mandal makes an effort to trace Gandhian Philosohy in Purulia district, West Bengal.

On the era of globalisation, no folk society is present in its pristine form. The Rajbansis of North Bengal have had a long experience of identity movements through socio-political uprisings. They are able to enrich their economy with advanced agricultural activities. Their achievement in modern education also help them in getting white colour jobs. They are the nucleus of socio-cultural life of North Bengal. Mr. Ashok Das Gupta has stated their present condition, problems and the prospects on the way to development.

Part-Three (Anthropometry and Health)

A comparison of working hours, fast food consumption and relevant tasks of Caucasian College students were measured anthropometrically and the result have been given in the article of Dr. Arupendra Mozumdar and Dr. Gary Liguori. Resident status also is an important variable in this concern. Alterations of environment reflect negative influence in health status of these college students. They expect that their research tract will be extended in respect to increasing interests of emerging area. It may play some referential role in health education, health administrators and financial matters.

Researches on health cannot be completed without considering the Socio-cultural milieus almost half (49.44 per cent) of the total patients among the people of Nadia district, West Bengal suffer generally in seasonal health problems. This valuable study of Dr. Abhijit Ghosal and Mr. Sovan Chakraborty has emphasized on the uses of traditional medical systems which is intricated with magico-religious trend of their society. Socio-cultural life and rituals also have influence on the people's perceptions.

Prevalence of under-nutrition is not confined as a single phenomenon but is returned as outcome of physiological problems as well as in the individual psyche. Quantification of under nutrition is effective through Mid Upper Arm Circumference (MUAC) and Body Mass Index (BMI). Nutritional statuses vary due to socio-cultural determinants as well as with ethnic variations. Dr. Subal Das, Mr. Satruhan Singh Shyam and Dr. Balram Oraon claim in their article that MUAC will occupy a prime indicator in under nutrition. This study is relevant for public health planning and implementation. Dr. Das and others have made this study in the tribal belt of Chattisgarh, especially on the malnutrition of the Gond tribe which is evaluated through MUAC.

While studying the health situation in poverty trodden rural Odisha, Ms. Anjali Dash has observed that morbidity expenditure in treatment of health problems is also high among the poor, and in this way they have to come under debt. So, health care facilities should be increased so that these become accessible to poor people to bring them as a healthy population. This is helpful to the people for doing more works and also for their involvement in our intellectual level as well as in building nation and make it for better tomorrow.

The contributors from different disciplines have endeavoured some unexplored areas and indicated the dimensions of research what we can find in future studies. Researchers through their empirical studies, have expressed their opinion after some sort of literature review or by following one or few cut off point or formula with some standard measurements. They have formulated their hypotheses for application and to follow a trend in human resource development. Health economics, funding in health care programs, financing in health researches are newly emerging areas which get importance to health planners from government and civil society levels. Bio-social researches among the tribal communities are not frequent and not regularly done in Anthropology and other interdisciplinary subjects. There is a fatal gap between collections of health related data of the tribal population and implication on the welfare of them. A more frequent research may create a thrust to review policy level decisions, increasing rate of funding in health researches, grass root level systematic observation and participation in bringing an effective phase in health care services of down trodden. Obesity plays an important role in physiological function of human body and also determines health behaviours. Anthropometric measurements, waist circumference and conicity index are used in Mr. Chandra Sekhar Roy, Dr. Ashish Mukhopadhyay and Dr. Mithu Bhadra's study to describe age variation among the adult male population of a village of North 24 Parganas district, West Bengal. They come to a wonderful conclusion on ageing.

Evaluation of nutritional status is an important aspect in the study of Anthropology. Dr. Kaushik Bose, Dr. Bigitendriya Debsharma and Dr. Subal Das in their cross-sectional study, have discussed the prevalence undernutrition using two different variables Mid Upper Arm Circumference (MUAC) and Body Mass Index (BMI). Dr. Bose and others have undertaken the study among adult male population of Munda and Oraon Tribes of Paschim Medinipur District, West Bengal.

Part- Four (Vulnerable and Essential of Our Populations)

Demographic variables of our society are vital to assess the socio-cultural milieus as well as health conditions of common people. Children and women are potential in strengthening entire health care services in the society. Geriatric researches in India are still in demand for the purpose of framing policies and programs at the community level. Biological studies on the capabilities of old age persons gradually reflect interesting conclusions which is effective to take clinical measures, domestic supports and protections from health problems.

Mother-child health issues are eternal factor of human society. Economic status and health care infrastructure play a crucial role to determine health status of the people, where mother and child health are in the most vulnerable point. Mothers of the basin of the river Balason start their motherhood at an early age. Low income induced under-nutrition is prevalent among them and remain in an important factor for their ill health. Hard work during pregnancy creates a vulnerable condition to their body and also have impact on the health of their children. Mr. Somenath Bhattacharjee in his mission, interprets the interrelated nexus among poverty, social situation and mother-child health.

The current century is the product of globalization. On the other hand, cosmology and knowledge of the world of indigenous society get platform to come forward for an integrated human welfare. Indigenous health care system is recently in central position of with programs and planning. Though these scopes an expanding the area of health care services is made, still studies in this area have unearthed a pitiable picture. Mr. Sudip Bhui through his article, indicates the role of the tribal women as healers in indigenous health care system on the rubric of worldview and cultural domain.

We live in our socio-cultural as well as in our physical environment. The structure and processes in our life depend upon these environments. Our old aged people have with their reducing capacity in subsistence and for regular health care remain dependant on the other members of the society. Instrumental Activities of Daily Living (IADL) to mitigate and induce comfort in life are increasing among the selected population. Mr. Mohan Chandra Dolai and Prof. Falguni Chakrabarty have analysed the differentiation of data of elderly section of the society with age-sex variation and spatial distribution. The minorities of our country get a special focus since last decade. A good number of secondary researches are available on this subject. Sufficient primary field based data are essential in grasping the real situation for their development. Their conservative worldview and community related unity have become crucial for following their future routes. Social stratifications, socio-economic statuses, and other variables in the equation of regional politico-economic circumstances, determine trends and dimensions of development. Researches among the Muslim community demand a unique model for the interpretation of their present conditions and delve out a new line of development programs.

Like the European countries the elderly people of India are also claiming a significant size on the total population. Health and nutritional problems of elderly population has received importance in the article of Dr. Bigitendriya Debsharma who conducted his field work at Chakdah Municipality town under Nadia district, West Bengal. Relevant anthropometric studies, calculating the BMI and MUAC have been utilized for the purpose of assessing the prevalence of acute under-nutrition at their population level. Researchers have prescribed the adult to take nutritious food to prevent the regular decaying of their body.

Flowers should be keep in pleasant environment for blossoming and spreading fragrant. Child labour is a painful experience in our society and alarming to human resources. Poverty compels these children to go for employment, and the hard work further affects their already existing ill-health. Government has made law and regulation to save them but our society is still not prepared to utilize these actions to protect children from harsh situations. Mr. Biswanath Gan in his article, requests the people to become more conscious about the protection of childhood and to take steps in abolition of child labour.

Social gerontology has been gradually expanding its field in the social science research for last two decades. Institutional supports in regulating life style is also developing speedily in India. In accordance with their increasing age they loss their potentiality for normal activities. The article of Sk. Siraj Ali, Dr. Bigitendriya Debsharma and Mr. Mohan Chandra Dolai has examined the social milieu of the very old (80+ years age) people in a municipal area of Purba Medinipur district, West Bengal.

Empowerment, governance and development become effective with the proper participation of individual irrespective of age, sex and class. Union and state governments have launched some development programs with the goal of bringing prosperity among the women. Here Ms. Bidisha Banerjee makes an endeavour to evaluate a series of development programs in perspective of the socio-cultural conditions in India with a special focus on West Bengal. She has recommended a number of complementary interventions in these programs to achieve qualitative progress.

We on behalf of the contributors, place this small endeavor in the way of great strant of researches in human resource development through the above mentioned elements and processes.

- *The Editors*

List of Contributors

Dr. Abhijit Ghosal, Assistant Professor, Department of Anthropology, Subarnarekha Mahavidyalaya, Paschim Medinipur, West Bengal.

Dr.Abhijit Guha, Professor (Retd.), Department of Anthropology, Vidyasagar University, Paschim Medinipur, West Bengal.

Dr. Abhradip Banerjee, Assistant Professor, Department of Anthropology, Government General Degree College, Singur, West Bengal

Dr. Arun Makal, Cultural Research Officer, Cultural Research Institute, Backward Classed Welfare and Tribal Development Department, Government of West Bengal

Dr. Anjali Dash, Research Associate, Centre for Social Studies (CSS), Veer Narmad South Gujarat University Campus, Udhana-Magadalla Road, Surat, Gujarat-395007 (INDIA)

Dr. Arupendra Mozumdar, Senior Program Officer, Population Council, New Delhi, India

Dr. Ashish Mukhopadhyay, Assistant Professor, Department of Anthropology, A.P.C. College, New Barrackpore, West Bengal.

Mr. Ashok Das Gupta, Research Scholar, Department of Anthropology, University of North Bengal, Darjeeling, West Bengal.

Mr. Avijit Halder, Freelance Researcher and Sociologist, Bangaon, North 24 Parganas, West Bengal(Died after his contributions)

Mr. Avik Roy, Assistant Professor, Department of Anthropology, Government General Degree College, Beliabera, West Bengal.

Ms. Bidisha Banerjee, Research Scholar, Palli Charcha Kendra, Visva-Bharati, Sriniketan, West Bengal.

Dr. Bigitendriya Debsharma, Assistant Professor, Department of Anthropology, Sitananda College, Nandigram, Purba Medinipur, West bengal, West Bengal.

Mr. Biswanath Gan, Research Scholar, Department of Anthropology, University of North Bengal, Darjeeling, West Bengal.

Dr. Brajaraja Mishra, Research Officer, Centre for Economic and Social Studies, Nizamiah Observatory Campus, Begumpet, Hyderabad, Andhra Pradesh.

Mr. Chandra Sekhar Roy, Assistant Teacher, Dalimba Jr. High School,Birbhum, West Bengal.

Dr. Dibyendu Maiti, Associate Professor, Delhi School of Economics, Delhi

Dr. Falguni Chakrabarty, Professor (Retd.), Department of Anthropology, Vidyasagar University, Paschim Midnapore, West Bengal.

Dr. Gary Liguori, Dean, College of Health Sciences, Co-Director, Academic Health Collaborative, Professor of Kinesiology, University of Rhode Island, Kingston, RI, USA

Mr. Hasibul Rahaman, Assistant Professor, Department of Sociology, Haldia Govt. College, Purba Medinipur, Weat Bengal.

Mr. Jagdeep Oraon, Assistant Professor, Department of Anthropology and Tribal Studies, Sidho-Kanho-Birsha University, Purulia, West Bengal.

Dr. Kaushik Bose, Professor, Department of Anthropology, Vidyasagar University, Midnapore, West Bengal.

Dr. Krishnendu Polley, Assistant Professor, Bidhannagar College, West Bengal.

Dr. Mita Sarkar (Das), Research Associate, Indira Gandhi Center for National Integration, Visva Bharati, Santiniketan, West Bengal.

Dr. Mithu Bhadra, Assistant Professor, Department of Anthropology, Dinabandhu Mahavidyalaya, Bongaon, West Bengal.

Dr. Palash Chandra Coomar, Joint Director of Census Operations (Retd), Directorate of Census Operations, West Bengal, Kolkata.

Dr. Prabhat K. Singh, Assosiate Professor, Department of Anthropology, Ranchi University, Ranchi, Jharkhand.

Dr. Rajib Chatterjee, Research Fellow, The Asiatic Society, Kolkata & Guest Lecturer, Department of Sociology, Rabindra Bharati University, Kolkata, West Bengal.

Dr. Pradip Kumar Mandal, Assistant Professor, Department of History, Manbhum Mahavidyalaya, Purulia, West Bengal.

Dr. Salil Kumar Dutta, Faculty Member, Department of Anthropology, Haldia Government College, Purba Medinipur, West Bengal.

Dr. Samar Kumar Biswas, Associate Professor and Head, Department of Anthropology, University of North Bengal, Darjeeling, West Bengal.

Mr. Santanu Panda, Research Scholar, Vidyasagar University, Paschim Medinipur, West Bengal.

Mr. Satruhan Singh Shyam, Research Scholar, Department of Anthropology, Delhi University, Delhi, India.

Dr. Somenath Bhattacharjee, Assistant Professor, Department of Anthropology, Assam University, Diphu Campus, Diphu, Karbi Anglong, Assam.

Ms. Sonali Giri, Research Scholar, Jadavpur University, Kolkata, West Bengal.

Mr. Sovan Chakraborty, ICSSR Junior Research Fellow, Department of Anthropology, University of Calcutta, Kolkata, West Bengal.

Dr. Srikrishna Mondal, Senior Faculty Member, Deptt. Of Anthropology, Mahishadal Girl's Collage, Purba Medinipur,West Bengal.

Dr. Subal Das, Assistant Professor, Dept. of Anthropology & Tribal Development, Guru Ghashidas Vishvavidayalaya, Bilaspur, Chhattisgarh.

Mr. Sudip Bhui, Assistant Professor, Department of Anthropology and Tribal Studies, Sidho-Kanho-Birsha University, Purulia, West Bengal.

Dr. Suman Hazra, Research Fellow, The Asiatic Society, Kolkata, West Bengal.

Mr.Suman Kalyan Samanta, Asst. Professor and Head, Dept. of Anthropology, Mahishadal Girls' College, Purba Medinipur, West Bengal.

Dr. Swapan Kumar Kolay, Associate Professor and Head, Department of Anthropology and Tribal Studies, Bastar University, Jagadalpur, Chhattisgarh.

Dr. Huidrom Suraj Singh, Assistant Professor, Department of Anthropology, Manipur University, Manipur, India.

Part I:
Indigenous and Minority Populations

1

Government s Approach to Tribal Development : Some Rethinking

Mita Sarkar (Das) Palash Chandra Coomar

Tribes of India have been receiving special attention from the days, the British Government got interested in them. Though different motives are imputed to what the British Government did or did not do for the tribals, the deterioration of the position of the tribal was largely due to the effects of the system of administration introduced by the British even though the result was certainly not intended. In this case, perhaps, O'Malley (1976) sums up well the position of the British Government Vis-a–Vis the tribes:

The British example goes to show how well intentioned designs can go haywire and even lead to disastrous results, if the same are not properly operationalized and implemented effectively. The purpose of this paper, however, is not to examine the role of the British Government in development of the tribals, as that itself is a subject for independent treatment, but to assess the steps taken by the Indian Government in the field of tribal development since independence.

INDIAN GOVERNMENT S POLICY TOWARDS TRIBALS

In the case of tribals, unlike other socially backward castes and classes, their development was to serve as an instrument to achieve a much larger goal, i.e. their assimilation in the national whole-which the Britishers were criticized for not aiming at. In the light of this goal, it is important to see what policies were evolved by the Indian Government. Policies are considered to be general guides to future decision making that are intended to shape those decisions so as to maximize their contribution to the goals of the enterprise. Therefore, policy formulation is ultimately an intellectual undertaking, in which realties are weighed, sanctions assessed, values considered and the planner attempts to mould a strategy for achieving what is sought. If one takes the above meaning of policy, then it seems that the Government of India lacks a clear cut and pointed policy towards tribals. Not only there is an absence of policy, but the different approaches or strategies adopted seem to be contradicting one another.

The so-called policies towards tribals can be classified broadly into three: (a) no change and revivalism, (b) isolationism and preservation, and (c) assimilation. After certain measures already taken establishment of contact between tribals and the rest of the civilization through communication facilities, education, commerce, government's institution of law and order and revenue, and the spread of the network of development agencies, it is no longer feasible to talk in terms of the first two policies. Technological advancement especially in the field of transport and communication has brought the culture of one community to the door step other. To talk under such situation in terms of "preserving" culture is like living in ivory towers. It sounds rather queer to hear social scientists talk to terms of preserving the culture of the tribals as if these tribes are carrying their "culture" in the test-tubes, or their "culture" is thriving in laboratory-controlled atmosphere.

Coming to the third criterion of assimilation, the question that can be raised here is, Assimilation into what? But before can take it up, let us discuss this policy of integration of tribes without imposition. Here, we will take only the first of the five principles (Panchasheel) formulated by Pandit Jawaharlal Nehru (1959) to guide the policy of the Government towards tribals. The principle lays down that, "people (tribal) should develop along the lines of their own genius, and the imposition of alien values should be avoided". It is a truism that any development or change in order to take place calls for, if no replacement, at least considerable modification in the existing beliefs, practices, customs and, above all, values. This is more so when such a development is planned and injected from outside. Even if one may consciously take all the care to see that one's own values do not unduly influence the values of the people to be developed, what about the influences which are inadvertently passed on. Are we not influencing the values of the tribals by providing them, our kind of education even though we may impart it in their language and through the teachers belonging to their group. In fact, in the absence of uniform values to be installed among tribals, what is imposed both inadvertently and also as a part of calculated design, are the values of us. This brings us to the question, raised earlier, Assimilation into what?

In the name of assimilation, it is generally advocated that the tribals should be brought into the mainstream of nationalism. What does it mean both in abstract and operationable term? Before trying to seek it's direct meaning let us try to drive some implied meaning out of it. The two meanings that can be implied from this are: (1) The tribals are yet outside the mainstream of nationalism; and (2) The non-tribals are part of the mainstream of nationalism. However erroneous it is to think that all non-tribals believe in nationalism. If nationalism means emotional integration, then it has to be achieved by :

- Identification with the dominant group (or group) by the minor groups.
- Mutual give and take of different groups, thus resulting in some composite system or group, and
- Co-existence of different groups but simultaneous acceptance of some minimum agreed common group goals, values, etc., by all groups.
- Even the non-tribal sections of the Indian society are far from such a meaning of emotional integration. Why single out tribes and castes may be questioned about their loyalty. Actually it has to be emotional integration.

Emotional integration does not automatically flow from mere administrative control of a region or from few economic welfare schemes. An egalitarian society and tolerant attitude of the people towards others can only built up a sense of unity among the different people. But tolerance for other groups or people cannot be developed if there is inequality, injustice, exploitation and discrimination in the society: also egalitarian society cannot be developed by tolerance for inequality, injustice, exploitation and discrimination. In fact, in the name of assimilation into the mainstream of nationalism or society, what is believed are : (1) On the part of government, obedience of tribals to its laws, and (2) On the part of non-tribals, into Hindu society. Officials most of them are Hindus-advertently and inadvertently engaged in achieving these objectives in the name of assimilation. Was the so called British policy of segregation not better than such kind of assimilation?

Actually, it is thought that there are some inanimate objects. The policies should concentrate more on development of the tribals - the development for the sake of development.

CONSTITUTIONAL MEASURE

We have provided for certain measures in the Constitution for the benefit of weaker section of the society. Let us see how far these are relevant for development.

Some special provisions are made in the constitution of India in the name of protecting and developing people belonging to some category. Broadly these can be categorized as : cultural, ethno-social, and areal (see Chart 1.1) provisions. Under the cultural rubric, only two types of minorities - religious and linguistic - are offered special protection pertaining to educational institutions of their choice and protection from any discrimination on the part of Government in granting them aid. Thus very limited special protection is offered to religious and linguistic minorities and it is mostly of "educational" nature. Similarly, special provisions and the protective measures incorporated for the backward classes are the most general, the smallest in number and the least in the political sphere. Even between the Scheduled Castes and the Scheduled Tribes, it is the Schedules Tribes who received more preferential treatment at the hands of framers of the Constitution. The provision for the creation of scheduled areas (Art. 244) (1) and the " Union Government's financial responsibility to the states in which there are Scheduled Tribes (Art.275) (1), and the extension of the executive power of the Union" Government in terms of giving directions to a State in the drawing up of plans and its execution necessary for the Scheduled Tribes are offered more protection and aid out of the consolidated fund of India and their development is more under the watchful eyes of the Union Government. These provisions are nothing but the replica of what is provided for the tribals in the Government of India Act of 1935. Should this mean that the framers of the Constitution did not have confidence in the State Governments as far as developments of Scheduled Tribes were concerned? In fact, since there is a provision made for grants to be made available to States out of the consolidated fund of India for the development of Scheduled Tribes, the subject of tribal development is excluded from the purview of the Finance Commission (Art. 275). No doubt, the funds coming from the consolidated fund of India will facilitate quick development but nevertheless the string of Union Government's approval is attached to this. The State Government is dependent on the Union Government whereas had the provision been made part of the

Chart 1.1

SPECIAL PROVISIONS IN THE CONSTITUTION FOR THE PEOPLE BELONGING TO SOME CATEGORIES

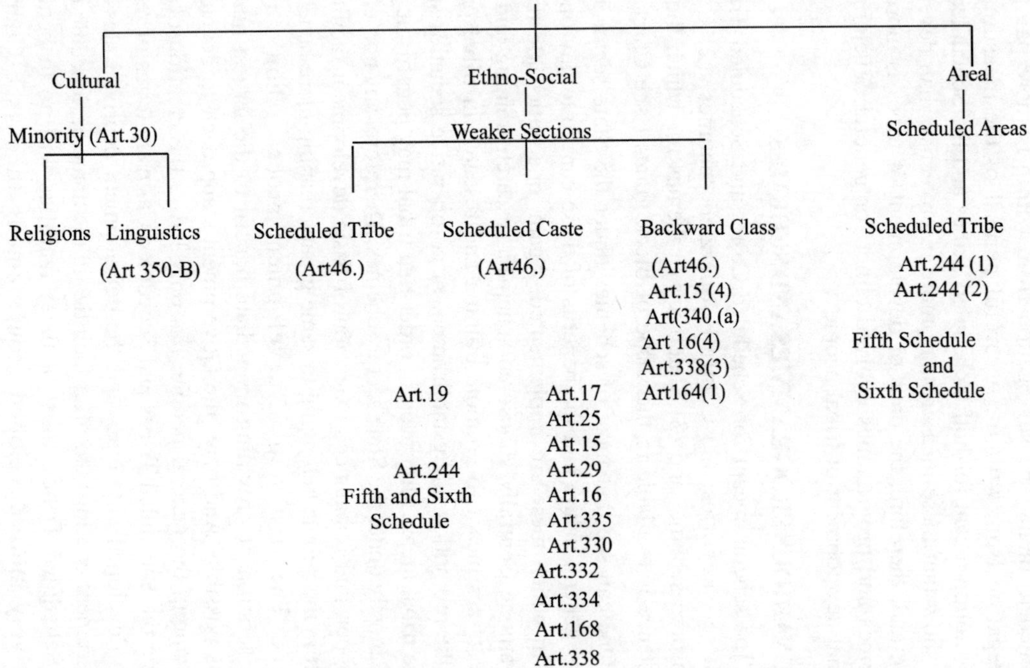

(based on Ghurey's Scheduled Tribes)

Finance Commission's terms of reference, the State Government would have received larger share in the name of the development of Scheduled Tribes as a matter of right. One is at a loss not to see the same protections offered to the Scheduled Castes whereas they, of all the Backward Classes, need such protection more for the social stigma of un-touchability attached to them. The segregation from within is more painful than segregation from without. A careful perusal of the measures in the Constitution meant for both Scheduled Tribes and the Scheduled Castes will show that these measures are more in protective than development sense and, therefore, the onus of development of tribes is more on the schemes and programmes evolved either for general development or special development of tribal people.

THE VARIOUS PROGRAMMES AND SCHEMES

The scheme meant for Scheduled Castes and Scheduled Tribes fall in three categories: (1) Centrally operated schemes, (2) Centrally sponsored scheme, and (3) State sector schemes for which the central assistance is available in the shape of block grants (see Chart 1.2.)

One can see that most of schemes under the State sector schemes are of general nature and the benefits of these can go to any one in the area in which these are implemented. Again, one noticeable feature is that among Centrally sponsored schemes, research training and special projects are meant to promote training and research in tribal problems and the promotion and establishment of co-operative societies specially in the tribal areas. Moreover, in order that tribal may benefits at primary level mostly under the State sector schemes. Therefore, any non-effective, improper, and imbalanced extension of basic development facilities will result in the people belonging to same groups reaping more benefits than others. The first step in development process should involve consideration of providing immediate benefit to the largest number as far as possible. And here, the Government's approach to development, like among the general people, has only led to the creation of classes among the Scheduled Tribes and Scheduled Castes in terms of relatively more developed elite class and the development deprived class. If the Government continues to offer facilities in the name of Scheduled Castes and Scheduled Tribes, most of these facilities will go to benefit the relatively more developed groups among them (see Chart 1.3). Development by its nature, creates classes among the beneficiaries. It is to counteract the ills of development process, designing and implementing of some purely welfare scheme side by side is wanted. Moreover, there should be linking of welfare schemes with development schemes.

Chart 1.2

THE PLAN PROGRAMMES FOR THE WELFARE OF BACKWARD CLASSES

Centrally Operated Schemes	Centrally Sponsored Scheme	State Sector Scheme
		I. Education
1. Direct distribution of Post-matric Scholarship.	1. Post-matric Scholarship	1. Pre-matric Scholarship and stipends.
2. Coaching and guidance	2. Girl's Hostel and examination fees	2. Exemption from tution centres
3. Overseas Scholarships	3. Career Planning and allied Schemes	3. Provision of education equipments
	4. Tribal Development Blocks.	4. Provision of mid-day meals.
	5. Promotion of co-operative Societies especially in Tribal Areas.	5. Setting up of Ashram Schools.
	6. Improvement in the working And living conditions of Sweepers and scavengers.	6. Grants for the consultation of school and hostel buildings.
	7. Welfare of denotified nomadic And seminomadic	
	8. Research Training and special Projects.	
		II. Economic Development
		1. Provision of land and Irrigation.
		2. Supply of Bullocks Agricultural implements, seeds and manures.
		3. Development of cottage industries.
		4. Development of Communication.
		5. Co-operation
		6. Colonisation of shifting cultivation.
		7. Supply of poultry, sheep, pigs and goats.
		III. Health, Housing and others
		1. Medical facilities
		2. Drinking water supply Schemes.
		3. Provision of Houses and House sites.
		4. Provision of legal aid. Grants to non official agencies working at the state level.

Unfortunately development and welfare are running as parallel lines and not as woven net work.

SOME RETHINKING

From Chart 1.3, it will be clear that though facilities from the top are offered to benefit the deprived sections, these are largely pocketed by the relatively more developed sections. The result is that not only here discontent and unrest are seen among the Scheduled Tribes and the Scheduled Castes, there is also intra-class wars – the poor belonging to one category fighting against the poor belonging to the other. Upsurges in Bihar and Maharashtra should be seen as writing on the walls which call for drastic change in the strategies for development. No doubt, there are scholars who are making out a case for equal treatment for all the poor and shedding of the distinction in terms of Scheduled Castes,

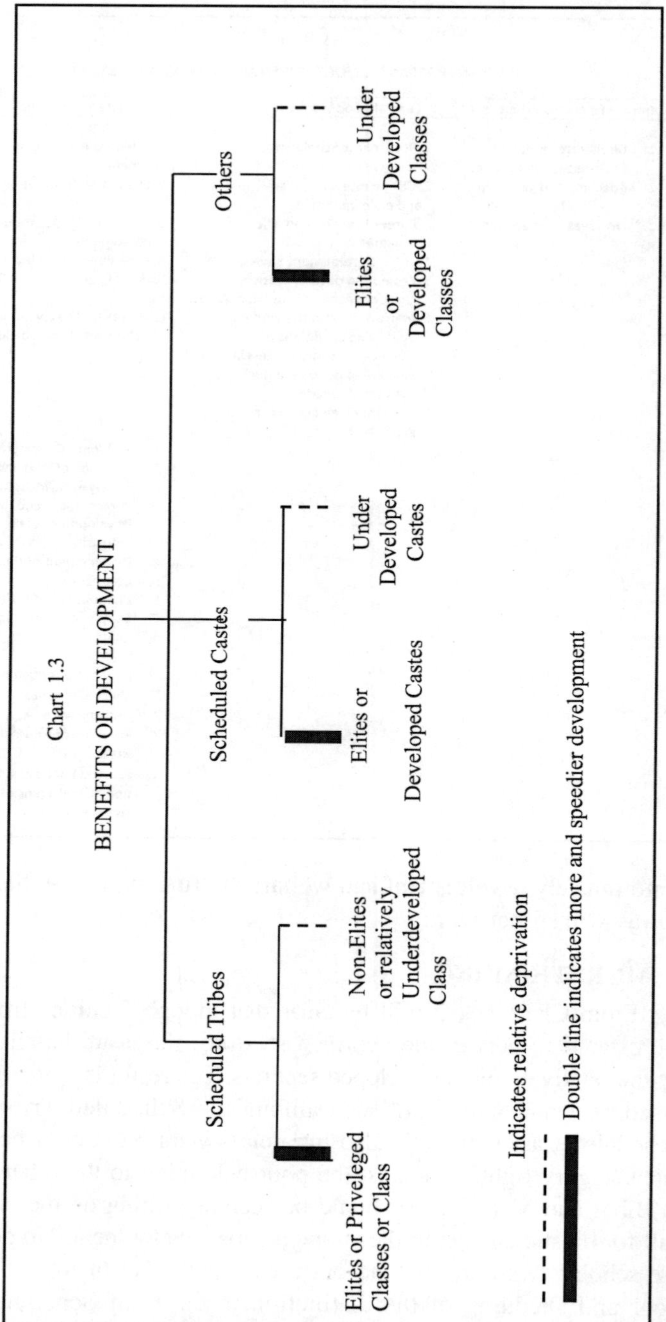

Chart 1.3

BENEFITS OF DEVELOPMENT

Scheduled Tribes and Other Backward Classes. For instance Karkal (1977) opines that :

"The difference in language, habitation, customs etc. alone need not make us feel more sympathetic toward them (tribes) than towards other poor whom we leave to their own fate. Those in sympathy with the Tribal people of a particular area only have said enough (against the injustices done to them by in scrupulous usurpers and landed properties), on their behalf. But this sorry tale is no different from what is happening in many other parts of the country, and to many non-tribal and poor people. The cure lies not in merely getting angry with the exploiters in one's own helplessness or even in taking up the fight on their behalf or in helping in the passage of legislation (and that too when implemented properly), which might relieve them of a part of their burden, but in so devising the means and systems (organization and programmes), that the tribal and non-tribals poor find a redress for the wrongs from which they suffer. And in this, the tribals do not, and should not stand on a different footing from the rest of our poor who need the same encouragement and social education." (Karkal:1977:42)

The reason for taking a long quotation from Karkal's paper is to show the current feeling among some scholars in proper prospective. One cannot help but agree with the first part of Karkal's observations. But in saying that the tribal poor and non-tribal poor be treated alike, we are losing sight of the main problem, i.e., how to identify the tribal poor from the rest of the tribals and the Scheduled Castes poor from the rest of the Scheduled Castes. The line of thinking taken by Pathy and others (1976) in this respect sounds more moderate, practical, and helpful to both the tribal and the non-tribal poor when they say :

"We have argued that since several tribal committees have developed antagonistic classes, and since some other's have remained relatively backward, the welfare measures shall have to be extended with proper caution. And that on the basis of the attributes which are the determining factors for social progress, the category may be reworked. Besides, those communities who have not developed class distinctions because of the predominance of communal economy and the society may be treated as tribes, and should be provided necessary attention. On the whole, there is a need to seriously rethink the terms, "tribe" and "weaker sections". (Pathy *et.al*:1976:406)

Transformation of society from caste lines to class lines is desirable but the process of change is creating class within castes and present approach of development talks only the "caste", the class distinctions from within go unrecognized. What is important is to rework the caste-class distinction into class-caste distinction. Let class precede caste. Chart 1.4 will amply exemplify the order in which preferences in development should be accorded to people belonging to different class-caste categories. This will enable us to identify and group together all the poor belonging to Scheduled Castes, Scheduled Tribes and Others, at the same time affording us opportunity to pay special attention to the needs of the people belonging to Scheduled Castes and Scheduled Tribes categories.

Rethinking on development policy of Government toward the weaker sections in general and Scheduled Castes and Scheduled Tribes in particular should consider the following observations:

(A) A comprehensive policy of development for all those falling in the categories 1 to 15 in the Chart 1.4 be evolved with provision for allocating development policies on the sectional basis, i.e., the Scheduled Caste people Below Poverty Line received the first preference but people belonging to backward classes and living under poverty line get precedence over the Scheduled Castes falling under the "poor" category.

(B) Special tailored policies of development for those who are Below Poverty Line (1 to 5 in the Chart).

(C) The Scheduled Castes be given preferences over the Scheduled Tribes, which is not so in the present scheme of development, especially because of the social stigma of untouchability attached to them.

(D) Among the Scheduled Tribes, preference must be given to those tribes who stay inaccessible areas, living in a primitive stage and are yet to establish contact with the outside civilization.

(E) The process of development should be as such that ultimately the distinctions of the Scheduled Castes and Scheduled Tribes whither away rather than allow it to perpetuate.

The Constitution while identifying certain communities for giving special treatment in development, has to be flexible enough to offer the Government with power to single out those belonging to the Scheduled Castes and Scheduled Tribes either for providing more facilities or for rescheduling them.

Chart 1.4

PEOPLE (ECONOMIC CLASSIFICATION)

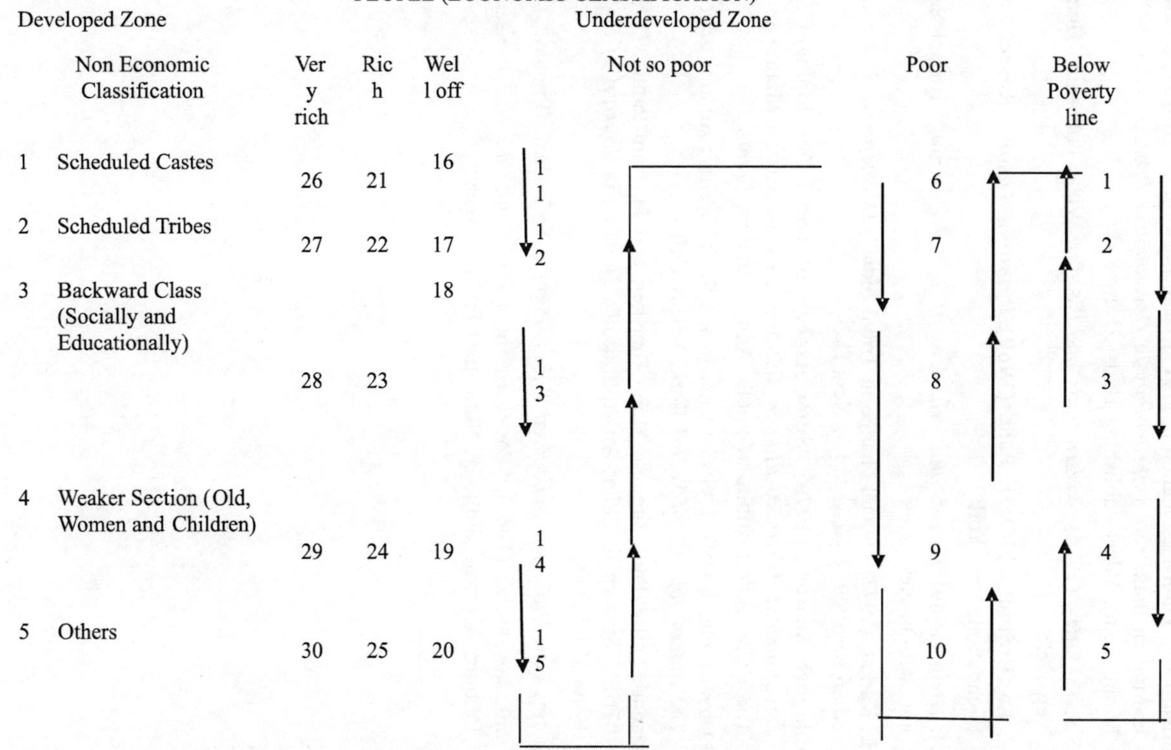

⟶ Arrow indicating relative preference in development in declining order .

Bibliography

Christop von Furer-Haimnendrop, (1977) "The Position of Tribal Population in Modern India", in *Anthropology in Development Process*. Hari Mohan Mathur (ed.), Vikas Publishing House, New Delhi.

L.S.S.O' Malley, (1976) *Modern India and the West*, Vikas Publishing House, New Delhi.

P.P. Le, Broton, and A.H. Pale. (1969) *Planning Theory*, Russel Sage Foundation. New York.

A.J. Khan (1969) *Theory and Practices of Social Planning*, Russel Sage Foundation. New York.

G.L. Karkal, (1977) "Social change in Tribal India", *Development Policy and Administration Review*, Vol.3. New Delhi.

Brahmdeb Sharma, (1976) "Some Aspects of Tribal Development", in *Development Administration in Tribal Area* Hari Mohan Mathur (ed.), The HCM State Institute of Public Administration, Jaipur.

V. Jagannandham, (1972) "Social Change and Social Welfare Administration", *The Indian Journal of Social Work*, Vol. XXXII.

Jaganath Pathy, Paul Suguna, Manu Bhaskar, and Jayaram Panda, (1976) "Tribal Studies in India: An Appraisal", *The Indian Journal of Social Work*, Vol. XXIX.

Ghurey, G.S. 1963. *The Scheduled Tribes*. Popular Prakashan, Bombay.

Nehru, Jawaharlal, (1959). "Foreward" in *A Philosophy for NEFA* (Second Edition), V.Elwin, Shillong, North East Frontier Agency.

2

An Approach to the Concept of Tribal Development

Mita Sarkar (Das)

Development is normally taken to mean change plus desired growth, that is, it has both qualitative and quantative dimensions. It may even say that the qualitative and quantative changes as have been / are being desired may be termed development. This brings us to the question of what changes as regards tribals have been / are being positively valued in our country and are thus, worthy of being termed tribal development. Here, it may be pointed out that, while hopefully both tribal and national development or what is commonly referred to as progress – shall proceed hand in hand, occasions may arise when one dimension of national development may be possible only at the cost of some dimension(s) of tribal development and vice versa. Here priorities may have to be worked out.

Tribal development is part and parcel of the overall modernization process. However, in the present state of the development in the tribal areas, their development process shall currently have to differ from that of the more developed non-tribal areas. Thus, it is hoped that, eventually, the tribal regions shall also become as developed as the non-tribal ones, and then both shall develop further in a similar manner.

It is generally emphasized that tribal development implies (1) development of technology, (2) emergence of new structures, and (3) emergence of new social values and attitudes. Such changes shall have to be carried out carefully so as to avoid destroying the fabric of tribal life until and unless the tribals have discovered new social moorings. Bringing about these changes in the tribal areas is bound to be doubly prone to problems as even the more developed non-tribal areas are having thus undergo numerous small cultural shocks as more and more modernization occurs.

Given the present states, three possible objectives of tribal development exist. One is to isolate tribals groups from the rest of Indian society and to allow them to develop within the context of their isolation according to their own wishes. The second is complete assimilation so that the tribals cease to exist as separate entities. The third is integration, which is developing a kind of adjustment between the tribals and non-tribals. The third appears most appropriate for our concept of tribal development. However, it has to be admitted that such integration may eventually, in the long run, lead to assimilation, but that would only be at a time when no further special provisions for tribal development shall be needed any more. In fact this may be deemed to be a systematic goal, i.e., bringing tribal areas within the main stream of national development, but not at the cost of individual tribals or of tribal groups.

It would be interesting at this juncture to take a look at Jawaharlal Nehru's very relevant ideas on tribal development in the present context. "We cannot allow matters to drift in the tribal areas", he said, and added, "the avenues of development should .... be persued within the board of frame-work of the following five fundamental principles: (1) People should develop along the lines of their own genius ..., (2) Tribals rights in land and forests should be respected, (3) We should try to train and build up a team of their own people ....., (4) We should not over-administer these areas or overwhelm them with multiplicity of schemes. We should rather work through, and not in rivalry to their own social and cultural institutions, and (5) We should judge results, not by statistics or the amount of money spent, but by the quality of human character that is evolved".

The tribal development can be attempted on a specific (piecemeal) basis, or on an integrated (holistic) basis.

In this context tribal development efforts have to consist of a package of (1) protective measures, (2) measures to provide special material benefits to enable the tribals to catch up with the more developed non-tribals, (3) attempts at increasing consciousness or awareness amongst both tribals and non-tribals to facilitate better harmony between the two, (4) measures to ensure personality development of the tribals, and (5) measure of area development of the tribal areas corresponding to similar developments in the non-tribal regions. It should be kept in mind that such measures should not merely be restricted to the Scheduled Tribes, but should also be made available to thedenotified and nomadic tribes.

Now brief spelling out of the measure listed above. It should however be kept in mind that since, in the absence of broad-base of enlightened tribal leadership which is now emerging but at a very slow pace, most tribal development is being attempted through external stimuli and hence workers and administrators in tribal areas shall have to be careful to keep reminding themselves that tribal society is much less complex and differentiated than any non-tribal society which the external worker/ administrator shall himself have experienced. Thus, tribal responses to, and comprehension or perception of, the measure being undertaken for this benefit may not always be what the external worker/administrator may have expected or desired. Special care shall have to be taken both at the implementation and at project formulation stages it has to be sure that the tribals understand and accept measures being carried out for their benefit. Development is not something that can be thrust upon people).

Project Measures: (1) Speedy implementation of existing land reform legislation that safeguards and enhances the property rights of tribals. (2) Provisions debarring tribals from mortgaging their lands. (3) Necessary legislative and administrative action to check land alienation and to restore such land as has got alienated from the tribals. (4) Appointment of special senior level field inspectors charged with implementing protective legislation and to ensure that no corruption and exploitative tendencies exist at lower levels. (5) Licenses may be issued for a specific quantity of liquor to be brewed locally and imbibed by tribals on special ceremonial occasions. (6) Steps to check the prevalence of bonded labour. (7) Legislative action to scale down tribal debts (or even write them off in specific cases). (8) Ensuring that non-tribal is able to make use of minor forest produce in the tribal areas, since this forms a major traditional economic source for tribals. (9) Ensuring that no private contractors are allowed to exploit major forest produce, the regulation of major forest produce being placed in the hands of the tribal development agency. (10) Reservation, as already exists, for tribals in matter of recruitment to government service and elections to public office.

Special Benefits: This could be done through following measures : (1) Provision of credit for agricultural purposes and to protect tribals from indigenous money lenders. (2) Redemption of debts and their conversion into long term loans with the Reserve Bank of India to assist local credit institutions (this, as is stated above, may also be classified as a protective measure). (3) Establishment of tribal cooperatives at the hamlet level, or for a group of hamlets, and the houses in their proximity, through which the tribal produce could be sold, credit and other inputs provided to the tribals, and essential consumer goods made available for purchase at reasonable prices under State government auspices, the Collector to exercise supervisory and disciplinary powers over functionaries of these cooperatives. (4) Assistance of all sorts for land improvement on farm development and soil conservation works to tribals already possessing land or those allotted it. (5) Provision of scholarships and other incentives to avail of education. (6) Evolution of special teaching techniques suitable for tribals. (7) Encouragement of traditional tribal cottage industries. (8) Provision of special healthcare and communications-development schemes since over the centuries tribals have got pushed into the less accessible and more illness prone tracts of land. Care shall also have to be taken to ensure that the benefits percolate all the way down to the tribals and are not siphoned off in between by the already better offs.

Increasing Awareness for Harmonius Co-existence: The various media shall have to be worked out forparticular places at particular points of time so that the message is communicated to the people without it appearing to be sermon.

This effort is to be directed more at non-tribals so that they readily accept tribals, not in a condescending or patronizing manner, nor with a sense of guilt at their own fortunate position, but as equal citizens of the country. Non-tribals, should also be motivated to train tribals in various skills and then to hand over local tasks to them as they become capable of handling such modern and complex tasks.

In tribal areas the effort should be find ways by which tribals can contribute not only to tribal development, but also to national development. This is because of feeling and the pride of having contributed to the mainstream of national development shall go a long way towards giving tribals a sense of belonging as well as confident optimism. Efforts at their involvement in terms of participation, even if only symbolic, are thus likely to go a long way towards providing a healthy, harmonious relationship between tribals and non-tribals.

Personality Development : This could be done through (1) Teaching in local tribal dialects. (2) Establishment of some conventional schools with hostel facilities and special scholarships for tribals. (3) The curriculum to include vocational guidance (as also guidance about availability of scholarships). The nature of the training given – civic, industrial or agricultural – to depend upon the specific needs of the area concerned. (4) The possibility of all teachers compulsorily serving in tribal areas for a fixed tenure before getting a government jobs elsewhere to be examined. Such teachers should however receive special training, facilities and allowances. (5) Simeltaneous use of formal and informal methods of teaching, including the use of folk media, such teaching to be based upon discussion, demonstration and participation, rather than on discourses. (6) Provision for functional adult literacy. (7) Exploration of various factors which could induce more tribals to go in for education. (8) Setting up, as suggested by Hooja, in his paper of at least one polyvalent centre in a tribal area on an experimental basis, where flexibility of approach according to individual or group needs would be a prime consideration. (9) Emphasis on making the tribal think about how and in what form can be contribute to (a) his community and (b) the nation. (10) Encouragement of traditional tribal festivals and group activities without vulgarizing them by turning them into exhibitions for non-tribal tourists.

Schemes for Normal Development: (1) The development and welfare schemes being implemented in non-tribal areas and the minimum needs programme should be equally applicable to tribal areas and, if necessary, special concessions should be made for such areas so as to ensure that the gap between them and the non-tribal areas does not widen. (2) Rural electrification, building of roads and the provision of drinking water, even if less economical than elsewhere, to be emphasized. (3) The setting up of medium, or large scale industries, if the geo-physical and economic conditions of the area are favourable. However, attempts should simultaneously must be made to ensure protection for the existing indigenous industries of the area and to minimize the shock of such modernizing agents. No industry should be set up without considering its impact on the proximate tribal society to avoid a repetition of something similar to the classical sociological example of the death of coal-station towns due to the diesalization of American railroads in the early 1950(s). (4) Efforts at enhanced agricultural production to be increased, especially because in many areas agriculture is a major source of tribal incomes.

While trying to operationalize the concept of tribal development, Anthropologists, suggested approaching the problem from the point of view of the six distinct cultural tribes zones that exist in India, i.e. (1) Anadaman and Nicobar Islands, (2) Western Ghat ranges and Nilgiri Hills (Mysore, Kerala, and Madras), (3) Purbachal, Mehgalaya and the Eastern and Western Himalayan Ranges, (4) Chota Nagpur Plateau and its extension (North-East Orissa, Bihar and Western (West Bengal), (5) Western Ghat Ranges, Dandekaranya and Chhatrishgarh (Southern Orissa, North EasternAndharaPradesh and South Eastern Madhya Pradesh), and (6) Malwa Plateau and the extension of the Vindhya and Satpura Ranges (Rajasthan, Gujarat, Maharashtra and Western Madhya Pradesh). L.P. Vidyarthi had paper suggested that national tribal zones can be set up. It is felt that such national zones could correspond to the above cited six tribal areas. Further, since they would cut across State boundaries, the possibility of such national zones being under the administrative control of the Central Government, with the State assisting it, should be considered.

The currently accepted approach towards tribal development that of integrated Sub-Plans for tribal areas, seems acceptable unless it is empirically proved wrong after it has been tried out. The Sub-Plan for tribal regions is a smaller plan within the State FiveYear Plan in which an integrated area development programme consisting of a project covering an area coterminous with existing administrative units, e.g. a Tehsil or Blocks, has been drawn up, focusing attention of the specific tribes in that region.

As an example let us examine the Sub-Plan strategy as set forth by the Special Schemes Organisation, Government of Rajasthan. Eight points have been emphasized. They are: (1) Additional resources made available specifically for integrated tribal development. (2) Keeping in mind the fact that the resources on which tribals traditionally dependent are getting depleted due to both natural and manual causes, alternatives are to be provided. Hence agriculture has to replace the forests as the economic base of the tribals and agricultural production has to be emphasized. (3) A linkage has to be established between economic development and tribal development. Hence economic programmes, especially in the agriculture, irrigation (specially minor irrigation), cattle, poultry and fisheries development, khadi and village industries, and mineral sectors, have to receive priority. (4) Infra-strcutural development is vital for economic progress. (5) Another aspect of the integration of tribal and economic development is the need for institutional re-organisation. Both the agency for the tribal administration and tribal cooperatives has to be organized anew. (6) Economic, infra-structural and organizational efforts are bound to fail unless a human resources development (particularly education) programmes is perfected. (7) Providing employment to tribals has to remain uppermost in our minds, hence a shelf of labour-intensive projects should be prepared and kept ready for implementation as and when funds become available. (8) Protective measures have to be intensified.

The preparation of a Sub-Plan involves: (1) Identification and delineation of tribal zones. (2) Identification of groups and diagnostic study of their society and culture. (3) Identification of the cultural parameters and socio-cultural barriers as well as facilitators of change and development. (4) Study of the different cultural units inhabiting the area covered by the Sub-Plan to formulate (a) the evolutionary sequences of the cultural traits of each unit, (b) social development processes and social complexities and (c) progressive functional differentiation in occupational specialization and (the) organizational remifications. (5) Assessment of potentialities, special problems and felt needs of the tribal areas to evolve an order of priority of development schemes. (6) Assessment of their resource avialbility for the Sub-Plan. (7) Formulation of sectoralprogrammes. (8) Devising a suitable administrative set-up.

It has been suggested, under the Sub-Plan scheme, that each State should appoint Tribal Commissioners from the Indian Administrative Service for the Sub-Plan regions, with specialist officers of the level of Additional/Joint Directors of the various government departments and experts from outside government be formed to serve in tribal areas. The Tribal Commissioner is to be deemed to have all the powers of the various Heads of Departments of the State Government as well as of the Revenue Divisional Commissioner to avoid having to refer day-to-day matters to the State Government. However, he is to work in conjunction with the Heads of Departments and Divisional Commissioners. The Tribal Commissioner is to be the head of a sort of mini-Secretraiat called the Tribal Commission which is to advise the State Government in the formulation of perspective, five-year and annual plans, with regard to tribal areas. Here the example of co-ordination in Kota is a good model.

Also being charged with ensuring implementation of the tribal plans, the Tribal Commissioner shall function through the concerned Collectors and the district administration, as well as through Panchayat and Community Development bodies, or Tribal Blocks where they exist. He shall also have a team of tribal extension officers who can be lent to the concerned VikasAdhikari (BDO) or other district official for specific tasks prescribed by the Tribal Commissioner. Further, he shall have some supervisory staff to assist him and the Collectors to administer the tribal development programmes.

It has also been proposed that the Tribal Commissioner, in addition to being subordinate to the Chief Secretary of the State shall be responsible to a Tribal Development Board consisting of important members of the Cabinet, Members of the Legislative Assembly, Members of the Perliament of the tribal area with the Chief Minister as its Chairman. The Tribal Commissioner, Collector of the area and some Secretaries to the State Government may also be co-opted as its members.

It is believe that the Tribal Commissioner should also have administrative control over the police in his territory. Further, the Tribal Commissioner should be competent to re-allocate funds within the Sub-Plan area, and that funds once earmarked for a Sub-Plan region should not lapse if unspent at the end of the financial year, but should automatically carried over for expenditure in the same region during the next financial year.

In the end, it is to point out that both the government and voluntary agencies would be agents for the tribal development. It is also to be hoped that more and more tribals shall themselves become agents for their own development.

Bibliography

A.H. Pale and Broton, P.P.L., (1969) *Planning Theory*. Russel Sage Foundation, New York.

Kahn A.J., (1969). *Theory and Practice of Social Planning*Russel Sage Foundation, New York.

Karkal G.L., (1977). *Social Change in Tribal India, Development Policy and Administration Review*. Vol. 3. New Delhi.

Sharma B., Hari Mohan Mathur (ed.), (1976). *Development Administration in Tribal Areas, Some Aspects of Tribal Development*, in The HCM State Institute of Public Administration, Jaipur.

Jagannadham V., (1972), Social Change and Social Welfare Administration.*The Indian Journal of Social Work*, Vol. XXXII.

3

Sahariya Development : A Micro Level Study of Madhya Pradesh

Swapan Kumar Kolay

India, 300 million are poor and still depending on nature or natural resources for livelihood and income generation. Of these an estimated 100 million are forest dwellers who are primarily dependent on forest not only for meeting their multiple household needs but also for their food security. Out of 68 million tribal population of the country, 50 per cent are directly dependent on forest for their livelihood requirements like food, fodder, medicinal plants, small timber and a variety of non-timber forest produces (NTFPs) which they collect from wild.

—At national level it is estimated that the value of NTFPs is nearly US $ I billion annually (Poffenburger, 1990). This huge and over increasing pressure and resulted to initiate the present forestry sector to emphasise towards poverty alleviation and livelihood improvements. Various forest programmes have been initiated like social forestry, community forest management, joint forest management, non-timber forest produce (NTFP) development and a range of Integrated Conservation Development projects (ICDP) including biodiversity and livelihoods, medicinal plant conservation and cultivation, etc. -NTFPs contribute significantly in tribal and rural economy as apart from own consumption (60 per cent) it is also sold in local market (Rao and Singh, 1996). Other estimates suggest that up to 35 per cent of income of tribal household in India comes from the collection and sale of unprocessed NTFPs (Giri, Bhattacharrya and Santra, 2001).

Forest Profile of Madhya Pradesh

Madhya Pradesh has the largest forest cover amongst all the states with 95221 sq km of forest cover or 31 per cent of its geographical area. This is around 12.44 per cent of the total forest cover of India. Most of the forests are under dry deciduous type that is ecologically fragile and in most cases are under extreme pressure of increase population and incidence of forest fire. Most of the north-western region of the state falls under this forest type. The population in the region is tribal dominated who is almost entirely dependent on forest for their livelihood. There is an alarming decline in the forest cover of the area due to the incidence of very high poverty and intense biotic pressure on forest resources. The dry deciduous forest of Sheopur district is rich in floral and faunal diversity. The mixed forest patches are rich in variety of trees and plant species bearing large variety of NTFPs including the medicinal and aromatic plants. It was observed that over three fourth (80%) of forest species yield commercially valuable NTFPs are traded in local market.

Madhya Pradesh is the abode of seven Partilularly Vernurable Groups (PTGs) and Sahariyas is one of them who are mainly living in the districts of Morena, Sheopur, Shivpuri and Guna. There are over 300 villages in the Sheopur Forest Division. In almost all of these villages are also vulnerable from the point of view of ecological stability and long term survival of threatened species.

The forests of the region are under intense biotic pressure mainly arising form cattle grazing. Illegal lopping, felling and unsustainable collection of Non Timber Forest Products (NTFPs). Due to scanty rainfall and intense grazing by cattle herds of Gujjars the ground flora is almost absent in most of the patches.

As the resource base has diminished and the demands of the resource has increased, the environmental services, recreation and NTFP have come to be appreciated as being equal to or more important industry than industrial timber and fiber, particularly in India. Many new stakeholders, from local forest user group through to powerful international Non-Governmental Organizations (NGOs), have gained a voice in the debate. Forest management has to take stakeholders into account for political and for instrumental reasons. Indeed a main driving force in the development of community forestry has been recognition that people living in forest areas have a major influence on the ecology and that they need to be involved if management is to succeed.

In income and consumption terms, there are three main components to overall role of forests and forestry in poverty alleviation:

Resources are used to meet current consumption needs, as a regular part of subsistence-level livelihoods.

Forests are used as 'safety nets', where people draw on available resources to meet emergency shortfalls and to keep from getting worse off in times of need.

Forest for 'poverty reduction' in the sense number of households below the poverty line is reduced (Bachler, 2005).

In the dry tropical forests of Sheopur there is rampant destruction of NTFP bearing tree/plant species. Apart from illegal lopping and cutting of the trees, there is widespread damage to the trees/plants due to unsustainable collection/harvesting. There are two broad categories of unsustainable harvesting/collection practices of NTFPs. In the first case the tree species, as in case of *Emblica offficinalis*, whose fruits are collected, is damaged due large-scale lopping and felling of trees. Further the fruits collected are immature, seeds of which are not viable for further propagation. Such practices have resulted into very poor regeneration status of species in the natural forest and pose threat to their long-term survival (Bhattacharya et al., 2002). There are hosts of factors both situational and external responsible for this present state. The spurt in the demand for NTFPs and market forces generated by this has contributed to this to large extent. The local traders of NTFPs in the small towns have traditionally instigated the tribal collectors of NTFPs into destruction of NTFPs trees in the unhealthy competition for making the most of the resource in short- term. At preset, most the NTFPs like fruits of certain trees are harvested completely from the natural forest, leaving nothing for further regeneration. Lack of awareness and training to the collectors is also a major cause. In the second category of unsustainable practices, the collection/ harvesting technique adopted by the collectors is putting the species under threat. One major concern is the technique adopted for the collection of gums and resins from trees like, *Boswellia serrata*, *Sterculia urens* and *Anogessius latifolia* that are found in large patch in the forest of this region. Due to faulty tapping technique employed, there are large numbers of deaths of such trees in the natural forest due to permanent damage to tree trunks. Since regeneration of such species takes a long time in natural forest, there is alarming reduction in the tree cover of these species.

High anthropogenic pressure due to over-grazing is another pressing concern in this area. Nearly 95% of the nearly 0.4 million cattle of Sheopur graze in open forest. There is almost complete absence of stall-feeding and grazing lots are also non-existent. Hence for the Gujjar community the forest is open access resource where they can leave their cattle for forage without any outside control. An estimated 1.5 times cattle graze in Sheopur forest compared to its carrying capacity. Ecologically, this has been a disaster. Rampant incidents of lopping, pruning and illegal felling are common place. Major species like *Ghot, Kardhai, Ber* and *Khair* are worst hit by unrestricted lopping. Degradation of local forest has dealt a body blow to the livelihood and income generation of Tribals. For gathering common forest products they have to work harder and travel farther. Seasonal time span for the availability of common NTFPs *like Anola* has shrunk from a month availability in forest a decade back to a week in recent times.

In recent times inter-community resource use conflict has also resulted into large-scale destruction of forest. The local cattle rearing community of Gujjars allegedly are responsible for much of the illegal lopping and cutting of forest for collection of fodder. The cutting of *Mahua* trees, which is venerable to the Tribals, by the Gujjars has further strained the social relations between Sahariya and Gujjars. To deprive the Gujjars from fodder, the Sahariya put local forest on fire, resulting in large area of forest destroyed in fire every year. To overcome these problems, International Centre for Community Forestry (ICCF) implemented some developmental activity which was supported by Ministry of Tribal Affairs, Govt. of India. The following objectives of these developmental activities are given below:

- To explore and promote participatory village level NTFP based income-generating activities.
- To promote and develop community initiated sustainable management of NTFPs with key emphasis on sustainable collection/ harvesting regime through awareness generation.
- To promote skill and capacity development through imparting training to NTFPs collectors.
- To develop local level institutions for effective marketing of NTFPs so those optimums benefits are accrued to the collectors with the use of techniques like Management Information System.
- To explore the scope of linking Joint Forest Management (JFM) activities for better NTFP management.

• To study the impact assessment of various activities.

Methodology

Basic information on occupation structures, caste, income and asset ownership was collected through household survey that covered all households in Sheopur district. A total of 310 household were chosen for more intensive study. Sample sizes for the villagers varied from 40-80 households, depending on the size of the villages and were selected through stratified random sampling. In addition to this, qualitative data were also collected from Sheopur Forest Division and various Forest Range Offices, key informants at the village level and poor households across all locations. Focus Group Discussion (FGD) was used as a tool to understand structures of power and patronage as well as exclusionary process and how these impacted on beneficiary selection.

Three quantitative surveys were conducted. The first was a census-where every household was covered. The questionnaire was pre-tested, revised and translated. It was designed to collect basic information on demographic, occupation structure, income, assets and access to pro-poor programmes.

–Next, a seasonal survey was conducted on for NTFP availability. The size of the sample was 40-80 households depending on the size and variability of the population.

The sample was selected by stratifying the population based on the census data. Proportionately more households were selected from the category of the landless poor to ensure that diversity within poor groups were captured.

Study Area

The project was implemented in the Sheopur Forest Division of Madhya Pradesh. This area is bound by river Chambal and district Morena in north and Rajasthan in south, river Chambal and Parvati form the western boundary and block Pohri, which is at 35 km from Shivpuri forms its eastern boundary. The topography of the area is flat with slight undulations. The project site is located at 25º 20' and 26º 15' North latitude and 76º30' and 77º39' East longitude in the Sheopur district which is situated in the north western part of the state of Madhya Pradesh bordering states of Rajasthan and Uttar Pradesh. It is located at a height of 238-498 meters above sea level. The average annual temperature of the region is 24.73º C and average annual rainfall is 764 mm.

The field work carried out in five villages namely (i) Goras (ii) Sesaipura (iii) Richi (iv) Ameth and (v) Panwara of Sheopur district, Madhya Pradesh (Table 3.1).

Table 3.1: Study Villages with Surveyed Household

State	*District*	*Block*	*Village*	*Number of Surveyed Household*
Madhya Pradesh	Sheopur	Karhal	Goras	80
			Sesaipura	55
			Richi	70
			Ameth	40
			Panwara	65
Total				310

Socio-economic Profile

The State of Madhya Pradesh has the sizeable tribal population of India. As per 2001 Census the total Tribal population of the State is 12,233,474 which is 20.27% of the total population of the State. Madhya Pradesh also boasts of large number of ethnic groups, which forms its Tribal population. India has 74 Primitive Tribal Groups (PTG) and seven of them live in Madhya Pradesh. The District of Sheopur, on the northwestern border of MP. is one such area where primitive tribal group "Sahariyas" forms the major population. The Sahariyas are mainly found in the Morena, Sheopur, Shivpuri and Guna district of Madhya Pradesh. Their usual food mainly consists of lesser millets and coarse cereals. Their economic condition is appalling. They have hardly any land of their own. They are virtually purchased as agricultural laborers at very nominal prices by landowners.

Another important element in the local demographic composition is the Gujjars, the cattle rearing community, which migrated to this district 4-5 decades back from the Rajasthan. Total population of the District is 5,59,715 with the growth rate of population from 2001 baseline being 3.33 per cent. For the whole district the tribal population is 21.53 per cent of the total, schedule castes are 16.16 per cent and rest 62.31 per cent are others. Interesting aspect to note here is the significantly high population of tribal in villages adjoining forest area. Survey done by the local Forest Department indicates over 40 per cent of population in the radius of 5 km from forest is those of tribal reinforcing the traditional belief of tribals being closer to the forest. Compared to this, only 26 per cent of the tribal are outside this radius. In fact Sahariyas are found mostly in villages within the forest or those very close to it. An estimated 3 out of 10 person in Sheopur subsists on annual income less than Rs.5000 - 6000 and only 14 per cent have income level above Rs 2,000. Villages deep inside the forest are deprived of basic facilities like health care, education, roads and potable water.

Tribal Community in Sheopur is heavily dependent on NTFP for generate income as they lack agricultural land and other traditional means of livelihood. In many cases the benefits from the NTFPs are accrued not only to the collectors but also to the primary processors who often live in the adjoining rural areas. NTFPs also serve as the source of food security to vast population who is squeezed out of forest and have little land for cultivation.

However at the local level the NTFPs play a crucial role in providing livelihood support to the forest dependent people mainly the tribals. Fuel wood, small timber, medicine, fodder etc. are traditionally extracted from the forest. Apart from this, NTFP collection/ harvesting is also a source of income to the local community. An estimated 80% of the tree/ plant species in the forest bear NTFPs of commercial importance. Approximately 90 different types of NTFPs are traded in the local market. Some of the important and highly valued NTFPs with their seasonal collection pattern are listed in Table 3.2.

Sheopur is a veritable showcase of large number of NTFPs, and an estimated 150-165 tons of which is collected annually from the forest. For almost whole the year round, over 300 villages in the District are vibrant with activities related to collection/ harvesting and processing of NTFPs or making preparatory survey of the forest in advance of collection season. The scale of activities may vary in intensity and spread over the year depending on availability of NTFPs. NTFPs like *Salai Gum, Aonla, Baheda, Satawar* and *Tendu Patta* are most important from commercial point of view. Salai gum collection contributes maximum to the local economy. Over the year the importance of *Salai gum* in the household economy has prompted local tribals to evolve indigenous system of tenure right on *Salai tree* to prevent any chances of conflict. In this system, the tribals have distributed the *Boswellia* trees in the forest among themselves on permanent basis for collection of gum. In the local forest *Nyctanthes arbor-tristis*, a weed, grows extensively. The stem of this weed is utilised for manufacturing baskets on a large-scale, which is then sold in the local market. In overall terms the NTFPs provides

Table 3.2: Important NTFPs of Sheopur and their parts used

Sl. No	*NTFP (Local Name)*	*Scientific Name*	*Part (s) used*
1	Aonla	*Embellica officinalis*	Fruit
2	Shatawar	*Asparagus racemosus*	Root/tuber
3	Bel guda	*Aegle marmelos*	Fruit pulp
4	Baheda Sabut	*Teminallia bellerica*	Fruit
5	Baheda Bakli	*Teminallia bellerica*	Bark
6	Shankhpushpi	*Convoluvlose pluricolis*	Whole part, Leaves
7	Hansraj	*Adiatum lunulatum*	Whole plant
8	Patol Patra	*Trichosanthes cucumerina*	Whole plant, leaves & root
9	Kankol Mirch	*Piper cubeba*	Fruits
10	Shivlingi	*Diplocyclos palmatus*	Leaves, roots and seed
11	Malkangani	*Celestus peniculata*	Seed
12	Amaltash Phali & Guda	*Casia fistula*	Fruits and Fruit pulp respectively
13	Mugdha Parni	*Centella asiatica*	Whole plant and leaves
14	Balaa Khareta	*Sida cordifolia*	Whole plant, roots, seeds and leaves
15	Kamal phul	*Mallotus phillppinensis*	Fruits, flowers
16	Gurmar	*Gymnema sylvestre*	Roots and leaves
17	Ber	*Zizyphus mauritiana*	Fruit and leaves
18	Nagarmotha	*Cyperus rotundus*	Tuber
19	Chitraka Mul	*Plumbago zeylanica*	Root and Bark
20	Indirajau	*Wrightia tinctoria*	Root, leaves, bark and seeds
21	Palash phul	*Butea monosperma*	Flower

Sl. No	*NTFP (Local Name)*	*Scientific Name*	*Part (s) used*
22	Varahikand	*Takka asperarox*	Tuber
23	Mahua phul and Gulli	*Madhuca indica*	Flower & Fruits respectively
24	Samhalu	*Vaitex nigandu*	Seed
25	Neem Gilo	*Azadirachta indica*	Fruits
26	Anantmul Kaladeshi	*Hemidesmus indicum*	Root
27	Harsinghar	*Nyctanthes arbotristis*	Seed
28	Khair	*Acacia catechu*	Seed and Gum
29	Kullu	*Steculia urens*	Gum
30	Dhawra	*Anogessius latifolia*	Gum
31	Salai Chid & Dana	*Boswellia serrata*	Oleo-resin & Seed
32	Tendu Patta	*Dyosporus melanoxylon*	Leaves

exclusive source of employment to the tribals for at least 8 months of the year and only about 1-2 month time the tribals are engaged in agriculture related activities. In terms of economic contribution, average estimated average household income from NTFPs is about Rs 15,000 (about US$300) for a year. In comparison average annual income from agriculture-related activities and other economic activities for a household is only Rs 6,400 (Bhattacharya and Hayat 2003).

These NTFPs are coming under increasing ecological threat due to loss of forest cover and destruction of NTFPs species. Destruction is mostly due to unsustainable harvesting of NTFPs prompted by unbridled commercialization of NTFPs. There is an urgent need to arrest the destruction of NTFP species in forest through capacity building of NTFP collectors and providing them incentive of encouraging their partnership in sustainable management of NTFPs. The key issues are thus awareness generation among the stakeholders and developing an institutional support to address issues/ problems related to sustainable management and utilization NTFPs.

According to an estimate, income drawn from the forest-based activities for villages within 5-km radius of forest is as high as 60%. In lean agriculture month like April-June, income of the tribals almost entirely comes from NTFPs like Tendu Patta and gum collection. To explore and promote participatory village level NTFP based income-generating activities appropriate technological and institutional interventions need to be introduced.

Looking the whole picture of the tribal dependency on NTFPs for their livelihood it is crucial to establish NTFP based micro-enterprise at village level to get better return from the NTFPs being collected in the area. To develop micro-enterprise, necessary input like capacity building, local level institutional infrastructure, development of marketing linkages and mechanization of processing of NTFPs are required to be introduced which will play key role in the development of the Sahariya community of the Project area.

Different Developmental Activities Conducted for the Sahariya

A series of activities were adopted beginning from selection of site, resource identification, training, assessment of available non timber forest products in the local forest area, the possibility of value addition for their marketability and also the potential marketing channel for the end products.

Socio-economic Survey

For the project implementation site selection was made based on socio-economic survey in consultation with local forest department, villagers and traders. Several parameters were kept in the mind such as Sahariya population, quantity of NTFPs being collected, accessibility to the villages and networking among the adjoining villages for the huge collection and processing of NTFPs. Based on above parameters and base line socio economic survey five villages namely Goras, Sesaipura, Ameth, Panwada and Richi were found suitable for the implementation of the project. The general information of the villages is shown in Table 3.3.

Identification of Potential Resources

After Selection of villages on the above criteria the village resources were identified in order to develop NTFP based micro-enterprises. The resource available were skilled manpower, availability of electricity, suitable cottage/working place, continuous availability of the sufficient quantity of NTFPs at the village and knowledge of local folk medicine system is desirable for the purpose.

Table 3.3: Village Wise General Information

General Information	*Name of the Village*				
	Goras	*Sesaipura*	*Richi*	*Ameth*	*Panwara*
Panchayat	Goras	Sesaipura	Richi	Ameth	Panwara
Sarpanch	Hari Singh	Kashi Ram	Soram adi	Mannu Adi	Usha Adi
President of Van Samiti	Bodi Ram Gurjar	Rajendra Gupta (Trader of NTFPs)	Mahendra Pratap Singh Chouhan	Gobind Singgh Yadav	Pahalwan Singh Yadav
Forest Range	Goras	Sesaipura	Karhal	Moravan	Karhal
Forest Sub-range	Goras	Sesaipura	Goras	Sesaipura	Karhal
Forest Beat	Goras	Sesaipura	Richi East	Ameth	Panwara
No of Hemlets	10	3	4	2	3
No of Tribal Household	321	143	318	136	150
Tribal Population	1605	695	1520	680	612
Source of Water	Hand Pump - 5 Sheep river & 1 bore	Hand Pump- 4, Bore - 1	Hand Pump - 2, Well- 1, Pond- 1 Kalari river & 1 bore	Hand Pump- 4, Bore- 1	Hand Pump - 8, Pond- 1, Bore- 25, Well- 1
School	Primary and Middle School	Primary, Middle and H.S. School.	Primary School	Primary, Middle and H.S. School.	Primary, Middle and H.S. School.
Hospital	PHC	P.H.C.	PHC, Goras	P.H.C.	P.H.C.
Electricity	Yes	Yes	Yes	Yes	Yes

Based on the analysis of various sources of income (Table 3.4) at Sesaipura and Goras villages have been installation of mini-pulveriser.

Table 3.4: Various Source of Income (%) in the Selected Villages

Sl. No.	*Name of Village*	*Source of Income*		
		Agriculture	*Labour*	*NTFP*
1	Goras	14 per cent	32 per cent	54 per cent
2	Sesaipura	9 per cent	30 per cent	61 per cent
3	Ameth	16 per cent	38 per cent	46 per cent
4	Richi	7 per cent	42 per cent	51% per cent
5	Panwada	13 per cent	38 per cent	49% per cent

Assessment/Quantification of Available NTFPs

For assessment of the NTFPs of the project site, primary data was derived from regular visit and meetings with the cross-section survey on local communities by conducting village PRA exercise, questionnaire and vegetation survey method (Table 3.5). It is estimated that nearly 10-15 tone of NTFPs (Bel, Anola, Shatawar, etc.) is being collected by the villagers (Chart 3.1). Also secondary data was generated through literature review visit to local forest department offices, revenue department, Sahariya Vikas Pradhikaran office to assess the quantum of NTFP production of the area (Chart 3.2).

This can be utilised for the processing in the pulveriser and for further value addition. The networking with the nearby villages can be established for the collection of greater quantities if needed.

Provisions for Income generation activities

Value addition and processing of NTFP play a vital role in ensuring higher returns to the collectors. The process of value addition can be applied from the stage of collection by adopting appropriate timings for individual NTFP, which will yield higher returns. After collection, grading of products based on size, quality, colour and stage of maturity also influences the product price. These products can be sold raw or after primary level processing like grinding, drying, de-seeding or de-pulping which can yield further higher returns.

Capacity Building

Since it is well accepted that capacity building operates as catalyst of change at various scales, number of training programmes, exposure visits and mass awareness campaign were conducted under the project for the local communities. Some of the activities were envisaged to enable the local community to envision, plan and implement actions in forest management relevant to generating and sharing benefits from forests:

Chart 3.1

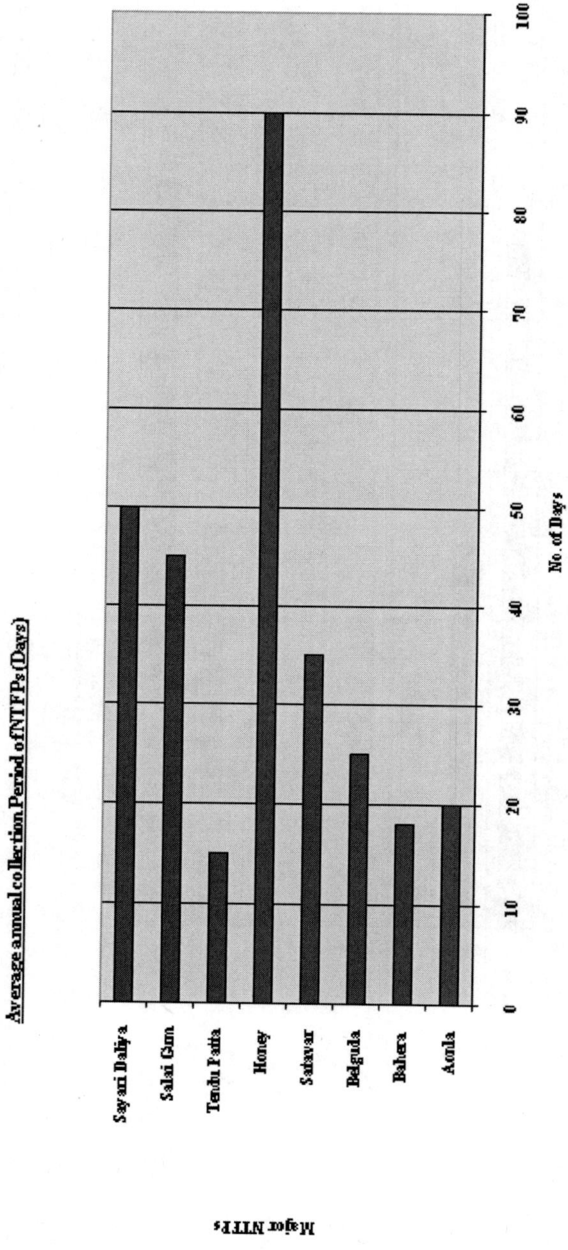
Average annual collection Period of NTFPs (Days)
Sayari Daliya
Salai Gum
Tendu Patta
Honey
Satavar
Belguda
Bahera
Aonla
Major NTFPs
0
10
20
30
40
50
60
70
80
90
100
No. of Days

Chart 3.2

Table 3.5: Estimated Production of NTFP in Sheopur: Quantity and Economic Contribution

Sl. No.	*NTFP*	*Estimated Production (Quintals)/No*	*Estimated Value (Rs. Lakh/US$)*	*Estimated Household Income (Rs/US$)*	*Average Annual Collection/manufacturing Period (Days)*
1	Aonla	500	10.00/2000	2200/44	20
2	Baheda	450	0.9/1800	600/12	10
3	Bael	200	1.2/2400	960/19.2	30
4	Marodphali	35	0.14/280	500/10	45
6	Malkangani	25	1.00/2000	450/9	60
7	Satavar	50	0.75/1500	1200/24	35
8	Mahua Flower	250	2.25/45000	800/16	30
9	Mahua Fruits	220	0.55/1100	600/12	45
10	Honey*	225	5.6/11200	500/10	30
11	Salai Gum	5302	159.06/319200	4500/90	120
12	Tendu Patta	18340.83	167.71	1200/24	14
13	Basket Making* (No.)	12000	0.36	1100	50

*Collected from select areas only.

(a) Training of stakeholders on business skill: For sustainable and smooth functioning of pulveriser machine, processing and selling of materials, training were imparted to the villager from time to time. In order to institutionalise the whole process, one village level committee was formed for the maintenance of pulveriser and monitoring purchasing and sale of raw and processed materials by keeping record in the register.

(b) Training of stakeholders on sustainable harvesting of NTFPs

(i) Scientific Satawar harvesting: Satawar is one of the important and prized plants for Sahariya community. The tuberous roots of Satawar is collected from the forest and sold in the local market. The local community practices unsustainable harvesting of tuberous roots of *Asparagus*, which is the chief cause of depletion of the plant population in the forest. To check this, unsustainable and destructive harvesting of *Asparagus* few training were imparted to the community members. Traditional collectors were trained on the scientific aspect of its collection. The main focus was on the training was on the fact that care should be taken to replace the dug out soil on the rhizome and at least 5% of the tubers should be left with the rhizome for fast recovery of the plants and for renewed yield.

(ii) Sustainable Kullu Gum harvesting: Kullu gum is harvested from the *Sterculia urense* (Kullu) tree. It is the second major source of income of Sahariya community. This is a very slow growing species, which takes nearly 20 – 25 years to maturity and for gum oozing. The gum collection practice adopted for by the Sahariya severely damages the tree due to uncontrolled harvest by deep incisions made on the trunk. As a consequence within a few years the tree dies of severe cut and wounds. To check the population of fast dying trees, villagers were trained of scientific harvesting method of kullu gum for sustainable yield.

(iii) Scientific harvesting of forest honey: Nearly 100 – 150 quintals of honey is harvested from the forests of Sheopur. Mainly rock bee (*Apis dorsata*) is found in this region. Although honey harvesting/ collection is a very old practice of Sahariya but the technique used by them is very unsafe and destructive in nature which not only affects the quality of honey but also the bee and hive population. Sahariya tribe people used to squeeze honeycomb for separation of honey, which also contains eggs, pollens, wax and other impurities in it. Therefore the villagers were trained for safe and scientific method of honey collection along with the existing honey hunter group. In this method only the honey-containing portion of the beehive is cut apart instead of removing the entire hive thus minimizing the chances of impurities and loss of the bee population. Thereafter the honey is extracted by using centrifugal machine. They were also provided with special kits and equipment including sting-proof dresses.

(iv) Training on Sustainable Harvesting of Aonla and Bel: Series of training were imparted to the villagers on sustainable harvesting of various NTFPs like bel, anola, etc. Earlier the villagers used very crude and destructive method of collection whereby they were causing severe lopping and trimming of the fruit bearing branches of the tree. In some cases even entire tree was felled to grab the harvest. All these resulted into reduced harvest next year and so on. Hence they were trained for sustainable harvest of the crop and made to understand the need of preserving the tree for their future progeny. Also some street plays and cultural activities were performed to make them understand the need of conservation of forest and forest produce.

(c) Training on Processing of NTFP at CSV, Wardha: In order to set up village level NTFP based micro-enterprise for the processing and value addition of various NTFPs 10 villagers were trained at Center for Science of Villages, Wardha. They were trained for processing of *Aonla, Bel, Harra, Bahera* and *Satava*r during the training for its primary processing as well as value added products like *Aonla murabba*, *Aonla Pachak, Bel murabba, TriphalaChurna, Satavari Kalp.*

(d) Mass awareness Campaign: For sensitizing the NTFP collectors to stop destructive harvesting of NTFPs and overcome from the exploitative marketing a mass awareness campaign through *Kala-Jatha* was organized in the selected village. In this context 10 days workshop was conducted at the Karhal range for presenting *Kala-Jatha's* activities covering folk songs and plays related to the campaign. This *kala-Jatha* was used for organising the whole campaign. Two plays and five songs related to conserving forest based produce and their values towards the livelihood of dependent population were highlighted. Posters and pamphlets were also distributed amongst the villages. Apart from the mass campaign time to time focus group discussion and meeting were also conducted at the villages to maintain sensitization towards the harmful and destructive practices.

(e) Development of Marketing Network: Processed material can be sold to local as well as distant market. Marketing linkages are to be developed by contacting traders, medicine man, pharmaceutical companies, Govt. departments (MPMFP Federation, Khadi Gram Udyog

Kendra) etc. To develop marketing skills amongst salesman, training on marketing strategies may be organized at the villages.

One NTFP based outlet is also proposed to be opened at the Forest range office, Karhal to publicize and sale the product in collaboration with local forest department. In order to sale the processed NTFPs generated by village institutions, distant marketing linkages have been identified and established. In this connection a tour was made to the Nursingpur forest division for having an exposure on processing of NTFPs for development of micro-enterprise. A tour was also conducted to MFP Federation for tying up marketing linkages between the rural institutions formed at village to the federation's outlet for selling the processed NTFPs. The Federation promoted the proposed marketing system against the 10% commission over the total sale.

(f) Formation of Self Help Group(SHG): The community being a very under privileged and backward one has hardly any organised effort to collect and utilise its available means of resources. Therefore few self help groups were formed to promote them for various types of income generating activities and developmental activities (Table 3.6). This would also be helpful for them to obtain institutional status as well as financial support in the form of help or loan for further strengthening.

Table 3.6: List of SHGs Rormed at Village for NTFPs Related Activities

Sl.No.	*Name of Village*	*Name of SHG*	*Name of President*	*Amount per Month Deposit (Rs.)*
1	Goras	Shri Savai Bhoj	Mr. Nanda	120/-
2	Sesaipura	Shri Ganesh	Mr. Murarilal	140/-
3	Ameth	Shri Ram	Mr. Hari Ram	120/-
4	Richi	Jay Durga	Mrs. Banti Bai	110/-
5	Panwada	Mahila Shakti	Mrs. Kanya Bai	150/-

(g) Micro-credit Disbursement: To start the NTFPs based micro-enterprise, disbursement of micro-credit as seed money for the purchasing raw materials and for further processing was considered to be crucial at the beginning. This credit may be taken back or given to other village to replicate after independent, stable and profitable running of pulveriser in previous village. The details of micro-credits are given in the Table 3.7 and Table 3.8.

Table 3.7: List of Samiti Formed in the Village for the Micro-enterprise Development

Sl. No.	*Name of Village*	*Name of Samiti*	*Name of President*
1	Goras	Lagu Van Upaj Prasanskran Samiti	Chunnilal Patel
2	Sesaipura	Lagu Van Upaj Prasanskran Samiti	Ramji lal

Table 3.8: Details of Micro Credit Disbursed

Year	General	Scheduled Tribes (ST)
1961	941	990
1971	930	982
1981	935	983
1991	927	972
2001	933	977

Establishment of Community Boiler

The traditional practice of boiling of NTFPs like bel and anola in the age old home made chulhas was not only time consuming and hazardous to the health and hygiene of the local tribals but it also resulted into huge loss of forest biomass being used as fuel by individual at their houses. Considering the loss of time, energy and resources it was decided to install a community boiler for boiling of NTFPs. It required less energy, fuel and effort of the person operating it and at the same time allowed quicker and safer mode of processing of NTFP saving their time and energy. Thus the villagers were allowed with more time to be utilized in other income generating activities or protection of forest resources.

Establishment of Mini-pulveriser

Through detailed discussion to the stakeholder three-phase electric operated mini-pulveriser with the capacity of grinding 7-10 kg NTFP per hour in two villages namely 1. Sesaipura and 2. Goras. Along with this pulveriser one electrically operated packaging machine was also provided for the packaging of powdered materials. The pulvilizer was used for grinding of NTFPs viz. *1. Asparagus, 2. Bel-pulp, 3. Trifola (Anola, Harra and Behera), 4. Arjun-bark* and several other medicinal leaves like *kalmegh, vitex negundo,* etc.

The pulveriser has contributed in the enhancement of the rate of same product in raw from they used to sell at throughaway price to traders.

This has increased the income generation about Rs 200-300 in compared to raw selling which was prevailing in the whole area.

Two full time trained workers were provided for operating this pulveriser and packaging machine. Efforts are also made to orient selected youths from intervention village to market their products at the local as well as distant markets. Opportunities were provided to attend with their product at *Van mela* during last seven years, through this exercise they got first hand exposure of direct marketing of their finished product in urban market. This is a common facility created from the project which could be of use for the local people of the village as well as other adjoining communities.

Social Dimension

- Social structure
- Social capital
- Cultural influence
- Health care

Economic Dimension

- Lower cost of production
- Cost of product development and marketing
- Efficiency and profit

Bio-physical Dimension

- Biodiversity
- Soil
- Climate
- Species habit and production
- Technology for harvesting

NTFP based Enterprise

Policy Dimension

- Price fixation
- Transit rules
- IPR
- Global and local demand
- Sharing rights and benefits
- Education

Livelihood Dimension

- Employment generation
- Regular income

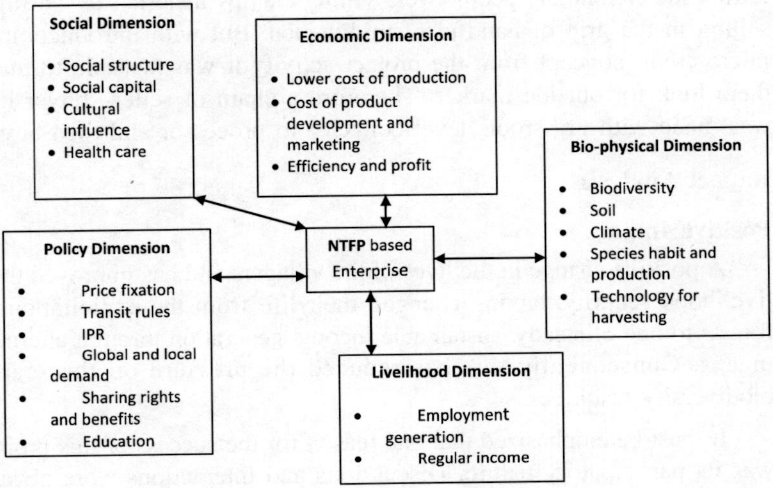

Fig. 3.1 : Model for Integrated Non Timber Forest Product (NTFP) based Enterprise Development

Development of Marketing Network

The strengthening of stakeholders capability to produce bulk of NTFPs processed or semi –processed with the help of community boiler

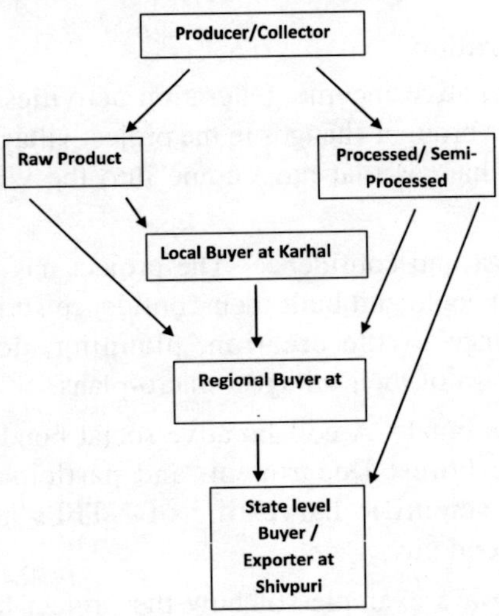

Fig. 3.2 : Possible Marketing Network of Local Non Timber Forest Products (NTFPs) to Generate More Income at Collector level

and pulveriser created the need for marketing network outside the village. Earlier the community people were selling the raw materials as a distress selling in the grip of handful of middlemen. But with introduction of micro-credit concept from the project activity it was possible to make them look for outside market. Therefore a chain of seller– buyer link was made with grassroots level collector to processor and then buyer.

Impact Analysis

Positive Impact

A positive change in the lives of the villagers and has improved their livelihood security, having changed their life from the exploitation of forests to one of steady, sustainable income generation through alternate means. Consequently this has reduced the pressure on the scarce biodiversity resources.

It must be emphasized that one reason for the success of this project was its participatory nature. Discussions and interactions were always held to find out what are the people's priorities they were encouraged to make their own decisions. Further, no free dole was given; instead, the people were motivated to work towards their chosen alternatives and pursue livelihood opportunities on their own steam for which assistance was provided. This helped them become stakeholders in their chosen alternate livelihood. Impacts of the projects are many folds, which are narrated in the following section.

Livelihood Generation

A list of alternative income generation activities taken up by the villagers which has brought changes in the project villages. Some specific instances of the changes that have come into the villagers' lives are outlined below:

- Building trust and confidence- The project has secured the trust of the local people and built their confidence so that they are able to take charge of the creation, planning, development and implementation of their villages' micro-plans.
- Creation of a bond—A collaborative social bond has been forged between the Forest Department, and participating villages to sustainable scientific harvesting of NTFPs and improve the grassroots economy.

The following are examples of how the project has benefited the villagers which in turn has make their understanding on Forest resources positively. The attitudes to reduce/abandon their erstwhile exploitation and degradation activities:

(a) There has been a direct resource dependency in more than six forests- dependants in the villages. The unsustainable NTFPs collectors who were dependent on the forest for livelihood have adapted to scientific harvesting technique unsustainable harvesting in general reduced by 50% in the project villages through protection and strict vigil by Forest Protection Committee (FPC).

(b) Villagers have taken up plantation rising in some areas resulting in NTFPs production for sell.

(c) Grazing incidence within project intervention and adjoining villages has been reduced by more than 50% mainly in the plantation areas due to awareness and vigil of protection by FPC.

In other instances, owners of cattle sold them and purchased NTFPs through SHGs loans. In Goras and Sesaipura villages, after the formation of a FPC, fire incidence in the adjoining forest has been reduced by 80%, grazing incidence reduced by 55%, fuel wood collection reduced by 40% which has appeared in the questionnaire survey asked to the local villagers in project area.

Table 3.9: Village-wise Data among the Sahariya Households on Scientific HarvestingEfforts of NTFPs Before and After FPC Formation and Project Implementation

Sl. No.	*Name of the Village*	*No. of NTFP Collectors followed Traditional Methods of Collections in Different Village*	*No. of NTFP Collector followed Improved Technique after FPC in Different Villages*
1.	Goras	70	258
2.	Sesaipura	66	129
3.	Ameth	46	145
4.	Richi	38	185
5.	Panwada	47	216
	Total	**267**	**933**

Source: Primary Survey Data—2010.

Table 3.9 shows the success of the project in achieving its ultimate goal of sustainable management and cultivation of valuable plants increased. Before the formation of FPC, no. of NTFP collectors followed traditional methods of collections in different villages in the entire target area was 267. This was increased to 933 after the project was implemented; recording a total percentage drop of 50% a very high increased indicating a high success rate.

In Goras and Sesaipura, a NTFP processing cum Herbal Clinic was built with the help of an initial investment from the project as well as peoples' contribution for different activities help the all villagers.

Out of the assistance of some amount will be allotted for alternative income generation activities through the SHGs, after successful recovery of loan would be enabled the FPCs to provide assistance, setting in motion a different Village Level Committee (VLC) revolving fund mechanism.

Greater awareness has been created among all the target villages on the need to has contributed sustainable harvesting of NTFPs, value addition, processing, nursery raising marketing and other income generating activity.

Mass awareness generation campaign *Kalla Jatha-rally* was organised jointly by the team and the villagers. This brought harmony and understanding in the minds of the local people thereby effectively propagating the conservation message. Due to the tremendous awareness generation capacity of the rally, Forest Department officials feel inclined to continue the programme every year so that the message will spread in a continuous on-going process.

Developing a Positive Attitude and Awareness

The sustainable harvesting and management of NTFP, approaches firmly established, the villagers now identify and dedicate themselves to the cause of conservation and have formed a positive bond with the different range official at Sheopur Forest Division.

By providing the villagers with more efficient cooking equipment, alternate sources of, income and biomass production as well as the capacity to access such alternatives (through the SHG loan scheme), the project has weaned the villagers away from the forest. Cattle have been disposed of, timely harvesting of NTFP have been greatly increased and as a result of which, the forest has begun to regenerate and recuperate. It is clear, therefore, the ultimate goal of the project-intervention villages is slowly but surely becoming an attainable reality.

It is also noteworthy that these villagers (members of FPCs), have come to realize the importance of the forest and are, in consequence, protecting it by preventing others from grazing/felling as well as informing the Forest Department about instances of gave violation—a clear case of the establishment of 'social fences'. Some FPCs have even levied fines against members discovered entering the reserve and engaging in destructive, anti- ecological activity. Seeing the concrete economic, social and environmental result of the project. It also gives an opportunity to test a new tool and means for forest protection. It gives a lot of satisfaction.

The activity has been able to bring to an end the hostilities of traditional adversaries- the Forest Department and the local people.

The following are the outlines of impacts of the project:

It helped in reducing the present exploitative marketing of NTFPs prevailing in area by providing them marketing linkages and marketing them self-sufficient through introduction of the concept of micro-credit.

Community has checked or stopped the present destructive harvesting of NTFPs by adopting scientific method of harvesting.

Forest ProtectionCommittee is now able to manage the whole activities related to micro-enterprise starting from collection to selling.

Economic return from the NTFPs collected have increased by two ways:

- Direct marketing from village to distant market by avoiding middlemen.
- Processing of raw NTFPs items before selling to the traders.
- Using the institutional infrastructure for controlling destructive harvesting has reduced NTFPs depletion from the forest due to unscientific and burgeoning exploitation.
- It may control the minimum price of NTFPs at the local market by developing networking amongst the village to village committees.

Conclusion and Recommendations

Hundreds of villages in the remote and backward areas of Madhya Pradesh depend on the forest as a resource for livelihood and income generation. It falls under the coping strategy followed by the Sahariyas in their day to day life. However, the NTFPs resources in the forest are affected by several means. Commercilisation of many NTFP species which were hitherto collected for household and subsistence purpose led to unsustainable harvesting regime which is threatening the long termavailability of many products. The commercialisation of several medicinal, dye and industrial gum products have severely impacted the production quality and the overall rural economy in tribal area.

Still in Sheopur district there is lot of potential to strengthen tribal economy by small interventions in these tribal pockets. These interventions should be with local resources, local people and with the local technology. In this regard following aspects have to be incorporated for forest based livelihood intervention:

- Village level procurement centre need to be developed which should have linkages with MFP primary cooperative society.
- At village level NTFP collectors group, SHG may be developed which need to be linked with nationalized/cooperative bank for providing micro-credit support to establish village/cluster level processing units/ micro enterprise.
- There is an urgent need for district level coordination with FD, revenue department, agriculture, panchayat financial institution to develop a district level plan, with the leadership of Sahariya Vikash Pradhikaran (Sahariya Development Authority) for forest based income generation activities.
- Large scale village household level nursery development activities need to be promoted for NTFP species for sustainable supply of these products for future generation.
- There are several important products which are collected by the tribal in bulk need to be harvested sustainably, various training programme, skill development programme needs to be organised throughout the year in these tribal pocket.

To integrated the tribals alienated from traditional practices of forest conservation, it is essential to strengthen the tribal institutions which are many instances. Market reform is key to ensuring remunerative return to collectors and making them empowered for forest conservation. In fact with the present exploitative market regime, mere transfer of usufruct rights to the collectors has little meaning. The recent changes made by the policy makers related to transit pass and its relation to sustainable harvesting of NTFPs also had limited impact due to extreme poverty of the Sahariya and very low literacy level and the fact that it failed to address entire chain of issues, mainly the market reforms. Recently, the Forest department and Indian Institute of Forest Management (IIFM), Bhopal has initiated several programmes for management of NTFPs which has yielded positive results even these efforts could be further linked with Prime Ministers proposal of 100 days employment in rural areas. It can certainly contribute to Indias, commitments to Millennium Development Goals (MDG) which is still a long way to go. The potential of NTFPs in poverty alleviation is enormous and can assist in all the 8 MDGs (Kaushal and Melkani, 2005). The Sahariyas of Sheopur are the tribals whose life is forest resource dependent. Through this project, IIFM was able to convince the policy makers, forest department, traders, communities, NGOs and academic institutions at local, national and international level that sustainable harvesting of NTFP with value addition and micro- credit are the effective means to meet the livelihoods objective as well as conservation objectives.

So from the above discussion it is clear that the effort of IIFM needs to be strengthened through continuous campaigning, capacity building training, micro-credit support and micro-enterprise to achieve the 100% poverty reduction in terms of number of household above poverty line and a healthy and productive forest.

References

Anon (1998).*Plan, Sheopur Forest Division.* Forest Department, Government of Madhya Pradesh, Bhopal.

Bahuguna, V.K. (2000). Forest in the Economy of the Rural Poor : An Estimation of the Dependency Level. *Ambio Vol. 29,*No. 3pp. 126-129.

Bechler, B.M. (2005). Forest Product Markets, Forest and Poverty Reduction, *International Forestry Review,* Vol. 7. No. 2.

Bhattacharya, P. and S.F. Hayat (2003). Issues in Substainable Management of NTFPs for Livelihood Generation of Tribals : A case from Sheopur District of Madhya Pradesh, India. Paper presented at the National Workshop on Non-wood Forest Products – New Mechanisms and Strategies. Organised by Government of India in New Delhi during 29-30 May 2003 pp. 37-47.

Bhattacharya P., S.K. Kolay and N.K. Bhagat (2006). Science and Technology Application for Enhancement of Rural Livelihood : Community Based Sustainable Management and Cultivation of Shatawar (Asparagus racemosus) in Chambal Ravine of Sheopur District of Madhya Pradesh, DST – Final Report (unpublished).

Champion and Seth (1969).*Forest Types of India*, Govt. of India.

Giri, T.K., P. Bhattacharya and S.C. Santra (2001). Ecology and Economy of Non Timber Forest Product in Village Life – A Case from Bankura District in West Bengal, *Annals ofForestry*, Vol. 9, No. 1 pp. 2.

Gutman, P. (2001).*Forest Conservation and the Rural Poor: A Call to Broden the Conservation Agenda*,WWF Macroeconomics for Sustainable Development Programme Office, Washington, D.C.

Kaushal, K.K. and V.K. Melkani (2005).India: Achieving Millennium Development Goals through Non timber Forest Products,*International Forestry Review* Vol. 7.pp. 92.

Proffenberger M. (1990).*Wasteland News,* Aug- Oct 1990 pp. 46-55.

Rao, A.R. and B.P. Singh (1996).Non wood Forest Products Contribution in Tribal Economy, *Indian Forester* (April).

Shrivastav, V.K. (2003).*Tribal Scenario of Madhya Pradesh and Chhatisgarh*. Sharon Publications.

Working Plan (2000). Sheopur Forest Department, Madhya Pradesh.

4

Indigenous Population: Their Problems and Prospects in Jharkhand

Prabhat K. Singh and Jagdeep Oraon

The indigenous population refers to culturally distinct groups that in various ways they had been affected by the processes of colonisation.However, they have preserved some degree of culture and political separation from the mainstream culture and political system.The term defines these groups as vulnerable to exploitation and oppression by the nation states.To save their rights in accordance with international law have been set forth by international organizations such as ILO and World Bank.The United Nations issued a declaration on the rights of indigenous population with a view to protect the collective rights of indigenous peoples to their culture, identity, language, employment, health, education and natural resources.

The term indigenous population is not applied uniformly in all cultures. The notion of an indigenous group depends on context and other issues. Indigenous peoples are referred in different countries in different ways such as indigenous ethnic minorities, aboriginals, hill tribes, minority nationalities, Scheduled Tribes, or Tribal groups etc. India, a country which has the second largest indigenous population in the world, is home to over eighty four million people classified as members of Scheduled Tribes, that is 8.2 percent of India's total population. Besides the

Scheduled Tribes, in addition, there are other too as the indigenous people as they have not been Scheduled in the Scheduled Tribe list of India. On the other hand, the official position of the Indian Government is that there are no indigenous people in the country. This position is seems to be of political nature and the government's claim is based on the flimsy ground. The ground is the country's complex migration pattern which means that unlike in other nation such as Australia or Canada. In India it is impossible to identify the original settlers of a particular region. Indian activists had taken the issues of indigenous people to the meetings of United Nations Working Group on IndigenousPopulations (UNWGIP) in 1982. These activists sought to claim indigenous status for India's tribal populations, peoples previously known as Adivasis, and who are officially recognised in government censuses as members of Scheduled Tribes. In 1987 the Indian delegates to UNWGIP represented a newly founded Indian council of Indigenous and Tribal peoples, affiliated with the World, India, a country which as the second largest indigenous population in the world,as members of Scheduled Tribes . Besides the Scheduled Tribes, in addition, there areindigenous people who have not been Scheduled in the Scheduled Tribe list of India. They claimed that India's Scheduled Tribe populations qualified for thenew transnational term "Indigenous peoples" because they were culturally different from mainstream Indian society, and especially because they had been internally colonized and dominated by a system of values and institutions maintained by the ruling groups of the country.

The Government of India reports in WGIP that there are no indigenous people in India, though, India had made an official acknowledgement at internationallevel of being one of the firstsignatories of ILOConvention No. 107 of 1957, thus ratifying it even though the revision No. 169 of 1989 is yet to be notified by India in relation to the indigenous people. The InternationalLabourOrganisation(ILO) gave considerableattention to the issueof the rights of indigenouspeople. A workable definition was given by theILO's Convention No. 107 of 1957, as "Those which having a historical continuitywithpre-invasion and pre-colonialsocieties...considerthemselves distinct from othersectors ofsocietiesnow prevailing in thosein those territories.... They form at present non-dominant sectors of society...". It is alsoamended slightly in No. 169 Of 1989.United Nations declared the year 1993 as the International Year of the Indigenous People. And, this international year of indigenous people was celebrated throughout the world with great pump and show particularly by the indigenous groups, India also did.

Indigenous and Tribal People with Particular Reference to India

In India, there are two categories of tribes:

1. Statutorily tribal people, they are called Scheduled Tribes.

2. Communities identifying themselves as tribal peoples and recognized as such by neighboring communities, but not in the status.

Neither the constitution of India, nor the Parliament has laid down the creation for recognition of Scheduled Tribes. The original list was notified by the President in 1950 in respect of the different states in consultation with the respective governments. Thereafter, there are many additions or alteration in states which have taken place in the Parliament. While in issuing the original notification the President had in general way taken into considerationthe categorisation of population in 1931Census and the list of "Backward Tribes" prepared under the Government of India Act 1935, in recommending to the Parliament, names of the communities to be added to or deleted from the list. The Union Government consulted the Governors of the respective states as well as the Registrar General of India (Census Commissioner)and the National Commission for Scheduled Tribes to get the states.

The numerical strength of general population and tribal population to the total population of the country is as follows:

Year	General Population	Scheduled Tribes (ST)
1961	428397442	6.87
1971	533534500	6.94
1981	665287849	7.83
1991	746302688	8.08
2001	1028610328	8.2

The higher population growth rate of ST does not entirelyreflect the natural growth of the ST population. During each inter census decades there has been fresh inclusion of the new names as STs. To some extent the higher growth rate is accounted for by the fresh inclusions in the list.

Tribal sex ratio in India is always higher than the overall sex ratio of Country. The data relating to the different census years are as follows:

Sex Ratio

Year	General	Scheduled Tribes (ST)
1961	941	990
1971	930	982
1981	935	983
1991	927	972
2001	933	977

Higher proportion of women among the STs would obviously mean higher probability of childbirths. Another very significant fact is thatduring large part of 1980 and early 1990s Nagaland, the tribal predominant state competed with Kerala about lowest death rate in the country. Now, Mizoram competes with Kerala for this honour.

Tribal Population Who have not been Statutorily Recognised as Scheduled Tribes:

There are several million tribal population who are not recognized as Scheduled Tribes even after the 60 years of first notification. From the Jharkhand and adjusting states who migrated to the tea gardens in Assam, are not considered as Scheduled Tribes till date. There are many others, the bretherens of major tribes of Jharkhand are also left for nowhere. In Jharkhand, there are more than four dozen communities struggling for inclusion in the list of Scheduled Tribes. Numerically a large community, the Kurmi is one of them.The Kurmis reside in Jharkhand as well as in the adjoining districts of states such as West Bengal and Odisha. The Kurmis have their tribal antecedence. The Kurmi is the offshoot of the main tribe Santhal. The Kurmis are still governed by their customary laws.These Kurmis are totemistic and differ from the Kurmis of the Gangetic plains culturally, socially, and economically. Santhals and Kurmis are culturally and physically very similar. The anthropometric measurements done by Risley and even in Peoples of India Project of Anthropological Survey of India reveal that they are very similar to each other. Some genome studies have been done by IICB (Indian Institution Institute of ChemicalBiology), Kolkata but data and resulthas not been published so far. However, the Jharkhand Government has forwarded the proposal to include the Kurmis in Scheduled Tribe list but the file is lying somewhere in the center.

Emergency of Indigenous

Tribals identity is at stake today. Identity problem is not all a problem unless identity is questioned or threatened by others. The people did not become conscious of being different, till they met others who came from a different region, spoke a different language, food habit and dressed differently. The tribals have been facing the same problem of their threatened identity. The tribals certainly want to maintain their separate identity and would like to be called the 'Adivasi' irrespective of their constitutional status as the Scheduled Tribes.

ScheduledArea in Jharkhand

The fifth schedule of Indian constitution happens to be one of the most important provisions for the administration of tribe dominated area.There are nine states having Fifth Schedule area namely – Jharkhand, Odisha, Chhatisgarh, Madhya Pradesh, Andhra Pradesh, Maharashtra, Gujarat, Rajasthan and Himachal Pradesh.These provisions have attracted considerable debate, attention controversies and conflict in Jharkhand, after the enactment of PESA (1996) & JPRA (2001). The landmark judgment of the Supreme Court in India known as SamtaJudgement has also opened new opportunities for the impoverishment and marginalised tribes in the Fifth Scheduled areas.

There are 14 districts of Jharkhand included in Scheduled areas covering 12 districts completely and 2 districts partially. In 1950 the following areas were notified as Scheduled:

Ranchi district

Sadar Chaibasa and Saraikela division in Singhbhum district

Sadar Dumka, Jamtara, Pakurand Rajmahal in Santhalpargana

Latehar Sub-division of Palamu district

Demographic Status in Scheduled Areas in Jharkhand

There have been considerable controversies regarding the 2001 Census. However, if one looks at the Census figures, out of 32,617 villages in Jharkhand, 17,353 were in the Scheduled Areas while 15,264 were in the non-scheduled areas. In the Scheduled Areas, 3,065 villages had no tribal population while in the non-Scheduled areas 10,323 villages were without tribal population.Around 12.8 per cent of the villages, the percentage of the tribal population has been less than 30 per cent and 0.01 per cent while in 17.7 per cent villages there has been no tribal population. In non-Scheduled Areas, 11.45 of the villages, the tribal population reported to be more than 40 per cent. In the Scheduled Areas in almost two-thirds of the villages tribal population is in majority, if the block level figures are analysed out of 112 Blocks. The tribal population in the Scheduled Areas has been below 30 per cent namely Barharwa (9.29), Udhwa (5.88), Sahebganj (5.78).

Percentage of Tribal Population to Total Population

	01-10	*11-20*	*21-30*	*31-40*	*41-50*	*50+*	
Scheduled Area	4.3	4.4	4.1	4.0	4.6	62.3	17.7
Non-Scheduled Area	10.2	4.1	2.7	2.2	2.1	9.3	67.6

Chotanagpur Tenancy Act (CNT), 1908 and SanthalPargana (SPT) Act, 1948

Besides the Scheduled Area Regulation Act 1969, there are Chotanagpur Tenancy Act 1908 (CNT Act) and SanthalPargana Act 1948 (SPT Act) which govern the tribal lands in Jharkhand and protect the tribal land from the alienation from tribal to non-tribal. In Chotanagpur region about two third of the total land belonging to the indigenous communities were alienated before the enactment of the CNT Act (1908) to protect the tribal land. As the land is only means of production and for that matter only means of survival. The tribals consider land as the mother of the people. The land cannot be owned, bought or sold. The land is sacred for them. And, thus, forms a major part of their being culture, religion, health etc. Land stands for their habitat, geographical territory, their ancestral homeland. They have the total right on the part of the 'mother earth' asthey call her, passed over to them by their foreparents. The land (*JAMIN*), the water (*JAL*) and the forest (*JANGAL*) that their habitatcontains belong to them. Since the time immemorial, since the dawn of human existence they have been exercising total control over the land and whatever beneath and above it (BosuMullick, *et. al.*1993).

Panchayati Raj Institution Extension to Scheduled Areas (PESA) Act

It is a Panchayati Raj Instituition Extension to the Scheduled Areas.It is enforced in Jharkhand also. This Act empowers people to redefine their own political boundaries. The Act also provides that *Gram Sabhas* and Panchayat at appropriate levels have the right to approve all development plans, control over all functionaries and institution of all social sectors, control minor water bodies, minor minerals and non-timber forest produce and land acquisition and displacement.The *Gram Sabhas* have also been given authority to control land alienation, impose prohibition, manage village markets and resolve internal conflicts through traditional modes. It has also reserved 50 per cent of the seats in Panchayats for the tribes and all posts of Chairpersons at all levels in the PRIs for the Scheduled Tribes.

Samata Judgement

It is a landmark judgement by the HonourableSupreme Court, after a case filed by an NGO named as Samata against the Andhra Pradesh Government for leasing tribal land to private mining companies in the Scheduled Areas. One major judgement was transfer of land in Scheduled Areas by way of lease to non-tribals, corporation aggregate, etc. stands prohibited.

The above four provisions:The Schedule Area, CNT and SPT Act, PESA Act and SamataJudgement have developed controversies and conflicts between the tribals and non-tribals.

And it is matter of more concern for the communities who more unscheduled Tribes the Moolvasis, aborigins, autochthonous, son of the soils and the original settlers of the area.They are being deprived at all levels, constitutionally and socially, politically, at level of programme implementation.

In Jharkhand there was continuous opposition of PESA Act, Panchayati Raj elections could not be held for decades due to this controversy and conflict even after several High Court orders. After Supreme Court order and under the pressure of Central Government, Panchayat Elections were held in 2010 December in Jharkhand. Scheduled Areas itself has discrepancies as we, mentioned above.

Very recently, on 25 January 2012, the Jharkhand High Court issued directions to the State Government to implement Section 46 of the CNT Act strictly. The Scheduled Caste and the Backward Caste in the state will not be able to sell their land without the permission of the Deputy Commissioner. The Scheduled Caste and Backward Caste people cannot transfer their land to anyone. However, the Deputy Commissioner can grant permission for selling their land to the members of SC and BC both the parties residing in the same district.

It is all happening after a long lapse of time. Much water has flown down in the rivers, Damodar and Subarnarekha of Jharkhand.

Bibliography

BosuMullick,S. Edwin Jay, Das AntoAkkam and Anita Jay Das (1993) *Indigenous identity Crisis andReawakening*,NawdinPrakasan Kendra, Delhi.

Bijoy, C. R. (1993) Emergence of the Submerged, *Economic and Political Weekly*, Vol. XXVIIINo. 26.

Das, V. (1992) *Castle over the graves*. InterIndia Publishing House, New Delhi.

Danda, A.K. (1989) Policies of Tribal Welfare in India in M.K Raha and P.C. Coomar (eds.) *Tribal India : Problem Development Prospect*. Vol. 1, Gyan Publishing House, Delhi.

Roy Burman, B.K. (1979) The Post Primitives of Chotanagpur Identity Dilemmas and Ethnic Relations in *Trends in Ethnic Groups Relations in Asia and Oceania*, pp. 102-41. UNESCO, Paris.

Sen, R. (1992) Tribal Policy of India,*Indian Anthropologist* Vol. 22 No. 2, pp. 77-89.

Singh, S.P. (1989) *Chotanagpur Tenancy Act. 1908*. Malhotra Brothers, Patna.

Singh, P.K. (1998) Two Hundred Years of Permanent Settlement and the Tribals in *Land and Forest Twin Tribal Problems*. (ed. Sahay and Bhowmick), ISRAA, Bidisa, West Bengal.

Singh, P.K. (2004) Economic Situations in the Tribes of Jharkhand, *Journal of Social Research*,Vol 32 No. 1 & 2, pp. 73-81.

5

How Rights Based Public Policies are Influencing Tribal Welfare in Odisha

Brajaraja Mishra

Introduction

There is wide concern over the years that tribal people have not been benefited from the various development policies, while the mainstream societies have prospered at their expenses, pushing them into the poverty trap (Mahapatra, 1991). The land is their main source of livelihood, level of sustenance, and basis of their very existence as communities. "The right to own, occupies, and uses land collectively inherent in the self-conception of indigenous people, and this right is generally vested not in the individual but in the local community, the tribe or indigenous nation" (UNDP, 2004). Tribals are facing a lot of problems to maintain their community rights over the land mainly due to obstacles come from demographic changes, population growth, reduction of their traditional territories, and lack of coordination with the forest officials. These people are ignorant of their rights and thus are highly exploited by the other communities (Human and Pattanaik, 2000). There is no security over the land resources that they are economically, religiously and spiritually linked up and most of time they are forced to lose their rights for the sake of economic development (UNDP, 2004).

In India tribals are the bottom of the society, poor and marginalised, oppressed and deprived off from the basic needs of life (Rath, 2006). There are over 700 Scheduled Tribes notified under Article 342 of the Constitution of India, out of which 62 Scheduled Tribes are residing in the 12 tribal districts of the State of Odisha: Balasore, Mayurbhanj, Keonjhar, Sambalpur, Sundergarh, Gajapati, Kalahandi, Rayagada, Koraput, Malkangiri, Nabarangpur and Phulbani (Ministry of Tribal Affairs, GoI, 2010). The Fifth Schedule Areas of the state constitute about 44.25 per cent of the total land area of the state (Padhi & Panigrahi, n.d.). The tribal population of the State, as per the 2001 Census is 81.45 lakh comprising 22.1 per cent of the State's total population and 9.66 per cent of the India's ST population which increased at a decadal growth rate of 15.83 per cent against the previous Census 1991. About 75.6 per cent of the rural and 61.8 per cent of the urban ST people are living Below the Poverty Line during 2004-05 (Ministry of Tribal Affairs, GoI, 2010). The child sex ratio has decreased from 998 in 1991 Census to 979 in 2001 Census. There is also a marked improvement in the literacy rate. The literacy gap which was 26.8 per cent during the 1991 Census has declined to 25.7 per cent in the 2001 Census. The tribes of Odisha though belong to four linguistic divisions namely (1) Indo-Aryan Speakers, (2) Dravidian Speakers, (3) Tibeto-Burmese Speakers, and (4) Austric Speakers, their life style, livelihood activities, resource ownership, socio-economic status, religious belief, etc. are quite similar. A major portion of the tribal habitat is hilly and forested. Tribal villages are generally found in areas away from the alluvial plains and close to the rivers. Most villages are uni-ethnic in composition, and smaller in size.

Tribal economy is based on customary and usufructuary rights over the land and forest resources which is mainly subsistence oriented (Padhi & Panigrahi, n.d.). It is mainly based on collecting, hunting and fishing (i.e. tribals like the Birhor, Hill Kharia), or a combination of hunting and collecting with shifting cultivation (i.e., tribals like the Juang, Hill Bhuiyan, Lanjia Saora, Kondh, etc.). The production process is characterised by extensive farming, simple technology, gender division of labour, small-scale units of production and absence of investment of capital. The common pool nature of resources supported by the customary rights prevents intensification of production, in the interest of conserving and sustaining the long-term productivity of the livelihood resources (Padhi & Panigrahi, n.d.). The social unit of production, distribution and consumption is limited to the family and lineage.

History of the Violation of Tribal Rights in Odisha

There is growing debate over the years about the long lasting injustice of ignoring tribal rights. They are restricted from their traditional and substantial livelihoods practices because of the implementation of the various forest conservation Acts and Rules and displacement and rehabilitation policy. Ministry of Tribal Affairs (MoTA) agrees the fact that, the rights of the tribals over the forest and forest produces is not adequately protected due to restrictions imposed by implementing various forest conservation Acts (Standing Committee on Labour and Welfare, 2002). During 1855, the colonial government issued a memorandum titled "Charter of Indian Forests", which mentions that all forest land belongs to the government property. Subsequently, the Forest Department was established and restrictions were imposed over the use of forest resources through implementation of the Indian Forest Act, 1865. The National Forest Policy came into force during 1952 which put further restrictions on access to forest and forest produces. The Wildlife Protection Act, 1972 came into force on dated 9th September 1972 which mentions that no person shall willfully pick, uproot, damage, destroys, acquire or collect and sell any specified plant from any forest land area. However the National Forest Policy, 1988 became a significant movement towards ecosystem conservation and enhancement of livelihoods by recognising tribal rights. But rules to implement the policy were not put in place until much later, and state governments in the meantime progressively reduced the traditional rights of the tribal people (Human and Pattanaik 2000).

According to the Orissa Land Reform Act (OLRA), 1960, lands belongs to a Scheduled Tribe (ST) cannot be alienated to a person belongs to non-Scheduled Tribe and the District Collector has the *suo moto* power to protect the tribals against any such transfers. But land alienation remains prevalent in Odisha even though it is officially unacknowledged (Fernandes *et al.*, 1988). The colonialism made it difficult to determine how much of land that tribal people have usurfructuary rights and how much they were lost in time (Padhi & Panigrahi, n.d.).While tribals are taking any loan from the moneylender, they are used to mortgage their land and the moneylender extracts whole produce in terms of interest payment. In subsequent periods when they are unable to repay their loans the moneylender becomes sole owner of the land. A study by Viegas (1987) in four districts of Odisha shows that, about 56 per cent of the total tribal land was lost over a period of 25-30 years due to various means, out of which 40 per cent were due to indebtedness and land mortgage, 23 per cent through personal sale, and the balance due to floods and other natural calamities. Faulty land settlement operations also another major factor of loss of tribal rights over the land (Mearns & Sinha, 1999). For example, in 1961 land settlement survey, 15 acres out of a total village area surveyed of 2647 acres in Niyamgiri hills of South-Western Odisha were declared as cultivable land (Roy Burman, 1987). But in reality many of these areas are owned by the tribal households.

According to the Tenth Five Year Plan, in India during the period of 1951-1990, as many as 213 lakh people including 85.40 lakh (40 per cent) of the tribals were displaced due to various development projects like dams, industries and mining (Standing Committee on Labour and Welfare, 2002). In Odisha various projects such as hydroelectric-cum-irrigation projects (i.e., Hirakud (1948), Balimela (1963), Machhkund (1949), Upper Kolab (1978), Indravati (1978), Mandira, Rengali (1973) and Subarnarekha mineral-based industries (i.e., Rourkela Steel Plant (1950), National Aluminum Company at Angul (1985), Hindustan Aeronautics Ltd (1962)); the bauxite mining project at Koraput (1981); and projects on cement, iron, dolomite and limestone have been developed which displaced lakhs of tribal people (Padhi & Panigrahi, n.d.). About 78.62 thousand hectares of forest land were transferred for promotion of such development projects (Fernandes *et. al.* 1988); Economic Survey of Odisha (various issues). According to Mohapatra (1999), over a period of five decades (1951-95), about 5.61 lakh tribals were displaced but only 35 per cent were rehabilitated (Table 5.1). All these projects have immense adverse effects on tribal welfare because they are facing a lot of problems in the rehabilitated place due to inadequate livelihood opportunities, and their indigenous beliefs and practices.

Table 5.1 : Number of Tribals Displaced and Rehabilitated in Odisha Due to Various Development Projects 1951-95

Sl. No	*Nature of Projects*	*No of Displaced*	*No of Rehabilitated*	
			Number	*Per cent*
1.	Hydro-electric Projects	325000	90000	27.69
2.	Industrial Projects	71794	27300	38.03
3.	Mining	100000	60000	60.00
4.	Sanctuary	50000	15540	31.08
5.	Miscellaneous Purposes	14746	5265	35.70
	Total	561540	198105	35.28

Source: Mohapatra (1999)

Evolution of the Rights Based Approaches to Resource Ownership

Universal Declaration of Human Rights (1948) had proposed a bundle of rights including rights to own property, and maintain a standard of living adequate to health and well-being that should be enjoyed by each person in the society (United Nations, 1991). These rights are synonymously used as the legal rights provided by the state (e.g., Fundamental Rights of the Constitution of India) to its citizens—basic life requirements that all humans are entitled to. Human rights are best to be understood as some supernatural terms and ideas arising from a particular set of alienating economic arrangements. Ideologically, they are considered both to conceal the particular interests of the bourgeoisie and to expose the limits of this class's liberal revolution (Marx, 1994). "When a new society establishes by people's control over the economic means of production, the apparatus of rights which functioned primarily to justify bourgeois possession of private property, would become unnecessary" (Engler, 2000). Given these juridical limits and this ideological prioritisation, it cannot be said that human rights are extended with impartiality to all persons - rather they are accorded in a manner that shows deference to certain groups of people (Miguez, 1977). When basic social human rights are not genuinely respected, those who face constant violation of these rights can take little solace in the pretentious language of universality. If a group of people is deprived off from their rights while other groups are enjoying, it creates envy and agony in the society. Biasness of human rights towards a specific category of people in the society raises the question of the ethical necessity of the ownership rights.

The answer to this questions liberalism principle says that it is the rights of the poor over certain resources. The Article 46 of the Directive Principles of State Policy states, "the state shall promote with special care the educational and economic interests of the weaker sections of the people, and, in particular, of the Scheduled Castes (SCs) and Scheduled Tribes (STs), and shall protect them from social injustice and all forms of exploitation". The Supreme Court of India (1997) further observes that, for poor/tribal, land is the most important natural and valuable asset, and imperishable endowment. It is a means of their sustainable living, maintenance of social and economic equality, enhancement of economic empowerment, and a safety net during acute crisis. Thus, assurance over the rights of land which they enjoy is necessary to promote social and economic justice in a democratic country like India.

There are certain principles which attract everybody's attentions towards justification of the rights of the tribals over the natural resources. It is widely felt that tribals—as a social class whose destitute circumstances are not of chance misfortune rather the byproduct of systematic exploitation. Using a combination of social-scientific analysis, religious reflection, and practical activity, it is needed to address the structural causes of poverty and power of the poor to transform the situation (McGovern, 1989). Development philosophers argue that, "it ought to respect the dignity and individual autonomy of all those whom it claims to help, including the poorest and the most excluded, including minorities and other vulnerable groups, often discriminated against; it ought to create opportunities for their participation - opportunities that are not dependent on the whim of a benevolent outsider, but rooted in institutions and procedures" (Uvin, 2007). Political thought also argues that any process of reform is dangerous when the changes it made are merely announced and accepted in theory without any necessarily conflicting engagement that accompanies real change (Engler, 2000). Thus, the Fifth and Sixth Schedule of the Indian Constitution speaks about the protection of tribals from the exploitation, to preserve the natural endowment of the land for their economic empowerment, and to cognate social and economic democracy with liberty, equity, fraternity and dignity.

But the national/states governments in most of the time deny the rights of the tribals to live and manage their traditional lands. They are forcefully exploits/assimilates/harasses tribals by enforcing strict legal provisions, which destroys their indigenous culture, tradition, livelihood, and social organisation (Singh and Kaur, 2009). "Human rights revolution" needs a revolution which must be lived by the majority in our world whose human rights are constantly violated and by those who would deprive them of these rights. It is also argued that, human rights are not established and intransigent ideals rather they are concepts continually being shaped and defined in historical struggle. Human rights have conceptual value and practical usefulness and hence in a world of persistent of injustice, the emergence and mandate of these rights may approach better social development. In addition, the human-rights approach clearly implies an absolute requirement of participation. This means that agencies should provide all relevant information to the people—in local languages if necessary, strictly monitor and ensure the security of the participant, and meet all the cost of participation (Uvin, 2007).

It is also necessary to understand the type of rights that should be passed to maintain equity. Legal thought mentions two types of rights—liberty right and claim right. Liberty right is the right that merely freedoms and do not correlated with any duties or obligations whereas a claim right is correlated with the duties of another or others. "These duties consist in either refraining from actions that would impede the right holder in his exercise of the right or, sometimes of performing actions that will give the right holder the thing he has a right to" (Curran, 2002). According to Hobbes, liberty right is an illusion—right of all men to all things is not better than no man had right to anything. If the rights are not protected the rights holder feels helpless like a person with no rights at all. Thus, people should get an adequate scope for better exercise of their rights by reducing the impediments involved in the transfer of rights.

Whether the rights of the people that should be protected are justifiable on humanitarian or welfare perspective? Some are of the opinion that it is the welfare right that ethically induces policy makers to distribute resources towards poor (Griffin, 2000). The Eight Nobel Path of Lord Buddha's mentions rights to livelihood as a basic human right. The Article 25 of the United Nations Universal Declaration of Human Rights (UNUDHR) includes all the major welfare rights. Political economy literature also states that the provision of basic needs of life is a human right. Thus the right to livelihood is a welfare right on the ground of ethics—rights of personhood, which is a necessary condition to govern efficient resource allocation in the society.

But sometime on the feasibility ground it is difficult on the part of the policy makers or other institutes to fulfill every demand of every person in the society. On the ethical ground also it is difficult on the part of a Government to fulfill all the claims of all persons (Griffin, 2000). Johnston and Button (1994) points out that humanity faces deprivation from the environmental rights because of at least three reasons. Firstly some people are living in the wrong place (near to mining areas, weapon testing place, storage of hazardous waste, boarders between two political regions, etc.) are most of the time displaces, alienated from their traditional holdings and experiencing increasing difficulty in maintaining individual and community welfare. Secondly, in the way of progress, national needs supersede the individual and community concerns. As such during the construction of dams, expansion of export-oriented agriculture, industrial development and tourism, maintenance of wilderness in some areas for protections of rare flora and fauna, etc. people are forcefully relocated (The Ecologist, 1993). Lastly, some time it is socially, culturally and legally acceptable to protect interest of some people while knowingly placing other humans at risk (Johnston and Button, 1994).

History of the recognition of welfare rights had very good and very bad consequences. We have many experiences of evils of fear, insecurity, ignorance, malnutrition and low life expectancy in the present society. There is also lack of self-reliance, self-respect, ambition, hope, inefficient policy paradigms and undermining of the valuable intermediate social institutions. There is no doubt that, with the best of intentions we have cured one set of ills and produced another—this is the nature of social change. The sensible response to it is not to prevent the changes but to admit to the new ills as they appear and try to cure them (Griffin, 2000). The cures will in turn produce their own new ills, and so on forever.

The Scheduled Tribes and Other Traditional Forest Dwellers (Recognition of Forest Rights) Act, 2006

The rights based approach which is famous as Forest Rights Act (FRA) has come into force on 1st January 2008. It recognises and vests rights of the Scheduled Tribes and other forest dwellers over the forest lands, who are residing in these areas for generations. According to the GoI (2007), "the recognised rights of the forest dwelling Scheduled Tribes and other traditional dwellers include the responsibilities and authority for the sustainable use of resources, conservation of biodiversity, and maintenance of ecological balance and thereby strengthening the conservation regime of the forest while ensuing livelihood and food security of the forest dwelling Scheduled Tribes and other Traditional forest dwellers". It also includes those people who were forced to relocate their dwellings due to state intervention. Thus, the underlying objective of the Act has been to strike a balance between the potentially conflicting interests of the forest dwelling communities and protecting forests and wildlife resources.

Rights assigned to people include a bundle of rights that is provided to secure both individual and community tenure rights over the forest land. With respect to the claims over the rights to access these resources and conservation of biodiversity, clear provisions are undertaken for active peoples' participation with adequate gender equity. In order to enjoy these rights these people are empowered for the protection of wildlife, forest and biodiversity, adjoining catchment area, water bodies, ecological sensitive areas, habitat of forest dwellers from any form of destructive practices that affecting their cultural and natural heritage and regulation of activities which adversely affects wild animals, forests and the biodiversity. There is also provision for the declaration of Critical Wildlife Habitats (CWHs) in the Protected Areas (PAs) to maintain wilderness of the area for the purpose of conservation of certain endanger species.

Odisha is one of the pioneering states to implement FRA in most of the Reserve and Protected forest landscapes. According to the source, there is a total of 5.25 lakes Individual Claims and 3239 Community Claims are received by the FRCs but only 56.16 per cent of individual claims and 24.64 per cent of community claims are approved at the final level (Table 5.2). But high rejection of the community claims is a disappointing fact since tribals generally depending on CPRs rather than have individual lands.

Table 5.2: Summary of Statistics of Implementation of FRA in Odisha as on 1st January 2012.

Nature of Claims		*Individual Claims*	*Community Claims*
No. Of Claims Received By the FRCs		*525748*	*3239*
Claims Approved By Gram Sabha	Area (Acre.)	659218.53	83986.55
	Families (No.)	403777	62435
Claims Approved By SDLC	Area (Acre)	514371.19	74367.12
	Families (No.)	313585	55706
Claims Approved By DLC	Area (Acre)	501727.46	71385.74
	Families (No.)	307104	54033
Titles Distributed	Area (Acre.)	475136.27	54255.40
	No. Of Titles	295246	798

Source: www.fra.org.in.

A report published by a Joint Committee of Ministry of Environment and Forest (MoEF) and Ministry of Tribal Affairs (MoTA), GoI chair by Dr. N.C. Saxena has reviewed the implementation of the FRA, 2006 in all the states of India. The Committee had adopted a participatory approach consisting of a number of meetings, email conversions, field visits, public consultations and workshops, and meetings with Government officials to analyse the effectiveness of the policy. The Committee had submitted a detailed report on December 2010. According to the report, Forest Rights Committees (FRCs) have been formed through a democratic process by Government officials and teachers rather than through election by *Gram Sabha* (GS). However, in some cases individual rights are not recognised. For example in two POSCO affected villages of Jagatsinghpur district, their individual rights are not recognised, even though they have genuine documentary evidences, on the ground that they did not follow the right procedure (through GS) and the documents are fabricated (Ms Neena Gupta Committee, 2010). Odisha has encouraged and sponsored civil society involvement in facilitating GS/FRCs. The nodal agency has issued several instructions to all District Collectors to involve the local civil societies, peoples' forum and their networks in facilitating the FRA implementation process. Besides this, the State Nodal Agency has been taking help from the civil society groups in identifying the implementation related issues and addressing it by issuing a clarification circulars time to time.

Most of the tribals are nomads. Their absence during the verification process makes it difficult to select actual beneficiaries. As a result, the Sub-Divisional Level Committees (SDLCs)/District Level Committees (DLCs) excluded a lot of people from the claimant list. Interestingly, all the titles are distributed are on revenue lands and reserve forests are excluded due to the absence of land records and proper maps (www.fra.org.in). In many areas SDLCs/DLCs were formed among the forest officials without approaching the Panchayat Raj Institutions (PRIs) and Primitive Tribal Groups (PTGs). The Government has diverted huge money from the Tribal Sub-Plan (TSP) and other funds to hire technical support groups to help GS/FRCs during the verification process. For example, in Sundergarh, Koraput and Malkangiri districts, NGOs were helped in sensitisation, facilitating evidence gathering, and monitoring (Saxena Committee, 2010). A lot of corruptions were found at various levels but no actions were undertaken against those persons.

Even though there are protests from the NGOs, people groups, and activists, people living inside the PAs have restricted access to land and forest produces. Forceful relocations are still prevalent in most of the PAs. There is clear provision that there should not be any forceful displacement from the PAs. People can stay in the Core area and have to enjoy all rights like other forest areas. Those who are relocated on their personal interest should have adequate rehabilitation packages. But the Forest Department (FD) did not provide clear information to the people and involved forced displacement in most of the PAs like Similipal and Sariska (Saxena Committee, 2010). The FD has a fixed format of community claims where options for most of the claims were absent. The format received by the communities in Similipal Tiger Reserve mentions that communities cannot claim firewood and nistar rights, did not mention the right to manage and protect forest, should not mention about the size/area of land, and collection and sale of NTFPs should be as per the Odisha Gram Panchayats (Minor Forest Produce Administration) Rules, 2002.

Shifting cultivation is the main source of living of the major tribals particularly of PTGs. But no such claims so far recognised. Those people who were forcefully resettled and their access to forest resources were restricted in the National Park (NP) or Wildlife Sanctuaries after implementation of the *WLPA*, 1972 however got eminent scope for their development due to implementation of the FRA. Odisha is too advance in the publication of data on both individual and community claims of PTGs. But like other states it fails document community rights. The state had issued a number of circulars specifically focusing the rights of the PTGs. There are several PTGs such as Juang in Keonjhar district, Dongria Kondh in Kalahandi district, Chakutia Bhunjia in Nuapada district, and Mankiridia and Khadia in Mayurbhanj district have benefited from the community rights (Saxena Committee, 2010). But there are also several instances rights of the PTGs are violated because of the ambiguities involved in the identification of the beneficiaries, management of resources, and recognition of the customary rights.

The forest official people have a lot of confusion about the community rights. They do not have any information about the verification process, criteria of individual and community claims, geographical boundary of the land, maximum limit of land that should be granted, claims of two communities over the same land and villages consisting of a mix of eligible and ineligible households (Saxena Committee, 2010). In Mayurbhanj district for instance, communities are informed that the boundary of the CPRs are pre-decided according to the official records under the Joint Forest Management or Community Forest Management. It may be a reason for clear identification of boundaries but involved the limitation of restricting of the communities to claim lands that they have customary rights. In most cases *Gram Sabha* does not allow or facilitated to play the role of determining community rights. Ms Meena Gupta Committee Report mentions that, three months of time have allotted to claim for the individual rights in *Gram Sabha*, but in case of the community rights, some date is fixed and no further extension allows in any circumstances which creates many ambiguities. In some cases, communities with help from the civil society groups have undertaken a comprehensive process of preparing the claims including discussion in the entire village, detail mapping and collection of evidence and initiation of the planning process but their claims were rejected in the latter stages. There are a lot of ambiguities involved with regards to the operation definition of the forest dwellers (Mohanty, 2012). Most of the non-Scheduled Tribes are told not to fill the claim on the fallacy that it is only meant for the tribes. For instance, over 200 villagers of Other Traditional Forest Dwellers (OTFDs) in Nayagarh district have community claims but their claims were rejected on the ground that they are not Scheduled Tribes. In some cases like Jagatsinghpur it has been officially publicised. The Government also did not approve claims of the women.

In some cases there is clear information about the approval/rejection of titles. As per the rule, officials from the tribal department, forest departments and revenue department jointly have to do verification of the claims. But the absence of the FD officials in time makes it difficult for verification of forest lands where tribals have community claims. As a result in most of the case only agricultural lands currently under cultivation were surveyed and excluded fallow lands (www.fra.org.in). There is a wide gap between the claims approved and the area mentioned in the title. In some cases it is about one tenth of the claims approved and there is no further explanation of such reductions. Some cases conditional titles are provided. For instance titled people have to protect wildlife areas and corridors, not encourage forest encroachment and take necessary steps to protect forests and wildlife which is even absent in the FRA provisions (Saxena Committee, 2010). There are some instances where cross-state claims were rejected. For instance Vasundhara, an Odisha based NGO reported three such cases where interstate claims were rejected: (i) bordering villages in Sundergarh have lands in Jharkhand, (ii) Mankadia communities of Mayurbhanj have claimed from the boundary of West Bengal and Jharkhand and (iii) The Cacti Bhunjia, a PTG community of Nuapada district have lands in Chhattisgarh.

Conclusion

This study explains about the history of the violation of the tribal rights in Odisha and the process of evaluation of the rights based approaches to resource ownership by taking the example of the recent development of the FRA, 2006. The impact of the 'property rights' has a mix of success and failures but may be considered as a better approach than the previous forest related welfare programs. Resource ownership has created some sort of food and livelihood security which promoted them to consume more nutrient foods, sent children to school, take care of the family health and sanitation, reduce conspicuous consumptions, improve socio-cultural relations, and induce propensity to save to meet unforeseen contingencies. It smoothens the consumption and production cycle through easy access to and allocation of scarce resources to the most useful needs. Thus, property rights institutions are playing most critical role in human resource development. Easy access to market, adequate and timely supply of inputs of production and irrigation, educational development, price security, etc. are the other associated factors also determining tribal welfare which needs to be improved simultaneously. The scope and coverage of these institutions are limited might due to the mismatch between different implementation agencies and the beneficiaries concerned. Some reasons are unavoidable and out of the practical coverage due to the short period, less funds, low human resource, lack of adequate information and differences in individual choices and preferences. But some of the limitations such as the principal—agent problem, exclusion of the beneficiaries, corruptions, knowledge gap, and coordination failure can be rectifiable and minimised by developing a sound Government machinery, allocating more economic resources, establishing a strong link between the Government officials and tribal people, and developing social institutions.

Bibliography

Brian, H. R. (1991). The Evolution of Human Rights Policy in Ontario. *Canadian Journal of Political Science , 24*, 783-802.

Curran, E. (2002). Hobbes's Theory of Rights: A Modern Interest Theory. *Journal of Ethics , 6* (1), 63-86.

Engler, M. (2000). Toward the Rights of the Poor: Human Rights in Liberation Theology. *The Journal of Religious Ethics , 28* (3), 339-365.

Fernades, W. E. (1984). *Forest, environment and forest dwellers economy in Orissa.* New Delhi: Indian Social Institute.

Fernandes, W., Menon, G., & Viegas, P. (1988). Forests, Environment and Tribal Economy: Deforestation, Impoverishment and Marginalisation in Orissa. New Delhi: Indian Social Institute.

Griffin, J. (2000). Welfare Rights. *The Journal of Ethics , 4* (1-2), 27-43.

Human, J., & Pattanaik, M. (2000). Community Forest Management: A Casebook From India. Oxfam: Oxford.

Johnston, B., & Button, G. (1994). Human Environmental Rights Issues and Multinational Corporation: Industrial Development in the Free Trade Zone. In B. Johnston, *Who Pays the Price? The Sociocultural Context of Environmental Crisis* (pp. 206-216). Washington D.C.: Island Press.

Mahapatra, L. (1991). Development for Whom? Depriving the Dispossessed Tribals. *Social Action , 41* (3).

Marx, K. (1994). Selected Writings. In S. Lawrence, *Indianapolis.* Hackett: Ind.

McGovern, A. (1989). *Liberation Theology and Its Critics.* New York: Orbis.

Mearns, R., & Sinha, S. (1999). *Social Exclusion and Land Administration in Orissa, India.* Washington D.C.: The World Bank.

Miguez, B. J. (1977). Whose Human Rights? *International Review of Mission , 66*, 220-24.

Ministry of Tribal Affairs. (2010). *Annual Report 2009-10.* New Delhi: Government of India.

Mohapatra, L. K. (1999). Tribals' rights to land and the state in Orissa. In D. Behura, & G. Pfeffer, *Contemporary Society Tribal Studies.* New Delhi: Concept Publishing House.

Ms Meena Gupta Committee. (2010). Report of the Committee Constituted to Investigate into the proposal submitted by POSCO India Pvt. Limited for establishment of an Integrated Steel Plant and CaptivePort in Jagatsinghpur District, Odisha. New Delhi: Ministry of Environment and Forest.

Saxena Committe. (2010). *Report on National Committee on Forest Rights Act.* New Delhi: Ministry of Environment and Forest and Ministry of Tribal Affairs .

Padhi, S., & Panigrahi, N. (n.d.). *Tribal Movements and Livelihoods: Recent Developments in Orissa.* New Delhi: Indian Institute of Public Administration.

Rath, G. (2006). Tribal Development in India: The Contemporary Debate. Delhi: Sage Publications.

Roy Burman, B. (1987). Historical Process in Respect of Communal Land System and Poverty Alleviation among Tribals. *Social Action , 37* (4), 391-420.

Singh, R., & Kaur, G. (2009). Human Rights of Indigenous People: A Reflection of Reality. *Asia-Precific Journal of Social Sciences , 1* (1), 117-126.

Standing Committee on Labour and Welfare. (2002). *Development of Primitive Tribal Groups: Twenty Eighth Report.* New Delhi: Ministry of Tribal Affairs.

The Ecologist. (1993). *Whose Common Future?* London: The Ecologist.

UNDP. (2004). Human Development Report 2004: Cultural Liberty in Today's Diverse World. New York: Oxford University Press.

Uvin, P. (2007). From the Right to Development to the Rights-Based Approach: How 'Human Rights' Entered Development. *Development in Practice , 17* (4-5), 597-606.

Viegas, P. (1987). Land Control and Tribal Struggle for Survival. *Social Action , 37* (4), 325-344.

Annexure 1 : Status of FRA, 2006 as on 31st January 2012

Status of Implementation of the Forest Rights Act, 2006 in the State (Odisha) (Individual Claims) (as on 31.01.2012)

Sl. No.	Name of the District	No. of Village in the District	No. of villages fully covered	No. of Claim received by FRCs	Gram Sabha Level			Sub-Divisional Committee Level			Dist. Level Committee Level			No. Titles distributed	Area (in acres)	No. of Titles distributed to PTGs	Area in acres
					No. of claims	Area (in Acres)	No. of families	No. of claims	Area (in Acres)	No. of families	No. of claims	Area (in Acres)	No. of families				
1	2	3	4	5	6	7	8	9	10	11	12	13	14	15	16	17	18
1	Angul	1632		8285	7250	4025	7250	3281	1970	3281	2503	1522	2503	2503	1522	991	416
2	Balasore	2691		4595	2785	1621	2785	2785	1621	2785	2785	1621	2785	1954	993	0	0
3	Bargarh	1207		3512	2630	3689	2630	1117	2374	1117	1017	1839	1017	961	1727	0	0
4	Bhadrak	1248	1210	202	202	11	202	175	10	175	175	10	175	175	10	0	0
5	Bolangir	1753		4796	4796	8710	4796	1079	2465	1079	1079	2465	1079	1079	2465	0	0
6	Boudh	1190	1164	3499	3242	4996	3242	1267	1832	1267	1108	1694	1108	997	1147	0	0
7	Cuttack	1857	69	5767	2324	1941	2324	1419	1077	1419	1419	1077	1419	1419	1077	0	0
8	Deogarh	774		11718	10118	16059	10118	4097	3766	4097	3982	3713	3982	3982	3713	799	494
9	Dhenkanal	1030		12529	12529	17390	12529	5550	7857	5550	5550	7857	5550	5051	7282	0	0
10	Gajapati	1528	1370	44615	28030	58842	28030	28030	58842	28030	28030	58842	28030	28030	58842	2106	3693
11	Ganjam	2831		12957	8533	16086	8533	5436	14037	5436	5075	13006	5075	5047	12943	459	1163
12	Jagatsinghpur	1230		49	48	32	48	47	32	47	47	32	47	47	32	0	0
13	Jajpur	1575		9170	1825	1057	1825	1815	1045	1815	1801	1045	1801	1801	1045	0	0
14	Jharsuguda	352		9204	9204	9427	9204	2354	2108	2354	2354	2108	2354	2319	2099	0	0
15	Kalahandi	2068	110	11378	10582	15293	10582	9927	14903	9927	9608	14531	9608	9176	14094	310	314
16	Kandhamal	2415	2335	56137	54216	86818	54216	53709	86260	53709	53606	85602	53606	53606	85602	1210	2693
17	Kendrapara	1619		4045	3233	1066	3233	310	449	310	305	442	305	305	442	0	0

Sl. No.	Name of the District	No. of Village in the District	No. of villages fully covered	No. of Claim received by FRCs	Gram Sabha Level			Sub-Divisional Committee Level			Dist. Level Committee Level			No. Titles distributed	Area (in acres)	No. of Titles distributed to PTGs	Area in acres
					No. of claims	Area (in Acres)	No. of families	No. of claims	Area (in Acres)	No. of families	No. of claims	Area (in Acres)	No. of families				
1	2	3	4	5	6	7	8	9	10	11	12	13	14	15	16	17	18
18	Keonjhar	2045	1021	52598	39976	71487	39976	37141	36443	37141	37141	36443	37141	36400	35921	4311	5851
19	Khurda	1355		2164	706	790	706	670	676	670	630	590	630	630	590	0	0
20	Koraput	1890	1188	33710	24873	43306	24873	24691	38325	24691	24621	38239	24621	23009	34881	0	0
21	Malkangiri	933	280	32893	31922	81294	31922	26965	73087	26965	26037	70082	26037	25183	64303	2329	5568
22	Mayurbhanj	3758	900	37554	27104	16244	27104	18586	11804	18586	18586	11804	18586	18586	11804	1281	807
23	Nawapara	658	89	9162	9137	21320	9137	5054	13211	5054	5054	13211	5054	4385	11395	204	602
24	Nawarangpur	867	454	36084	35040	66730	35040	32423	65630	32423	32423	65630	32423	30411	58832	0	0
25	Nayagarh	1516		3334	2808	3945	2808	2708	3945	2708	2654	3902	2654	2620	3891	0	0
26	Puri	1613		1169	1169	80	1169								0	0	0
27	Rayagada	2469	1602	30053	28147	43823	28147	16714	27243	16714	15212	24795	15212	15212	24795	2682	4371
28	Sambalpur	1262	628	29853	19319	21875	19319	12353	16805	12353	12019	16347	12019	10814	14976	0	0
29	Subarnapur	825	3	1561	1409	3298	1409	334	651	334	326	642	326	326	642	0	0
30	Sundargarh	1668	1668	53155	22744	37963	20620	13548	25904	13548	11957	22638	11957	9218	18074	463	423
	Odisha	47859	14091	525748	405901	659219	403777	313585	514371	313585	307104	501727	307104	295246	475136	17145	26397

Source: www.fra.org.in

Annexure 2 : Status of Community Rights as on 31st January 2012

Status of Implementation of the Forest Rights Act, 2006 in the State (Odisha) (Community Claims) (as on 31.01.2012)																	
Sl. No.	Name of the District	No. of Village in the District	No. of villages fully covered	No. of Claim received by FRCs	Gram Sabha Level			Sub-Divisional Committee Level			Dist. Level Committee Level			No. of Titles distrib-uted	Area (in acres)	No. of Titles distri-buted to PTGs	Area in acres
					No. of claims	Area (in Acres)	No. of families	No. of claims	Area (in Acres)	No. of families	No. of claims	Area (in Acres)	No. of families				
1	2	3	4	5	6	7	8	9	10	11	12	13	14	15	16	17	18
1	Angul	1632		2													
2	Balasore	2691		434	40	126	400	24	76	240	2	52		2	52		
3	Bargarh	1207		2	2	4											
4	Bhadrak	1248	1210	0													
5	Bolangir	1753															
6	Boudh	1190	1164	104	1	12											
7	Cuttack	1857	69	19	15	6580	469	3	7	115	3	7	115	3	7	0	0
8	Deogarh	774		61	60			6	14		6	14		6	14		
9	Dhenkanal	1030		57	53	158	1473	46	106	938	46	106	938	46	106		
10	Gajapati	1528	20	109	20	3343	179	20	3343	179	20	3343	179	20	3343		
11	Ganjam	2831		62	52	290		34	272		24	130		24	130		
12	Jagatsinghpur	1230		0													
13	Jajpur	1575		0													
14	Jharsuguda	352		8	8	9	120	2	5	2	2	5	2	2	5	0	0.00
15	Kalahandi	2068		169	169	21500	8817	169	21500	8817	155	21107	8191	140	18535	5	192
16	Kandhamal	2415		165	3	3	50	2	1	35	0	0	0				
17	Kendrapara	1619		145	103	108	336										
18	Keonjhar	2045		379	346	7783	23544	328	7428	23544	328	7428	23544	322	7419	20	283

Sl. No.	Name of the District	No. of Village in the District	No. of villages fully covered	No. of Claim received by FRCs	Gram Sabha Level			Sub-Divisional Committee Level			Dist. Level Committee Level			No. of Titles distrib-uted	Area (in acres)	No. of Titles distri-buted to PTGs	Area in acres
					No. of claims	Area (in Acres)	No. of families	No. of claims	Area (in Acres)	No. of families	No. of claims	Area (in Acres)	No. of families				
1	2	3	4	5	6	7	8	9	10	11	12	13	14	15	16	17	18
19	Khurda	1355		2	2	0											
20	Koraput	1890	796	330	58	2781	2950	58	2781	2950	58	2781	2950	51	1781		
21	Malkangiri	933	282	131	117	4197	10863	79	3015	8123	73	2911	7797	68	2203		
22	Mayurbhanj	3758	43	45	45	20624	3549	45	20624	3549	44	19394	3319	42	19394	16	14644
23	Nawapara	658		35	35	2497	2260	20	1920	1528	20	1920	1528	5	20		
24	Nawarangpur	867	20	84	74	1311	1480	32	1051	864	32	1051	864	20	408		
25	Nayagarh	1516		91	2	500	64	2	500	64	2	500	64	2	500		
26	Puri	1613		0													
27	Rayagada	2469		20	20	316	126	20	316	126	8	15	37	8	15		
28	Sambalpur	1262	497	340	175	10897	5155	78	10623	4493	78	10623	4493	37	325		
29	Subarnapur	825	3	15	15	164	600	6	7	122	1	1	12				
30	Sundargarh	1668	1668	430	27	786		17	781	17							
	Odisha	47859	5772	3239	1442	83987	62435	991	74367	55706	902	71386	54033	798	54255	41	15121

Source: www.fra.org.in

6

Emerging Problems of the Indigenous People on the Way to Development

Samar Kumar Biswas

The tribal populations are living in different corners of India and primarily lived in hilly, forested, and isolated areas. From time immemorial, they are the inhabitants of India and presently more than eight per cent of total population of this country has been occupied by them. After Africa, India is the second largest tribal population of the world. They vary in strength in different states from twenty to several lakhs, and primarily they are concentrated in Madhya Pradesh, Jharkhand, Odisha, Maharashtra, Bihar and the North Eastern States of India and so on.

The characteristics of tribals are normally :

1. each tribe has a common name;
2. members of the tribe live in a common area/territory;
3. they have a common dialect/language;
4. they are culturally homogenous;
5. they have a common occupation and generally they are based on simple economy;
6. they have own political organization; and
7. they have common ancestor and religious faith.

Primarily, they depend on nature for maintaining their daily livelihood. Hunting, gathering, pastoralism, agriculture, artisan type, day labour, etc. are the basic economy of the tribals. In respect to nature, their prime sources of economy are forest, land and water sources (like river, wetland, etc.).

Depending on forest, they collect various forest materials, mushrooms, fruits, roots, tubers, honey, beams, branches, grasses for house making, wooden log for plough making, household and utensils; various fibers, cocoons and other raw materials for making various crafts, clothes, etc.; fodder for their domestic cattle, medicinal plants for treatment, *kendu* leaf, resign, fuel, and so on. Apart from this, sacred grooves are also very important in respect to their socio-religious life. Depending primarily on hunting, forest is an integral part of them, as they hunt different animals which fulfill their demand of food and nutrition. That tribal people who depend on pastoralism, pasture land is very important for them. Most of the tribals rear various domestic cattle as subsistence economy from where they get various nutritious foods and so on.

From water sources, they collect various aquatic flora and fauna like fish, snail, mollusc, fruit, root and tuber of aquatic and semi-aquatic plants from where they get the nutritious foods and so on also.

A major section of the tribals primarily depend on agriculture. They practice both *jhum* cultivation and settled agriculture. Most in cases, now they are practicing monocrop cultivation. They however can produce various crops, such as maize, paddy, wheat, *rai*, *cowni*, *bazra*, oilseeds, numerous vegetables, fruit plants, roots and tubers (potato, beat, carrot, yam, etc.), spices and so on.

Moreover, their way of living is very simple. They enjoy a lot through celebration of various social and religious ceremonies, festivals, etc. They have their own social systems controlled by themselves. They share their joys and sorrows through these occasions. They are peace-loving, cordial and obedient.

However, tribal people in India and other parts of the world are known by different names. They are mostly vulnerable groups. From the views of polity, economy, social-cultural paradigm and religious matters, government in those respective countries can not neglect the bulk. Respective authorities should provide safeguards to them according to the State's constitutional provisions. In this global paradigm, this issue of excluded groups who are so close to nature and possess their own intellectual reasoning and therefore capable of providing certain types of global public services and alternative solutions of so many problems could not be so far neglected. International LabourOrganisation has postulated some indigenous rights on the global basis and not specifically concentrating on a single indigenous community, included all of them under the category of indigenous peoples. Indigenous Rights encompass the domains like general policy (1-12), land (13-19), recruitment and conditions of employment (20),vocational training (21-23), handicrafts and rural industries (21-23), social security and health (24-25), Education and means of communication (26-31), contracts and co-operations across borders (32), administration (33), general provisions (34-36)- applicable to all the indigenous communities brought under the common umbrella of Indigenous People (ILO, 1991).

With the passes of time, non-tribal people began to enter into the hinterland of the tribals and gradually started to settle permanently with the tribals. Gradually, they started to exploit the tribals through occupying and monopolizing their natural resources and so on of the tribals. Not only that, they also began to deprive and exploit the tribals physically, mentally, and economically. Apart from these, several organizations, government and state machineries overloaded by the outsider non-tribal people cause the tribals loosing many things. Due to establishment of various dams, hydro-electrical power projects, thermal power plants, big industries and so on, the concerned authorities have acquired huge amount of tribal lands. However, the tribals have been displaced. Though they have got the compensation, but the tribals have lost their unity and solidarity. With their displacement, not only their habitations but also their kinship, culture, polity, economy, and religious life have been affected a lot. Even in several cases, many of the tribals have not got the compensation and rehabilitation. It is noteworthy to mention that in many cases the tribals have been partially benefited due to the above facts.

In respect to development, non-tribals have come in close contact with the tribals and started to exploit their natural resources rapidly. In this regard, they started to destroy the forest, which is deforestation. Due to this, social, economic, religious, political and cultural lives of the tribals have been severely affected. Due to deforestation, the tribals who depend on hunting and gathering as well as pastoralism have been affected a lot. Due to scarcity of medicinal plants, traditional treatment system has been affected to a great extent. Source of nutritious foods, hunting, games, mushrooms, honey, fruits, tubers, yam, etc. have been remarkably reduced. Due to these facts, the food, nutrition as well as health of the tribals have been seriously hampered. Therefore, due to deforestation, the tribals not only lost the source of economy or mental satisfaction, but also their survival was on the way of crisis.

In this regard, it is to be mentioned that the tribal areas which have been covered mostly by the forest, but now-a-days these are replaced into deforested areas. Officially designated forest land in India between 1951 to 1980 India had lost 4.3 million hector of forest land. The area cover under the forestof the country as per 2007 assessment is 6,90,899 km.^{2} which is 21.02 per cent of the geographical area of the country. Very dense forest constitutes 83,510 km.^{2} (2.54 per cent), the moderately dense forest 319,012 km.^{2} (9.71 per cent) and open forest constitutes 2,88,377 km.^{2} (8.77 per cent) of the Geographical area. The scrub accounts for 41,525 km.^{2} (1.26 per cent), (FSI, 2009). Thus, many of these forests are in poor condition. Ultimately, the forest situation in India is poor and this scenario is very serious in case of tribal because the economy of a vast majority of them depends on forest. The scarcity of forest area brings a watering situation to tribal economy.

Apart from deforestation, in many areas several dams, barrages, hydro-electrical plants, etc. have been already or being constructed. Due to this fact, the natural flows of the rivers and streams have been affected severely. Even in many cases, these have been dried out. As a result of this, the tribals who depended on it for fishes and other aquatic animals and plants as well as nutrition were hampered a lot. Thus, it directly affected the food, nutrition and health of the concerned tribals.

The tribals normally depend on natural resources such as forest, rivers, streams, etc. and comparatively, they are less dependent on monetary transaction system. Therefore, if the natural resources are lacking, obviously they are bound to face the problems related to health as well as survival and gradually they have become marginalized. Grabbing the land of the tribals by the others is widespread in allover the India. The land alienation is not an issue of the present day. That was stated approximately more than three hundred years ago. But it was culminated during the *Zamindari* period as well as during the British. It was expected that after independence, such deprivation would be abolished. At the present context, we are not going in detail about the Dalit Movement, Dr B.R. Ambedkar, Neo-Buddhism, policies of inclusion of the excluded, dedication of these people in interest of the country and nation, and legacy of Deccan history and the various social movements for equality and justice still relevant in present Human Rights Movements. But we must say that after all these great efforts, especially in this era of globalization, it has been evidenced that day by day these oppressions have been increasing since India's independence. Some examples are to be cited here:

The reports from the Ministry of Rural Development, Government of India 2007-2008mentioned that 5.06 lakh cases of tribal land alienation have been registered in various states of India covering a total of 9.02 acres of land, of which 2.25 lakh cases have been disposed off in favour of tribals causing just the area of 5.00 lakh acres (Indigenous Rights Quarterly, 2008). We can see various cases of alienation and restoration of tribal land in different states of India. In Madhya Pradesh, out of 29,596 cases, not a single case has been ruled in favour of the tribals. Similarly, in Tripura, out of 29,112 cases, 20,043 were rejected,andin Odisha, an overwhelming 43,213 out of 104,644 cases were gone against the tribals. These are serious matters of concern (IRQ, *ibid.*). In Assam, we can see how the non-tribal people have brought plots from the community land of the indigenous tribal groups in the name of schools, societies, trusts, etc., but ultimately used them for individual benefit and commercial purpose (The Assam Tribune, 1st February, 2007).

Cultural Research Institute (CRI), Government of West Bengal conducted few surveys to know the nature of land alienation of tribal communities in 1960-1961, 1960-1965 and 1972-1073. CRI observed that land transferred to the non-tribals was enormous. CRI also conducted a survey over 407 *mouzas* in 12 C.D. Blocks under erstwhile West DinajpurDistrict over 15,148 people and found that 31.4 per cent were landless agricultural labourers, and there were also marginal farmers who had their own land but also used to work as agriculturallabourer (Sen, 2011).

In respect to establishment of tea gardens, in Terai-Duars region of North Bengal areas, many of the tribal peoples like the Oraon, Munda, Santal, Mahali, Asur, etc. were brought from Chotonagpur areas and gradually started to live here permanently as tea garden labourers. But now-a-days, many of the tea gardens have been closed. On the other hand, they were uprooted from their motherland, Chotonagpur where they could not go back and further, they are not getting job opportunities due to lock out of the tea gardens. Even they are not getting opportunity to work in other sectors too as labourers,and presently, they are facing tremendous crisis in order to maintain their livelihood. Therefore, their traditional ways of living as well as cultures have been deeply affected.

In West Bengal, many of the tribal land have been alienated. It was known that around 4,500 acres of tribal land in Uttar DinajpurDistrict have been illegally occupied by the non-tribal tea-planters. In MaldaDistrict, huge amount of tribal land have been illegally transferred to the non-tribals. In this district, a survey on 16 *adivasi*(tribal) villages and observed that in every *adivasitola* (tribal hamlet)two-thirds tribal peasants' land come under the possession of non-tribals. It was also known that 45,000 acres of tribal land have been illegally transferred to non-tribals at Samukhtala of AlipurduarSub-division of JalpaiguriDistrict of North Bengal, i.e., northern West Bengal (Sen, 2011).

In this concern, the Totos, a Primitive Tribal Group of West Bengal, living in Totopara village under Ballalguri*Gram Panchayet* of MadarihatSub-division, JalpaiguriDistrict of West Bengal close to the Indo-Bhutan border, lost huge amount of land and forest resources. In earlier, this village was covered by dense forest and village was occupied by themselves only. But now-a-days, the forest is almost absent in this village, even bamboo, shoreaand some other valuable plants. These plants were cut down by bamboo traders and also due to illegal logging without any notion of conservation. Forest Department is now maintaining the neighbourhood forestland and seldom aware of the fact that how far life of the Totos is depend on these forest resources.

In earlier, the land of this village was recorded 1996.76 acres under the name of Toto heads, but now they are the owner of only 343 acres of land (17.18 per cent) as because 81.72 per cent of lands have already been handed over to the non-Totos. In this concern, it was known in 2003 that 73.92 per cent of the total families were populated by the non-Totos, with 700 Nepali families, 25 Bihari families, four Bengali and Muslim families each, and two families of each Garo and Mech origin. This influx has caused many problems for the Totos as non-Totos are now sharing the natural resources of them. Their authority over power, politics and traditional resources started to decline (Biswas, 2009 and 2012). In earlier, they could depend on their own resources for maintaining their daily livelihood primarily, but now-a-days it is very difficult for them. It is known that around 57 per cent of the Toto families had to depend on Bhutan for earning their common minimum livelihood. In spite of their hard struggle and tough work, 86 per cent Toto families could earn not more than Rs 2,000 (INR) per month. However, to maintain their livelihood, many were forced to take loans from money-lenders (Biswas and Bhattacharjee, 2011). Even in case of modern politics,their representation was very low.

In order to maintain their daily livelihood, now the Totos are facing several problems as major portion of land has been alienated and the forest areas have been reduced to a great extent. Crop cultivation is not possible to a great extent. This primitive tribe, Toto, who could depend on forest for several purposes like food, fruit, root, rhizome, tuber, yam, fodder, honey, mushroom, fuel, medicinal plant, gomes, house construction material, etc. in the past, but now-a-days these are not available in these areas or they have to go into dense forest for the same. The major portion of their land has been alienated. Now they are facing problems to graze their domestic cattle.

Further, due to the same as well as scarcity of land, they could not produce sufficient amount of crop. They have shed off their traditional orange cultivation cum porter-job of the orange as well as shifting cultivation or *jhum*cultivation (slash-and-burn cultivation) due to various reasons. They have now accepted permanent agriculture that they learnt from the Nepali. But problem is that they do not possess good arable land as compared to the Nepalis and others. Even, some of the Totos have become agricultural landless. From the nature, some of their prime needs, such as food, shelter, medicine, and objects used in their religious life were previously fulfilled and satisfied. But due to deforestation and land-alienation, these fulfillments have been affected adversely. On the other hand, they are bound to accept and adjust with the modern ways of living. But to accustom the modern way of living, such as education, health treatment and shelter, they need strong economic support. But how is it possible? As already they have lost their economic resources, land, forest, etc. Simultaneously, the development of alternative economy has not been done properly here. They are not in a position to earn from the alternative sources of economy. So, they are facing the extreme crisis in their daily life which is the prime obstacle in the way for their development.

In this concern, another example may be given. The Drukpa or Dukpa a very little known tribal community are living in BauxaDuar area of Kalchini C.D. Block of AlipurduarSub-division, JalpaiguriDistrict of West Bengal. They are living in eleven villages and Bauxa Fort market of this area. According to the study of Biswas, there were 232 Drukpa families with 1,194 people of which 542 were females and rest 652 males. This area is very remote, nearly isolated and hilly region covered by dense forest too. This BauxaDuar area is in the extreme north east part of JalpaiguriDistrict of West Bengal and very close to Indo-Bhutan border.

The major problems of this area are poor transportation and lack of communication followed by education and health, etc. (Biswas, n.d.)

Majority of the Drukpa people can only speak in their mother tongue, *Dzongkha* falling under Tibeto-Bhutan linguistic group. Very few of them can speak in Nepali, Hindi, Bengali and English, but not fluently. Surface transportation is nearly absent (Biswas, n.d.). To communicate with other places, they face a lot of difficulties, and thus, they try to avoid going outside normally. However, their main challenge is regarding linguistic communication. Due to unknown of other languages, they have to face problems as they could not share their views with others. Even, in serious health situation and illness, when they are bound to take admission in hospitals or go to the nursing homes and doctors, they usually try to avoid Indian health facilities, rather they prefer to go to Bhutan as because they are incapable of communicating with the majority Bengali physicians of West Bengal State as well as Indian physicians. Most of them do not know the Bengali or other languages in appropriate way. Due to this linguistic problem, development of education is being affected adversely. The local teachers, who are actually the outsiders to the Drukpas do not show their interests to come to BauxaDuar and *vice versa*. The students of Drukpa community fail to understand the teachers' language as they are not from the Drukpa community and do not know their language.

However, there are no good schools in and around this locality with better infrastructure and modern up-to-date curriculum. Thus, after completing the primary education, most of them cannot take admission for secondary education at Kalchini or Alipurduar areas which are far away and also lack of proper surface transportation. Naturally, most of the Drukpas lost their interest for high school and higher education or other educations. In addition to that, as because of their inability to understand and communicate with other language groups, they do not feel the anxiety in taking admission in outside schools for high school education and beyond.

However, the Drukpas, the local orange cultivators and step cultivators are facing many problems in their daily life. Particularly due to absence of proper communication and surface transportation, and language problems, their education, health, economy and other developments are being affected a lot. Thus, for their very development and progress, the above matters should be thoroughly considered. Otherwise, it will take time more, and the progress will be slowed down.

From the above discussion, study and observation, it may be concluded that most of the tribals occupy the major section of the Indigenous Peoples category universally when we are thinking of a Global Village and their Indigenous Rights and their alternative services to the Nation. But, we are actually just talking and re-talking. What we do in favour of these aborigines and so called indigenous? They are obviously facing so many challenges in different paradigms. That might be just scatteredandlocal or quite generalised. Most of the tribals of India as well as West Bengal have lost their economic resources such as forest, land and water. It was observed through the study that the in cases like Totos and Drukpas, inhabited in remote part of West Bengal Duars along with Indo-Bhutan international boundary are facing severe problems to maintain their common minimum livelihoods. Their economic resources have been shifted to the others. The same is happening in cases of other tribal communities too.

These simple indigenous peoples have no sufficient representatives in modern polity and they are not in a position to say anything or policy making. However, if we want inclusiveness, sustainability, taking these neglected human resources under confidence, overall development, and assure their development, progress, mainstreaming, then we should have to give the emphasis on their economic, educational, social, cultural, political, and health issues, relation with nature as well as transportation and communication with other groups. Further, sufficient tribal representatives from indigenous communities must be addressed to the politics for their proper development. Developing their human resources and their active participation in education, health, administration, sports, etc. are needed. If they have strong economy and education and way of communication and power in politics and policy making as well, then other problems including health and so on may be solved very simply.

References

Biswas, S.K. (2009), Socio-Economic Crisis and Its Consequences on a Little Known Tribal Community in West Bengal, India, in E. Kolig, V. SM. Angeles and S. Wong (eds.) *Identity in Crossroad Civilisations*, 8:97-114 : Amsterdam University Press, Amsterdam

Biswas, S.K. (n.d.) *The Drukpas of West Bengal, India* (under publication).

Biswas, S.K. and S. Bhattacharjee, (2011), Depletion of Resources and It's Impact on Food, Nutrition and Health: An Anthropological Observation, in U.V. Somayajulu, C.P. Prakasam, N. Audinarayana and K.E. Vaidyanathan (eds.) *Health, Poverty and Human Development Perspectives and Issues,* 201-215 : Global Research Publications,New Delhi

Biswas, S.K. (2012), Ignorance, Exploitation and Poverty: A Case Study Among the Totos, in D. Midya (ed.) *Indigenous People in India: Identity, Empowerment and Discontent*, pp. 111-119 : APH Publishing Corporation,New Delhi

Concern over Transfer of Tribal Lands to Non-Tribals, *The Assam Tribune,* 1 February, 2007.

Forest Survey of India, (2009), *India State of Forest Report 2009*: Ministry of Environment and Forest,Deharadun

International Labour Organization, (1991), "Concerning indigenous and tribal peoples in independent countries, 1989", *Convention No. 169 inInternational Labour Conventions and Recommendations,* Vol. 2 (1919-1991) : International Labour Office, Geneva

Land alienation of Tribals in India, *Indigenous Rights Quarterly*III(4), October-December, 2008.

Sen, P. (2011), Separatism in North Bengal. *Frontier* 43(40) April 2011.

7

Conservation Through Religious Practices: A Case Study of Hussain Dighi of West Bengal

Hasibul Rahaman

Introduction

Since time immemorial, a reciprocal relation has been maintained between nature and human society. This reciprocal relation leads to nature worship which has been considered an important determinant of the origin of religion by E.B. Tylor and Max Muller. But in the post modern era, development is now being considered as hot cake. As we all know that without destruction of nature, development is not possible enough. From holistic approach, we are welcome development without any hesitation in the one hand and side by side the people of India would like to keep the natural resources for the sake of their own safety and also for otherness on the other.

Conservation and sustainable use of biodiversity for the benefit of both present and future generations, an ethical concern, has now a global political and legal sanction in the form of Conservation on Biological Diversity signed by almost all countries. Yet, irreversible loss of biological diversity and inequitable distribution of resource base remain serious problems. While deficiencies of State driven conservation approaches have been brought out, proven examples of perfect conservation approaches are lacking. With increase of population pressure and biological resource demands set by fast economic growth ambitions, threats to protected areas are getting more and more serious (Ramakrishnan, *et.al.* 1998). Conservation has become popular, and even the term 'ecology' appears in daily press and is heard of in commercial television.

Man and environment research has been neglected since the 1930s, when the 'environmental determinism' became widely recognised (Detwayler, 1971). For the preceding several decades the occurrence of many man's cultural characteristics were largely attributed to the nature of environment where they were found, often without much evidence. The idea, promulgated by Frederich Ratzal, Ellsworth Huntington, Ellen Semple and others became firmly entrenched in Sociology and Anthropology before it was gradually discredited and replaced by other explanations.

In the present day, many forms of nature worship in India still abounds. All forms of life from hedges to fig, trees and from crabs to peacocks and tigers continued to be considered sacred and inviolable in relation to a variety of primitive cults (Guha: 1994). Amongst these varied religious practices, a significant form is the sacred lake and its preservation in the community context. Assessment of the sacred lake or pond and its surroundings as well as subsequent conservation remains a key issue in the environmental conservation programmes in the present time. An idea behind protecting a particular area by declaring as sacred is based on religious, spiritual, cultural and social factors.

Generally a pond is considered as common property resource (CPR) and is used by the local people. So, a pond constitutes an important component of community living and gets entangled with several religious, socio-cultural, ecological and economic functions. Under the traditional system protection and regulated use of a lake or pond was largely a result of the community's collective stake in its natural resources. External interventions as well as institutional and technological changes have adversely affected this stake arrangement (Jodha : 2001).

Many traditional societies throughout the world have institutionalised in variety of different ways large or small cultural landscapes or sacred ecosystems as a part of their belief system. In the Indian context, too cultured-linked ecosystem management is to be found in many of the societies, which have a large number of natural resource-linked institutions. The concepts of sacred lake, sacred pond, sacred grove, etc. represent various stages of social selection (Depommier and Ramakrishnan, 2002).

Environment is the topic of the day. Conservation of environmental nature has become priority (Ghosh, 1991). This, however does not mean conservation or preservation should be at the expense of human need. Religious spiritualism on the other hand is the soul of any culture or civilisation.

So, there is need for a new approach to nature conservation, it has to emerge as a people initiative rather than State enforcement.

Objective and Methodology

The main thrust of the present paper is to examine nature of conservation through religious beliefs and practices.

The present study is exploratory in nature. It is exploratory in the sense that it will examine all the aspects of sacred pond from ethnographic point of view. In order to understand the traditional method of conservation faced by the people living around the pond, an intensive field work has been done. In the present study data has been collected mostly through field work and complemented with secondary data.

The study was conducted mainly on Hussain Dighi and its surrounding villages. This particular pond has been selected purposively taken into consideration of some important subjects like the religious history of the place, indigenous knowledge system applied for conserving of this pond, nature of society and the socio-cultural and economic life of the people adjacent to the pond. The data has been collected by applying several methodological tools and techniques like interview, case study, observation etc. Aged person, *Fakir* (beggar), Panchayet personnel and pilgrims were interviewed randomly. During fieldwork the following questions were asked by the author to understand the method of conservation. The questions have risen in this regard are:

i. What types of activities are performed by the pond?

ii. What is the people's perception for maintaining the sacredness of the pond area?

iii. Who are the sacred specialists of the pond?

iv. How many types of sacred performances are observed in the pond area?

v. Whether festivals, fairs etc. are held or not in or around of the pond?

vi. From which places do the pilgrims come here? Why and When?

vii. Are locals getting benefit from the tourists?

viii. What are the indigenous method for conserving the lake and its surroundings?

A Brief History and Ecological Features of Hussain Dighi

The Hussain Dighi is situated at Daspara (Gram Panchayat) of Uttar Dinajpur district of West Bengal and which is 30 km. far from NH-34. It is a round shaped pond. According to BLRO (Block Land Revenue Officer, Chopra Circle) records, the area covered by the pond is around 25 bigas. There is no proper documentary source in connection with the depth of the pond and no fixed kind of mouth. Once upon a time, the pond was bounded by little amount of forest and the local people had close interaction with it.

As per field view is concerned, villages are being considered as neighbours of the Dighi. They are Gondugochh, Glantigarh and Tepagoan etc. The villagers are the followers of Islam.

Myth or Oral History of the Dighi

Though, the local meaning of Dighi is pond. Hence, the Hussain pond has commonly referred as Dighi. From Durkheimian sense, it is considered as sacred because it is worshiped by the locals in general and Muslims in particular.

During fieldwork, it is tried to find out what is the actual history behind this name. This question was asked to an older generation and their replies vary from person to person. The most acceptable answers are being explored here.

Someone views are that Hazrt Imam Hussain was the grandson of Prophet Muhammed. Imam Hussain and Hassan were being considered as martyr for the hosting of Islamic flag and tried to carry on forefather's tradition. They were cruelly killed by their enemy Egit and not only that they were not allowed to drink water.

As we can say, no one knows that in which year it (Dighi) was made. The local says that it is the symbol of Feratkul (river) for the reason that its water is green and clear and similar to Feratkul which they heard from local Hajis (those who visited sacred Macca). And for this reason it is popularly called Hussain Dighi.

As stated, the above oral history differs from the others. Another section of an older generation thought that the entire area was under the kingship of Hussain Shah. During his monarchy a pond was dug for the sake of the farmers. From perspective such a name was given to the pond.

In connection with the name of Hussain Dighi, another myth is that an unknown religious beggar *(Fakir)* called Hussain had resided beside the Dighi. According to local's opinion, he would always keep silent and devoted himself towards God. He did not feel uneasy if anyone wanted to talk with him. Gradually, in this way, the neighbouring villagers were able to make a rapport with this sacred man. The villagers generally rushed to him, when they felt any problem and the *fakir* tried his level best to eradicate their problem. Hence, this sort of oral history suggests another reason why the pond is called Hussain Dighi.

Role of Religion in Conservation

Out of all the religions existing in the world, Islam is one of the latest and therefore, most modern. It originated from Judaism. For this reason Moses (Mussa) and Jesus (Isha) are undoubtedly considered as their prophet (*Paigamber*) while Hazrat Muhammed was last in the line. The theology of Islam is well connected with modern and scientific thought and can be compared with modern philosophy such as Marxism and no doubt it fully matches even today's social structure. But in today's pragmatic scenario the actual theory of Islam is now being interpreted to benefit the Mullahs all over or rich Sheiks of Arab world which obviously contradicts with the Islam which preaches equality (Ghosh: 1991).

People, environment and religion etc. are interrelated to each other. It is interesting to note that religion works a bridge between man and environment. Therefore, environment has to be conserved as through nature, we can perceive Allah's presence all-around. If we consult the Islamic literature, we can say that conservation of environment does not mean that we should discard modern development since according to changing need, the modern development is also very much a just requirement. Only thing, appropriate steps should be taken that modern development takes place without harming the environment.

In case of environmental sociology, too, international processes and discourses have not been examined in much detail by Indian scholars.

While the spread of industrialisation and urbanisation in the Western generated an extensive literature on the transformation of the fundamental ecological categories of time and space, of changes in the nature of work and leisure, public and private spheres, such as cultural ecology has been absent from India. While environmental sociologists in India have largely ignored the macro framework of ethno development. They have produced numerous micro-framework of development in the form of industrialisation and urbanisation and its impact on human population.

The articulation of environmentalist ideology by social movements was also influential in spurring sociologists to discuss not only the inequitable effects of development projects, but also launch a wider critique of the development paradigm, denouncing the value upon which it was based. In a discourse which laid claim to a Gandhian heritage, scholar like Ashis Nandi (1987), attacked the ideology of domination over nature (and women) that underlay Western science and technology. So, environmental sociology should study how people are connected with ecology and how they can conserve it (nature, i.e. pond)?

Management is an integral part of conservation. As per field data concerned, there is no fixed managerial board for this purpose but it indicates us that Shabaddin has been taking care of this sacred pond. As because, he is descendent of *fakir* decent. A small hut has been found beside the pond and the *fakir* used it as like as chamber of religious activities. As we knew that every Thursday and second half of Friday (2 pm to 5 pm) in a week, he used to sit at the hut and those days the visitors are come for *manat* (vow). The civil background of the visitors are—married, unmarried, widow, widower and divorced and occupational color is plural like—-cultivators, labourers, housewives and students. The nature of *manat* varies from visitors to visitors such as:

i. household peace
ii. getting children
iii. to cure the disease
iv. academic success
v. for agricultural productivity, etc.

There is a clear guideline for visitors that, they are directed to come over the pond in *pak* (pure) condition. Moreover, no visitors are allowed to bath with this water but they are allowed to procure a bottle of water for medical purpose. Generally, the visitors come over to the pond along with white cock, dry fish, nunia rice as a gift for the *fakir*. The *fakir* uses it as a personal income but there are no demands from his side. Even then, the visitors are willingly to give little amount of money as visit fee. According to the *fakir* with the help of this money, he nurses the Dighi, like-–scavenging.

It is interesting to note that there is no hard and fast rule with respect to caste, varna and religion for visiting this place but they are directed to follow the Islamic norms during visiting time of this pond. And it is considered as the symbol of religious secularism because the *fakir* used to sit over the Dighi on Thursday and Friday in a week for the visitors. As we all know that most of Hindus are taking oath for fasting on Thursday in the one hand and Friday is prayer day to the Muslims on the other.

Taboos and Rituals associated with the Dighi

The term conservation, preservation is considered as the wing of religious prescription rather religious taboos. As like as other sacred places it is also treat as sacred so that it has some taboos for conserved its sacredness which has close linkage with nature conservation. The most observed taboos are as follows :

i. Women are strictly prohibited from entering the sacred area of the Dighi due to the belief that they are impure (menstrual cycle being the most commonly cited cause).
ii. The people who are in *Napak* (impure) situation are not permitted walk over the Dighi.
iii. The visitors are clearly directed that they are not allowed to throw the plastic and material in the pond.
iv. Fetching fodder or fuel wood is strictly prohibited because the myth prevails that the use of such kind of materials over the sacred pond will hurt the sentiments of the grandson of Prophet Muhammed.
v. The villagers are not allowed to use the water of the pond for the purpose of domestic animals or for sanitation.

Rituals

The neighboring population of Hussain Dighi is primarily dominated by Muslims but if we think from broader perspective, the whole area is characterized by diverse ethno-culture.

We are well informed that ritual is an integral part of religion. There are a number of rituals these are observed over the Dighi. In view of field work, it is to be noted that first *Baishakh* of every Bengali New Year a *mela* (fair) is held around the Dighi.

However, preparation for this grand fair, that is providing infrastructural facilities like construction of *mela* huts which will accommodate the pilgrims etc. is done under the direct supervision of the *fakir* of Hussain Dighi and during the *mela* time he has the sole responsibility to build a committee. Market is an attraction of the *mela* and it continues for two days. In the *mela* traders dealing various essential religious articles of consumption as well varieties of cosmetic items from the home town Islampur and Kisanganj of Bihar. The pilgrims comes all the way from a distant places like—part of Dakshin Dinajpur, Siliguri and also from Bihar. The attraction of the religious fair brings the mendicants and ascetics , beggars and leapers, the anti-social persons like—cheals, the pickpocketers also tread their way in this *mela*. The committee members that lend their service to control and organize the *mela* and small police force from Chopra Police Station and some Border Security Force (BSF) personnel are deployed to help and manage the huge assemblage.

The huge gathering over the Dighi includes people of heterogeneous origins with respect to caste, class, religion and sex also. Though they are usually coming to the *fakir* for *manat* (vow) following the Islamic custom. It can be rightly pointed out that in connection with fair the ceremony of sacred bath is firmly forbidden. In spite of that here we noticed a close linkage between little and great tradition.

At night of those days the *mela* committee organizes a *jolsa* (religious discussion). The local Hindu and tribals are willingly participate in this holy meeting which has popularly called as *Ors*. In this sacred meeting all participants in respect of caste, class, religion etc. are taking oath to conserve it. And from this perspective we can observe the notion of religious syncretism based on Hussain Dighi.

Conclusion

The area, surrounding the pond is covered by the dominancy of tea garden and a number of people are associated with garden activities. The workers in general and owners in special do not bother in regard to environmental pollution and pay any attention to its sacredness. They are consciously and unconsciously using the water of the pond without taking prior permission from *Fakir*. As a result, right now this sacred pond is under challenge and threat. The local people of the area and its neighbours cannot tolerate this kind of situation which is created by the tea planters but they are not in a position to start a movement against the tea planters because some of them are also working in the gardens. Moreover we can observe that the local government like Gram Panchayat and along with the Office of the BDO (Block Development Officer) does not take any serious step against tea planters. In this unethical situation the poorer local people find out only way to be religious practices, which are also known to us as indigenous method and technique to conserve it.

Indigenous peoples themselves have repeatedly claimed that they have fundamental rights regarding an application of indigenous knowledge because it is necessary to their cultural survival (Mauro and Hardison: 2000) and similar situation have found in this study area. According to locals, they are deprived from pond benefit because the outsider tea planters enjoy every benefit from the pond and trying to control over it. So this kind of attitude of outsiders will agitate and in future the locals are bound to generate a movement because this is a sentimental matter.

From a holistic point of view, it is to be noted that change is a universal dimension of society, which has been found from theological to positivistic stage. In the era of developmental discourse, there have rapid changes are taking place throughout the world. Following the line of length, in the name of the marker of development, there have been noticeable changes like - demography, education, social, political and economic aspiration etc. found around the pond area. As a result, human interaction has been found in the various forms of developmental activities like – modernisation the pond area and use of water of the pond for agricultural activities, etc.

As per the record of field view, at present, the rituals are known to small number of people, most of whom belong to an older generation (above 50 years). Most of the people especially those who belong to a younger generation (below 40 years, 73 out of 100 interviewed) admitted that the religious belief was central to sacred pond conservation is taking into consideration as superstition. Only 20 per cent of the people were interviewed, seemed to know the significance of sacred pond conservation.

Taking into consideration an emic approach, it can to be said that it functioned as an integral part in the social and cultural life of local people. As we know that the locals are closely associated with the sacred Dighi which we have found since savagery stage and it is going on till today. In order to keep an ownership over the sacred pond, they are practicing indefatigable religious activities. Hence, this sort of function suggests that it is a symbol of cultural heritage and bears an indignity so that it can attract the tourists. As because, indignity of otherness is always an attractive dimension to the tourists. Last but not least, it is very much important therefore to keep to original state. Awareness of new generation and participating management are the key aspects for its further conservation.

Recommendation

Here are some suggestions and recommendation offered by the respondents of the field survey for saving Hussain Dighi from deteriorating situation.

i. The Gram Panchayat should take the responsibility to look after the Dighi.

ii. Tourism department should take developmental project for its modernisation so that tourists can be attracted.

iii. Restrictions on pump machine in pond as it pollutes the water and hamper its sacredness, etc.

Finally, we would rather say that Government should take necessary action for keeping it in its originality and that priority should give to locals. The indigenous peoples should not be treated as clients or mere stakeholders in the process, but should be invited to participate in all levels of decision making and management, finding representation on steering committee, planning boards, advisory bodies.

Bibliography

Depommier D and Ramakrishnan PS (ed.) (2002). *Traditional Ecological Knowledge, Conservation of Biodiversity and Sustainable Development*. Institute of Francais de Pondichery, Pondichery.

Detwyler T R (1971). *Man's Impect on environment*. MacGraw-Hill Book Company,New York.

Ghosh G K (1991). *Environment: A Spiritual Dimension*. Ashish Publication House, New Delhi.

Guha R (eds) (1994). *Social Ecology*. Oxford University Press, New Delhi.

Jodha N S (2001). *Life on the Edge: Sustaining Agriculture and Community Resources in Fragile Environments*. New York: Oxford University Press.

Mauro F and Hardson PD (2000). Traditional Knowledge of Iindigenous and local Communities. International Debate and Policy Initiatives. *Ecological Application*. 10(5): 1263-1269.

Nandi A (1987). *Tradition, Tyranny and Utopia: Essays in the Politics of Awareness*. Oxford University Press, New Delhi.

Niyogi T K (1998). Sacred bath ceremony and myth-ritual complex at Gangasagar. *Journal of the Anthropological Survey of India*, 47: 25-47.

Pattanaik S (2007). Conservation of Environment and Protection of Marginalized Fishing Communities of Lake Chilika of Orissa, India. *Human Ecology*. 22(4): 291-302.

Ramakrishnan P S, Saxena K G and Chandrashekara (ed.) (1996). *Conserving Boidiversity for Sustainable Development* New Delhi: Indian National Science Academy.

__________, (1998*) Conserving the Sacred for Biodiversity Management.* : Oxford and IBH Publishing Co. Pvt. Ltd., New Delhi

__________ (2002). *Traditional Ecological Knowledge, Conservation of Biodiversity and Sustainable Development.* Institut Francais De Pondichery. Pondichery.

Sargent F(eds.) (1974). *Human Ecology.* New York: North-Holland Publishing company.

Xaxa V (1992). Oraons: Religion, Custom and Enmvironment. In Geeti Sen (Eds). *Indigenous Vision: People's of India; Attitude s to the Environment.* Sage Publication, New Delhi.

8

Stratification among the Muslims of North Bengal

Rajib Chatterjee

Muslims occupy one of the most important positions in the society of West Bengal and consider the largest religious minority group. They have a population of about 25 per cent according to 2001 Census and concentrate almost all the districts of West Bengal. Historically, North Bengal, the northern most six districts of the Indian state West Bengal, stood apart in the context of Islamisation during the seventh century and later but distinctly aloof from the rest of Indian Muslims. There were clear indications of mixed culture among the Muslims living there. 'Popular Islam' was considered as apt term to describe the religious rituals followed by these Muslims. Though, Islam in its principles does not permit the differentiation of its followers or Muslims in caste, class or any other form of groups. But in reality the group distinctions is noticed among the Muslims and particularly in North Bengal, the Muslims are highly diverse in their culture and practices. The local or little tradition often minimizes the Islamic great traditions or the principles of egalitarianism. There are two ways of trying to understand what Islam and Muslims is all about in North Bengal. One is by interpreting it theologically which is the ideal or 'textual Islam' and another 'contextual Islam' or how actually Muslims of North Bengal practice their faith i.e. from the people's perception. If, someone tells, 'Muslims of North Bengal observes such and such practices; one might ask 'which Muslim'? That means heterogeneity is an established fact in the peoples mind instead of monolithic believe though theoretically Islam advocates an egalitarian social order. A cultural synthesis with respect to great tradition of Islam and local cultures has been noticed among them which emerged a unique pattern of society among the Muslims of North Bengal.

Islam: The Journey from Equality to Inequality

The term social stratification is used for structured social inequality. It involves hierarchy of social groups. Social inequality simply refers to the existence of socially created inequalities while social stratification is a particular form of social inequality. It refers to the presence of social groups which are ranked one above the other. Ideally Islamic tradition is based on egalitarianism and non-hierarchical social order applicable to people of all colours and cultures yet pluralistic society among the Muslims is very old due to its contact with diverse social and cultural situation. Since its very inception Islam changed from the kin based egalitarianism of Arab bands to religion based egalitarianism which later transformed into a feudal authoritarian pattern. At the initial stage the Islamic society of Arab was divided into clan and tribes. But when it spared to distant lands, Muslims started to classify themselves according to their lineal and social connections with the Prophet and Caliphs. And when it came to India, the caste structure of Hindus made the situation complex as a large number of the Hindus were converted into Islam. The Indian Muslims are broadly divided into three categories 1) *Asraf* or*Khas* who claim a foreign descent and 2) the *Ajlaf* or*Aam,* i.e., the indigenous converted from high castes and 3) *Arzal* or *Raizal,* i.e. degraded section from low caste Hindu and animists. There is a clear rural-urban division throughout migration for employment has exposed them to urban culture at milieu. Even amongst the peasantry, there is class differential between the land-owning class and the landless. Partition of Bengal has affected the Muslim population because of migration of particularly the elite class to East Pakistan (now Bangladesh). Cross-cultural exchanges amongst the Muslim community between West Bengal and Bangladesh also have an influence over the lives of Muslims in West Bengal.

Population Characteristics of the Muslims of North Bengal

The Muslim penetration of the region dates back to medieval period. The involvement of Muslims dated back when BakhtiarKhalji started invasion in Tibet. In later period the political intrusion of Mirjumla and HussainSah also brought many Muslim communities. And moreover the simplicity of Islam and the Sufis attracts many people to proselyte.

Moreover, many Muslim groups were also invited to migrate because of their specialized services. However, Muslims particularly in North Bengal have diverse origins. But majority of them are indigenous convert. Dominated by an agrarian economy, they responded very little to the questions of upper India's Muslim identity. Common cultural practices of seeking blessings of the *pir*, *fakir*, *darbesh* and intermingling during religious festivals particularly amongst the subalterns built up a strong secular tradition among the Muslims of North Bengal.

In Islamic great tradition the principles of egalitarianism has minimized the social distances and stands for a perfect equality of all individuals but in reality distinction is noticed as the country India as a whole and Bengal or North Bengal in particular is a place of diverse communities of diverse religious orders and a large number of the Muslims are indigenous converted from Hindus, Buddhists and other religions. Therefore, the structure of popular Islamic or Muslim society is also changed either due to the constant interaction with other socio-cultural groups or due to the caste system of dominant Hindus. Mendelbum also states that the Indian Muslims share some of the basic socio-economic characteristics of the places in which they live in. And Risely in 1901 identified a large number of non-Muslim characters among the Muslims living in Bengal.

However, the Indian Muslims are broadly divided into three categories (i) *Asraf* or*Khas* who claim a foreign descent and (2) the *Ajlaf* or*Aam,* i.e. the indigenous converted and (3) *Arzal* or *Raizal,* i.e. degraded section, though theoretically Islam advocates for an egalitarian social order. Superiority or inferiority of a *biradery* or caste like group is determined by the relative pure or impure nature of the occupation associated with each section. Siddique (1974) identified nearly 60 endogamous castes like ethnic groups among the Muslims of Kolkata. Mondal (1997) identified 15 important ethnic and occupational Muslim groups of Siliguri, a sub-Himalayan city of Darjeeling Himalaya.The census of India, 1901 listed 133 Muslim groups who had some features of Hindu caste system like hierarchy of social groups, endogamy and hereditary occupational activity, etc. (Mondal, 1997).

Social Groups among the Muslims of North Bengal

During the early British periods, the region North Bengal indicates the places of the districts of Jalpaiguri, Dinajpur and Rangpur. The first census of Bengal in 1872 offered to classify the Muslims of North Bengal in to the following categories viz. *julha, mughal, sayed* and *sekh*. But only a negligible number of Muslims represented the above said categories and thus the large numbers of them were considered as unspecified. In the year 1881 the second census replaced all the above noted Muslim categorized and offered only two categories for enumeration viz.*Shia* and *Sunni*. But again a large number of them were remained unspecified out of neither this two. In 1891 census all the previous categories were altogether offered to the Muslims of Bengal and very interestingly the majority of the Muslims replied them as *Sekh* which they had rejected earlier in the census 1872. However, the Muslim population of present day North Bengal districts is significantly divided into social groups of varied backgrounds. These are of sects, sub-sects, theological schools, *khanquah*, *silsila*, social status and ethnic or regional backgrounds.The Muslims are largely divided into two broad categories – *Desi* Muslims and *Bhatia* Muslims.This are the two most popular classifications made by the Muslim themselves in various places of North Bengal or more particularly in the districts of two Dinajpur, Jalpaiguri, Darjeeling and Cooch Bihar.

Desi Muslims includes indigenous converted from Rajbansi and other caste Hindu groups. And the *Bhatia* Muslims include the migrants from lower Bengal, Bihar and other parts who have a foreign ancestry. In North Bengal three Muslim groups are popularly known as *Desi*Muslims viz. *NasyaSekh*, *Paharia* Muslims and *Badia* Muslims. *NasyaSekh* are the decedents of local converted from various caste and tribal background and a large section among them are the indigenous converts from *Hajong, Koch, Mech* and *Rajbansi* communities. As they are fallen from their original caste or tribe thus knows as *nosto* or *nasya*. *Paharia* Muslims concentrated only in three hill Sub-divisions of Darjeeling District. They are a hybrid population and originated after the marriage of Muslim male and Nepali females of Darjeeling hills. They are very much inclined to the hill cultures and identical with their other hill communities except in their religious faith. *Badia* Muslims are found in Malda,Uttar Dinajpur and DakshinDinajpurDistricts along with Darjeeling plains. They are a unique society among the Muslims who had a traditional occupation of castration of cattle. Basically they were pastoral group. They believe that they were in the regular army of SherSahSuri as soldiers. But they are good cultivators in North Bengal.

Bhatia Muslims are the decedents of Muslim groups who migrated from low lands of Bengal and various other parts of India to Cooch Bihar during the reign of Koch Bihar Maharaja. Actually they were invited by the Raja to serve the kingdom because of their specialized services. Their

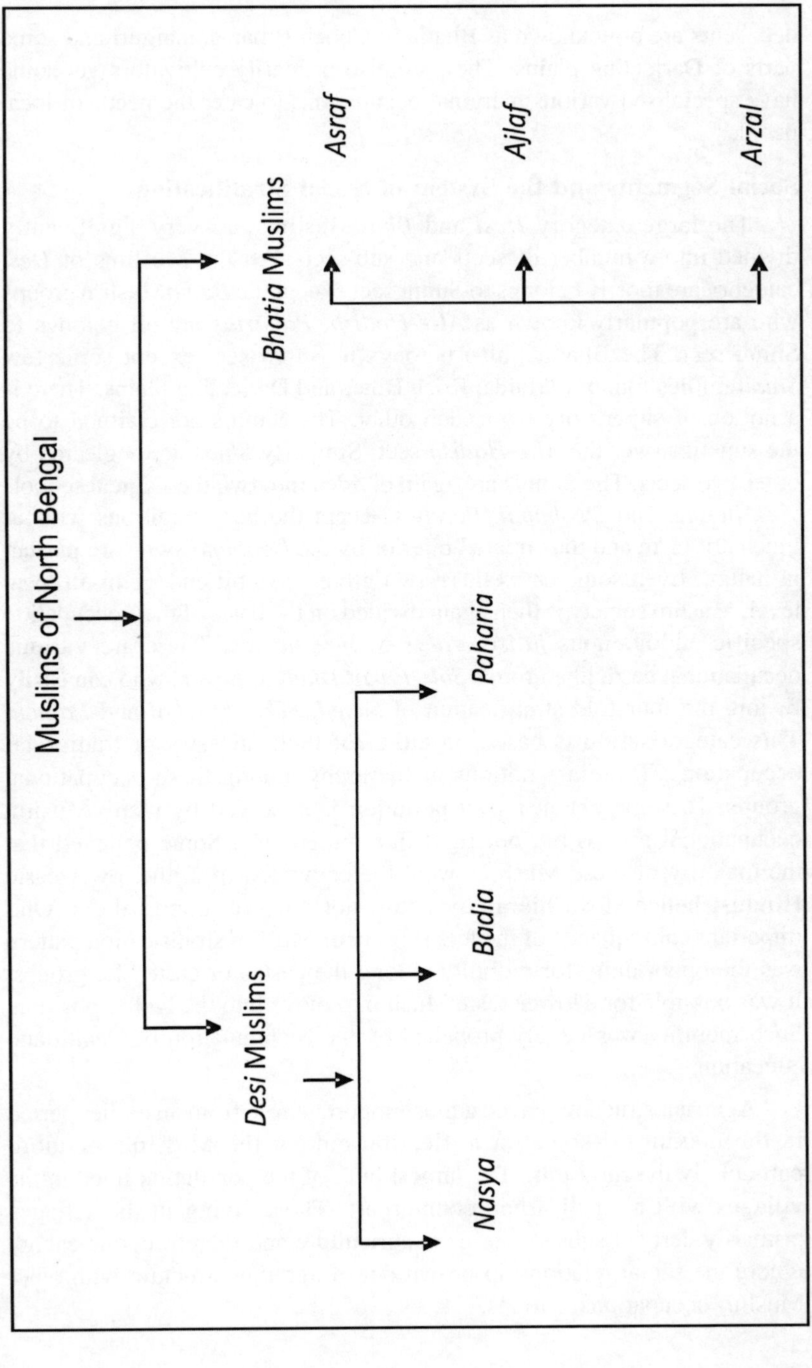
Muslims of North Bengal
Bhatia Muslims
Asraf
Ajlaf
Arzal
Desi Muslims
Paharia
Badia
Nasya

decedents are now known as Bhatia in Cooch Bihar, Jalpaiguri and some parts of Darjeeling plains. They are also primarily cultivators yet some have specialised various marginal occupations to cater the needs of local people.

Social Segments and the System of Social Stratification

The large category *Desi* and *Bhati*Muslims are very significantly divided into a number of sects and sub-sects. All the Muslims of *Desi* category are mostly belongs to Sunni sect except the *Badia*Muslim groups who are popularly known as *Al-e-Hadish*. *Paharias* are all belongs to Sunni sect. The Bhatia's also belongs to Sunni sect except some few *Shia* families found in Malda, Koch Bihar and Darjeeling plains. There is a notion of superiority over each other. The Sunnis are claimed to be the superior over the *Al-e-Hadish* sect. Similarly *Shias* are neglected by other two sects. The Sunnis are again divided into two theological schools viz., *Berelvi* and *Deobandi*. *Berelvis* accept the little traditions without much criticism and thus treated inferior by the *Deobandis*who are puritan in nature. Even some cases these two groups exhibit endogamy in local level. Muslim society is then again divided on the basis of their occupation specific endogamous *jatis*or *zaats* or *biratharies*. There are various occupational caste like groups *Sah, Fakir, Dhunia, Ansari* who can easily fit into the four fold stratification of *Sayed, Sekh, Mughal* and *Pathan*. This categorisation is based on either of their ancestry or traditional occupations. There are notions of hierarchy among these occupational groups. To some extent purity pollution is observed by many Muslim occupational groups but not rigid like the Hindus. Some believed that the majority of these Muslims were the converted from the lower caste Hindus; hence steep hierarchy could not emerge among them. One important consequence of the less rigidity of Muslim stratification pattern was the opportunity for mobility among the castes or caste like groups. It was possible for a lower caste Muslim to move into the higher position. Such mobility was largely propelled by the accumulation of wealth and education.

Agrarian structure played a most important role from an earlier period in the making of social stratification among the Muslims or more particularly the rural folk. The largest bulk of the population lived in the villages with a small urban counterpart. Those living in the villages primarily derived subsistence from agriculture and therefore, one cannot ignore the social relationship grown out of agrarian structure with other Muslim occupational groups.

Emerging Status Groups

However, a process of change in status is gradually seen among the Muslim groups of the region. During my stay in various places of North Bengal, I observed that the people are now categorised into certain status groups irrespective of their traditional *jati* or *jat* identity. Previous categorisation*Uchajat* and *Nichajat* are now replaced by *Bhadralok* and *Chotolok*. Each of these two groups has separate social positions and roles and determined their educational background and economic positions. Though marriages are usually taken places within the *jat* boundary yet status played a crucial role as now a days marriages take places with in the own status groups. Due to separate socio-economic boundary each groups have limited scope to maintain face to face social relations. Hence, a process has been taking place rapidly towards a transition from traditional to a modern social structure.

Concluding Remarks

Although the Quran insists on the radical equality of all Muslims, caste (*jat, jati, biraderi*) remains a defining feature of the Muslim society of North Bengal as a majority of them are the indigenous converts from high caste, low caste and animist groups. From above this discussion it is revealed that the Muslims of North Bengal is primarily divided in to two distinct groups in terms of their ancestry or place of origin in spite of egalitarian characteristics. And the most striking features among these two groups are their distinct cultural identity which is being strictly maintained by both of them.The arrangement in hierarchical order of different sects, sub-sects and segments and *jat* or *jatis* ultimately shaped the structure of the society. And thus a gap between text and context is seen among the Muslims of North Bengal. Even today marriages continue to take place within the original caste group. This is how Muslim society comes to be characterised by the existence of multiple endogamous castes like groups.

However, the differences in social stratification are now interpreted by the differences in material prosperity which is a shift of status from social group to status group. Lavish living and extravagant expenses indicate one's wealth accompanied by status and power. However, upper strata are gradually becoming educated, and a social difference between the educated and non-educated is emerging. Gradually, a *bhadralok* class also appears among them with a distinct lifestyle based on modern education, etiquette and culture. And a process has been taking place rapidly towards a transition from traditional to a modern social structure.

Bibliography

Ahmed, Imtiaz (Ed.) (1973).*Caste and Social Stratification among Muslims in India*.Manohar Publications, New Delhi.

Ahmed, Imtiaz (Ed.) (1983).*Modernization and Social Change among Muslims in India*.Manohar Publications, New Delhi.

Ahmed, Imtiaz (Ed.) (1984).*Ritual and Religion among Muslims in India*.Manohar Publications, New Delhi.

Ahamed, Imtiaz (Ed.) (1985).*Family, Kinship and Marriage in India*.Manohar Publications, New Delhi.

Ahmad, Aziz (1964).*Studies in Islamic Culture in the Indian Environment*.ClarenDon Press, Oxford.

Ansari, Ghaus (1960).*Muslim Caste in Uttar Pradesh: A Study of Culture Contact.* The Ethnographic and Folk Culture Society, Lucknow.

Bhattacharaya, Ranjit Kumar (1991).*Moslems of Rural Bengal: A Study in SocialStratification and Socio-Cultural Boundary Maintenance*. Subarnarekha, Kolkata.

Chaudhuri, B. and Sabur M. A. (Eds) (2008).*The Minorities*.Calcutta University,Kolkata.

Davis, Marvin (1983).*Rank and Rivalry: The Politics of Inequality in Rural West Bengal.* Cambridge. University Press, Cambridge.

Hunter, W.W. (1871).*The Indian Musalmans*.Trubner& Company, London.

Madan, T.N. (Ed.) (2001).*Muslim Communities of South Asia: Culture, Society and Power*. Manohar Publications,NewDelhi.

Mondal, Sekh Rahim (1977).Structure of Kinship among the Muslims in a West Bengal Village.*Man and Life*, Vol. 3.

Mondal, Sekh Rahim (1979).Kinship, Inheritance among Muslim: Socio-Cultural Consequences. *Social Scientists*, Vol. 7.

Mondal, Sekh Rahim (1987).*Elite and Middle Class in Bengali Muslim Society: A Study in Modernization Problem of a Minority Community: An Occasional Paper, No. 1*.Department of Sociology and Social Anthropology, University of North Bengal, Darjeeling.

Mondal, Sekh Rahim and Bhadra R. (Ed.) (1991).*Stratification, Hierarchy and Ethnicity in North East India*.Daya Publishing House, New Delhi.

Mondal, Sekh Rahim (1994).*Dynamics of Muslim Society.* Inter-India Publication,New Delhi.

Mondal, Sekh Rahim (1996). Do the Muslims have Caste? – A Critical Appraisal. *Journal of The Indian Anthropological Society*, Vol. 31, No. 2.

Mondal, SekhRahim (1997).*Educational Status of Muslims: Problems, Prospects and Priorities*.Inter-India Publications, New Delhi.

Mondal, Sekh Rahim (1997).*Muslims of Siliguri – Aspects of Their Society, Culture and Relationship with the Metropolis.*Institute of Objective Studies, New Delhi.

Mondal, Sekh Rahim (1998).Dynamics of Social Stratification among Muslims in Rural West Bengal, in *Muslims in Free India their Social Profile and Problems.*M.K.A. Siddiqui (Ed.) Institute of Objective Studies, New Delhi.

Mondal, Sekh.Rahim (1998). Muslim Minority in Koch Behar: Their History, Society and Culture.*Islam and the Modern Age*, Vol. 29, No. 1.

Mondal, Sekh Rahim (2006). Muslim Society and Culture in Bengal: Tradition and Change, in *Islam and Muslim Communities in South Asia.*NadeemHasnain (Ed.) Serials Publication, New Delhi.

9

Muslims of Darjeeling Hills: Issues of Their Development

RajibChatterjee

Muslims have a substantial presence in Darjeeling hills which is situated in the northern most corner of the state West Bengal though the district Darjeeling has a significantly low percentage of Muslim population of 5 per cent (2001 census) which constitute one of the least Muslim populated districts in India. In India Muslims are considered as a backward community in terms of their education, economy and other social-cultural attributes which is ubiquitous. And the situations in Darjeeling hills are also very terrible as no such activities are initiated exclusively for the development of Muslims though government funds sanctioned only for the betterment of Scheduled Castes and Scheduled Tribes in Darjeeling Himalayan region. The Darjeeling Gorkha Hill Council (DGHC) for the last 20 years spent not a single penny for the sake of the development of hill Muslims. However, Muslims in Darjeeling hills are primarily a community migrated from the plains since British annexation to the tract during 1835. The colonial history of Darjeeling reveals that, the rapid growth of the town in flocked a huge number of Muslim groups specialised in various occupations to serve the Europeans and their native companions in the late thirties of nineteenth century. They came from various corners of inside and outside India and later domiciled permanently after marriage with native girls. Irrespective of their all ethnic and social-cultural variations, they constitute a uniform cultural identity intermingled with the popular hill cultures by adopting their life ways. Hence, there is a need of serious research for assessing the extent, nature and cause of Muslim backwardness and marginalisation for the sake of strategies to ameliorate their condition.

A Brief Sketch of the People

It is very difficult to say the exact time of Muslim migration in this mountainous hill region as of the lack of historical records. There are various popular myths among the Darjeeling Muslims regarding their migration to the Himalaya. But these are not validated by authentic evidences. However, these hill Muslims have a colonial history which reveals that the Europeans during the early part of 19th century encouraged a large number of Muslim groups to Darjeeling as the town was acted as a district head quarter and the centre of all type of administrative activities during the early British periods. Dr Campbell's supervision to the growth of trade and commerce added a new dimension to the importance of Darjeeling as a centre of 'trans-frontier' trade and an entry port for Central Asia. This encouraged a huge number of Muslims to migrate and gradually some of these non-familial male individuals later got married with the native Nepali girl and domiciled as a permanent resident. These families are the early Muslim families of Darjeeling hills. After that many Muslim groups have also later settled permanently for their business purposes. Muslims are predominately urban community there and concentrated in the urban areas of Darjeeling, Kurseong and Kalimpong town.

Table 9.1 : Muslims of Darjeeling Hills (2001)

Name of the Sub-division	*Population*
Darjeeling Sadar Sub-division	5698
Kurseong Sub-division	3199
Kalimpong Sub-division	3063

(Source:2001 Religious Census report)

Broadly, Muslims in Darjeeling hills are still engaged in their traditional occupations. They are broadly in self-employment. They are engaged in various marginal occupations as per their traditional caste occupations.Some are still in the occupation of animal slaughter. Some are in fish trading. Besides, a considerable number of them are in various small marginal businesses like bakery industry, household utensils made of steel and brass, wielding, cloth merchant, tailoring, etc.Economically these Muslim groups are lagging behind. Only the Kashmiri and Tibetan Muslim families are well to do. Since colonial times, these two groups are engaged in the business of woolen garments and *pashmina*.

Major Fundamental Development Bottlenecks

Muslims in Darjeeling hills had a rich heritage and their innumerable contribution towards developing the hill regions for habitable to all is indisputable.Their strong attachment to their habitation is without a shred of doubt. Despite having this they are reduced to be a marginal community for various reasons which create tension and anger among them. The Darjeeling Muslim development deficits may be interpreted from the perspectives of social exclusion and alienation. The images of the Muslims have been constructed by the dominant society as "non-indigenous", have created a barrier and mental ghetto which stimulus in their identity crisis and security issues. The socio-political situations of Darjeeling hill region also have a great role in their relative backwardness. This often alienated them from the dominant society of the hills and ultimately deprived them from progressive aspects.

During the colonial times Muslims enjoyed and were privileged migrants as of their special services which had a great necessity in social lives. But soon they lost all their social status and privileges as after independence, some socio-political factors creates obstacle to join them in the progressive aspects of the hills. Nepali population was increased due to immigration. These migrants or immigrants started small scale businesses or engaged in marginal occupations and for the first time, the Muslims faced tough competition with their Nepali neighbours even in their traditionally specialised economic avenues. Economic instability effects in the education of their children as it entails additional expenditure on the one hand and the family deprived of his contribution on the other. Poverty is undoubtedly the chief cause contributing to the increase in percentage of illiteracy. But this situation cannot be fully blamed on poverty. Inquiries for those capable of giving education to their children reveal that they suffer from a sense of deprivation and frustration. Uncertainty in securing jobs after a particular level of education frustrates them. That is why majority of the guardians do not think their sons would adopt any profession other than their hereditary one. Persons belong to the lowest income groups stubbornly by stick to their traditional occupation and never think of getting out of it.

Their socio-economic condition presents a dismal picture there. They are deprived of due representation in public employment even at the lowest level. As the formal administration was under DGHC led by GNLF

(Gorkha National Liberation Front), the whole administrative positions are owned by Nepali speaking caste and tribes of Darjeeling Himalaya. The Muslims are not allowed to join in any permanent position in DGHC offices. They are also denied equal opportunity in the private sectors. Their representation is indeed very poor in local services. Economically they are very poor. The majority of Muslims in Darjeeling fall in lower income group. Majority of them engaged in fish and beef market as per daily wage of Rs. 60. There are two government *madrasas* in Darjeeling town for both male and female each. But these *madrasas* are facing various types of constraints and impediments. As the recurrent process is under the control of Hill council, there is no recruitments of *madrasa* teachers since 2003. Books are not supplied to *madrasa* since last 10 years. Mead day meal is stopped from 2008. Ultimately all these provoked drop out of Muslim students in government *madrasas*. Moreover, after finishing *madrasa* education, the modern missionary led English medium schools are not interested to give them chance in their schools. As a result, the literacy level of the Muslim community is much below. Because of the hurdles at the lower level of education, the share of Muslim students at higher and professional level is also much below.

The absence of proper civic amenities and infrastructure facilities were a major complaint voiced by the Muslim community. Muslims in Darjeeling hills are predominately an urban community and living *basti* type settlement of Darjeeling, Kurseong and Kalimpong town. But infrastructural facilities are not reached to them as the place is overlooked by the Municipality. Muslims have virtually no access to government development schemes.

Muslims are often not able to avail of the reservation benefits available to OBCs as the officials (as most of them are from Nepali speaking ethnic communities) do not issue the requisite caste certificates. It was also alleged that many eligible Muslim OBCs (Other Backwork Classes) were not included in the official list which results in denial of several benefits to the Community. Many Muslims faced ill-treatment at the hands of authorities when they apply for new ration cards.

Concluding Observations and Issues of Affirmative Action

It is however, true that after Independence, Muslims were being used merely as a vote bank by all the political parties and no Worth-while administrative action to improve their socio-economic condition was taken by any government. For more than fifty year of India's Independence no such developmental initiatives were taken for the betterment of Muslim life. The Sachar committee report reveals the fact that even the Muslim dominated districts or states are far behind from the map of socio-economic development. The places like Darjeeling, where Muslim concentration is very low, never come into the media hype as because of their numerical strength as well the geo-morphological position of the tract. In Darjeeling hill areas, the Muslims are almost an "entrapped minority". The geomorphologic pattern of the place secluded them from the rest in one hand and in other the majoritarian attitude (i.e. the Nepali communities) alienated them from the positive developmental aspects of Darjeeling hills.

Darjeeling is excluded from the industrial map of the state. Surely, the economic viability and environmental feasibility do not welcome the industrialists. Unemployment is a big problem to them. Youth of Darjeeling hills irrespective of their creed are now starting many specialized services or jobs which are traditional occupations of Muslims. The displacement from these traditional occupations has contributed to Muslims being deprived of their means of livelihood and has led to fuel in the Muslim grievances. Education is undoubtedly troubled Muslims and diverted them from utilizing the positive aspects of progress and advancement of hills. But small scale industries have a great potentiality as the Muslims preferred self-employment. Ideally, development processes should remove or reduce economic and social obstacles to cooperation and mutual respect among all groups living in Darjeeling hills. But it is equally necessary for Muslims themselves to come out and achieve their own empowerment. Muslim masses themselves must be awakened. Like Urdu poet Iqbal says, "*Allah does not change the condition of the people unless they strive to change themselves*".

Bibliography

Ahmad, Aziz (1964).*Studies in Islamic Culture in the Indian Environment*.Claren Don Press, Oxford.

Chatterjee, Rajib (2007).Socio-Economic Profile of the Dhunias of Sub-Himalayan Darjeeling.*Islam and Muslim Societies*, Vol. 3, No. 1.

Mondal, Sekh Rahim (1983).For a Sociological Understanding of Indian Muslims.*NBU Review*, Vol. 6. No. 2, pp. 95-108.

Mondal, Sekh Rahim (1994).*Dynamics of Muslim Society*. Inter-India Publications, New Delhi.

Mondal, Sekh Rahim (1997).*Muslims of Siliguri: Aspects of Their Society, Culture and Relationship with the Metropolis*. Institute of Objective Studies, New Delhi.

Mondal, Sekh Rahim (2001).Tibetan Muslim Refugees in India: The Problem and the Prospects in *Refugees and Human Rights*. S.C. Roy (Ed.) Rawat Publications, Jaipur.

O., Mally, L.S.S. (1907).*Bengal District Gazetteer: Darjeeling*. Longos Press, New Delhi.

10

Transformation of Material Culture with Reference to Occupational Change among the Kharias of Purulia District in West Bengal Srikrishna Mondal

Srikrishna Mondal

INTRODUCTION

The Hill Kharia, a hunting and gathering tribe, belong to the proto-australoid racial stock and mainly inhabit Bihar, Madhya Pradesh, Maharashtra, Jharkhand, Odisha and West Bengal in India. In Purulia, West Bengal the Hill Kharia are found in 7 out of 16 Police Station situated at the eastern side of the district. They are found in different districts like Bunkura, Paschim Medinipur contiguous with Purulia in West Bengal, in Mayurbhanj district of Odisha, in Singbhum and Dalbhum district of Jharkhand. S.C. Roy (1935) made an exhaustive ethnographic study. The Kharias are sub-divided into three main sections on the basis of geographical location, economy and culture. These are Dudh Kharias, Dhelki Kharias and Hill Kharias. The total population is about 9,57,971 (2001 Census). The Dudh Kharias are the most advanced and educated section of tribe who are mainly inhabit at Ranchi. They live in settled villages away from the forest and hills. They have as their neighbours various Hindu castes with whom they come into frequent contract. They have taken to agriculture and other occupation. The Dhelki Kharias can be found in Gangpur, Jaspur and Raigarhdistricts of Madhya Pradesh. They also live in settled villages and have come in close contact with neighbouring communities. Agriculture is their main economic source.

The Kharias who used to live in and around hilly tracts are known as Hill Kharias. Sometime they also referred to as *'Pahari Kharia'*. The peasants, among whom they lived, called as the Khariya. They are also known by the mythical term Sabar. The Purulia district with the largest concentration of the Hill Kharias is in Manbazar P.S., which also happens to be the largest Police Station of the district. Approximate population of the Hill Kharias is 15,000 in Purulia district. The Kharias originally belong to a nomadic tribe wondering in a large territory in search of food. They were forest dwellers and traditionally hunter and food gatherers, who used to maintain their livelihood by collecting edible roots, tubers, herbs and fruits from the forest and hunting the animals, they were totally depend on the forest. Their life was intricately related with the forest ecosystem. Their adaptation to the environment is direct and simple. Their previous mode of subsistence pattern receded due to the deforestation and ecological changes.

E.T. Dalton in his book "Descriptive Ethnology of Bengal" (1872) has described about the mythical concept of Kharia origin. Their mythical belief is that they originate from peahens egg. They lived at Rotasgarh in Patna. Later on they migrated to the areas near the Koyal River.

According to Mukhopadhayay these Kharia people with small and scattered population, live in remote and isolated areas. They are still in pre-agriculturist stage and mostly depended on outmoded forest economy, mainly depended on the *jungle* (forest) produce. At present due to denudation of the forest areas these people have been ecologically and economically displaced. The interactional pattern between the Kharias and the village peasantry has not fully crystallized. The Kharias are main engaged in committed crimes from petty thefts to burglaries, robbers, large dacoits and even murder. That means that about 98 percent of these people remain engaged in anti-social activities (Mukhopadhyay, 1989).

The Kharias are not only the primitive and backward, but they also remain involved in criminal activities. They were alleged to be notified as a Criminal Tribe under the Criminal Tribe Act of 1924. Act was repealed in 1952 and the Kharias have officially been declared as a "VimuktaJati" (De-notified Tribe). In all villages, theKharias migrated in different period of history either in search of employment or selection of habitat due to some social reasons. Incomes of most of the members derived from selling of fuel, laborers for agricultural works. A few of them have got a very negligible area of land. Due to different ecological constraints and poor economic condition of farming population growth of the villages has been arrested.

Now most of the Kharia people lead a settled life. Their economic condition has been changed from nomadic hunting gathering to settled agricultural activities. The material culture and social relation have been changed in relation to change of subsistence pattern.

Area of Study

Three villages namely Kulabahal village under Hura C.D. Block, Babuijore village under Puncha C.D. Block and Pargora village of Bundwan C.D. Block have been selected for the present study. Being a migrant community, the Kharias of the Kulabahal are able to preserve very little originality, because of the easy accessibility to the Purulia town, whereas the village Pargora being located as the fringe of the forest, gives the Kharias residing here less exposure to the modern life. Pargora and Babuijore villages are located at the vicinity of forest. The total population of the studied villages has been given in Table 10.1.

Table 10.1 : Distribution of the Scheduled Tribes, Scheduled Castes and OBC/General in Three studied Villages (Census 2001)

Name of the C.D. Block	*Name of the Village*	*Scheduled Tribes Population*	*Scheduled Castes Population*	*OBC/ General Population*	*Total Population*
Hura	Kulabahal (JL No. – 47)	386	75	719	1,180
Puncha	Babuijore (JL No. - 12)	154	0	899	1,053
Bundwan	Pargora (JL No. - 88)	196	0	159	355

Methodology

The present study is based on the empirical study carried out during July and November 2005 and December 2006 among the Kharias of Kulabahal village under Hura C.D. Block, Babuijore village of Puncha C.D. Block and Pargora village of Bundwan C.D. Block. The data have been collected by using the standard tools and techniques of Social Anthropology.

Ecology of the Area

The district Purulia belonging to the Western border of West Bengal, is virtually an extension of the Chhotanagpur plateau and bears a topographical feature which stand in quite contrast with the other plain areas of the state. The district is located in the humid sub tropical climate region or comes under plateau region characterized by arid and dry zone and is specified as chronic Drought Prone Area (DPA).

The basic economy of the district is agriculture. But it is severely constrained by drought condition. Because of erratic and scanty rainfall, there is frequent failure of crops leading some times to famine or near famine situation. The hilly undulated terrains put up a further constraints and substantial portion of land, is a uncultivable waste. The situation is harshed by poor communication system, inaccessible to inferior parts, particularly during rainy season. The rate of literacy is somewhat lower

Table 10.2 : Age-group wise Distribution of the Kharia population of the Studied Villages

Sl.Nos.	*Age-group (in years)*	*MalePopulation (Percentage)*	*Female Population (Percentage)*	*Total Population (Percentage)*
1.	Upto4	26 (9.96)	25 (10.28)	51 (10.05)
2	5-9	31 (11.87)	26 (10.69)	57 (11.24)
3	10-14	32 (12.26)	23 (9.46)	55 (10.89)
4	15 -19	20 (7.66)	27 (11.11)	47 (9.27)
5	20-24	18 (6.89)	18 (7.40)	36 (7.10)
6	25-29	23 (8.81)	20 (8.23)	43 (8.48)
7	30-34	20 (7.66)	28 (11.52)	48 (9.52)
8	35-39	19 (7.27)	14 (5.76)	33 (6.50)
9	40-44	20 (7.66)	15 (6.17)	35 (6.90)
10	45-49	14 (5.36)	11 (4.52)	25 (4.93)
11	50-54	12 (4.59)	7 (2.88)	19 (3.74)
12	55-59	6 (2.29)	5 (2.05)	11 (2.16)
13	60-64	5 (1.91)	12 (4.93)	17 (3.35)
14	65+	15 (5.75)	12 (4.93)	27 (5.32)
15	Total	261 (51.78)	243 (48.21)	504 (99.98)

N.B. : Percentage is in respect to Total Population.

than elsewhere in West Bengal. The topography of the district is hilly and undulated. There are numerous hillocks in south, forming a continuity with the Dalma range. The district gifted with wide and scattered forests and some wild animals. Due to the constant erosion in the sloped area, indiscreet cutting and grazing etc., the forest resources have now become scanty.

From Table 10.2, it is observed that the total population of the studied villages is 504, out of which 261 (51.78 percent) are males and 243 (48.21 percent) are females. The total population has been categorized into various age groups on the basis of age and sex. The total male population is 261, out of which 26 (9.96 percent), 31 (11.87 percent), 32 (12.26 percent), 20 (7.66 percent), 18 (6.89 percent), 23 (8.81 percent), 20 (7.66 percent), 19 (7.27 percent), 20 (7.66 percent), 14 (5.36 percent), 12 (4.59 percent), 6 (2.29 percent), 5 (1.91 percent) and 15 (5.75 percent) belong to the age group of 0-4, 5-9, 10-14, 15-19, 20-24, 25-29, 30-34, 35-39, 40-44, 45-49, 50-54, 55-59, 60-64 and 65 years and above age groups respectively. Similarly the total female population has been categorized on the basis age and sex and their total number is 243 (48.21 percent) of its total population. Out of this total, the frequency of female is 25 (10.28 percent), 26 (10.69 percent), 23 (9.46 percent), 27 (11.11 percent), 18 (7.40 percent), 20 (8.23 percent), 28 (11.52 percent), 14 (5.76 percent), 15 (6.17 percent), 11 (4.52 percent), 7 (2.88 percent), 5 (2.05 percent), 12 (4.93 percent), are belongs to the age group of 0-4, 5-9, 10-14, 15-19, 20-24, 25-29, 30-34, 35-39, 40-44, 45-49, 50-54, 55-59,60-64 and 65 years and above respectively.

It is significant to note that highest population is 57 belong to the age group of 5-9 years out of which 31 and 26 are males and females, respectively. The highest age-group 65 years and above has 27 persons. Out of them 15 (5.75 percent) and 12 (4.93 percent) are males and females, respectively.

Table 10.3 shows that the types of family among the Kharias in the studied villages. In this table the types of family have been categorise into six groups viz; nuclear family joint family, extended family, conjugal family, broken family and single family respectively. The total number of the families are 113 out of which 51 (45.13 percent), 27 (23.89 percent), 11 (9.73 percent), 13 (11.50 percent), 7 (6.19 percent) and 4 (3.53 percent) belong to the nuclearfamily, joint family, extended family, conjugal family, broken family and singlefamily respectively. The total number of nuclear family is 51 out of which by 22 (19.46 percent), 12

Table 10.3 : Family Types among the Kharias

Name of the Villages	*Nuclear Family (No. &Percentage)*	*Joint Family (No. &Percentage)*	*Extended Family (No. &Percentage)*	*Conjugal Family (No. &Percentage)*	*Broken Family (No. &Percentage)*	*Single Family (No. &Percentage)*	*Total Family (No. &Percentage)*
Kulabahal	22 (19.46)	9 (7.96)	5 (4.42)	7 (6.19)	2 (1.76)	1 (0.88)	46 (40.70)
Babuijore	12 (10.61)	11 (9.73)	2 (1.76)	4 (3.53)	5 (4.42)	1 (0.88)	35 (30.97)
Pargora	17 (15.04)	7 (6.19)	4 (3.53)	2 (1.76)	0 (0.00)	2 (1.76)	32 (28.32)
Total	51 (45.13)	27 (23.89)	11 (9.73)	13 (11.50)	7 (6.19)	4 (3.53)	113 (100.00)

N.B.:Percentage is in respect to Total Family

(10.61 percent), 17 (15.04 percent) belong to the villages of Kulabahal, Babuijore and Pargora respectively. Similarly joint family of the villages are 27 out of them 9 (7.96 percent), 11 (9.73 percent), and 7 (6.91 percent) belong to the Kulabahal, Babuijore and Pargora respectively.The total number of extended families are 11 out of which 5 (4.42 percent), 2 (1.76 percent) and 4 (3.53 percent) belong to the villages of Kulabahal, Babuijore and Pargora respectively. It is also found that there are conjugal families and their number is 13 out of which 7 (6.19 percent), 4 (3.53 percent), 2 (1.76 percent) belong to the villages of Kulabahal, Babuijore and Pargora respectively. The next category is broken family where one of the parents live. The total number of broken family is 7 out of them 2 (1.76 percent) and 5 (4.42 percent) belong to Kulabahal and Babuijore respectively. It is significant to note that there is no broken family in the village of Pargora. From the above study it also highlights that there are also 4 families comprise only single member out of which one single family (0.88 percent) each in Kulabahal and Babuijore villages and 2 (1.76 percent) families are present in Pargora village.

The table 4 shows the level of literacy in the studied villages. The level of literacy has been classified into 5 categories viz., Illiterate, Can-Sign, Primary, secondary and higher Secondary level of education. The total population of the villages are 504, and out of them 270 (53.57 percent), 104 (20.63 percent), 106 (21.03 percent), 22 (4.36 percent) and 2 (0.39 percent) are belong to the categories illiterate, can-sign, primary, secondary and higher secondary level of education respectively. From this it is seen that out of 261 male members, 118 (23.41 percent), 55 (10.91 percent), 68 (13.49 percent), 18 (3.57 percent) and 2 (0.39 percent) belongs to the category of illiterate, can-sign, primary, secondary and higher secondary level of education respectively. The female of literacy level is indicating that of the total 243, 152 (30.16 percent), 49 (9.72 percent), 38 (7.53 percent) and 4 (0.79 percent) belongs to category of illiterate, can-sign, primary and secondary level of education respectively. It is significant to note here that there is no female member belonging to the higher secondary level of education. The people of the villages are less interested to send their children to school. A few of male students are going to the school outside the village and stay at ashram hostel for education.

From the table 5, it is found that the landless Khariafamilies are 43 (38.05) in number out of the total family. Out of 43family, 17 (15.04 percent), 16 (14.15 percent) and 10 (8.84 percent) are belong to the villages of Kulabahal, Babuijore and Pargora, respectively. The landless

Table 10.4 :Literacy Level among the Kharias

Sex	Literacy Level					
	Illiterate (No. &Percentage)	*Can Sign (No. &Percentage)*	*Primary (No. &Percentage)*	*Secondary (No. &Percentage)*	*Higher Secondary (No. &Percentage)*	*Total (No. &Percentage)*
Male	118 (23.41)	55 (10.91)	68 (13.49)	18 (3.57)	2 (0.39)	261 (51.78)
Female	152 (30.16)	49 (9.72)	38 (7.53)	4 (0.79)	0 (0.00)	243 (48.21)
Total	270 (53.57)	104 (20.63)	106 (21.03)	22 (4.36)	2 (0.39)	504 (99.99)

Table 10.5 :Family-wise Land Holding Pattern of Kharia Tribe

Name of the village	*Amount of Land*						
	Landless (No. & Percentage)	*Upto 10 Katha (No. & Percentage)*	*11-20 Katha (No. & Percentage)*	*21-30 Katha (No. & Percentage)*	*31-40 Katha (No. & Percentage)*	*41 Katha and above (No. & Percentage)*	*Total (No. & Percentage)*
Kulabahal	17 (15.04)	11 (9.73)	03 (2.65)	04 (3.53)	06 (5.30)	05 (4.42)	46 (40.70)
Babuijore	16 (14.15)	11 (12.38)	02 (1.76)	04 (3.53)	00 (0.00)	02 (1.76)	35 (30.97)
Pargora	10 (8.84)	04 (3.53)	05 (4.42)	04 (3.53)	06 (5.30)	03 (2.65)	32 (28.31)
Total	43 (38.05)	16 (14.15)	10 (8.84)	12 (10.61)	12 (10.61)	10 (8.84)	113 (99.98)

families do not have agricultural land but made their houses on the *patta* land which are provided by the Government. Rest of houses has some amount of land for agricultural purpose. This amount of land is categories into five groups according to their landholding capacity.

These groups are (1) who have land upto 10 *kathas* (local unit for area of land), (2) who have lands 11-20 *kathas*, (3) who have lands 21-30 *kathas*, (4) who have lands 31-40 *kathas* and (5) who have lands 41 *kathas* and above. In the village Kulabahal the above mentioned categories have 11(9.73 percent), 3(2.60 percent), 4(3.53 percent), 6(5.30 percent) and 5 (4.42 percent) *kathas* of land respectively. In the village Babuijore the land holding capacity of the families are 11 (12.38 percent), 2 (1.76 percent), 4 (3.53 percent) and 2 (1.76 percent) are belong to the said category respectively. It is significant to note that the category of 31-40 *kathas* of landholding families is not found in the village Babuijore. In the Pargora village the landholding families with 31-40 *kathas* of land have the highest number. The total number of families with 41 *kathas* and above are 10, out of which 5 (4.42 percent), 2 (1.76 percent) and 3 (2.65 percent) are belong to the villages of Kulabahal, Babuijore and Pargora respectively. The Kharias are of opinion that they have more less agricultural land and whatever they have are mainly of mono cropped and depend on monsoon. As a result the production of crops varies in relation to seasonal variation. The production of food substances is not adequate to them.

Sex Occupational Category

Table 10.6 depicts that the occupational pattern of the Kharias in the district of Purulia. The total members of the Kharia population are 504, out of them 261 (51.78 percent) and 243 (48.21 percent) belong to males and females, respectively. Majority of the people earn their livelihood through labour activities. It is highlighted that 46 (9.12 percent) persons are depend on forest products to maintain their life and out of them 20 (3.96 percent) and 26 (5.16 percent) are males and females respectively. At the same time some persons collect *Sal* leaf for plate making, which is also their one of their profession. Out of them, 9 (1.78 percent) and 15 (2.97 percent) are males and females, respectively. Some persons who have some amount of agricultural lands, they are engaged in agricultural activities to produce agricultural crops for maintaining their livelihood. The number of these persons is 56 (11.11 percent) out of its total population. Among them 40 (7.93 percent) and 16 (3.17 percent) are males and females respectively. The members of the younger

Table 10.6 : Occupational Status among the Kharia Tribe

Sex	Occupational Category						
	Agriculture & Agricultural Labour (No. & Percentage)	*Daily & Migratory Labour (No. & Percentage)*	*Forest Collection (No. & Percentage)*	*Sal Leave Processing for plate making (No. & Percentage)*	*House-wife & Cattle Rearing (No. & Percentage)*	*Students & Unable for any kind of work (No. & Percentage)*	*Total (No. & Percentage)*
Male	40 (7.93)	80 (15.87)	20 (3.96)	9 (1.78)	15 (2.97)	97 (19.24)	261 (51.78)
Female	16 (3.17)	38 (7.54)	26 (5.16)	15 (2.97)	63 (12.50)	85 (16.86)	243 (48.21)
Total	56 (11.11)	118 (23.41)	46 (9.12)	24 (4.76)	78 (15.47)	182 (36.11)	504 (99.99)

generation who are physically stronger, act as migratory labourers in various activities in the nearby town and other parts of the state. Their number is 118 (23.41 percent) of the total population. Out of them 80 (15.87 percent) and 38 (7.54 percent) are males and females respectively. Besides, some persons are also engaged in household activities and cattle rearing and their number is 78 (15.47 percent) out of the total population. Out of them 15 (2.97 percent) and 63 (12.5 percent) are males and females respectively. It is significant to note that due to the impact of modern system of education, the Kharia boys and girls are presently going to school for their education. The total number of students and unable for any kind of work are 182 (36.11 percent) of its total population. Out of them 97 (19.24 percent) and 85 (16.86 percent) are male and female student, respectively.

Social Aspects of the Kharia Life

Food Habit

They take rice as staple food twice a day. They drink tea with ground nut. They take meat of the animals like rat, squirrel, fox, cow, goat, buffalo, snake etc., when available. They also eat leafy vegetables. Children take meal thrice a day according to availability. They catch fish from streams and river for consumption. Sometimes they also starve irregularly in the summer and long day rainy season. During lean period they often suffer from lack of staple food.

Small patch of land for agriculture does not mitigate their food requirement. The production is very much insufficient to sustain their hunger. Most of them are marginal farmer and wage earner. Availability of animal meat is gradually reducing due to deforestation and lack of sufficient animals. Various types of leafy vegetable plants they collect from nearby forest and surrounding habitation.

Addiction Pattern

They traditionally prepare '*Hardia*' (rice beer) and '*Mahua*' (local country liqure). Beside they take *Biri* (country made cigarette) made from local *Kendupata* and *Canabis*. They drink alcohol at the time of ritual performances of the Mahato community. Now in the Babuijore and Pargora village both male and female regularly drink alcohol. They are so addicted to alcohol that sometimes they sell rice which is given by Panchayat Office for the purchase of alcohol. Even, they sale their tile of own house to buy alcohol from local people or market.

Development by Non Government Organization

The Government Organizations play the most significant role in rehabilitating the Kharia-Sabar community and restoring their lost dignity. There is some Non Government Organization (N.G.O.), who also takes initiative for their development particularly of their health and disease, household industry, agricultural operations and so on. The Paschim Banga Kharia Sabar Samity has also been able to make significant contribution to the cause of the Kharia Sabar through the untiring effort and commitment of its core members. Smt. Mahasweta Devi admirably assisted the Sabar Samity of Rajnowagar village. This *Samity* (association) also takes initiative for their education. Presently they are continuing one primary school. There are about 82 registered students. Butamong them 30-40 students only attend the school regularly. One Kharia Sabar Hostel was set up at Pargora village of Bandwan C.D. Block under State Tribal Welfare Department where 20 students permanently stay for their education.

Development by Panchayat

The Government of West Bengal has initiated several schemes for alleviating the harshness of living condition of the Kharia, including employment generation and provision of land and credit. Panchayat has helped to setup a Kharia house from Indira Abash Yojana. They also give 30 kg. of rice per month to a Kharia family under Annapurna Yojana with free of cost. They also give 40 kg. of rice at the rate of Rs. 2 per kg. under Antodaya Yojona. Self Help Groups are formed by the Panchayat member in the Kharia hamlet. Self Help Group project is also formed in the village Kulabahal and Pargora. Men have also formed a self help group in the Kulabahal village. This money is utilised in the purpose of making broom sticks, *salpata* (Sal tree leaves) plates and ropes.

Joint Forest Management

It is the participation of local people or tribal people for forest development. It helps to engage as wage earner in various activities, like tea plantation and preservation of sapling etc. They remain engaged in making *salpata*, *mahua* seeds collection and *kendupata*, deposit at forest office and receive Rs. 30 per day. The Kharia people also remain engaged as day labourer for felling the trees. On the other hand, illegal felling of trees has come under control through the participation of the local Kharia people.

Conclusion

Historically, the root of the Kharias was stigmatised in the colonial period. The Kharias belong nomadic tribe, wondering in search of food for occupying large territories. They were forest dwellers and traditionally hunters and food gatherers, who used to maintain their livelihood by collecting edible roots, tubers, herbs and fruits from the forest and hunt the small animals. They were totally depended on forest.

Though forests were the main source of Kharia economy, still because these were declared as the protected areas, they are unable to harvest the produces properly. The outsider money lenders, *Zamindars* and *Izzera* class (lease) from Hindu peasant community brought wide transformation of the region materially and culturally. The forests were to be first denuded by the merchant, land holders and colonial Governments during the first decade of twentieth century. The administrative machinery brought the Kharias under the preview of Criminal Tribe Act 1924. Once done, it was enforced by law and became a mode of social oppression. Thus during the first decade of the century, the Kharias were deprived of the forest economy which forced them to come in contact with the village society for seeking shelter and occupation but in most villages the Kharias were given shelter not as functional tribal group or as normal inhabitant. The village landlords allowed the Kharia families to settle in tract of the village area so that they could exploit them as labourers. However a client-patron relationship was developed between homeless Kharias and landlords. As a whole the Kharia in many villages were obliged to serve the landlords because they were dependent on landlords or the village peasants for their habitation and socio-economic security.

Their previous mode of subsistence pattern receded due to the deforestation. They try to lead a settled life in the village and adjust themselves with the agricultural stage of living. But agricultural obstacles in the laterite stony soil forced to them alternative means of livilihood. Now they partially depend on forest resources, and also on agricultural labour. The scope of wage earning opportunity within the village as well as in the neighbouring village is not adequate. Due to poverty and lack of better income, the grown up boys of Kharia families have taken '*Bagal*' (cow herder) profession as alternative occupation.

The Government of West Bengal and Government of India have initiated several schemes for alleviating the living condition of the Kharias in regard to their house type, agricultural land, domestic cattle and poultry, birds, employment generation as day labourers. They are gradually trying to adjust themselves with the rural folk of Bengal.

SUGGESTION

Keeping from above discussion in view I have put forwards some suggestions for the development of the Kharias:

1. Extension services for agriculture are weak. At present small plot of land distributed among the Kharias but the quality of land is not good to carry out agriculture properly. Only 4.16 percent Kharia adults have some agricultural land and landless are of 15.47 percent. The agricultural extension works should be employed in a better way.
2. Joint forest management program must be more strengthened to engage the Kharias at various activities like tree plantation and preservation of sapling, collection of seeds and protection of forest etc.
3. Free supply of high-yielding seeds, chemical fertiliser, pesticide etc. will help the Kharias to do agriculture.
4. Training should be provided about cultivation at undulating topography. The irrigation facilities should be provided if possible. Also, necessary training is required about cattle and poultry rearing. Subsidised loans and free distribution of livestock should be provided.
5. Knowledge should be provided about preparation of agricultural land for better crop production and prevention soil erosion.
6. School education of children up to Madhyamik and adults education program would be arranged.
7. Marketing facilities should be improved for supporting the activities of co-operative marketing and purchase of forest and agricultural produce.
8. Awareness Programme Camps should be arranged for community health and modern medicine. Development of knowledge of traditional ethno-medicine and schooling of children should be given priority.

Bibliography

Acharya, P.K. (2002). Fund Allocation, Expenditure and development of Primitive Tribal Groups: A Case study in Orissa. *Man and Life* : Vol. 28 Nos. 3-4. pp. 223-237.

Banerjee, H.N. (1959). 'The Kharia of Modhupur, Singhbum District and Neighbouring Regions'. Bulletin *of the Department of Anthropology*, Vol. 8, No. 2, pp. 91-202.

Banerjee, H.N. (1962). Socio-Ritual Status of the Kharia in the Ethnic Background of Manbhum. Bulletin *of the Cultural Research Institute, West Bengal*. Vol. 1, No. 2, pp. 16-28.

Bharal, G.P. (1968). Denotified Communities and Their Problems of Rehabilitation. The *Indian Journal of Social Work*, Vol. XXVIII, No. 4.

Biswal, Debendra Kumar. (2002). Impact of Eco-Degradation on Food and Ethno-medicine of the Shifting Cultivator Primitive Tribes in Orissa. *Man and Life* Vol. 28, Nos. 3-4. pp. 251-260.

Chandra Ramesh. (2000). *Environment Forest and Tribes*, (Anthropological Concomitance) Rawat Publications, Udaipur.

Dalton, E.T. (1872). *Descriptive Ethnology of Bengal*, Calcutta.

Das, Rajat Kanti. (2005). *Development from Tribal Perspective : A study of Santal, Bhumij and Kharia – inhabited Villages of Midnapore, West Bengal*. Kolkata.

Das, T.C. (1905). *The Wild Kharias of Manbhum*, Calcutta.

Das, T.C. (1936). *The Wild Kharias of Bhalbhum, Anthropological Paper No. 3*, University of Calcutta, Calcutta.

Datta, B.N. (1935). Kharias Ethnological Notes on some of the Castes of West Bengal, *Man in India*, Vol. 15, pp. 196-224.

Enthoven, R.E. (1922). *Tribes and Castes of Bombay*, Bombay.

Majumdar, B.C. (1927). *The Aborigines of the Highland of Central India*, The University of Calcutta, Calcutta.

Mukhopadhyay, Chandidas. (1989). Crime and Criminals of Purulia Asian *Studies* Vol. 7, Calcutta.

Mukhopadhyay, Chandidas. (1989). Kharias, *Socialist Perspective*, Vol. 12, Calcutta.

Mukhopadhyay, Chandidas. (1989). Folklore a Vehicle of Ethnic Protest *Folklore*, Calcutta.

Risley, H.H. (1891). *Tribes and Castes of Bengal*, Vol. 1, Calcutta.

Roy, S.C. (1935). Past Migration of the Kharia Tribe. *Journal of the Bihar and Orissa Research Society*.

Sinha, Dikshit. (1984). *The Hill Kharia of Purulia : A study of impact of poverty on a hunting and gathering tribe*, Anthropological Survey of India, Calcutta.

11

Assessment of Developmental Inputs among the Lodhas of Paschim Medinipur in West Bengal

Santanu Panda

Introduction

This chapter deals with an empirical assessment of the utilisation of the development inputs under the Rastriya Sama Vikas Yojona (RSVY) scheme of the Central Government in two Community Develpoment (C.D.) Blocks of Paschim Medinipur district in West Bengal. The author of this paper along with three other research investigators were engaged in an empirical assessment study by the district administration. The assessment of the utilisation of the development inputs were specifically designed to collect field level data regarding the implementation of development inputs under the scheme. The RSVY scheme is a recent initiative undertaken by the Planning Commission of the Central Government. The scheme aims at focused development programmes for backward areas which would help reduce imbalances and speed up development .Under the RSVY the Central Govt. aimed to cover 100 backward districts in India. Already 50 backward districts have been covered during 2003-2004 and a sum of Rs. 15,000 crores per year was provided to each of the district for a period of three years and a total of Rs 45 crores per district have been released to the State Governments on hundred per cent grant basis in instalment.

About RSVY (Rastriya Sama Vikas Yojona)

Under this component a District plan is to be prepared for each identified backward District showing the flow of funds from all sources namely, state plan, centrally sponsored scheme; central schemes, externally aided projects etc. as well as the specific schemes for the additionally under the RSVY. The schemes is to be used as an additionally. The state Govt. should first use all available resources & Funds under the RSVY are to be used to fill critical gaps, which stand in the way of rapid development. The RSVY Components of the District plan could also include schemes for drought proofing, agriculture and horticulture, etc.

About the Lodhas

In West Bengal there are 38 Scheduled Tribes distributed mainly in the southwest and the northern parts of the state (Bhowmick:1963). The Lodhas are mainly found in the western part of the state in the districts of Purulia, Bankura and Paschim Medinipur along with tribes like Santal, Munda, Bhumij and Oraon who are numerically and economically in a much better condition than the Lodhas. The Lodhas generally live in and around the forest covered areas of the southwestern districts of the state and still largely depend on forest for their livelihood.

In one of the pioneering anthropological study, the Lodhas were depicted as a semi-nomadic community who used to move from one place to another in search of livelihood (Bhowmick 1963). According to Bhowmick, the Lodhas of erstwhile Medinipur district depended mainly on food gathering and hunting and some of them were found to be engaged in agricultural as well as non-agricultural activities as hired labourers of the higher caste and wealthy families of the villages. It was also found that among the Lodhas earning from particular types of occupation was not sufficient in the majority of the cases to maintain their families, so they had to practice a variety of occupations to sustain their livelihood (Ibid.).

The Government of Independent India repealed the Criminal Tribes Act in 1952. Even after de-notification as criminal tribes, the Lodhas continue to suffer from the social stigma and the non-tribal neighbours still behave unsympathetically towards them. Over the decades, the Lodhas gradually changed their occupation from hunting gathering to agriculture as an alternative means of livelihood owing to deforestation (Danda, 2002).

The Census of 1981 shows that the total population of the Lodhas including the Kharias and the Kherias in West Bengal is 53,718. The Lodhas are concentrated in Medinapur District and their total number according to the Census of 1981 was 16,534. Besides West Bengal, they are also found in the Mayurbhanj and Baleswar districts of Orissa, Originally, they inhabited hilly rugged terrains covered with jungle. Their mother tongue is Lodha, which is close to Savara, an Austro-Asiatic language. They are fluent in Bengali. Traditionally they were forest dwellers but now they have started cultivation either as owner or as agricultural labourer and are also engaged in hunting and fishing. More than 80 per cent of them follow Hinduism with traditional belief in spirits and nature (Mandal, H. *et. al.* 2002:).

Objectives

The following objectives are taken for study :

1. To study the impact of various types of developmental inputs on the socio-economic life of the Lodhas.
2. To find out the reasons behind such non-utilisation of developmental inputs.

An attempt would be made to formulate some suggestions for their better implementation.

Materials and Methods

The present study has been concerned with all Lodha families, who belongs to Scheduled Tribes community of Binpur-II and Nayagram C.D. Blocks of Paschim Medinipur district. The members of other communities of these two C.D. Blocks are not undertaken for the present study.

The primary data for the study has been collected through intensive anthropological fieldwork conducted for about two consecutive years.

Both qualitative and quantitative data were collected through census, structured and unstructured questionnaire and also with the help of genealogy, case studies, participatory observation, focus group discussion and panel interviews.

In order to carry out this research a micro-level anthropological study was conducted. This micro level study were mainly based on participant observation which were included the collection of both quantitative and qualitative data on the demographic, economic, political and socio cultural dimensions of the selected Lodha settlements within the study area. Besides these basic information, case studies on the delivery and utilisation of various developmental programmes (including programmes under RSVY scheme) were collected. The Lodha settlement clusters were selected on the basis of previous field work experiences in the area. All attempts were made to cover all the Lodha village/settlements in which some kind of development inputs have reached.

Lodha Settlements in the Two C.D. Blocks

We have selected the Lodha settlements for our survey in consultation with the District Planning and Development Cell, who keeps the record of the development inputs given to the Lodha community under the RSVY scheme. Within the stipulated period of the impact assessment project we have been able to visit 12 Lodha settlements of Binpur-II and Nayagram C.D. Blocks and conducted basic census and survey on occupational diversity of the Lodhas who received some kind of development input from the district administration. Along with the basic surveys, we have collected quantitative and qualitative data regarding the nature and type of development assistance as well as the utilisation of the inputs by the beneficiaries at the household level.

The total number of households in our sample has 269 and the total population is 1,024 and there is predominance of females in the sample. Among the 12 Lodha settlements, 6 belongs to Binpur-II C.D. Block and the rest was located in the Nayagram C.D. Block. The number of households is larger in Nayagram C.D. Block than Binpur-II C.D. Block and the largest Lodha settlement (49) in our sample comes from Nayagram C.D. Block while the smallest (seven) belongs to Binpur-II C.D. Block. The average of the number of households in Nayagram C.D. Block is 30.3 while the same average is 14.5 in case of Binpur-II C.D. Block.

Table 11.1 : Profile of the Surveyed Lodha Settlements

Name of village	*Male*	*Female*	*Total Population*	*Number of Households*	*Mean Household size*
Amlasole (Binpur-II)	21	39	60	18	3.3
Chakadoba (Binpur-II)	27	40	67	18	3.7
Chirakuthi (Binpur-II)	20	20	40	08	5.0
Dhobakacha (Binpur-II)	22	26	48	10	4.8
Rimradanga (Binpur-II)	37	46	84	26	3.2
Sankhabhanga (Binpur-II)	10	11	20	07	2.8
Ambhisole (Nayagram)	55	69	124	32	3.8
Bansiasole (Nayagram)	42	33	75	19	3.9
Banksole (Nayagram)	62	66	128	33	3.9
Palasia (Nayagram)	59	46	105	25	4.2
Sitalpura (Nayagram)	42	46	88	24	3.7
Singdhui (Nayagram)	105	80	185	49	3.8
Total: 12	**502**	**522**	**1024**	**269**	**3.8**

Table 11.2 : General Descriptions of Development Inputs

Name of Development Inputs	*No. of Beneficiaries (Per cent)*	*No. of used Inputs (Per cent)*	*No. of Inputs Sold (Per cent)*	*Not yet been able to Cultivate (Per cent)*	*Unused Solar or in Bad Condition*
Solar Light	94 (37.75)	44 (46.80)	47 (53.20)	-	03
Patta Land	31 (12.45)	11 (35.48)	-	20 (64.52)	
House	50# (20.08)	46 (92.00)	-	-	
Cattle	36* (14.46)	06 (16.67)	22 (61.11)	-	
Total	211	107	69	20	03

Notes : # 4 houses which were built under the scheme were found to remain unutilized as those were not suitable for living.

* 8 goats have died within a week after they were given to the beneficiaries.

( ) Represents percentage out of the total number of households.

[ ] Represents percentage out of total number of beneficiaries.

From Table 11.2 we have found various types of Development inputs given to the Lodhas. Solar lights have been received by 94 (37.75 per cent) families out of 249 but 46.80 per cent utilised it. Plots of patta land have been given to 31 (12.48 per cent) families out of 249 but only 35.48per cent of them were found to cultivate on them.

There were 50 (20.08 per cent) beneficiary families out of 249 under the housing schemes and most of them (92.00 per cent) were found to live in the houses constructed under such schemes. A total of 36 (14.46 per cent) families out of 249 were given poultry birds and/or cattle. Only six families (16.67 per cent) were found to rear the cattle and/or poultry bird. In most of the cases, the cattle and/or the birds have either sold or died.

Table 11.3 : C.D. Block Wise Description of Development Inputs

Name of C.D. Block	*Solar Light*			*Patta Land*		
	No.of Beneficiaries (Per cent)	*Used (Per cent)*	*Sold (Per cent)*	*No. of Beneficiaries (Per cent)*	*Used for Cultivation (Per cent)*	*Not yet been able to Cultivate (Per cent)*
Binpur-II	20 (21.27)	01 (5)	19 (95)	10 (32.25)	01 (10)	09 (90)
Nayagram	74* (78.72)	42 (56.76)	29 (39.19)	21 (76.74)	10 (47.62)	11 (52.38)
Total	94	43	48	31	11	20

Note : *3 Solar lights were found to be out of order in the Nayagram C.D. Block at the time of survey

This table 3 shows that the total number of beneficiaries under the RSVY and Indira Awas Yojana (IAS) schemes of Binpur-II C.D. Block is lesser than the Nayagram C.D. Block. The development inputs are utilised more by the beneficiaries in Nayagram C.D. Block than that of the Binpur-II C.D. Block. In Binpur-II C.D. Block only one family out of 20 who received the solar light was found to utilize it whereas, 10 (32.25 per cent) families received Patta land but only one was found to cultivate the same. In the Nayagram C.D. Block, 56.76 per cent of the beneficiary families utilised solar lights while 39.19 per cent families have sold the solar lights. In the same C.D. Block, 47.62 per cent families utilized patta land for cultivation whereas, 52.38 per cent families were unable to cultivate it.

Findings and Observation

- The Lodha families of two C.D. Blocks are in a very poor condition because all family members depend on forest resource collection and agricultural labour.
- It was found that 31 persons (12.44 per cent) got patta land out of 249 household in 11 villages of two C.D. Blocks.
- During our interviews 20 informants reported that land pattas were issued and given but the beneficiaries have not yet seen the plot. The Land and Land Reforms Department officials have not given any proper guidance to the beneficiary families about the location of the land.

- In some cases the patta was issued in favour of the father but they could not cultivate the land after the death of the father because when the father was alive other persons were forcefully cultivating the same land.
- The beneficiaries sold some of the high technology developmental inputs like solar cells distributed to them. The poor and landless Lodha families were found to sell the solar cells to the wealthy neighbours. The Lodhas also did not know how to use solar cell.
- Lodhas got houses under IAY scheme, which were constructed by Govt. Department, but houses were not suitable for their living. Because in the house there is no window in the room. They were also found to live in a single room with goat, cow, hen etc.
- Lodhas got bullock and plough for cultivation from Govt. but they have no agriculture land, so they sold the bullock and plough to the neighbours.

Recommendations

1. The Lodha families to whom patta land have been issued on paper should be given the actual right of possession with full protection by the District administration and the Panchayat against all kinds of encroachment.
2. In some situations, adequate land may not be available for distribution to the landless Lodha families. In those cases, measures may be taken to reclaim uncultivable barren lands with irrigation facilities for distribution.
3. Solar cells should not be given to individual Lodha families without enquiring their socio-economic condition. If these are to be given to the individual Lodha families, the members of those families should be given proper demonstration/training for using such technical gadgets.
4. The house building plans should also have been made in consultation with the beneficiaries themselves to give honour and importance to their specific needs.

Bibliography

Bhowmick P.K. (1963), "The *Lodhas of West Bengal*" ISRAA Kolkata.

Bhowmick P.K. (1981), "Rehabilitation of a 'Denotified Community' The Ex-Criminal Lodhas of West Bengal (pp. 6-8)" Pub: Royal Anthropological Institute of Great Britain and Ireland. No. 44, Source: Stable URL: http://www.jstor.org/stable/3032233.

Danda, A.K. (2002). 'Predicaments of a marginalized community: The Lodha' *Journal of Anthropological Survey of India.* 51: 103-111.

Devi Mahasveta. (1983). *Lodhas of West Bengal,* Published in Economic and Politicall Weekly, Vol. 18, N0, 22.

Devi Mahasveta. (1985). *The Savara Tribals of West Bengal,* Economic and Politicall Weekly, Vol. 20, N0, 35.

Mandal, H. *et.al.* (2002). 'West Bengal', in *India: An Illustrated Atlas of Tribal World.* Anthropological Survey of India: Kolkata.

Panda, S. and Guha, A. (2009) 'Development Inputs among the Lodhas in a District of WestBengal: Problems of Implementation and Recommendations' *Journal of the Indian Anthropological Society,* .44: 69-75.

Roy, Shyam Sundar. (2009). 'What good is Independent India for the Lodhas?' *The Statesman,* 4 December 2009, p. 15.

Verma. R.C. (1990). '*Indian Tribes through the ages*.' Ministry of Information and Broadcasting. Govt. of India.

Part II: Dimensions of Human Resource Development

12

How to Develop Human Resource to Learn Anthropology in a Better Way ?

Abhijit Guha

In simplest terms, Human Resource Development (HRD) basically involves a series of planned and coordinated activities done by the members of an organisation to improve their level of performance. Experts in the field view HRD as a process consciously initiated by human beings. Anthropology is a discipline which studies human beings from biological and social points of view in a holistic framework. HRD specialists take help from the anthropologists because the process of HRD ultimately deals with humans. In this paper, I would make an attempt to outline the process which are needed for Human Resource Development in the learning of anthropology with the help of some examples from my experiences of learning anthropology for more than 25 years in a rural milieu with my students in the Department of Anthropology, at Vidyasagar University, West Bengal.

Encountering the Hurdles

I will first point out some of the difficulties I encountered in teaching anthropology to the students of Vidyasagar University. The first and foremost difficulty which I noticed among the students is that they do not read books outside anthropology. I believe that the students of anthropology must read a lot of story books, novels, short stories, poems, dramas, articles, travelers' accounts, science fictions and the like in Bengali as well as in English. Since all books deal with human affairs and variety of human conditions, reading of books outside anthropology helps a lot to get interest in human variety and problems. I found that my anthropology students do not read story books even for entertainment.

A related problem is lack of language skills of the students of anthropology at Vidyasagar University. Here majority of the students of anthropology cannot write correct sentences in English or even in Bengali. They make a lot of spelling mistakes and they rarely consult dictionaries and encyclopaedias. These are serious handicaps in learning anthropology. A good teacher in anthropology should encourage the students, particularly the beginners to read a lot of story books. The next thing is to practice writing. The students should write and try to publish them in local newspapers, magazines etc. The teachers may guide them in this adventure. Once a student of anthropology reads a good amount of story books, prepares small pieces of write-ups a lot of HRD in learning anthropology would be done.

The third difficulty of the students of anthropology at Vidyasagar University lies in their expression of thought through speaking. Most of the students lack the skill and power to present their ideas in a logical and coherent form. These become visible during classroom interactions with teachers, presentation of papers in seminars and Ph.D. registration programmes. But the most notable evidence of the lack of communication skill of the students of anthropology at Vidyasagar University is the virtual silence of the students when a speaker waits for questions from the audience after the presentation of a lecture. In my opinion this lack of courage to ask questions is related to the first two difficulties of our students. It had our students been well-read in out of syllabus books and possessed a fair amount of general knowledge and could construct correct sentences while speaking, they could definitely ask questions more frequently to speakers who delivered lectures at our department.

Potency of the Students of Anthropology

I will now describe some positive qualities of my student of anthropology at Vidyasagar University. Out students are very much field oriented. They always like to go to field and observe human activities. It was my students who first took me to the villages is Paschim Medinipur district in which land for industries were being taken over by the

Government for industries. I later conducted my fieldwork and completed my doctoral work by conducting fieldwork in the same area. Two students (a boy and a girl) aroused my interest to study the problems of joint forest management in a village near Karnagargh area. They also did excellent work in collecting records from the Office of the Forest Department. Another student and he is now a teacher of anthropology in a college wrote an excellent article in Bengali on the conservation of bamboo groves in a tribal village in Paschim Medinipur district. A student of the first batch in my department did excellent fieldwork in a village in the Nayagram C.D. Block on land which emerged in a river as a common property resource and we have written articles and I gave lectures based on the results of his fieldwork in many seminars and workshops. My current Ph.D. students have chosen many interesting problems through their observations in the field and I have been continuously writing with them on their problems and they are also presenting papers in various seminars and conferences. My lesson from the fieldworks of my student is that whenever I allowed the students to think independently to select their own problems and field sites, good results have come out. I just gave them good books and papers to read and further inspired them to read new things but never forced them to select research problems. I have to function strictly when they show something written by them. In the classes, I have seen that whenever students are allowed to talk in the class seminars, they try hard to talk in English and they do it. I never found any student who did not like the class seminars.

A Short Ethnography of My Learning from the Students

I will now describe a specific case of my own learning from my students at Vidyasagar University. I have already mentioned in brief about this in the previous section. Let me go into the details of the case.

During the mid-1990s three students of the Department of Anthropology went to do fieldwork for their M.Sc. dissertations in a village named Paschim Amba, only eight kilometers from the Medinipur railway station. They selected a hamlet inhabited by the Koras and started measuring human bodies and collected data on family, marriage and kinship following the standard anthropological methodology. In one usual afternoon in the Department, when we were discussing about the colourful Kora marriage ceremony, a student remarked, 'The colour and pomp of Kora marriage will soon go away since their lands are being taken over for a big pig iron industry of the Tatas.'

The remark of the student was a sufficient jolt for me and one Sunday morning in 1995, I landed up in Paschim Amba village where I first met a peasant leader named Trilochan Rana who was then leading a militant movement against the acquisition of agricultural land for private industries by the State Government. In Trilochan Rana's house we met a good number of peasants hailing from Amba, Maheshpur, Kantapal, Gokulpur, Baharapat, Shyamraipur and other villages of the area. Very quickly they started to narrate quite enthusiastically the gloomy story how their lands have been taken away for the industries. Trilochan Rana depicted how they were trying to protest against this kind of anti-peasant policy suddenly adopted by the Left Government of West Bengal in the wake of liberalization in India. Ironically, Mr. Rana, who was a former Naxalite, took refuge under Congress party to organize this peasant movement. 'But Sir, how coming from a University you can help us in this struggle for survival?' At that moment, I could not give any direct answer to this straightforward and pointed question.

While returning to Medinipur, I was thinking of the possible course of my individual action on land acquisition. Should I take up research on this problem? In fact, I had to struggle within myself for a long time on this issue simply because it was not just passing through the railway station Gokulpur twice a week like the service-holders commuting from Kolkata to Medinipur. Anyway, after my maiden visit to the field many events occurred and I had to go to those villages several times accompanied by the students. During this period I took two firm decisions. One was to do my Ph.D. dissertation on this problem and the other was to support these dispossessed peasants by writing popular articles on the various adverse effects of land acquisition on the socio-economic life of the enterprising Sadgope caste cultivators and poor Lodha and Kora families living on both sides of the south-eastern railway track between Medinipur and Kharagpur railway stations. Gradually, a feedback with the peasants developed and while collecting data I took an active part in organizing a public meeting within Paschim Amba village in collaboration with the district unit of the Association for the Protection of Democratic Rights (APDR). This ultimately culminated into a deputation to the District Magistrate on the adverse economic and environmental impacts of land acquisition in this area. But it also became clear that the APDR leaders who were definitely 'educated Bengali *bhadraloks*' were not very much interested in fighting in favour of the rights of the poor sharecroppers and marginalized tribal peasants dispossessed from their major means of production under the New Industrial Policy adopted by the West Bengal Government.

What I could ultimately sustain was continued research on land acquisition for development projects by combining field and archival materials and dissemination of my research findings in various academic and popular forums. The methodology of my research can hardly be called 'purely anthropological' let alone 'neutral' since my holistic perspective did not end in village but went far beyond into the files, notes and Gazette Notifications at the Land Acquisition Department of the District Collectorate to the West Bengal Assembly Proceedings. My entry into such a politically sensitive field site was made possible by my students who stayed with me from the beginning to the completion of my Ph.D. and they are still there with me.

Concluding Remarks

To sum up, I will say that learning of anthropology with the students is a challenging experience for me. If our students could read more story books, practice to write popular articles, use the computer to read and write on anthropology and do fieldworks in their own localities on their chosen problems and if the teachers always encourage them to search for new problems on which anthropological knowledge gained from the classrooms could be applied, then Human Resource Development in the learning of anthropology would be much more interesting that the way they exist at present. At least this is my experience of teaching anthropology at Vidyasagar University.

13

Issues and Problems in Agricultural Development: A Study on the Farmers of West Bengal

Arun Makal, Abhradip Banerjee, Avik Roy, Suman Hazra and Krishnendu Polley

Introduction

Agricultural development is one of the most talked about issues as a major portion of our population is still engaged with the agricultural industry. The widespread modernization of agriculture, development of many modern techniques and improvement in farm productivity all are the basic characteristics of agricultural development (CSSC, 1974; Bhalla & Tyagi, 1989).

Due to this reason most of the strategies of development even with its focus on different domains often emphasize upon rapid agricultural development in general and its modernisation in particular. The prime economic objective of agricultural development is to contribute to increased per capita incomes. Moreover, agricultural development promotes the proper conditions for farming so that planting, harvesting and processing of crops can be done effectively, which ultimately can reduce poverty and save lives (Mellor, 1966). Undoubtedly, such an approach has brought change in today's agricultural practices. There has been an overall improvement in agriculture all over the world and India is not an exception.

Over the years Government of India has tried to promote agricultural development. With their many initiatives Government of India have tried to convince farmers so that they can adopt modern techniques for the cultivation of their crops and most importantly for the improvement of production. But often the issue of access to these facilities came in the way. Because, still maximum numbers of farmers of our country live in the villages, they have no proper idea regarding the usage of modern farming techniques. Moreover, they do not have correct information regarding modern methods of soil preparation and use of high yielding seed varieties. Often their low level of education and lack of communication has resulted into a general lack of awareness regarding the modern research and inventions on agriculture. Consequently, these factors haven't helped agricultural development to be as successful as in many other parts of the world.

Quite naturally a number of studies have been undertaken to understand the issues and problems of agricultural development (De walt, 1994; Antweiler, 1998; Purcell, 1998; Sillitoe, 1998; Martin *et. al.*, 2002; Sillitoe *et. al.* 2004; Ellen, 2006). Moreover, many researchers (Hendy, 2000; Berrigan, 1979; Engel and Salomon, 1997) are also concerned with the topic of sustainable agricultural development and sustainable farming systems. The discipline of anthropology has also played a significant role in understanding the emerging issue of modernisation of agriculture. Mostly scholars (Rhoades, 1984; Sillitoe, 1998) have often emphasized upon the local procedures and strengthening farmers' voices in negotiating definitions and implementation of sustainable agricultural development (Cleveland, 1994, Sumberg & Okali, 1997). Netting, (1974) recognized that there is a positive correlation between indigenous farmers' ecological knowledge and the sustainability of their farming system. He pointed out that there is often an assumption that "traditional cultivators" are more sustainable than "commercial and industrial agriculture" that is unjustified without supportive data (Netting, 1993).

The situation in West Bengal is not much different. A high percentage of farmers in West Bengal are small and their farm or land sizes are little in size. They fully depend upon the agriculture. These people often sale their produces for earning livelihood and supporting their families. In addition, large numbers of farmer families depend on agricultural products for daily nourishment. Farmers in the State of West Bengal try to use many modern technologies to improve their farming. But, they face many problems in the application of modern farming techniques. Because, these rural farmers have no knowledge regarding modern farming techniques on the one side, on the other side, they have no such amount of money to accumulate modern inputs of farming. To overcome these problems most of the farmers in the State of West Bengal use their traditional or local knowledge in association with modern techniques to fulfill their farming activities. Not only in West Bengal, one can find similar situation all round the world – where farmers who have been managing different traditional agro-ecosystems seems to have found their way out in their own experience and deliberate experimentation. Even at times their gathered knowledge is so complex and sophisticated they could be applicable to the farming context.

Objectives, Methods and Study Areas

The present study attempts to investigate issues and problems of agricultural development among the farmers in the State of West Bengal. It tries to explore how various factors of modernisation and development affect both life and agricultural economy of the farmers in West Bengal, so that it can provide some glimpses regarding how farmers use their local knowledge and information to keep pace with the overall agricultural development of the country and the state.

The present study purposively selected farmers of the four districts in West Bengal i.e. Burdwan, Purba Medinipur, Hooghly and South Twenty Four Paraganas; who are primarily engaged with the cultivation of rice and other crops like potatoes, flower, groundnut, sesame and guava. These four Districts have been selected on the basis of pattern of land holdings, soil, climate, crop varieties, mixed crop cultivation, market orientation research and labor pattern.

The district Burdwan is better known for its predominant agricultural activities in comparison to other Districts. The District is truly called the granary of West Bengal due to its highest position in the production of paddy. From this region, rice is exported to the different districts within the State and even in the neighboring countries. Nearly all the varieties are produced in this region, which can be primarily classified into three types depending on the cultivated seasons like autumn rice, winter rice and summer rice. These three seasons are named according to the season of harvest of the crop. Autumn paddy is known as *aus*. The pre-monsoon *aus* covers May to September. The winter or monsoon paddy, known as *aman*, is grown from June to December. The summer or dry season paddy is popularly known as *boro*. The sowing time of summer paddy is November to February and harvesting time is March to June. The growing season of *boro* sometimes overlaps with *aus*.

The District Purba Medinipur is predominantly an agricultural District where paddy is the principal crop. Besides, different crops like groundnut, wheat, potato, sugarcane and betel leaf are produced here in large quantity. Aquaculture and shrimp farming has been taken up in a big way in the coastal belt. Floriculture and horticultural activities are concentrated in a major portion of Tamluk Sub-Division. Floriculture and sericulture are also widely practiced here.

The District Hooghly is one of the remarkable positions in the arena of agriculture. In this District, about 70 per cent of the population derives their living from agriculture. The agricultural economy of this region mainly depends on the cultivation of different cash crops like jute, sugarcane, potato and vegetables. The District is also famous for jute industry and is the hub of the jute trade in West Bengal and even in India. Other important industries of the District are the automobile industry and a textile industry. The continuous increase of pressure on the land due to the industrial development, the agricultural families have become victims of losing the land. This district is also well known for potato cultivation. Tarakeswar is a largest producer in the production of potato, which is even more than the average production of potato in the state. Therefore the domestic economy is completely served by the products produced locally.

In the District South Twenty Four Parganas, rice, sugarcane, chillies, coconuts, potatoes, timber and betel nuts are the principal agricultural products. The agriculture mainly supports the local rural economy. A considerable amount of people draw their livelihood from the agricultural sector. A large number of populations of this District depend on fruit farming. The District is very famous guava producing region of West Bengal. Guava is third most important fruit crop of the State after mango and banana. Baruipur Sub-Division of South Twenty Four Parganas is the biggest guava grower in West Bengal. Besides, more than one thousand families of this Sub-Division earn their livelihood from fruit cultivation. Different other significant guava cultivated regions of South Twenty Four Parganas are Kalyanpur, Shankarpur, Shikharbari, Hariharpur, Govindapur and Ramnagar.

Various standard research methods like Observation, Case Studies, Focussed Group Discussion have been used for the purpose of collection of data for this studty. Farmers from each of these Districts were consulted to understand their practices of crop farming and especially emerging problems and issues around different crops. Particular cases have been taken to understand local agricultural practices, development of agriculture, problems of the farmers and how they make an impact upon the life of the farmers. Moreover, Focused Group Discussion has been used to understand how these farmers try to solve their problem through their appraisal, analysis and plans.

Emerging Issues and Problems

The emerging issues of agriculture in West Bengal begin with the problem of agricultural and rural infrastructure. The problem of agricultural infrastructure includes problem of irrigation, soil conservation, and soil testing services. Besides, it also includes problem of land, labor, capital, modern agricultural inputs and preservation. The other major problems faced by the farmers of the State include environmental problem, and problem of production, production costs, problem of market infrastructure and price fluctuations. On the other hand, farmers of our State also face different difficulties due to the development of modern agricultural technologies.

Problem of Irrigation

Irrigation is an important problem among the all farmers in every villages of West Bengal. For example, flower farmers in the Panskura region of the District Purba Medinipur cultivate paddy once in a year which is in the rainy season because of limited water sources. They also cultivate only some season flower due to water or irrigation problem. There is no Governmental facility for irrigation in all the farming villages. Flower farmers in the Panskura region have personal mini pump for irrigation. Some farmers use *tulu* or shallow pump in their pond to fulfill their irrigation activities. They do not get any help from the Government in such cases. Due to the development of modern irrigation techniques nowadays farmers in the Khanakul region of the district Hooghly face a number of new problems which include power failure; high diesel price; and occasional unavailability of diesel. Besides, high irrigation charge is also a problem particularly faced by the poor farmers. Large and medium farmers gain most from the private irrigation system and they are benefited by cultivating their sizeable chunk of land.

Problem of Land

Farming lands in West Bengal are decreasing day by day due to growth of population. For example, the guava farmers of Baruipur region in the District South Twenty Four Paraganas expose that land is a major problem in favor of guava cultivation. On the other hand, land is also noticed an important problem among the flower farmers of Purba Medinipur District. Farmers of Panskura region comment their difficulties for land, saying, *"Land prices and values have increased over time. Several Governmental and Non Governmental agencies often acquire our land for industry and road. We are given compensation, but those patches of land beside the main roads are more costly for us. We remain always afraid of losing our land due to this recent development of communication efforts"*.

Problem of Soil

Soil problem is an important issue in farming. The fertility of soils is destroying day after day due to use of more chemical fertilizers. Farmers in the Khanakul region of the District Hooghly consider that soil of that region was excellent for potato farming about two to three years ago. But recently some problems are identified within soil which is an important cause for reduction of potato production.

Problem of Labour

Labour demand is adversely affected by the mechanisation process. Wage employment was gradually being displaced by the increased mechanisation of agriculture in the villages. The labor required for operating various activities relating to the major crops such as flower, potato, groundnut, betel leaf, sesame and guava declined over time. Besides, machines are also being used in other operations such as carrying, threshing etc. which considerably curtailed the labor requirement for a range of post harvest operations in the village. This in turn results in unemployment of those laborers who are traditionally engaged to this profession. On the other hand, it is noticed that paddy, betel leaf and flower farming need many labors for farming operations. Availability of labor and labor cost are major constraints for paddy, flower and betel-leaf farming, which all require considerable manual labor. But of availability laborers is difficult, which forces farmers to invest in equipment such as tractors and harvesters. Sometimes farmers hire seasonal migrant laborers because *"they can work all day during the hot summer"*. Besides, labor cost is increasing day by day. As a result, some farmers employ a few laborers during the entire year and hire a few more seasonally such as for collecting and harvesting paddy.

Problem of Capital

Finance is a problem among all farmers of the State. Farmers of the Hayatpur village in the Khanakul C.D. Block of Hooghly District are very suitable for potato cultivation because of fertile alluvial soil of the river. But the farmers have financial limitation. Thus, small farmers of the village do not get profit by potato cultivation. Sometimes they do not get good price by trading potato from the *mahajon* (local big trader). Other example is found among the guava farmers of the Baruipur region who clarify that they do not get any assistance from the Government to get loan for cultivation. On the other hand, as regards the rural finance, the lending procedure of the banks had remained unchanged over time and the poor farmers had to face formidable difficulties in accessing bank loan. Informal moneylenders who extend credit at an exorbitant rate of interest overwhelmingly dominate the rural finance. The farmers could not sell their produces at the procurement centre. The poor farmers either mortgage the harvest to village moneylenders or sell it to intermediaries. In this way the poor farmers and sharecroppers in the farming villages could not benefit because they could not invest in cultivation, they had to depend on rented land and had to borrow from moneylenders at an exorbitant interest rate.

Problem of Preservation

Farmers stated tjat storage is a problem after the harvesting the crops. There is no good cold storage near the villages. Sometimes proper preservation of potato is done in the cold storage.

Problem of Modern Agricultural Inputs

The modern agricultural inputs include high yielding improved seed varieties, chemical fertilizers, pesticides and weedicides. Recognizing the widespread availability of the chemical fertilizer, the farmers had been confronting problems such as availability of substandard fertilizer; their higher and unstable price; ignorance of farmers about the application of fertilizer, and fertilizer crisis. On the other hand it is observed that, availability of pesticides increased over time at the local level. However, the price of pesticides recorded an upward trend and there has been more fluctuation in its price level in recent past. The farmers opined that the quality of pesticides had deteriorated over time and could not kill pest and predators as effectively as before. The increased uses of pesticides have been causing various environmental problems such as the decline in fertility of the soil. Lastly, nowadays it is noticed that mechanical and manual weed control methods are being replaced by chemical control methods. In the Panskura region 50 per cent of the flower cultivated areas are treated with weedicides. But recently all types of farmers (i.e. large, medium and small) cannot apply these chemical weedicides on their flower plants due to its high price.

Environmental Problem

The environmental problem is mainly occurred by nature which mainly include problem of climate, disease and pest. Therefore, the environmental damages are seen in all cropping systems. Sometimes, plants or seedlings of flower are ruined due to weather. Environmental damages are found in case of flower farming. More rain, hailstorm and storm destroy the flower plants. Drought is a big problem for flower farming. Crop damages due to flood are observed in the Khanakul region. Here flood destroys the whole cropping patterns and systems almost every year. It destroys the paddy of rainy season and also affects the lives of hundreds of farmers and destroys agricultural land, livestock and farming constitution. On the other hand, fluctuating weather sometimes causes advent of a number of diseases in case of potato farming. Other example is found among the flower farmers who notice that different diseases and pests destroy the flower plants. Farmers of the Hayatpur village in the Khankul C.D. Block suggest that the production of potato is decreasing due to disordered weather. Again, good weather can also be a problem if it leads to market saturation and falling prices.

Problem of Production

Low production is now a problem among the all crop farmers. In the Khanakul region, about 100 bags of potato were produced from the one *bigha* (one *bigha* = 0.133 Hectare) land just one year ago. Now, only 20 to 40 bags potatoes are produced from the one *bigha* land. On the other hand now the production costs of all the crops like rice, potato, flower, betel-leaf has been increased due to the higher price of seeds, fertilizers and pesticides.

Problems Related to Market

The market related problem include low price of produced crop in the market, price fluctuations, distance of the market, market saturation, insufficient profit, insufficient place of selling, informal-marketing-system, and export problem. At present, most of the farmers are facing problems due to fluctuating market price. In the competitive market economy, the farmers are not getting sufficient profit by selling their produced crop. Sometimes farmers do not get good price of flower in the market. Up and down of flower market is totally depending on high and low production of flower. Recently flower farming is increasing in different villages of the different districts. As a result the productions of flowers are increased and the profits are decreased. Again farmers notice that when the flower markets of Mumbai and Delhi goes down then the flower market of Howrah and Kolaghat go down automatically.

Export of the crops in the markets is also a significant problem which is seen in case of betel leaf and potato. These problems result into the wastage of crops during export. On the other hand, guava farmers of the Baruipur region explained that the main difficulty to the trade was transport. Tonnes of guavas go waste every year because they fail to take them to the market on time.

Selling of produced flowers by the farmers is another problem. In the local area there is no market for flowers. In Howrah, the wholesale market for flowers, the wholesalers do not allow the farmers to sell their flowers directly to the flower traders. The farmers have to sell their flowers to the wholesalers at a low profit. Actually there is no formal marketing system, wholesalers on their own wish increase or decrease the price of the flower.

Conclusion

The above discussion of different local difficulties among the farmers of West Bengal has raised a number of important issues. These issues are vital for real development of agricultural situation and the farmers of our State. Present study further reinstates the realities of developmental policy involving agriculture and their actual implementation at grass root level.

This study has identified that West Bengal farmers prefer to cultivate staple food crops, followed by accompanying food crops and lastly pure profitable crops. On average, farmers produce three different crops per year such as staple i.e. paddy; accompanying i.e. potato and various green vegetables and pure profitable crops i.e. flower, betel-leaf, potato, groundnut, sesame and guava. These crops are dominant, profitable and having market demand in several regions of the State. Therefore farmers of the state prefer to cultivate these lucrative crops. Conversely, they cultivate paddy only for consumption. As a result paddy cultivation is decreasing all over the State.

Then again, there are some other reasons behind the decrease of paddy cultivation. For example, the occurrence of floods in the some paddy growing areas affect paddy every year. Khanakul and Palashpai regions are the most flood affected region of the Hooghly District. In every year a disastrous flood occur in these areas which affect all the villages and destroy agricultural land, livestock, farming constitution and life of the farmers. In addition, farmers of the some region fail to cultivate paddy due to lack of irrigation like Mahatpur village of Purba Medinipur. On the other hand, fragmentation of paddy land has made some holdings no longer viable for sustained production. Finally, on top of all that, the increasing cost of production on one hand, and decreasing farm gate prices on the other, have caused many farmers to stop paddy farming due to marginalisation of net farm returns.

Precisely, this Study has noticed that farmers of West Bengal need many supports for improvements of farming systems. Farmers claim extension programs and financial supports. Prices of all inputs of farming are increasing day by day. Most of the farmers interviewed complained that farming is becoming increasingly unprofitable, not only because the negative impacts of climate and disease, but also because production costs keep increasing while commodity prices continue to decrease. Farmers use large quantities of fuel to operate machinery and irrigation pumps. So raising fuel prices seriously reduces their profit margins. Studied farmers consider that the low prices, low profits and volatile markets of commodity crops are greater problem than climate variability, because crops do better with irrigation than with rain.

Therefore, Governmental supports regarding above said farming problems are immediately required. On the other hand, the developmental efforts in farming system are required with effective participation of varied sections of farmers in the State.

Bibliography

Antweiler, C. (1998). Local Knowledge and Local Knowing : An Anthropological Anlaysis of Contested Cultural Products' in the Context of Development. *Anthropos.* Vol. 93. pp. 469-494.

Berrigan, F. (1979). *Community Communications : The Role of Community Media in Development.* UNESCO, Paris.

Bhalla, G.S. and D.S. Tyagi (1989). *Patterns in Indian Agricultural Development : A District Level Study.* Institute for Studies in Industrial Development, New Delhi.

Cleveland, D. A. (1994). Can Science and Advocacy Coexist? The Ethics of Sustainable Development. *Anthropology Newsletter.* Vol. 35. No. 3, pp. 9-10.

CSSC. (1974). *Green Revolution: The Unfinished Task.* Minerva Associates, Calcutta.

Dewalt, B. R. (1994). Using Indigenous Knowledge to Improve Agriculture and Natural Resource Management. *Human Organization.* Vol. 53. pp. 123-133.

Ellen, R.E. (Ed.) (2006). *Ethnobiology and the Science of Humankind.* Blackwell Publishing House, Oxford.

Engel, P.G.H. and M.L. Salomon (1997). *Facilitating Innovation for Development. A Raaks Resource Box.* Royal Tropical Institute, Amsterdam.

Hendy, David (2000). *Radio in the Global Age.* Polity Press, Cambridge.

Martin, G.J., A.L. Agama, J.H. Beaman and J. Nais (2002). *Projek Etnobotani Kinabalu : The Making of a Dusun Ethnoflora (Sabah, Malaysia), People and Plants Working Paper 9.* UNESCO, Paris.

Mellor, J.W. (1966). *The Economics of Agricultural Development.* Cornell University Press, Ithaca.

Netting, R. McC. (1974). Agrarian Ecology. *Annual Review of Anthropology.* Vol. 3. pp. 21-56.

Netting, R. McC. (1993). *Smallholders, Householders: Farm Families and the Ecology of Intensive, Sustainable Agriculture.* Stanford University Press, Stanford, CA.

Purcell, T.W. (1998). Indigenous Knowledge and Applied Anthropology : Questions of Definition and Direction. *Human Organization.* Vol. 57. pp. 258-272.

Rhoades, R.E. (1984). *Breaking New Ground: Agricultural Anthropology.* International Potato Centre, Lima.

Sillitoe, P. (1996). *A Place Against Time : Land and Environment in the Papua New Guinea Highlands.* Harwood Academic, Amsterdam.

Sillitoe, P. (1998). The Development of Indigenous Knowledge : A New Applied Anthropology. *Current Anthropology.* Vol. 39. pp. 223-52 Participating in Development : Approaches to Indigenous Knowledge. P. Sillitoe, A. Bicker & J. Pottier (Eds.) pp. 1-23. Routledge, London.

Sillitoe, P, J. Barr and M. Alam (2004). Sandy-clay or Clayey-sand? Mapping Indigenous and Scientific Soil Knowledge on the Bangladesh Floodplains. In *Development and Local Knowledge : New Approaches to Issues in Natural Resources Management, Conservation and Agriculture.* A. Bicker, P. Sillitoe & J. Pottier (Eds.) pp. 174-201. Routledge, London.

Sillitoe, P. (2006). Ethnobiology and Applied Anthropology : Reapprochement of the Academic with the Practical. Special Edition of the *Journal of the Royal Anthropological Institute.* pp. S119-S142.

Sumberg, J. and C. Okali (1997). *Farmer's Experiments : Creating Local Knowledge.* Lynne Rienner, London.

14

Recruitment Procedure and Status of Workers: An Observation on Industries of Two States in India

Salil Kumar Dutta, Dibyendu Maiti and Avijit Halder

Introduction

The steadily rising rate of economic growth in India has recently been around 8 percent per year and there is much speculation about whether and when India may catch up with and surpass China's over 10 percent growth rate(Sen,2011).Development can be investigated independently of whether Governments and institutions articulate their objectives in terms of expanding capabilities, or increasing economic growth, or any other possible sets of social goals (Alkire, 2010).In this era of reforms, industrialisation was one of the pillars of India's development strategy from the 1950s to the early 1980s. The rates of growth across Indian states started diverging more in the 1990s over the 1980s is accepted even by the sympathizers of the reform. The highest rates of industrial growth were observed in the states of Andhra Pradesh and Gujarat which grew at more than 10 percent per annum. In contrast, Indian states of Assam, Odisha, Madhya Pradesh and West Bengal grew at 3 percent or less per annum. However, despite increasing convergence of the industrial policies of all the Indian states since the early 1990s (Kohli, 2009),(Chakravarty& Bose, 2009), their performances have been rather divergent. From the late 1970s and early 1980s, it was increasingly felt that trade liberalisation and new industrial policies were required for industrial growth. This began to be implemented from the mid1980s; Government of India has pursued policies of liberalisation, privatisation and globalisation in order to enhance competitiveness and to accelerate the economic growth rate since the early 1990s and the most decisive break with the trade policies of the past came in 1991, when the Government of India was situated in a balance of paymentcrisis. Since then, the reform programme has included the removal of most licensing and other non-tariff barriers on all imports of intermediate and capital goods, broadening of export incentives, removal of export restrictions, elimination of the trade monopolies of the state trading agencies, the simplification of the trade regime, reduction of tariff levels and their dispersion, the full convertibility of the domestic currency for foreign exchange transactions, and so on. For example, the maximum tariff was reduced from 400 percent to roughly 15 percent by 2005-06, and its standard deviation during this period went down from 41 percentage points to around 15(Dutt, 2003; Krishnaand Mitra, 1998 cf.Maiti and Marjit,2009). This is also true in the case of non-tariff barriers. This was also accompanied by devaluations of the Indian rupee and the introduction of an explicit dual exchange market in 1992. In addition, more flexibility was given to Foreign Direct Investment (FDI) and foreign capital inflow gradually led to a governmental withdrawal from producing activities (Hasan*et al.,* 2007).The centrepiece of industrial regulations in India had been a system of industrial licensing, but this has been gradually withdrawn in recent years. All these liberal trade and industrial policies are seen to have assigned a significant role to the market for accelerating growth and creating employment. This must have implications for formal-informal distribution across industries, depending upon their international competitiveness. Market competitiveness imposes pressure to cut costs, particularly the monitoring cost for in-house production, leading to fragmentation and vertical disintegration. Contracting out to the informal sector at low cost for similar work is one of the better options for cost reduction and therefore, informal contracts are expected to increase.

It is argued that the process of economic liberalisation that was initiated in the early 1990s has played an instrumental role in this regard. It is clear that some Indian states took advantage of economic liberalisation to a greater extent and showed a higher rate of growth than others. High rates of growth in recent years have encouraged economists and policy analysts to attempt to understand the underlying process of this rapid industrialisation and to explore whether such growth has contributed to a reduction in poverty across states. But which reform factors contributed and to what extent is not clear in the existing literature. It is argued that the forms and functioning of institutions, influenced by social, political and cultural factors at the state level in a large federal democratic country such as India, must have led to differential regional development (Maiti, and Marjit, 2009).

Contract Labourer

The term 'contract labour' is applied to labourer who are employed through a contractor and does not necessarily have a direct employment relationship with the end of employer. Rather, it is the contractors and contract labourers who have a contractual relationship. On the other hand, migrant labourers are those who are forced to migrate from rural to urban areas or from agriculture to industry in expectation of higher wages as pull or push factor. In principle, these two types of labour are different, but since the migrant labourers are often employed on contract, they were treated as contracted labour for the purposes of this study (http://labour.nic.in).

Objective of the Study

This study tried to look forward on that secret which effects on hampering the growth of employment generation which striking on poverty eradication and the status of workforces in particular and growing industry in general in India.

Reason Behind the Study

In order to know the industrialisation process, a survey was conducted in two States namely; West Bengal and Gujarat in the year 2009. The two States are different in many respects, contemporary evidence and research findings from many scholars and agencies, including the 2005 World Bank Survey report, suggest that Gujarat has fared best in terms of recent industrial performance and investment climate and is growing faster than other states in the post-reform period. On the other hand, West Bengal belongs to the worst climate category. In fact, the states are distinctly different in terms of their political and cultural environments.

The Methods of the Study

The study explores both secondary and primary information. A number of features of industrialisation and formal firms were collected from the Annual Survey of Industries (ASI) and Centre for Monitoring Indian Economy Pvt. Ltd. (CMIE)databases. Reports of the National Sample Survey Organisation(NSSO), Government of India, on the informal sector were also considered to see the pace of informalisation. The primary data had been collected from the empirical settings of the firms in the two States at the same period.

Study Design

The objective of this study is profoundly linked to the socio-economic, political and especially social factors behind the recruitment procedures and the deal.The two sample States were purposively selected because of their differences in socio-political environments and strength of labour market institutions. So a detailed primary survey was conducted to fulfill the lacuna of secondary data. West Bengal's labour legislation and strong trade unions places it in the pro-worker category. In contrast, trade unions and labour legislation are comparatively weak in Gujarat.

Information on firms was collected from the secondary database at first, while it was not extensive. To satisfy the empirical situation one statespecific and three common industries were selected for detailed study. The common industries chosen were cement, iron and steel and cotton textiles, and the statespecific industries were jute from West Bengal and man-made fiber from Gujarat.

A list was prepared of each industry by location from the secondary data set. Ten to fifteen samples for each were selected randomly from two or three clusters. Fifty firms from each State were selected for detailed survey. Therefore, the total sample units numbered 100 from each firm, management, trade union leaders, suppliers and two workers (one permanent labour and one contract labour) were interviewed. During 2008-09, we gathered information via a structured open ended questionnaire on formal and informal institutional networks for input and output transactions, the terms and conditions of those contracts, the forms of intermediary agencies, the role of trade unions for in-house and outside production, ethnic relation in contracts and other formal and informal norms. The management staff of the firm was met at first and other stakeholders later for verification. A pilot survey was undertaken to experience the reaction of the respondents and also to identify the location and forms of production units and then made some rearrangement of the questionnaires. A final survey was then conducted for detailed study.

Data Analysis

The Annual Survey of Industries and official records of industrial statistics for the formal sector, reports that the share of contract labour in organised manufacturing varies from 15per cent to 26per cent across States. However, it is observed about 70 to 75per cent in the sample States. Barely one percent of workers are recruited through a formal procedure. In Gujarat, most of them are recruited and controlled by relatively experienced workers of the firm. They mostly have a good relationship either with management or the owners or both directly. In West Bengal, they are recruited by trade unions through their peer group linkages with a nexus of political persons and bureaucrats. In both cases, the intermediaries charge fees to both parties, and this equilibrium is mostly stable because both parties have interests. For West Bengal, workers join trade unions in order to increase the probability of retaining their jobs for an extended period and to protect their own interests. In Gujarat, the story is the same, but the actors are different. Here, labour contractors play the same role as the trade unions in West Bengal, with the exception that they do not have political affiliations. They receive a specified amount on per worker that they supply to a firm. The incentive that workers have is just one: the availability of a job. It emerged from the survey that a large proportion of the workforce in Gujarat is composed of migrant workers from the States of West Bengal, Odisha and Bihar. A general question that may arise is if the labour contractors do not have political affiliation, what gives them bargaining power? The answer lies in Gujarat's huge scope for alternative employment. Withdrawal of workers from a firm poses more of a danger to the firm than to the contractor because getting another job contract for the firm is not that difficult. Here emerges another crucial difference between the two States. For workers in West Bengal, losing a job is more problematic as the scope for alternative employment is almost negligible.

Recruitment Procedures and Types of Workforce in the Studied Industries

The observation found that three kinds of workers are hired by the organised and registered firms: directly hired permanent labours, directly hired contractual labours and contract labours supplied by the contractors. Among these, the dominant share of permanent workers are directly hired by firms is only 29.9per cent in Gujarat and about 24.2per cent in West Bengal. Therefore, 70 to 75per cent of the workforce is hired on a contractual basis, either directly by the firm or through contractors or the experienced old worker of the same organisation. Those very people at times play a vital role to supply the manpower. Since the Contract Labour Regulation (Regulation and Abolition) Act, 1970 (http:// labour.nic.in) also allows the use of a contractor in order to hire these workers, firms can come to rely on them. As a result, the share of contract labour supplied by contractors is 53.6per cent in Gujarat and 15.1per cent in West Bengal. In contrast, the share of contract workers directly employed by the firm is 16.4per cent in Gujarat and 60.7per cent in West Bengal.

It is has been come out in the observation that recruitment procedure in campus is very few in West Bengal, which almost absent in Gujarat. If it happen then for the technical personnel are recruited through the process. As two kinds of contract workers found in studied States; hired directly by a firm's management and through labour contractors or the suppliers. Therefore, the form of intermediation suggests that labour, particularly contract labour, is benefiting from the industrialisation process. Moreover, in a politically less active State, it is reported that contractors receive incentives for each worker that they supply. As a result, firms rely on them for workforce as, labourutilises their services for work and contractors or the suppliers enjoy a power over the negotiation with both sides. From this perspective, the contracting system seems to operate quite smoothly. On the other hand, these contractors are largely trade union and politically influenced persons in West Bengal. The direct commission that they receive from a firm undermines their credibility and explains why they apply pressure on the firm to undertake direct recruitment even for contract labour. This has a depressing effect on the industrialisation process, and informality is thus also prevalent in the process of labour recruitment. Recommendation by friends/relatives is a major source of labour recruitment in Gujarat, whereas recommendation by a trade union leader or the dominant political party in the vicinity is the major instrument for recruitment in West Bengal. The role of trade unions and political parties in the recruitment process has been negligible in Gujarat. A recommendation through middlemen is another part of recruitment in Gujarat and also a bit applied in West Bengal.

Status of Workers and their Benefits

The share of permanent workers who are having union membership is observed from the analysis of data is about 39.1per cent and 34.8per cent in Gujarat and West Bengal respectively. It is also important to note that none of the contract workers in Gujarat is a member of a trade union, but in West Bengal it is about to 24.1per cent of contract workers hired by the firm and 35.7per cent hired by contractors are members of a union. The findings also focused on other aspects of labour service, that is, provision of social security benefits, which covers items like Employee's State Insurance (E.S.I.), Provident Funds, etc. The observation shows that the law stipulating that firm owners/contractors are to pay these benefits to contract workers is routinely ignored in Gujarat and that these laws are not entirely obeyed in West Bengal either. However, although the manufacturing units in Gujarat religiously deny social security benefits to their workers, they always pay them the minimum wage (the statespecific figure was Rs.100 for skilled workers in 2006-07). In this respect, West Bengal suffers considerably by comparison. The minimum wage criteria are frequently violated in the West Bengal manufacturing units (Rs 75 being the minimum wage for semi-skilled workers in 2006-07, state specific). Indeed, there are some spinning units in West Bengal and some well known cotton mills paying workers less than Rs. 75/- per day, even the workers sometimes works more than the stipulated hours with a cheap food packet! The issue of wage increment does not have much relevance because revision of wages in both States is rarely carried out.

Conclusion

The process of economic liberalisation that was initiated in the early 1990s played an important role in our country. It is evident that some States took advantage of it to a greater extent and showed higher rates of growth than others (Maiti and Marjit, 2009). The forms and functioning of institutions are influenced by social, political and cultural factors and must produce differential results in regional development. Hence, here the study considered West Bengal and Gujarat, for a field survey in order to examine the actual or the real situation of the industrialisation process. The States are distinct in terms of investment climate and political behaviour. The intention was to observe the labour induced industries in West Bengal and Gujarat to know the empirical reality.

The observation found that in both States the rise of competitiveness as well as the prevalence of a large unorganised sector has led to firms tending to squeeze in-house production and largely use non-market informal institutions (for example, social groups, political and other peer groups) for transaction, which are based on mutual trust and longterm relations. Such establishments not only reduce operation costs but also ensure marketing networks. In these transactions, there is a strong influence of political and trade union contracting in West Bengal, whereas ethnic relation and an invisible peer group of middlemen play a similar role in Gujarat. Both of these negotiators have the motivation to earn agency fees. They usually take the advantages of the hardships. This is also true for hiring of labour. Most of them are controlled and recruited by a firm's relatively experienced workers in Gujarat and by trade unions in West Bengal through their peer group linkages. In both cases, the intermediaries earn fees from both sides. This equilibrium is relatively stable because both parties have interests. For West Bengal, workers connect trade unions in order to ensure the probability of retaining their job for a longer period and to protect their own interests. The picture is a bit different in Gujarat, here, labour contractors or the workforce supplier play the same role as the trade unions in West Bengal. The only difference being that they (in Gujarat) do not have political affiliation. They charge a specified fee for each worker that they supply to a firm. Workers have just one incentive; to procurement of a job. It comes into view in the study that a large proportion of the workforce in Gujarat is composed of migrant workers from the States of West Bengal, Bihar and the adjoining State Rajasthan and they are generally recruited through personal contacts such as friends and relatives. Their achievement is that they can find employment in Gujarat, and however low their wages, they can able to send some money to home to carrying on their families. The employment opportunities in both the States from which the workers migrate are meagre, which acts as a major contributing factor to migration. The observation again reveals that, in Gujarat, the scope for alternative employment is huge and for this reason labour contractors/ suppliers need not any political affiliation, what gives them bargaining power. Withdrawal of workers from a firm poses more of a danger to the firm than to the contractor because securing another job contract with the firm is not a difficult task. Here emerges another crucial difference between the two States. In the case of workers in West Bengal, losing a job is more problematic as the scope for alternative employment is almost negligible. This is the reason behind the importance of trade unions to workers in West Bengal. However, the benefits for contract workers are largely ignored. In Gujarat, contractors receive incentives for labour supply, and both firms and labourer approach to them for their requirements. The incentive for contractors in West Bengal is that the resolution of issues via public forums undermines their political credibility and they therefore press for direct recruitment. However, since direct recruitment is considered undesirable by the corporate sector on account of cost, the combination of these two factors has a depressing effect on industrialisation.

The Government passed the Contract Labour (Regulation and Abolition) Act in 1970 in order to protect contract labourers in the manufacturing sector. Under section 10 of this Act, the State can prohibit the use of contract labourers in any production activities in a factory. The relevant authority takes into account the nature of the work and comparative practice when deciding whether to prohibit the use of contract labour. Central and State Governments have issued periodic notifications prohibiting the use of contract labourers in specific processes and activities. They can be employed in non-core activities like cleaning and maintenance, packing, welding, painting and warehouse activities. Moreover, the Act seeks to promote the health and welfare of contract labourers. Canteens, rest rooms, drinking water, toilets, washing facilities and first aid facilities have to be provided for them. The contractor should pay wages to the workers on time. The rights of contract workers are covered in the Minimum Wages Act, Employee Provident Fund Act and Employees' State Insurance Act. Employers cannot claim that a bonus or gratuity constitute 'wages' under the Act as it does not consider a bonus or a gratuity to be a part of wages. So, although the use of contract labour involves flexibility, the law also provides some benefits and rights to those workers. As per this regulation, industrial officers should make regular visits to the plants/ manufacturing units in the organised sector to enforce the law, but this enforcement mechanism is not clear. Central authorities are reported to receive complaints from contract workers and trade unions that contract workers are performing the same or similar work performed by workers employed directly by the principal employer. There is much truth in the complaints received by the Ministry of Labour and this was validated by our survey. Some of our survey observations vividly depict the extent to which contract workers are exploited. The most striking feature is that most contract workers cannot be a part of the trade union, so the trade union cannot officially fight for their interests. The benefits prescribed by law for contract labourers are routinely ignored. All the permanent workers receive social security benefits from the firms in our study, such as provident funds, medical insurance and employee's insurance. In contrast, only 11.8per cent of contract labourers hired directly by firms in Gujarat and 13.0per cent of those hired in West Bengal are reported to receive at least one of these benefits. Interestingly, none of the contract labour supplied by the contractor receives these benefits in Gujarat, but 57.1per cent of these labourers receive social security benefits in West Bengal.

There are two kinds of contract workers in both States: directly hired by a firm's management and hired through labour contractors or suppliers. Therefore, the form of intermediation suggests that, particularly contract labourer, is benefiting from the industrialisation process. Moreover, in a politically less active State, it is reported that contractors receive incentives for each worker that they supply. As a result, firms rely on them for workers, workforces utilises their services for work and contractors enjoy a power over the negotiation with both sides. From this perspective, the contracting system seems to operate quite smoothly. On the other hand, these contractors are from largely trade union and politically influenced persons in West Bengal. The direct commission that they receive from a firm undermines their credibility and explains why they apply pressure on the firm to undertake direct recruitment even for contract labour. This has a depressing effect on the industrialisation processand informality is thus also prevalent in the process of labour recruitment. Needless to say that it is important to give attention carefully by the Government so that the procedures of recruitment as well as improvement of the status of workers come with a better welfare and can bring proper utilisation of human resources in our country.

Bibliography

Alkire, S. (2010).Development A Misconceived Theory Can Kill.inChristopher W. Morris (Eds.)*AmartyaSen Contemporary Philosophy in Focus*.pp. 191-220, Cambridge University Press, U.K.

Chakravarty, D. and I. Bose (2009).Industrialising West Bengal? : The Case of Institutional Stickiness.*IPPG Discussion Papers*, Series Number Thirty Two, pp.4, U.K.

Dutt, P. (2003). Labor Market Outcomes and Trade Reforms: The Case of India.in R. Hasan and D. Mitra.(Eds.)*The Impact of Trade on Labor: Issues, Perspectives, and Experiences from Developing Asia*, Elsevier Science B.V.

Dutta, R. (2003).LabourMarket, Social Institutions, Economic Reforms and Social Cost.in S. Uchikawa (Eds.).*Labour Market and Institution in India, 1990s and Beyond*, Manohar Publication, New Delhi.

Kohli, A. (2009).*Democracy and Development in India – From Socialism to Pro-Business.* Oxford University Press, New Delhi.

Krishna, P. and D. Mitra (1998). Trade Liberalization, Market Discipline and Productivity Growth: New Evidence from India.*Journal of Development Economics*, Vol. 56.pp. 447-462.

Leftwich A. (2009).Analysing the Politics of State-Business Relations: A Methodological Concept note on the Historical InstitutionalistApproach, *IPPG Discussion Paper*, U.K.

Maiti, D. (2008).Organisational Morphology of Rural Industries and it Dynamics in Liberalized India: The Case of West Bengal. *Cambridge Journal of Economics*, Vol. 32, pp. 571-592.

Maiti, D. (2009). Institutions, Networks and Industrialisation: Field Level Evidence of Fragmentation and Flexibility from India.*IPPGDiscussion Paper,* Series Number Twenty Six, U.K.

Maiti, D.and S. Marjit(2009).The Institutional Determinants of Informalisation and its Effects on Growth and Poverty in India.*IPPGDiscussion Paper,* Series Number Thirty, U.K.

Marjit, S. and D.Maiti (2006).Globalisation, Economic Reform and Informal Labor, in B. Khasnobis and R. Kanbur, (Eds.)*Informal Labor Markets and Development*. MacMillan-Palgrave, Helsinki.

Ministry of Labour and Employment, *Contract Labour in India*, Government of India.

National Sample Survey Organisation.*Survey of Unorganized Manufacture*. 1989-90 (45th Round), 1993-94 (50th Round), 1994-95 (51st Round), 2000-01 (56th Round) and 2005-06 (62nd Round).Department of Statistics, Government of India, Delhi.

Planning Commission, *Number and Percentage of Population Below Poverty Line, 1973 to 2004-05,* Government of India, Delhi.

Sen, A. (2011).*The Telegraph,* Editorial, 26 May 2011, Vol.XXI,No.319, pp.10, Kolkata.

World Bank (1990).*World Development Report 1990*. Oxford University Press, New York.

15

Availability of Drinking Water Facilities to Maintain Quality of Life in the Medinipur Municipality Areas of Paschim Medinipur District : An Anthropological Evaluation

Sonali Giri and Suman Kalyan Samanta

Safe drinking water, sanitation and good hygiene are fundamental issues to health, survival, proper growth and development of a society. However, these basic necessities are still a luxury for many of the world's poor people (UNICEF, 2006). From the point of view of health and hygiene, safe drinking is considered to be the most important. So to provide the pure and uncontaminated drinking water to the people is one of the most important duties of the administrative authorities. There is no doubt that water and sustainable development are inextricably linked. Once viewed as an infinite and bountiful resource, water today defines human, social, and economic development. Without adequate supplies and management of fresh and safe water resources, socio-economic development simply cannot take place.

Safe drinking water generally is so obviously essential to health that the risk being taken for granted. Efforts to prevent death from diarrhoea or to reduce the burden of such diseases as ascaris, dracunculiasis, hookworm, schistosomiasis and trachoma are doomed to failure unless people have access to safe drinking water and basic sanitation (UNICEF, 2006). Better quality of drinking water is an essential condition for maintaining a good health condition of people both for rural and urban areas. In most of the cities there are more households than water supply connections, indicating that either there are many shared connections or households depend upon public taps. The data indicates that many households have their own sources of water supply while others complement to own sources of supply with that of the public agency (National Institute of Urban Affairs, 2005). The uses of water in a community are many, and the requirement in quantity and quality are also varied. Conventionally, it has been convenient and economical to provide a single water supply sufficient in quantity to serve all uses and suitable in quality to meet drinking requirements, even though only a small fraction of the total water supply is actually used for drinking (Park, 2009).

Methodology

In the present study an attempt has been made to understand the role of water specially on the health status of the town dwellers as well as availability of water resources and distribution of water in the urban areas that means in the neighboring areas of any urban centre's. At the same time due importance has been given on the concept of use and basic pattern of use as practised by the town people. Preferences have been given on the drinking and domestic use of water as well as availability, acceptability and regular practice of use. Considerable variations have been observed as per the economic class and locality difference not only that in respect of time a significant variation has also been observed. Another considerable parameter in the present study is to assess the available water distribution related infrastructural facilities in the town areas.

Selection of Study Area and Studied People

The present study has been conducted in the Medinipur Municipality areas of Paschim Medinipur district. This is the district head quarters of erstwhile Midnapur district and present Paschim Medinipur district not only that it is one of the major part of Medinipur-Kharapur Development Authority. In this connection it is to mention here that the State

Government considers it as the future megacity along with few other towns of the State. Naturally several plans and programs have been implemented for the development of the area. Medinipur is a historical town as a result the town has developed in an unplanned way. Not only that, it is one of the most important towns of south western part of West Bengal. For this reason people gradually came here and settled permanently, so the population of the town increases day by day in a rapid manner. But the question of infrastructural facilities and the requirement of basic needs i.e. water both for drinking and domestic use come to the forefront in the present discussion. Under such a circumstance, the Medinipur town has been selected for the present study and on proposed the implementation of the Medinipur-Kharagpur Development Authority Megacity project in the said area it is a very timely and pertinent issue.

Methods Used

The specific field survey has been conducted on the several wards and localities of the Medinipur Municipal areas. General field survey has been conducted mainly in the slum areas like Minabazar, Mirzabazar, Patnabazar, Sepoybazar, Rajabazar and in some residential areas of the town such as Bidhannagar, Sarat Palli, Rangamati, Ashokenagar, Arabindanagar. At the same time the availability of water facilities in the fringe areas of the town also surveyed.

For the purpose of the present study Case Study, Interview and Observation methods were adopted. On the basis of random sampling young, aged, knowledgeable persons of the locality were selected. Sampling also covered people from different wakes of life such as service holders, businessmen, teachers, practitioners, quack doctors and others. Data have been collected specially on the availability of water resources; use of water in various daily livelihood purposes of the households, water distribution system of the town, role of the Municipality in supplying water, as well as special emphasis has been given on the health profile and other cultural aspects. One of the authors has a very prolong contact with the study areas over more than a decade. As a result personal observation and personal experience also help to conduct the present study in a more scientific way. Besides some household surveys, personal interviews of different persons, those who have directly or indirectly very long experience or contact with any types of water supply related activities also have been taken with due importance. In this connection it is also mentioned here that different secondary data sources and office records have been considered with prime importance.

Essentiality of Drinking Water Facilities in the Urban Areas :

During the five decades since independence, India has witnessed phenomenal development of water resources and self-sufficiency in food grains, rapid expansion in the urban areas, energy and industrial sectors. About 85 per cent of India's urban and rural population availed the facility of drinking water infrastructure. However, this achievement has been done at the cost of groundwater depletion, water logging, water quality degradation and pollution and increasing salinity levels affecting large areas. Sectorial demands for water are growing rapidly in line with urbanization (estimates suggest that by 2025, more than 50 per cent of the country's population will live in cities and towns), very fast population growth, increasing incomes and rapid industrial growth, as a result, per capita water availability has been falling (Planning Commission, 2002).

Status of Drinking Water in West Bengal

Before going to discuss the study area, it is important to know the present situation regarding the quality and distribution of drinking water at the State level specially in urban areas. Generally West Bengal is one of the leading States in India. Several development projects have been implemented from time to time by both State Government and Central Government. West Bengal Government is providing adequate and safe drinking water to 90.41 per cent of the rural population. This has been achieved by implementing 1068 Piped Water Supply Schemes and 4,98,443 spot sources. Similarly, 80 per cent of the urban population in 126 Municipalities (including KMDA area) is covered by Piped Water Supply Scheme. Since 1977, Piped Water Supply Schemes (PWSS) have received much needed attention and support of the Government. Rural population coverage through PWSS was only 0.70 per cent in 1977 which is 35.88 per cent as on 31.03.2009. Adverse geological conditions have resulted in contamination of drinking water by presence of excess Arsenic, excess Fluoride and excess Chloride to 31 per cent of rural population and 53 per cent of the urban population of the State (P.H.E.P of Government of West Bengal, 2012).

Now the State Government has already shifted their objectives regarding availability and distribution of drinking water. In this changing scenario the State Government is determined to provide safe drinking water to all the inhabitants of the State during the Eleventh Five Year Plan period. This would be achieved by tapping sustainable sources and implementing Piped Water Supply schemes wherever feasible and spot tube wells in other areas. Efforts are being made to increase the number of schemes based on non-conventional sources like rainwater, ponds, abandoned open cast mines and springs in hill areas.

Drinking Water Supply System in the Urban Areas of West Bengal

There are considerable areas of West Bengal which are urban areas. Due to rapid urbanization a very vast area of West Bengal gradually come under urban areas. A large number people are living under these Municipal areas. There are 85 Municipal towns in Non-KMDA part of the State. Pipe Water Supply Schemes have been extended to each of them by the P.H.E. Department of the State Government. However, there is deficiency in service level and also in coverage by distribution network. By 31.03.2009, population coverage in Non-KMDA Municipal areas has reached 88.60 per cent. At present, major augmentation has been taken up in Medinipur and some other Municipalities of southern part of West Bengal (P.H.E.P of Government of West Bengal, 2012).

A Brief Outlook Medinipur Town :

Medinipur is the district headquarters of Paschim Medinipur district. It is situated on the banks of the Kangsabati River (variously known as Kasai and Cossye). This area had taken a pioneering role in India's freedom struggle. A large number of freedom fighters who had bravely faced the gallows are the sons of the soil of Medinipur. In order to free their motherland from the yokes of bondage, they had willingly sacrificed themselves in the freedom pyre. In the 2011 Census, Medinipur Municipality had a population of 169,264, out of which 84,977 were males and 84,287 were females. The 0–6 years population was 15,172. Effective literacy rate for the 7+ years population was 88.99 per cent. On the basis of the above information it can be said that demographic, health, education, nutrition and related other information are very important considerable point for the said population as per some external and internal factors.

Prominent Water Resources, Climatic and Geographical Condition of the Area :

The quality of water and adequate supply of water are considered to be the two most important factor for health. It is absolutely an established truth that the water reserve conditions as well as availability of water of any area are directly or indirectly depending on the several factors. Specially, the water condition of any area is mainly depending on the different climatic and geographical features such as annual rainfall, temperature, soil type etc. When the climatic and weather condition of the Medinipur Municipality is considered then it is observed that Medinipur is located between 22⁰57’10" and 21⁰36’35" North latitude and between 88⁰12"40" and 86⁰33’50" East longitude and is 23 metres above sea-level. WikiMiniAtlas

The climate follows a hot tropical monsoon weather pattern. Summer last from April to mid-June and the temperature varies from 30°C to 45°C . Daily heat is often followed by evening rains known as *kalboishakhis* or dust-storms (*loo*). Monsoon rains last from mid-June to late August or even September with rains from the southeast monsoon contributing the lions-share of the annual rainfall of around 1500 mm. Winter last for 2 to 3 months and are mild in nature and temperature varies from 8°C to 14°C. Soil near the Kangsabati River are alluvial with a high-degree of clay or sand, whereas soil towards Rangamati are lateritic. Vegetation includes eucalyptus and *sal* forests on the northwest side of the town. Throughout the year the Municipal authority is much more depending on the Kangsabati River water as well as on underground water. But in the summer they have been facing severe water crunch in the river (District Statistical Hand Book, Paschim Medinipur, 2008).

The Present Condition of the Quality and Portability of Drinking Water of Medinipur Municipality

In the present study an attempt has been made to get a very clear picture about the town people’s dependency on the quality of drinking water they regularly intake. Due to some basic difficulties the researcher could not be able to conduct the microorganism test of the regularly useable water specially the drinking water. In these circumstances the researcher depends on a famous research work conducted on the Medinipur Municipality areas by Chakraborty and Roy of Vidyasagar University published in 2012. In the said study they have given emphasis to record the distribution pattern of the “fecal coliform” of water samples collected from tap water from Sepoybazar of Medinipur town.

Drinking water samples were collected from two sources and the bacteria were isolated from this collected water sample. From this experimental study it is concluded that the Medinipur town’s drinking water (Sepoybazar area) contain very few bacteria. Among five isolated bacterial colonies, four colonies were formed whitish and only one was formed as yellowish colonies and three colonies were formed opaque and two colonies were formed transparent colony. The isolated bacteria from drinking water of two different sources were characterized by different Bio-chemical and Physiological tests. By the Gram staining, it has been concluded that all the isolated bacteria from drinking water were Gram-negative bacteria. Screening of isolated bacteria with MacConkey agar plate, it has been found that some of these bacteria are lactose fermenting bacteria and some of these bacteria are non lactose fermenting bacteria. Screening of isolated bacteria with TCBS agar plate, it has been concluded that some of these isolated bacteria are sucrose fermenting bacteria but others are not. By the Protein Hydrolysis test, it has been observed that some of these isolated bacteria have protease enzyme and exhibit protease activity. Screening of isolated bacteria with blood agar plate, it has been concluded that all the isolated bacteria were non-pathogenic. By the antibiogram, it has been observed that some of these isolated bacteria were found to be resistant towards Chloramphenicol antibiotic but other were mild sensitive towards these antibiotics. All the isolated bacteria were sensitive towards Streptomycin and Tetracycline. Most of the isolates were sensitive towards Ampicillin and Norfloxacin.

Prevalent Common Water Borne Diseases as Observed in Medinipur and its Adjoining Areas

One of the most important finding about Medinipur and its adjoining areas is that water borne diseases are very common out come due to regular intake of impure and contaminated drinking water. As bulk demand of drinking water in the Medinipur Municipality areas have been supplied from both river and underground surface water and somehow river and underground surface water have been contaminated by Gokulpur Industrial Estate, Kharagpur Industrial Estate and some other sponge iron factories situated here and there. Another major factor for prevalent of water borne diseases among the inhabitants is the pollution of ground and surface water from increased fertilizer and pesticide use in agriculture in the adjoining wide spread agricultural fields and from industrial waste sources. An emerging threat to water quality of the said area is due to the use of Persistent Organic Pollutants (POPs). These are chemicals that degrade very slowly and remain in the environment for years (Water Aid, 2012).

On the basis of discussion with the local doctors, common people, health personnel, students and scholars of the said areas on the water borne health problems and diseases the following prominent health related symptoms and feelings have been sorted out. And also justified that these problems primarily occurred due to use of poor quality of drinking and domestic water.

Dr. P.K. Bera is a general physician who has a more than 20 years of experience to treat the patients in Medinipur town areas. He shared his experiences regarding the health and hygienic consciousness of the town dwellers and tried to highlights on the water problem in the Municipal areas at the same time giving a brief idea about the water borne diseases in the area. To him :

I am residing in the Patnabazar area of this town. I have been privately practicing in the town for more than 20 years. There are three places like as Dwaribandh, Kuikota and Rangamati where I have chambers for private practice. Most of my chambers are situated in the neighboring slum areas as well as residential areas of the town. Both poor, mediocre and upper class people are my patients so I am quite aware about their problems. It is generally observed that most of the patients, coming from slum areas have suffered from various types of skin diseases as pond water is the only resource for their domestic use. Most of the ponds in the Medinipur Municipal areas remain in a very unclean condition and most of the cases pond water is contaminated so it has very adverse effect on the human health condition. One of my observations is that there is a very large size-pond in front of the famous Twin Mosque i.e., locally addressed as 'Jora Masjid' is very close to my residence as well as my chamber. It is a very holy pond especially to the Muslims. Every day approximately 10000 local people and other visitors use this pond for their domestic purposes. Beyond that during the time of famous 'Urus' festival which is an international fair of the Muslims. On this occasion, a very large number of travelers come from other countries to this place. During this festive period approximately lakhs of people use this pond for domestic purposes. There is a very popular belief that anybody who take a full bath in this pond he or she will cured from the diseases or from any physical or mental abnormality not only that any expectation or desire will be fulfilled. Although there is no scientific basis behind this belief, but ultimately water of the pond contaminated. This contamination generally promotes to increase the frequent and severe skin diseases among its users. Not only that most of the patients frequently suffer from various types of digestive problems, dysentery and different worm related side effects. Very frequent losses of hair, skin rashes and some other problems are the common features of the patients. Most of the time generally the children have suffered from diarrhea and blood dysentery. Generally the people belonging to the middle and higher economic classes have better consciousness than the people belonging to the poorer section of the society or the slum dwellers and it is my another observation that they have suffered less from water borne diseases in comparison to the slum dwellers. In most of the time the economically and educationally better off people have used Municipality supplied pipeline water or deep tube well water for the purpose of cooking and drinking as well as in domestic purposes also. They generally avoid the pond water for their domestic use rather they frequently use well water. My another observation is that many slum dwellers use well water for their cooking and drinking purposes but due to lack of proper purification of these well water sometimes it may cause harmful effects like as food poison, heavy toxicity, and other problems.

Prominent Water Borne Problems in the Studied Areas

Parameters	*Common health impact*
Pesticides	Weakened immunity, Drinking water primarily contain higher percentage of chlorides that cause reproductive and endocrinal damage.
Persistent Organic Pollutants	High blood pressure, hormonal dysfunction, and growth retardation
Salinity	Objectionable taste to water, generally affect osmotic flow and movements of fluids.
Iron	Generally the excessive higher percentage has a poisoning effect on a child as it can damage blood tissues, Digestive disorders, skin diseases and dental problems.
Fluoride	Immediate symptoms include digestive disorders, skin diseases, dental fluorosis
Arsenic	Immediate symptoms of acute poisoning typically include vomiting, esophageal and abdominal pain, and bloody 'rice water' diarrhea.

Prominent Sources of Water for Domestic Use

Although the elite class and financially well-off people are using Municipality supplied water for their daily domestic purposes, especially for bathing, washing clothes, cleaning the household utensils and other essential purposes. But a large number of town dwellers are using wells and ponds as their main sources of domestic water. A considerable number of town dwellers are using water of neighbouring Kossai River for their domestic purposes. There are numbers of large or medium sized ponds within the Municipal areas. Most of these ponds are Government or vested property but due to improper and inadequate maintenance most of these ponds become almost polluted and contaminated. But the matter of surprise is that a large number of town dwellers are using water of these ponds for their domestic purposes. Besides these ponds maximum numbers of town dwellers especially the poor and mediocre economic standard people are using well water for their daily purposes. There are approximately 10,000 wells used as one of the dependable sources of domestic needs.

Main Sources of Water for Cooking

From the point of good health condition, safe and good quality of water is essential for the purpose of cooking, because in most of the cases digestive problems come out due to the use of poor quality of water for the cooking process. In the studied areas several trends have been observed regarding use of water in the cooking process. In the elite areas of the town most of the people have used tap water for the purpose of cooking. Especially the lower income group families and slum dwellers have used well water as well as tap water for the purpose of cooking. Even they have a popular concept that the pulses have not boiled in a better way in the tap water or well water but pulses boiled fully if it is boiled in pond water. So a good number of slum dwellers of Medinipur town areas have used pond water in their cooking process. Sasthi Dula is a 60 year old woman who has a very long experience in cooking in different messes and hostels and also in different households of the town. To her :

I have been residing in the Patnabazar area of the town for a very long time. I have been engaged more than 35 years in cooking in different boys and ladies messes and hostels of the town. During the time of cooking either in mess, hostel or in my house, I have used tap water, well water as well as pond water also. I always prefer pond water to boil pulse because in pond water it become fully boiled but to prepare soup I have used tap water or well water which one is available at that time. It is observed that pulse is a very common item in the menu list of messes or hostels and I have used pond water for preparing any pulse item. On the basis of my personal observation it can be said that most of the females in this area known to me follow the similar cooking procedure.

Major Sources of Drinking Water

Every year, unsafe drinking water, coupled with a lack of basic sanitation, kills at least 1.6 million children under the age of five years which is more than eight times, the number of people who died in the Asian Tsunami of 2004 (UNICEF, 2006). The emphasis on the means of achieving safe drinking water has changed. Internationally, in the past, there had been a trend towards adding more and more parameters to standards with an associated requirement for sampling and analysis. This is an approach which is still found in many countries, including India (WSP Report, 2010).

The inhabitants of Medinipur Municipality are mainly depending on the supplied water that has been provided by the Medinipur Municipal authority. Beside the supplied water several other sources have been used as the alternative sources of drinking water. As per the collected information from the field it is observed that most of the people have a very soft heart and common sentiment about the water of river Kongsabati. The river Kongsabati is flowing by the side of the Medinipur Town. In most of the cases it is observed that the river Kongsabati is considered to be a holy river especially to the town people. In real sense some of the people of the town depended on the water of river Kongsabati. From the case study the information collected it became clear that almost in all the seasons the people have been facing water crunch especially in the summer. There are total 24 wards existed in the town. There are 169,264 people are living in the Medinipur Town areas as per the Census of India, 2011. In this connection it is also mentioned here that there are 37,392 households remain scattered throughout the town areas. The Municipality supplies 17.72 MLD water daily for the requirement of the town people which is considered to be very insufficient to the town people.

Availability of Water Related Infrastructural Facilities in Town Areas

The Municipality authority has taken an elaborate arrangement for providing the drinking water to the town people. Generally the Municipality regularly supplies water through approximately 513.69 km. long underground pipe lines. The prime sources of water of the town are Kangsabati River water and the underground water. There are total 43 Government deep tube wells in the town to supply drinking water. At the household level well is considered to the major, dependable and low cost sources of water especially for the purpose of domestic use. Although the numbers of Government wells are very limited but the private wells are maximum in number. During the survey it has been observed that in a number of cases in the residential areas of town, people have their personal deep tube wells. In this connection it is also mentioned here that in most of the economically and educationally better off areas most of the town dwellers have household water connections. Beside these there are approximately 4065 public water taps through which the

Municipality supplies drinking water to the town people completely in free of cost. There are five over head water tanks in the Municipality areas from where drinking water has been supplied to the town people. These are situated at Baisakhi Palli, Gatebazar, Station Road, Swarat Palli and Battalachak. The approximate capacity of these overhead water tanks are approximately 2 lakhs gallon, 1 lakh gallon, 1.25 lakh gallons, 50 thousands gallon and 2.5 lakh gallons. There are approximately 240 large size ponds which are mostly vested or Government property commonly used as the domestic water resources. A large number of town people have regularly used these ponds for domestic purposes.

Regularity of Water Supply System

In most of the areas of the town, the Municipal authority has provided drinking water to the town people through the underground pipe line system. But in some newly expanded areas of the town the underground water pipeline is yet to be installed. There are two types of water supplying systems offered by the Municipal authority. They have been provided water through private household connection as well as through public taps. It is generally observed that households of financially strong and elite class mainly prefer household water supply line connection, where as in most of the fringe areas, slum areas, poor and undeveloped areas, the Municipal authority distributes drinking water through public taps. In some cases Municipal authority distribute water through mobile water vans. The town dwellers generally get water two times daily for four hours i.e. from 6.00 AM. to 10.00 AM. and 4.00 PM. to 8.00 PM.

Major Problem Areas

On the basis of the official records and directly or indirectly collected information from the Municipality areas it can be said that in almost all the time the water of Kangsabati River has been used as the prime water sources for domestic and drinking purposes. But during summer and winter season the water level of the Kangsabati River decreases very drastically which ultimately results a very serious water scarcity in the Municipality areas. As a result most of the people have been facing trouble for scarcity of both drinking and domestic water. Sometimes the Municipal water supply system became irregular. In the slum areas especially in the Sepoybazar, Mirzabazar, Minabazar, Patnabazar are high density population region, but the flow of pipe line water is very slow and inadequate for which there is a very large number of people who remain standing in the long queue in front of the public taps. As reported by the residents of these slum areas although the Municipal authorities have been distributing drinking water through mobile water vans but as per the demand, the supply is very negligible. In the summer and winter seasons most of the wells become dry as a result most of the household have been facing a tremendous scarcity of domestic water. In the slum areas, most of the people have been sharing pond water for their regular domestic use. Obviously it is observed that most of these ponds are either Government or vested ponds and due to lack of any proper maintenance, the pond water become contaminated and unhygienic so skin diseases, dysentery and some other types of physical problems are very common features to these people. Johora Bibi is a resident of Minabazar. She has been facing some water related problems. She has expressed her opinion in this way –

I am residing here in a rented two room house. Along with my husband, three daughters and one son I am residing here for a period of more than twelve years. I have used pond water for the domestic purposes such as for bathing, washing cloths and garments, cleaning of utensils etc. Generally my children have suffered from itching, skin rashes, dysentery. For the purpose of cooking I have used tap water and sometimes when tap water is not available or for my busy schedule I can't able to collect tap water, I have used well water collected from the wells of the neighbours. Regular collection of tap water is a very problematic matter to me because in the morning and afternoon I remain engaged as a housemaid in three households. As because for collection of water from public tap, I have to wait for a very long time in the queue in front of the public water taps. Although sometimes the Municipality authority supplied drinking water through the mobile water vans but it is not enough as per the requirement.

Conclusion

Generally it is observed that for successful advocacy of health and hygiene condition of the inhabitants of a particular area, good and proper management of water resources is to be taken up by the concern authority. To advocate the development of water supply system, water distribution infrastructure and the demand of water supply, the authority should update the basic information. From the study it becomes clear the Medinipur is an old town and due to various reasons there is a rapid influx of population. Due to unplanned, unscientific and haphazard ways of development, it is one of the prime obstacles behind the smooth distribution of good quality water supply in the Municipal areas. Water crunch during summer and winter seasons as well as lack of consciousness of significant number of town dwellers, authorities and others create a very panic situation that ultimately present not a very fair situation of the town regarding the use of water and water resources.

Bibliography :

Chakraborty, S.P. and S. Roy (2012). Assessment of the Quality and Portability of Drinking Water of Midnapur Town and Pidraloha, Paschim Medinipur. *International Journal of Life Science, Biotechnology and Pharma Research*, Vol. 1, Issue, 1.

Government of India (2014). *District Census Hand Book, Paschim Medinipur*, Series – 20, Part – XII-B, Directorate of Census Operations, West Bengal, Kolkata.

Government of West Bengal (2008). *District Statistical Hand Book. Paschim Medinipur,* Bureau of Applied Economics and Statistics, Kolkata.

Government of West Bengal (2012). *Activities and Achievements in Rural Drinking Water Supply and Other Areas.* Public Health Engineering Department, Kolkata.

National Institute of Urban Affairs (2005). *Status of Water Supply, Sanitation and Solid Waste Management in Urban Areas.*

Planning Commission, Govt. of India (2002). *Water Supply and Sanitation : A WHO – UNICEF Sponsored Study*, New Delhi.

Park, K. (2009). *Preventive and Social Medicine*, Bhanot, Jabalpur.

UNICEF (2006). *Meeting the MDG Drinking Water and Sanitation Target: The Urban and Rural Challenge of the Decade*. WHO Press, Geneva.

Water and Sanitation Programme Report (2010). *Water Safety Plans for Rural Water Supply in India : Policy Issues and Institutional Arrangements.*

Water Aid (2012). *Drinking Water Quality in Rural India : Issues and approaches*

16

Gandhian Thought in Manbhum District: An Historical Study

Pradip Kumar Mandal

Manbhum District was formed by the British Government in 1833. Manbhumkhas or Manbazar was the headquarter of this *jungle mahal* (forest based) District. This District was situated at the border area of South-West Bengal. At the time of partition of Bengal in 1905 Lord Curzon divided Bengal and this portion of Bengal transferred to the state of Bihar and Orissa. From that time to till independence Manbhum District remained in Bihar. In1956, division Manbhum District was devided in two parts- Dhanbad Sub-division remained in Bihar and Purulia Sub division consisting 16 Police Stations transferred to West Bengal.

Gandhian philosophy, his notion on freedom movement, and his economic and social welfare policy- all ideas reflected in the Manbhum District during the Gandhi era. Here we will analyze Gandhian political ideology on freedom struggle and the economic policies which were implemented by the congress leaders of Manbhum District.

The Nationalist Movement led by Gandhiji deeply inspired the people of Manbhum. They joined in the freedom struggle in the name of *satyagraha* and *boycott.* The people of Manbhum boycotted courts, legislature, educational institutes and foreign goods. They also decided not to pay taxes to the British Government. Nibaran Chandra Dasgupta resigned from the post of head master of Purulia Zilla School and joined *Swadesi* Movement as announced by Gandhiji. Similarly, Atul Chandra Ghosh, Upendra Mohan Dasgupta, Gobinda Chandra Bhattacharya and other left their legal profession and took active part in the Non-Cooperation Movement. National Primary School was established at Jhalda.

Gandhiji visited Manbhum in two phases. First time he visited during the conference of Bihar Provincial Congress Committee on 12th – 13th September, 1925. The conference was held at Purulia. Gandhiji's speech on use of *Khaddar*, Spinning, and problems of untouchability deeply inspired the common people of Manbhum District. During the time of Civil Disobedience Movement, the people of Manbhum took part to celebrate Independence day on 26th January, 1930. As soon as Gandhiji broke Salt Act at Dandi, the people of Manbhum also implemented his Civil Disobedience agenda under the leadership of Nibaran Chandra Dasgupta. After the suspension of the second Civil-Disobedience Movement Gandhiji visited Purulia for the second time to uplift of harijans and he also visited Nibaran Asram to see Nibaran Chandra Dasgupta who was then seriously ill. In Quit India Movement Manbhum played a significant role. Violent activities were created in this movement. But, Atul Chandra Ghosh, President of Manbhum District Congress Committee did not approve violence and he announced to take part the Congressmen in Non-violence method as enunciated by Gandhiji.

Economic ideology of Gandhiji also inspired the people of Manbhum. During the time of Non Co-operation Movement constractive activities were made under the leadership of Nibaran Chandra Dasgupta. He established *Silpasram* on 1921 inspired by the ideal of simple living of Gandhiji to develop poor people. *Swadesi matches*, soaps, *khaddar* etc. were manufactured by this *silpasram*. Very soon *Silpasram* became centre place of constructive programmes of the Congressmen.

In the year 1940, 'National Week' was observed all over the District of Manbhum. Sixty-nine *Satyagrahi*s were attended in Satyagraha Camp at Sevagram. It is important to note that all 69 *Satyagrahi*s made a total contribution of 1,62,681 yards of yarn. Gandhiji was highly impressed and he sent a message.

Sevagram

07-08-40

Dear Atulbabu,

I congratulate the 69 Satyagrahis on their substantial contribution of 162681 yards of yarn. I hope they will continue to make progress.

Yours

Bapu

Apart from that, on 1940 a National Basic School was established at Majhihira village of Manbazar P.S. by Chittabhusan Dasgupta. The aim of this school was to teach poor and uneducated people through vocational activities like spin, wooden work, khadi making, etc. on the line of Gandhian economic philosophy. This school trained the local people on spinning and encouraged them to cultivate *karpas* for self-employment. Thus the 'khadi economy' was started for economic progress and self-employment.

Gandhi tells the Government, public leaders and the capitalists and industrialists, "you have money and power but the villagers have the advantage of numbers. Their capital is labour. When they become aware of the value of their capital they will rule life. You cannot afford to antagonise them. Wake up therefore before they are driven to desperation. Give them the line clear." Even Gandhiji thought that after independence there is no need for Congress as political party. His aim was to build a 'Lok Seva Sangha' for development of Indian people. The leaders of Manbhum followed this Gandhian thought. They established Lok Sevak Sangha in 1948 by giving resignation from District Congress Committee.

Even co-operative society and panchayat system also established in the Manbhum District for public welfare. Lokbrati Society was formed in Purulia for the development of farmers. This society advised the farmers to use fertilizer, preservation and use of high-production seeds. This society also distributed good seeds in reasonable price. Thus Lokbrati Society set an example for uplifment of economic condition of the people of Manbhum. Similarly, Manbhum District Congress Committee introduced Panchayet system in Sadar Subdivision of Purulia in 1946. The principal object was to establish Gram Swaraj as envisaged by Gandhiji. These Panchayet effectively implemented the welfare programme for the rural people. So we can see that Gandhian Philosophy was implemented in Manbhum for a long time.

Bibliography

Bhattacharya, Buddhadev (1969).*Evolution of Political Philosophy of Gandhi,* Calcutta.

Bondurant, John (1959). *Conquest of Violence : The Gandhian Philosophy of Conflict*. Oxford Universal Press, Oxford.

Brown, Judith (1972). *Gandhi's Rise to Power : Indian Politics : 1915-22*. Cambridge University Press, Cambridge.

Copland, H. (1911).*Bengal District Gazetteer, Purulia.*

Dab, Jayanta Kumar (2007). *Local Politics and Indian Nationalism, Purulia: 1921-1947*, Kolkata.

Mandal, Pradip Kumar (2013). *Manbhum Jelar Bhasa Andolaner Itihas*. Kolkata.

17

A Folk Society on the Way to Modernisation: Opportunities and Challenges

Ashok Das Gupta

INTRODUCTION

Development is intensively connectively with political and economic aspects. In Indian perspective, most people live in rural society segregated into various agrarian rural structures. Here, the economy could be broadly classified into production oriented and trade related types; and simultaneously categorized into Traditional, Mixed, Nationalised, Macro and Micro-financing now moving towards globalization and global economy. In this global era, what should be the mode of development? Perceptions of Policy Planners at Global/ National/Regional stages may require help from multi-disciplinary approach, especially anthropology which is holistic study of mankind and also emphasizes on socio-cultural aspects through qualitative in-depth micro study (community wise or cross cultural; synchronic and/or diachronic).

People in traditional politico-economic system should move in the direction of civilisation, but this is a fact that they are confined within Nature-Human-Super-Nature relationship. The latter is related to culture which is Psychic Unity of Mankind or results out from Psycho-Biological need. But, study of culture now more emphasises on symbols, cognition/ world view new Ethnography and post-modernism.

Culture of the subject group plus development process (input) result into sustainable development (output): development in such case is more nature-friendly and pro-people; maximum people gaining the status of stakeholders are attracted to it and benefited from the policy. Other than this could be reason behind outsiders' interference where a policy would be always challenged by another and therefore no development work could be performed or be slow down from a steady or faster pace.

And in such a condition, womenfolk could play an important role. This issue is going to be highlighted through a brief discussion on Rajbanshi community of northern West Bengal.

THE RAJBANSHIS

Rajbanshi (also treated as Rajbanshi) is a community that has unique social and economic institutions guided by political and religious organisations. These peoples are situated in Sub-Himalayan South Asia but to a specific region namely North Bengal. The region is a borderland formed of northern part of West Bengal state of India attached to eastern Indian and north-eastern Indian states, China (Tibet), Himalayan countries like Nepal and Bhutan, Himalayan Indian state of Sikkim, and independent country of Bangladesh. Rajbanshis are basically living at lowland agricultural pockets in North Bengal somewhat different from various types of highlanders once thrived up on forest resources, so called mines, estate system and transnational trade.

Rajbanshis are not beyond of Hindu agrarian caste system; but also attached with quasi-egalitarian forms of Hinduism and show affinity with several trade-oriented religions. Rajbanshis are speaking of pre-Aryan, Aryan and post-Aryan impacts continuous with Colonial rule and post-Colonial democracy.

In this era of globalisation and Global Market Economy, Rajbanshis feel industrial revolution about 300 years back. They are in favour of agricultural revolution 12,000 years back; but they are realizing more and more per-agricultural livelihood with cognition of forest produce, medicines and drug, spices and silk, handlooms and trade, gold and treasure, self-sacrifice, mechanical solidarity and different gender realities and forgotten beliefs. They are for sure in a confusion of agriculture versus pre- and post-agriculture overlap. Issues like country-town nexus, identity, and culture as the earliest non-written book (Little Tradition) documenting Indigenous Knowledge System with Global Public Service to folk life are in new pace.

Rajbanshis, living as an ethnic group in northern West Bengal state of India consisting of six districts (Cooch Behar, Jalpaiguri, Uttar Dinajpur, Dakshin Dinajpur, Malda and Darjeeling), was basically folk community centuries ago, but with time accepted agriculture on the basis of joint extended family system. Once being *Pundra* or *BratyaKshattriya* category, they are linked up with the mythical pre-historic Pundra Kingdom and fall within extended ruling category of Hindu social caste hierarchy. These people might have affinity with forest based tribal groups like Mech, Rabha and Bodo in Sub-Himalayan Bengal, but definitely with the Khen and the Koch. They sing Kushana song. Indigenous statehood was developed around thousand years back in the name of Kamtapur followed by distinct Koch Bihar Kingdom (mid-16th to mid 20th century) during Mogul-Rajput and British India. Rajbanshis also exist in neighboring Nepal foothills, Bodoland Autonomous Territory of Assam (North East India) and Purnia region of Bihar. The six Districts mentioned above together with sixteen Districts in Rajshahi Division of North West Bangladesh (formerly East Pakistan and East Bengal) were the actual North Bengal now partitioned. Geographically, it is a highland called *Barind* land bordered with Teesta-Torsha and Mahananda River Systems to east and west all initiated from Sikkim and Bhutan (once Sub-Tibetan buffer states in Himalayas). Cooch Behar cum Jalpaiguri enjoyed statehood, but rest on *Barind*land and Mahananda plains of North Bengal had no such traditional statehood- they are more attached with Gangetic Plain in every aspect. In this era of globalization, when discrimination is growing, like all other communities, the Rajbanshi fractions are now demanding for separate statehood. They address their ethnicity, especially dialect, link with North East India and tribal or communal affinity as markers for separate identity from majority Bengalis with whom they stay for long. Hard to believe that they are the same Rajbanshis who once underwent status mobilisation from *Bratya Kshattriya* to *Kshattriya* pure line and majority accepted *Vaishnavism,* a quasi-egalitarian sect among the Hindus as a whole upon traditional *Tantric* (magical) practices, Shiva cult, animism, Buddhist remnants and other minor religious groups. They once participated in land-reformation programme, irrigation projects, rural banking, cooperatives, rural governance and self-help groups in a way of micro-financing, but many of them now consider agriculture less profitable and flee to suburbs. They are rapidly losing their indigenous knowledge traits considered as the way of survival up to few decades ago; only a few out of them could survive because of culture. In *Barind* land fractions, they proceed towards tea, pineapple, corn, spice (chilly), horticulture (gerbera) and illegal drug (hemp propagation) rather than fruits and vegetables and lowland crops like paddy, jute, flex, cane, bamboo, aurum and *marua*. On social ground, the issues could be viewed from three different angles: local, national and international. Locally, a society could be just a quasi-egalitarian community, or it might be classified into caste-like strata or there might be a strict caste hierarchy categorically distributed into three major sections: Upper Caste with maximum status (Brahmans and a few others), Dominant Caste with highest level of status mobility and Lower Caste with the lowest status. Lower Castes however have certain community like approaches and own ways of status mobilisation or a sense of self-reliance. Continuum was there in-between tribes and lower castes. Tribes in some cases accept agriculture as their prime occupation and behave like caste: they enjoy the most prestigious rank among tribal world. Lower castes in agriculture sector often on their community line mobilize their status from excluded categories to included ones. In such a way, they like Dominant Caste undergo through *Sanskritization* and/or imitate any superior Reference Group asking for certain reformations on either religious or secular paradigm. They in a sense become Dominant Community. The inter-relationship among Upper Caste, Dominant Caste and Dominant Community is very crucial for the political turmoil of a State or Nation-State.

Rajbanshi ("dynasty of king"). According to the local myths, their ancestor Koch king Hajo established the kingdom of Kampur by the end of 15th century. There is also another legend concerning the ancestry of the Rajbanshis. When *Parshuram* had started destroying the *Chhetria* dynasty in India as his father's revenge, the *Chhetri* kings and their people escaped to save their lives. Ancestors of Rajbanshis themselves being *Chhetries* fled and started living in the forests of Nepal's Morang and Jhapa by hiding. In context of Nepal, King Prithvi Narayan Shah annexed the kingdom of the Rajbanshis into a unified Nepal state. From the perspective of physical anthropology, the body structure of the Rajbanshis of Nepal looks like that of Mangol-Dravid people. However, in complexion, they bear a resemblance to the Aryas. The Rajbanshis call themselves the descendants of Suryabansi and reveal their clan (*gotra*) to be Kashyap. They follow *Chhetri* character and customs and add Singh and Rajbanshi to their names. The Koches call themselves the Rajput *Chhetris*. It is also said that *Koch*, *Bhadai*, *Paliya*, and *Deshia* including the Rajbanshi caste are the Dravidian castes of north-east and east Bengal. They are also thought to be the mixture of the Mongolian blood but they use Brahmins as priests in some of their religious rituals and follow the Hindu religion. There is no discrimination by status and level in their community. They can marry their co-lineage partners under the conditions of seven generations' gap. The Kamata kingdom appeared in the western part of the older Kamarupa kingdom in the 13th century, after the fall of the Pala dynasty. The rise of the Kamata kingdom marked the end of the ancient period in the history of Assam and the beginning of the medieval period. The first rulers were the Khens, who were later displaced by AlauddinHussain Shah, the Turko-Afghan ruler of Bengal. Though Hussain Shah developed extensive administrative structures, he could not maintain political control and the control went to the Koch dynasty. The Koch Rajbanshi's called themselves Kamateshwars (the rulers of Kamata/Kamatapur Kingdom), but their influence and expansions were so extensive and far reaching that their kingdom is sometimes called the Koch kingdom. Under his highness Maharaja Naranarayan the then King of Kamatapur, the Koch dynasty flourished to the highest extent. And his brother Shukladhwaj Singha (famous as Chilarai) was one of the greatest heroes of that time and he prominently dominated the eastern part of Kamatapur which now known as Assam (previously Assam is known as Prag Jyotispur) now it is known as Asom which is an integral part of The Republic of India. The Rajbanshi community has a rich heritage and culture which had been inherited from the ancient civilisation. The Rajbanshi community has their own dialects, culture, and way of living. The culture reflects the humbleness, peace, unity and harmony with nature, as Rajbanshi are primarily animist. A few rulers, kings, queens, princes and princesses of the Koch dynasty are His Highness Maharaja Naranarayan, Prince Chilaray, Maharani Gayatri Devi, (Princess Gayatri Devi later on married Prince of Jaipur Man Singh) which had helped a strong relationship between the two kingdoms. Maharaja Ajit Narayan Dev of Sidli (Capial at Bidyapur) Kingdom was also part of the Koch dynasty (Sanyal, 1965; Das Gupta, 2010; Wikipedia, 2012).

Most Rajbanshi are farmers who only grow enough food for their own families. They also rearing some animals. Some Rajbanshi have begun to earn money by their excellent weaving. Rajbanshi houses are made of wood, bamboo, thatch and mud. The Rajbanshi houses are grouped in villages. Some villages have only ten houses. Other villages have as many as one hundred houses. Most Rajbanshi houses include just one family of parents and their children. Rajbanshi fathers are the head of the household.

RAJBANSHI IN AGRICULTURE

A century before Rajbanshis did not cultivate paddy varieties throughout the whole year, but only in a specific season; so cultivation is seasonal and not yearly. They preferred rice cultivation in the monsoon season which is unique to South Asia, South East Asia and South China. Rajbanshis then with very low population and minimum need left the cultivation ground for a season or a year or several years. This type of practice they considered good for maintenance and increase of the soil productivity. They did not cultivate at fixed place overtime; rather time to time they changed the place of crop-cultivation. They called it *jhum* cultivation where the bush and trees of the selected area were cut off to let them rotten and then burnt with fire before planting the crops (slash and burn type of cultivation). This type of Swedish cultivation can be further grouped into slash and burn cultivation in true sense within the forest areas (now banned) and secondly, bush-fallow cultivation. Land used for slash and burn cultivation used to be left for next 5-7 years. In that way, soil got back fertility and forest and bushes returned back. In late winter when soil was covered with deciduous leaves of *shorea* and teak grown up in mixed type forest, they set up fire in order to prepare piles of ash providing manure into the soil. Savanna grasses are grown up here along with evergreen forest and deciduous vegetation and diversified flora of ferns, pteridophytes, lichens, mushrooms herbs, orchids, epiphytes and shrubs. *Thadda, chopsi*and*mailsa* are long grass varieties eaten up by elephants and rhino. However, under the clear sky pleasant sunshine of autumn freed the soil from harmful insects, vectors and pests. Light raining in late winter and temperature fall at night made the ash more fertile, and proper situation arose for the earthworms. Seeds were spread unevenly in late summer or at the time monsoon just launched the Himalayan terrains causing flash floods Sub-Himalayan valleys. Soil is covered with sand, lime, clay, loam, bolders, conglomerates and gravels.

Rajbanshis left that *jhum* cultivation with introduction of wooden plough and applied the technique of sowing the saplings rather than the seeds with help of a digging stick. Later, Rajbanshis started preferring settled crop cultivation basically in the flood prone areas and utilized irrigation techniques. They have generally classified the soil type into three: *danga* (highland), *nichu* (lowland) and *jola* (marshy land). There is complete absence of large farm houses and therefore land is distributed into small pieces. Small to middle scale peasants have become the land owners and the rest becoming landless labours, share croppers and other attached with agriculture oriented jobs. The earthen boundaries of these demarcated landscapes are called the *aal* and used by the cultivators to go into the field. Wider *aal* is also utilized for vegetable propagation which is a unique feature in its own. *Danga* is preferred for vegetable cultivation, production of wheat and *marua*, habitation and kitchen garden, bamboo propagation, sacred groove and grazing. The *nichu* land is considered appropriate for rice cultivation. In winter, the Rajbanshis at the *nichu* land cultivate several types of vegetable along with *makoi* (corn) on the sloppy landscape; whereas propagate wheat on the *danga* region. The low land areas are used for production of pulses and mustered (along with other rapeseeds like *rai* and *tisi*). Pulses are of different varieties: *maskalai*, *thakurkalai*, pea, gram, moog and *khesari*. *Jola* region is good for jute, water hyacinth and arum, while the slopes for the ferns. Sandy river bed in foothill areas is good for spices, watermelon, poppy, cardamom, ginger and garlic as well.

Rajbanshis used to cultivate paddy and jute. Rajbanshis prefer rice cultivation. Paddy sowed in winter season is the *boro* type, whereas *joli*, *aush* and *amon* are propagated in marshy land, during summer-early spring and early monsoon-late spring respectively. *Kaon* or *Kamon*, basically a typical boro, is a variety of rice with smaller grain size. It is not too tasty as other improved qualities of paddy. *Kaon* is a suitable example of domestication and gradual improvement of a wild variety into the category of a crop. It grows reluctantly in the natural environment of North Bengal on and aside the *aal* (the divider and pathway inside the crop field). At a time, Rajbanshis used to eat hotchpotch of boiled *Kamon* or *Kaon*. *Kaon* was served as hotchpotch in festivals. The high yielding hybrid rice varieties and other types of vegetables replaced later both Kaon and traditional verities of rice. Along with rice cultivation of the winter verities, *aal* is often modified for the cultivation of various vegetables grown at higher landscape. It increases the profit amount of the cultivator. However, Amon varieties they have preferred the most are *Kukra or Kukurjali*, White *Nunia*, Black *Nunia*, *Tulaipanji, Swarna, Kalam, Kamon/ Kaon, Payejam, Mala, Dighe, Banshiraj, Aralia, Baran, Nalach, Kechardam, Harigachhi, Bayaj, Fulbete, Ropa* and so on. Some *aush* verities are *Pakshiraj, Tepishal, Nayachur, Muktahar, Bhadma, Chapari, Kotki, Shate* and so forth. *Mala* ripens first. Rajbanshis have the concept of six seasons like summer (*Greeshma*), rain (*Varsha*), autum (*Sarat*), foggy (*Hemanta*), cold winter (*Sheet*) and spring (*Basanta*); each with two months out of total twelve. Rajbanshis usually cultivated rice in the season of monsoon and cut it in the season of *Hemanta* - a typical season between autum and winter when the dews started falling on earth. Sowed with the first monsoon rain of June, this Mala variety blooms so fast and hence, the rice grains are found available in stalks before the annual festival of *Durga / Bhandani* that is the worship of Mother Goddess in the very next *Sharat* / autumn season (September-October). It could not wait until the season of *Hemanta* like other rice varieties.

In settled cultivation, after collection of the crops of rainy and spring seasons and their harvest throughout the month of *Hemanta*, crops are again cultivated in winter. Rajbanshis raise their stock throughout the first part of winter season. On the last date of first month of winter season, *Poush*, Rajbanshis go to the cow shade and bind a bundle of crop on the bamboo pole. Rajbanshis go on pilgrimage to their supreme deity, *Jalpesh*, once at the season of autumn with the prayer for good production of the winter crops, and then again in rainy season in the next year. Black cloud in north- east indicates heavy storm with lashing rain. Rain started in Saturday continues for seven days, whereas in Tuesday lasts for three days. For paddy and jute cultivation, bright sunshine in day time and rain in night are highly required. In spring, breezing wind comes from the south and in winter, cold wind from north and north-west affect the common people. Raining in spring causes damage to the ripening crops in the field and if there is lashing, the effect would be more serious and deadly. Heavy rain in late autumn and/or early summer is also deleterious. Indeed, in every step of agriculture practices, there are some exclusive folk attributes in the form of myth and festivals throughout the year that always say something about the Rajbanshis Folk Life and their Indigenious Knowledge System (IKS). *Kukurjali* was very sacred to them and they generally served meal with the rice from this paddy on ceremonial occasions like rite-de-passage, religious festivals and agricultural ceremonies. Black *Nunia* is dark in color; when the crops are full grown, the field looks black and the air is filled up with a sweet fragrance. Grains of Black *Nunia* are relatively smaller, but very much tasty; it is sold in market in higher price level than the hybrid varieties due to its low production. Common *Nunia* is also there, seed coat color is golden. Rajbanshis are concerned about high nutritious value of *Nunia* rice. Handfull of *Nunia* rice can fill the stomach for the whole day. A handful of Nunia paddy (taken for cook) could provide a higher amount of cooked rice. *Kalam* is the rice with thin elongated grains and also of good taste.

Males often perform their work on mutual understanding among the close relatives or neighbours. The same process of sharing the work could be seen in case of child care; the villagers kept their children under the guidance of aged fellows in the village when parents have to move into the field. Females actively participate into sowing, harvesting or thrashing. Males are also involved in preparation of wooden plough from good-quality non-degradable teak grown up reluctantly in the neighbouring forest areas of mixed type common in sub-Tropical regions.

Rajbanshis yield another variety of paddy, *Dharial*, which is known for its pressed shape and therefore used exclusively in production of the preserved rice products (*muri*-puffed rice; *chira*- bitten rice; *khoi*- pressed rice). The production amount is supposed to be higher in rainy season, but due to flood or irregular and untimely rain fall, the quantity could not always reach to the optimum level. The costly irrigated cultivation process in the dry winter season with relatively low crop production often assures the Rajbanshi cultivators a fixed amount of income. In winter irrigation facilities are required. With the help of bucket and bamboo pipes, water is taken out of wells or from the canals formed by numerous small river flows. In the time of ripening of crop, they have to take special cure so that cattle, birds, rat, bat or elephants could not eat it up. The ripened crop after being harvested with the help of a sickle, they lay the crop down on the field in clusters. In this way, crop becomes sun-dried. Paddy straws have been burnt off so as to produce manure and destroy the pests before the next cultivation begins. The remaining paddy grains on the field are eaten up by the birds and mouse; the latter brings it to its underground house and preserve in the dry soil. In house on the thrashing floor plastered with cow dung, paddy is thrashed by hand. A pair of bullocks keeps running over these cereals and in this way, the grains are separated from the straw. Then the straw and the grain are raised on separately into the store. Sowing, harvesting and thrashing of paddy are mainly governed by the womenfolk. Women know well what distance to maintain between two bunches of paddy sapling. They also know what the number of saplings would be in each bunch depending on the weather of a particular year. Women know more about the natural weather indicators. They in their folk life practice various magico-religious performances and utter various proverbs. Flowering in bamboo will bring in rats from jungle that then would destroy the whole crop causing natural famine and leaving only mushrooms, ferns and lichen soup. Lashing thunderstorm in summer causes bad mango production and is also responsible for low paddy yield. Frog leg muscle and mollusks and snails are full of protein. Decrease in number of frog will negative to natural modes of pest and insect control. Excess snails are deadly to cultivation. Palm, cane, date are the sources of sugar and palm is best for local climate. Areca is the main economic resource of every village. *Guwa*or *chegua* or *guai* is the local name of areca. *Buguri* or plum is also collected and preserved as pickle. Women are involved in fishing in local ditches and small fishes there along with *nadiali* fishes in local steams are converted into dried fishes by just leaving the fish pieces in dry sun beam without using salt or turmeric. Dung-cum-stick is the best quality fuel. Paddy cultivation can be followed by ground nut. *Motihari* is the best variety of tobacco. Heavy raining in autumn is also fatal to paddy and jute cultivation: the sowing period should be postponed or be selected on the basis of ground reality. High to prune the aurum to get maximum yield is another hidden techniques. Dye from local flower and gum from aurum are very crucial. Colors from soil and *khoir* tree are remarkable. Ethno-toxicant from aurum for fishing is also important. Those toxic substances cannot herm crabs as well as mosquito larvae eating fish varieties. Women also know well about floriculture at pots, bonsai, nursery, open garden, special manure, weeding, shedding, pruning, and the wind courses from mountains and seas important for flowering. Pest control by light trap, food systems in ecology, ash, azadirechta cake or spray, mixing pattern of organic manure and chemical substance, adding of bone dust and raw fish rotten, and other means are unique inventions of Rajbanshi women folk. They know the inadequacy of salt in local environment and hence prepare salted puffed rice. They not only intake lime with areca and betel, but also apply it in pond purification. They have invented some good techniques for fishing of pond fishes, river fishes and fishes with extra respiratory organ. Activity of fishes, fish eating birds and ants are natural indicator of weather to them. Controlled use of ant, termites and earth warm are friendly in gardening. Duck, goose and swans that control the population of snails in the pond is actually helping fish cultivation and also their stool is a good source of fodder for the fishes. They know about the shrubs like *bichhilara* controlling infectious diseases in poultry. They know about the grasses and plants that increase the milk productivity of cows. Women are really good will kitchen garden in *uchu* or *danga* or upland places where they propagate vegetables and spices. Turmeric, zinger, peppercorn, chilly, cardamom, cabbage and broccoli, cauliflower, mustard, rapeseeds, sunflower, bitter gourd, gourd, potato, sweet potato, carrot, beat, *chalkumra* or *panikumra* (Pumpkin), lady finger, brinjal, snake gourd, cane and bamboo, jack fruit and guava, *kaon*, *marua* and maize are the basic vegetables.

Rice is consumed in various ways, such as, boiled rice with salt, rice with pulses, vegetables and other non-vegetable items. They stored the rice in dry preserved condition. They first wet the rice, then fry it hot, and press in *chham* (husking machine) with *gyin* (leaver/handle) manually so that the rice portion comes out from the seed coat; the seed coat is used both as manure and fodder; whereas the pressed rice, *chura*, is served with card which is till the most auspicious item for any kind of religious ceremony or festival for the Rajbanshis. The community is fond of *dahi (curd)*, and unsaturated fat, i.e.,*ghee*. Fresh milk from the cow is immediately kept in earthen pot in cold place and in this way they prepare the card (*goleyadahi*). So, *dahi-chura* was one of the most delicious items for them. *Foktoi* is a pulse-like dish prepared from mixture of fried dust of *chura* and garlic which is cooked in boiled water with mustered and chilly. They also prepare *vapa*, another exclusive rice item with some specific economic attribute to the Rajbanshi society. Here, they take some rice dust and prepare a soft watery lye of it, then give shape of disk-like cakes that they cook on steam one by one. For steaming, they again take a *handi* (earthen cooker) on fire with boiling water inside and the vapour coming out of the single pore at the centre of the lid automatically bakes the rice cakes into delicious *vapa* cakes. Till now they fry their home-made soft rice and take this fried rice (*chalbhaja*) with tea in the early morning. They boil rice in water which is their main food item (*bhat*) and also consume the nutritious watery emulsion of the boiled rice, *fen* or *telani*, with garlic. Husked rice in home in *chhum-gyin* is only decoated but the nutritious cotyledon part remains attached. Rajbanshis pour slight water over cooked rice and preserve this for the whole night which becomes another item (*pantabhat*) for the breakfast meal. Watery cooked rice could be further fermented so as to prepare alcoholic substance added with sucrose and dust of rice coat (kind of fodder). Rajbanshi females used to engage in preparation of *dahi*, *ghee*, *chura*, *muri*, salted *muri*, husked rice and *vapa* within homestead whereas the males go to the field and participate in the process of crop-cultivation. Females generally prepare the *vapa* at night and then early in the morning go outside for selling the cakes at the exchange of other goods - a typical barter system. They collect rice by selling the *vapa*. And from these collected rice, they feed their family and again produce the rice cakes for next day selling. Prosperous families do not let their women to go into the field, maintain joint-extended families to meet the manual labour and generally apply day labours on temporary basis.

Role of Rajbanshi women folk is very interesting to observe. Traditionally, we can find out them associated with various sectors of the folk life: cooking and other domestic work, fuel collection, child raring, animal husbandry and poultry, pre and post agricultural performances, pond and other water management, fish processing, kitchen garden, floriculture, food processing, production of rice cakes and pulse cakes, fruit preservation, manure manufacturing, curd production, fern and yam collection, mushroom collection and cultivation, areca cultivation, betel cultivation, ethno-medicinal plant propagation, management of sacred grooves, management of bamboo and cane bush, spice cultivation, handloom industry on jute-flex-silk, embroidery, dye yielding, oil extract from rapeseeds, pottery, salt in puffed rice, tobacco product manufacture, marketing sector, sucrose preservation from various resources like palm and cane and dates, and so forth. On this basis, certain kinds of Self-Help Groups can be arranged. That would a part of micro-financing. Women living in rural sector therefore would be interested in saving in their accounts in rural banks. Co-operatives would be formed. Easy bank lone is necessary. Access to credit is a part of gender empowerment. But role of the males and their behavior to other gender would then be of much concern.

A section of Rajbanshi community is thinking that micro-financing is not the ultimate solution. So, they are moving to other job sectors. Government jobs, jobs in rural government bodies, rural centres for mother and child care, and such things cannot be the only options. Both men and women are moving towards informal job sectors. Job opportunity is much higher there, but job security in comparison to formal sectors is definitely much lesser.

Migration to suburban and urban sectors in search of blue collar jobs sectors in developing countries is a trend. Women are indulged in working as domestic helpers, seasonal agricultural labours in big farm sectors, manufacturers of *bidi* (traditional cigarette), girl child labours and others. Illegal logging, stone crushing industry and sand collection in local rivers, soil cutting and brick manufacturing, pottery and clothing industry with a better opportunity to marketing cum entrepreneurship, fast food industry, mushroom industry, floriculture especially of gerbera, mixed cropping and pisci-culture, small tea gardens and pine apple cultivation are emerging job sectors. Migrations to urban and suburban zones are of two types: some migrate to the relatives living near the urban sectors and others in slums.

Rajbanshis have therefore three conceptualities: "I don't need urban, I like to be in safe with my traditional peasantry"; secondly, "we will go to urban but not at the stake of rural transforming into urban" and thirdly, "if we don't cultivate crop, what will be our food-practice then?" The agrarian Rajbanshis can use their biodiversity and agricultural resources to improve their life.

Folk to Modernity: In the Context of Indigenous Knowledge

Raised first in the 1990s under the domain of Human Resource Development by World Bank, the term indigenous has become highly integrated with the concepts like Sustainable Development and Folk Life. Mostly undocumented, originated from the very reflection of the nature and natural happenings in day-to-day life upon the Folk Mind, shared by a huge bulk of population spread out from forest to village, and of course, the most functional in form for their continuous loss and gain, discovery and rediscovery with time. Indigenous Knowledge traits could not remain kept apart from the known modern knowledge traits and are quite able to formulate a new sub-system with some universal attributes under the Global Knowledge System, mainly for two basic reasons. These are:

1. A lot to be learned from the traditional societies, the folk communities and the holders of the Little Tradition to make up the side effects, hazards and damage caused by unidirectional and unjustified implementation of modern technologies and modern developmental works; reducing the folk agitations and ensuring share of profit to all.
2. Need of mutual understanding between folk and modern societies for establishing a sustainable way of planned development to gain the highest degree of support from all associating parts of the society so as to
    2.1. attain suitable economic growth and growth in both culture and civilisation,
    2.2. produce a good quality human resource,
    2.3. and achieve properly organised way of living, avoiding the probabilities of conflicts like between majoritarians and

minoritarians or of global-local nexus or even a clash in the frame of ethnicity or religious communality.

There are many folk societies living on the community basis chiefly within or aside the forest, using the forest products for their daily use, with the sense of a common territory, common dialect, non-subsistence type of religion, traditional health and politico-economic systems of their own, homogeneity, simple way of living, and mechanical solidarity that make them fallen under the category of 'folk'. The main features that create the difference between the folk and the rest are their non-adaptive domains and their high level dependence on nature that plays a great role behind the formation of a system of indigenous knowledge traits in order to maintain their daily life. The closest to the folk society is the peasant society whose basic criterion is the fruitful application of peasantry type of economy where the agricultural produce is not all distributed among the group members or clan or tribe in a village on community basis through barter or reciprocity deeply associated with myth and customs of folk life making it unique in feature, but marketised by means of monetary economy and therefore a country-town nexus has eventually formed there. In past, the villages in India showed strong willpower to remain their solidarity or unity that provided it a specific nature of local-level self-sufficiency which could not be disturbed by any kind of political alteration at the regional or even in a broader perspective.

The folk in their traditional condition may lack the modern amenities simply considered as the various styles of a civilisation, but in reality they should contain some kinds of civilisational level by means of cultural traditions and social relationships established with both outside and in inside. Still the folk communities have their own technological apparatus differing strikingly from the modern amenities. The simplicity in their technologies is the prime factor behind considering these societies primitive. These technologies might be so simple, but on the other hand, they are highly effective in protecting the feed back system built up within the relationship of nature and the folk communities. These technologies thus have played great roles in proper maintenance of their daily life and therefore, very influential in the determination of their cultural identity.

The artifacts they produced with the very help of their traditional technologies from the natural products construct their material part of culture. Using these artifacts, they exploit the nature which creates certain types of division of labour, and in order to maintain the same, they create some rules in the names of folkways, norms, and customs according to their beliefs, values and morals that uniformly regulate their behavior and construct their social aspects (socio-facts). With this aid of traditional artifacts and primitive type of technologies used systematically according to the socio-facts, the members of a folk community would perhaps be able to regulate the nature and natural happenings. In due course of regulating the nature, they develop the magic and when the belief in supernature comes into, the concept of sacrifice so as to appease a supreme entity in the form of religion, various related customs, cultural performances and specialists automatically appears. That has been the set of magico-religious activities associated with the traditional ways of disease remedy/supporting the mental strength/agricultural or post-agricultural performances or other kinds of traditional economy/ rites de-passage and other social ceremonies actually responsible for the gradual development of folk dance, folk songs, folk lore, folk riddles, folk literature, folk rime, folk plays, folk cookery and folk recipes, folk craft, paintings, myths and other related issues like folk notion of time day-week-season-year, folk architecture, folk play, folk dialect, and so forth. These symbols actually reveal out the World Views of the folk peoples, and open the closed chapters of their cognition. These all including material culture of a folk community construct the folk culture; again this folk culture associated with the socio-facts plus folk economy, folk politics, folk religion, and folk way of disease treatment figure out the folk-life. Ultimately, parallel with the Global Knowledge System, another system by the knowledge traits of the indigenous communities, Folk Wisdom and non-reflective domains (specially related with socio and psycho-facts) have been developed at the local level. That system has been found distributed asymmetrically (within the genders, age groups, labour divisions and social strata). Moreover, this system could be worked out from the tactics used to maintain the daily life properly, and related with the non-subsistent parts, though being highly functional in nature: produced and reproduced, developed and lost with time. This is called as the Indigenous Knowledge System (IKS). The set of indigenous knowledge traits builds up a system called indigenous knowledge system working as the regulator of folk life. The system would include everything present within a folk life (both functional and related non-functional). So, the system ranges from all the material and the non-material, tangible and intangible, verbal and non-verbal aspects of life among the members of a traditional or better to say, an indigenous community to the domains of folk song, folk proverb, folk etymology and chants, folk music, folk tales, folk literature, folk dance, folk painting, folk sculpture, folk recreation, folk play, folk art and craft, folk cookery, folk settlement patterns, folk architecture, the notion of time, weather forecasting, dialectology of folk speech, superstitions, myths, legends, riddles, folk religion, folk lore, sense of right and wrong (folk ways), norms (regarding kinship relations and rites-de-passage), folk customs (regarding household affairs, agricultural operations and other social behaviour), various types of organisation (political, economic, religious, and social), ethno-medicinal practices, folk technology, folk agriculture and other production domains. The words we use to denote indigenous knowledge are not still significant and confusing, since these terms are affected by high risk of inter-subjectivity and often used interchangeably. Whether we speak off the terms like Indigenous Knowledge (IK), Indigenous Technical Knowledge (ITK), Ethnology, local knowledge, folk knowledge, traditional Knowledge, Traditional Environment/ Ecological Knowledge (TEK), People's science, there are always arguably enough overlap. This Indigenous Knowledge System (IKS) not only includes the indigenous technological knowledge traits, but also the set of knowledge traits used to maintain a folk life and that is why, IKS is also termed as Peoples' Knowledge. The folk peoples are closely associated with the nature and therefore, the Indigenous Knowledge System is also found to be closely attached with the nature; this close attachment gives IKS the name of Indigenous Ecological/Environmental Knowledge System. So, known by various names, IKS is found closely attached with social, cultural, natural and human capitals within the non-reflective population. It could also be classifies into various systems of gender and age-group. Though being functional in nature, IKS is closely associated with various non-functional symbols of human life. On the basis of community study, IKS could be divided into various domains like Agriculture, Animal Husbandry and Poultry, Ethno-Fishery, Artisan, Disease Treatment Ethno-Medicine and Folk Remedy, Post-Agricultural Practices, Traditional Economic and Political System and associated Technologies, Material Apparatus and related socio-facts, and psycho-facts expressed by means of various symbols (Das Gupta, 2011).

Indigenous Community: A community being closely associated with forestry and peasantry with a given set of indigenous knowledge traits is treated as an indigenous community. These indigenous communities are once considered as the ethnic minorities staying inside or close to the forest region, more exclusively the scheduled categories like the Scheduled Tribes in India. But now the label of indigenous community or indigenous population is considered in a broader perspective so as to include the whole sector of rural communities, close or remote to the modern access, maintaining the attributes of Folk Life, indigenous technological skills, traditional ways of Environmental Management System, Disaster Management, Weather Forecast, Agriculture, Animal Husbandry and Poultry, Ethno-Fishery, Disease Treatment and Ethno-Medicine, traditional economic and political organisations and so on, at least to some extent. Such characteristics might be found beyond any forest-based tribal community and into the circumference of agriculturist tribal communities as well as caste societies and the complex type of agrarian rural society based on peasantry. They might be even connected with the urban-industrial sectors basically through the rural to urban migration, womenfolk and various types of communication by means of kinship, economic and religious ties. So, the IKS has actually a wider periphery but it gradually vanishes along with the increasing distance from the original habitat of the folk community associated with a specific type of ecosystem and bio-diversity.

Shift from one ecosystem to the other has the potentiality to put an impact upon the ways of living. The affected community thus may have to enter into a struggle for its acclimatiation in that new environment and to accommodate with the earlier inhibitors, or to use other type of material apparatus than their traditional ones, and to acculturate certain other kind of values and norms through the way of culture contact. They may have to select new words and terminologies into their own language which could alter the way of speech, methods for biodiversity management and develop the knowledge system, and technologies involved in production, food and food ways as well as transform their age-old beliefs and ideas, ideology of the life and way of justifying the truth, and even non-subsistent domains like traditional ways of health-care, interaction of man nature super-nature, economy and polity. Ultimately the effect would be expressed up on both the subsistent and non-subsistent parts of the folk life.

Therefore, IKS could also be found beyond the folk community within which it originates, might be in a diluted form, through the very processes of migration, diffusion or culture contact between culture areas facilitating the process of acculturation of cultural traits. So, now basically the village peoples in a broader sense are collectively included under the category of indigenous community, and when the discussion is going on the issue of protection and violence of the rites of these indigenous communities and their folk life, it is all about the Indigenous Peoples. The terminology 'Indigenous Peoples' is synonymous with the terms like aborigines, aboriginal peoples, native peoples, first peoples, first nations, and so on known differently in different parts of the World.

Indigenous Peoples: Now the term 'Indigenous Peoples' is being used in a greater sense and that includes the scheduled, the non-scheduled and the excluded tribal communities and any non-tribal community with IKS and sharing the Folk Life; therefore giving an assurance of long-existed close attachment with the locality inhabited. Its periphery has now been expanded from the forest dwelling stalks up to the rural communities overlapped by both folk life and peasantry.

This concept of indigenous peoples is closely associated with the study of poverty, human rights, indigenous rights, land and forest rights, bio-piracy and illegal knowledge transfer, globalisation and market system, human resource development and implementation of modernity, setting up of urban-industrial sectors and economic growth, anti-globalisation anti-capitalist movements and need of sustainable development to condemn these agitations and the risks of terrorism and national disintegration by forming a balance between the World Views of traditional and the concepts of modern societies, decision-making system for the Policy Makers in Governance about minority development-poverty eradication-economic growth-community development in terms of health, education and social welfare, and so on.

There is actually no internationally recognized definition regarding Indigenous Peoples; it is a contemporary terminology used by various internationally recognized institutions like United Nations, International Labor Organisation and World Bank. It is highly related with Indigenous Communities, Indigenous Knowledge System as well as Indigenous Rights.

ON-GOING CHANGES IN THE AGRICULTURE DOMAIN AND ROLE OF IKS:

The categories like indigenous community or ethnic minority or tribal group or under-privileged sect or even a countryside dweller fallen under indigenous peoples are nothing but receivers of some provisions supplied to them by the state to come out from the stage of backwardness. However, these provisions could not always be fully utilied by all the peoples of a deprived community, especially those who actually required these. This happened due to dominance of the privileged class within their own community, insufficiency of proper awareness, absence of communication and lack of a suitable guideline by the State Machinery. Some other intermediates and bureaucrats could take the opportunity of their positions and corruption and mismanagement on the other severely damage the Public Sector. Again, fall of the Private sector opens the path of the smooth journey for privatization, marketisation and capitalist economy. Along with this would eventually come the concepts like ultimate profit, spreading the market to the access of all globally, increase number of the consumers as much as possible, provide the consumers certain efficiency to purchase things, allow them to have the taste of a good livelihood and increase consumerism. Produce numerous quantity of products to constantly supply the bulk their new and advanced mode of requirements, well as anyhow lowering the price level of the product so as to sell it among purchasers as many as possible. To do this, the producer would try to create a market worldwide, form a homogeneous culture in favour of His thinking, establish. His monopoly over that market, invent new type of effective technologies that would reduce the production cost, violation of labour laws or changing the same in his favour, appointments-on-temporary basis and on job security, low-cost labour, replacement of labour by machines and unemployment, illegal trade, bio-piracy and illegal technology transfer, lowering the price level to bring the highest portion of the market within access as well as collecting the good quality raw materials in relatively low from a place with immense scarcity. The suppliers of raw materials thus get assured for a fixed market and permanent source of income. It would be actually looking exploitative while being viewed from the side between the disparity between the profit levels of the raw material suppliers and the capitalist producer. But at the same time, the income level and status of living in the paradox of pure economy are developing for the peasants as well as the workers and officials in the factory. At the same time, one kind of environment for investment by medium and big scale factories is growing there creating new jobs and income sources for many in permanency or temporary basis. The Democratic State could not go totally against the working category or complete favour of the capitalist private investor and a way of negotiation it takes for its own favour (such as taxation, human resource development, improvement in the standard of living, poverty eradication and solve of the unemployment problem at least in a private sector and its subsidiaries). The factory owners, businesspersons, investors and companies are also aware of the fact that the workers working in the factories may also be consumer of their products. They have to maintain the power of purchase things within the common peoples; compromise with the state and public to maintain a harmonious situation good for trade and economy as well as maintain good terms with the raw material suppliers (intimately involved in global public service). The factory could provide some facilities or techniques or information to the indigenous community; but the latter with the help of its rich knowledge traits about the locality, ecology and bio-diversity could contribute to nature and the private companies or the public or the State Machinery in such a manner that on other could do the same. So, establishment of a negotiable line, understanding of each other, proper communication and mutual understanding between global and local, private and public, traditional and modern, State and Multi National Companies have been required by all from the Policy Makers to the Economists, Politicians to businessmen and suppliers, producers, distributors, retailers and consumers. Unless privatisation, industrialisation, investments and marketisation do not cause for massive scale land alienation against certain will-force of the commoners, damage their cultural identities and non-reflective domains, remove them from their share of profit, proceed against State interest and do not disturb the welfare steps taken by the government (in favour of workers, cottage and small scale industries, self-help groups, co-operatives, protection of the village systems and local merchants); in a country like India where the economy is still capitalistic, villages are mostly caste oriented and semi-feudalistic, democracy exists within the diversified ethnic peoples and doors are open to the globalisation since more than a decade, the Global and Private sectors could sustain, collaborate with the State and the Peoples and even utilize the good side of the IKS with the helps of indigenous communities. So, a global concern for the indigenous communities in the name of Indigenous Peoples and protection of the indigenous rights are here needed not for the betterment of those communities only, but also to check their complete transformation. Therefore, indigenous peoples could be used in generating ethnic violence on one hand on the issues for violation of indigenous rights; on the other hand, same could be applied so as to protect their rights, bring development in the way they want and the kind of share of profit they demand to them, incorporate them in the developmental process in an integrative way, draw to outline of sustainable way and appease them not to go into any ethnic disruption or get involved in any provocation. Only then, their cultural identity, folk life and non-reflective domains remain unchanged. Ultimately the situation for suitable application of IKS in Global Service would arise.

Some related discussions are going to be held below (referring the Rajbanshi community of Bidhan Nagar, Siliguri Sub-Division, Darjeeling District, West Bengal state of India):

Application of new verities and genetically modified items could often exert a negative impact upon protection of the old verities useful in sustenance of a biodiversity, an ecosystem, human life and the culture. And again, safe, good quality, local, hygienic, resistant, disease free and easily acclimatising variety may also grab attention of many especially when as a domesticated crop it has been growing naturally, in a complete organic manner and applying no toxic or non bio-degradable substance in the form of manure or pesticide; therefore often involving the IKS of the local indigenous community. This type of process has found in Bidhan Nagar region of Siliguri Sub-division, Darjeeling District of North Bengal (northern West Bengal); where the multinational food processing company Calipso India Private Limited provides a permanent market for the pine apple and other vegetables to the local peasants- these producers have now a permanent market where they could sell their products at a fixed price, obviously higher than before. But here the level of profit made by this multinational company remains concealed. The factory provides the cultivators organic manure produced from the waste rubbish of pineapple and vegetables. Many peoples get jobs in the factory at various positions and more other in transportation system. No doubt the standard of life has been increased in Bidhan Nagar region, application of harmful chemicals has been reduced in the filed, not even any genetically modified variety has been introduced nor the cost of irrigation and electricity needed in the cultivation of dry season paddy have come to be seen there. But replacement of food crops by pine apple and pine apple economy must cause some sort of socio-cultural changes among the Bidhan Nagar peasants most of which are Rajbanshis followed by Bengali castes and caste like Muslims speaking mixture of local Rajbanshi, Maithili and Bengali dialects. Here, the concept of Indigenous Peoples is necessary for the safeguard of the IKS as well as the overall protection of the Indigenous Community that cultivates the pine apples in their land.

In the same Bidhan Nagar region, establishment of small tea gardens growing parallel with the Tea Estates at the end of 1990s was highly opposed by the local peasants. They were afraid of land alienation. That ultimately led to the initiation of ethnic movement in the name of indigenous statehood Kamtapur and Kamtapuri language. Eventually, a new branch of separatist movements for the very formation of a new state was emerged out. That even got a passive support from the other frustrated peasants of Bidhan Nagar (falling under the Phansidewa Legislative Area). The region is mostly populated by Bengali speaking people, Scheduled Caste Categories including the Namasudra and Rajbanshi along with some religious minorities, tea garden Adivasi labourers and other Scheduled Tribe categories, and fractions of Nepali and Hindi speaking population (chiefly from Bihar). Here, concept of the Indigenous Peoples is needed for protection of the land rights exclusive provisioned for an indigenous tribal community having long time attachment to the land or the region. Here Indigenous Peoples would be applied to overcome the fear of loss of cultural identity, ethnicity, income source, Folk Life and traditional knowledge-belief-faith of livelihood; in order to check any kind of disharmony; establish proper communication with an effective mode of awareness; understand the Folk Mind and make a bridge between contrasting endowments like traditional and modern as well as local and global. As that were successful; many of the Rajbanshis on their own responsibility have initiated tea-plantation on their soil. However, people there have now been habituated with small-scale tea gardens. They supply their products (raw tealeaves) to the local tea factories. Tea is an easy way of income. However, many of these peasants primarily were not in a condition to set up tea gardens. That was an adverse situation because of two basic reasons- knowing nothing about tea cultivation and secondly, lack of funding. Rural bank is there in the C.D. Block, but many have already taken up small loans and therefore they have to go to local money-lenders. Some on contract basis lease their small scale farming lands to the outsiders for five to ten years for tea plantations and thereafter they get back their piece of land with a well established tea plantation. The local peasants now do not sell their lands to any outsider that they did before for an assurance of getting a job in that tea garden. Rather they are more intended to establish tea plantation of their own.

Unlike the tea plantation process, in pine-apple cultivation, the risk of land alienation is absent and therefore its impact remains more or less positive among the folk peoples in Bidhan Nagar area. Rajbanshis of Bidhan Nagar have now become quite detached from their traditional life pattern and IKS.

Rajbanshis are now more focusing on vegetable cultivation, mushroom production, floriculture, fruits and areca nut, alternative crops, and poultry rather than their traditional jute and paddy oriented conventional production system and animal husbandry. Even the local farmers are now doing mixed and complex type of vegetable cropping. Many of them prefer to use vermicompost and organic manure. Rajbanshi indigenous knowledge on biodiversity would help them to set up such intensive vegetable cropping. Rajbanshis are even using fallow lands and doing alley cropping. They are now demanding for cold storage. Vegetables, leafy vegetables and arcea nut propagation as well as fishing in local water bodies are common here in Bidhan Nagar area. Many of the local people are now attached with alternative jobs in town, suburb and their own ruruban pockets. Small scale irrigation projects and Teesta-Mahananda canal are really helpful in vegetable propagation in uplands that were once cover up with bamboo bushes and sandy lowlands full of grasses, marshes of cane and arum, and moist slopes with arum. Pulses in winter are more profitable than wheat and maize. Experimentally, the area can be selected for brinjal, betel leaf, lemon grass, shorea, teak, catechu, silk cotton, and even orange. Bidhan Nagar is a sub-Himalayan Terai belt in Mechi-Mahananda basin. The cold wind coming down from hills is good for cultivation of exclusive garbera flower. Many peasants are also earning money by production of vegetables in off-season. Potato in winter and autumn is being produced reluctantly. Many leafy herbs also grow up in the same potato field and assure extra income. Pointed gourd or *potol* is also grown up in huge quantities on lattice- this vegetable is planted twice a year and yield is available throughout the year. Radish and potato of so many kinds are available. Many peasants are now yielding jute seeds. Winter and monsoon vegetables are produced in huge quantities and these have good demands in local market. Vegetable production has altered the socio-economic situation of the countryside. For disease control however, they are using pesticides and herbicides.

So, the IKS of the Rajbanshi Social Fold (progressing on the track of modernity) is very essential to work out and in this process the non-functional domains could play an important role and ultimately the basic pattern of the folk life would therefore reveal out in front of us. And the most important thing is that only after getting this IKS, we could properly apply the modern knowledge upon the folk life and the nature in which it resides. From proper adjustment between traditional and modern technologies as well as between IKS and advanced knowledge system, we could achieve actual way of conserving the bio-diversity, because from this biodiversity the indigenous community maintains its folk life and therefore protects it in its own indigenous feed back management system. To do it appropriately, the community needs a banner like Indigenous Peoples and aid from indigenous rights. Correct adjustment among folk life, proper management programs and indigenous rights could postulate a sustainable development. And this adjustment could only be achieved when there is a definite balance between traditional and modern knowledge systems. Impetus is also needed from the domain of intellectual property rights and patent laws especially to check bio-piracy and illegal technology and knowledge capital transfer.

CONCLUSION

Rajbanshis exploit natural resources as they exploit the same by means of agriculture, kitchen garden and village biodiversity. This decides their mode of production, social structure and World View: institutions, organisations and culture are not above of that. And in Rajbanshi culture and folk life, agriculture covers a huge area. They may not leave their agrarian rural structure. Various inputs into their agrarian life give rise to different outputs overtime illustrating their historicity. This agriculture brings them so closer to majority Bengali people.

An indigenous community therefore shows a typical nature of cultural lag as the intrinsic part of its culture still remains the same and continues to be expressed symbolically through their non-functional domains like religion, even when the adaptive domains like agriculture related instruments/ material subjects/ technologies have been changing rapidly since modernisation input begins. And womenfolk have the right potentiality to do the rightful thing and access to credit: traditional to mixed to macro to global through microfinance in rural sector: the prime way to credit access.

So, development should be sustainable and pro-people considering relationship between human population/ human concentration and quality plus quantity of resource/ mode of resource exploitation (traditional to modern). Planning Commissions and politicians along with the intellectuals and experts should consider the aspects and interests of all the people according to their World View regarding society and nature. Without knowing each other as much as possible; exchanges of thought and message in order to create the equilibrium are not done. Only at that time, development would be uninterrupted at the highest level. Development in farming sector and agro-based industries would therefore become evident. Farmers in many parts of the world are conserving traditional varieties even as they modernize and adopt improved varieties. This pattern is illustrated by reference to Asian rice agriculture. A new approach to conservation is needed that builds a collaborative program between farmers, crop scientists, ecologists, biogeographers, and social scientists. A first step is to analysse farming systems that already conserve traditional crop varieties.

No doubt, there is a huge scope of rural entrepreneurship, micro-credit and gender empowerment in agrarian rural sector, India. The ways might be NGO and other Self-Help Groups. A lot to walk and a lot to do. We cannot neglect the womenfolk- half of the human resource: it is just a feeling and that empathy should meet the reality.

Bibliography

Das Gupta, Ashok (2010).The Relevance of 'Indigenous Peoples', In *Environment and Sustainable Development in India*,R.K. Sen, A. Mukherjee and P.K. Pal (Eds.)pp. 137-156.Deep and Deep Publications, Delhi.

Das Gupta, Ashok (2011).Does Indigenous Knowledge have anything to Deal with Sustainable Development? *Antrocom Online Journal of Anthropology*, Vol. 7, No. 1,pp. 57-64.

Sanyal, C.C. (1965).*The Rajbansis of North Bengal.* Asiatic Society, Kolkata

Wikipedia (2011), *Rajbanshi*, Accessed 10th December, 2012.

Part III:
Anthropometry and Health

18

Employment Status and Its Association with Health and Lifestyle among College Students

Arupendra Mozumdar and Gary Luguori

Employment during college has been established as a part of life for many students in the United States. The escalating cost of higher education and declining federal and state aide, coupled with the rising cost of living, continue to increase college students' concerns about financially supporting their tuition and livelihood during college (Ehrenberg and Sherman, 1987). As a result, a sizable proportion of full-time college students now also work in paid jobs during the academic year (Stern and Nakata, 1991).

Research on employment in college students includes describing trends, work-patterns; and the profile of working students (Stern and Nakata, 1991; Harding and Harmon, 1999). College students that work at high-quality part-time jobs tend to develop career-related skills and increase their level of career maturity (Healy *et. al.*, 1985; Pascarella *et. al.*, 1994). Also, working on or off campus does not appear to negatively affect the development of academics (Pascarella *et. al.*, 1994). Other research has indicated that moderate amounts of employment may even be related to higher academic achievement (Hood *et. al.*, 1992) and greater satisfaction with college (Pennington *et. al.* 1989).

A nonlinear relationship exists, however, between hours worked and the previously mentioned positive outcomes. Students who did not work or who had a heavy work schedule (more than four hours per weekday or more than 20 hours per week) reported slightly lower grade point averages (HPAs) (Hood *et. al.*, 1992) and were less satisfied than the students who worked 11 to 20 hours a week (Pennington *et. al.*, 1989. Working a full-time or part time off-campus job was also found to be negatively associated with academic performance, knowledge, development of interpersonal skills, and satisfaction with almost every area of the university environment, compared to students working on-campus (Astin, 1993).

Although a number of studies have been published on the relationship between employment status and academic performance, very few have explored the relationship of health-related factors with employment. Typically, research on the influence of time spent at work has shown negative associations with personal health. Leslie *et. al.* (1999) reported an association of insufficient physical activity among non-working college students in Australia. More recently, Adams and Colner (2008) used American College Health Association/ National College Health Assessment (ACHA/NCHA) data from 28 colleges and universities to report a significant negative relationship of working hours and frequency of fruit and vegetable intake among college females. Miller *et. al.* (2008) focused on the relationship of work hours with selected health behaviours and academic progress among students of a south-eastern university, and found a higher frequency of binge drinking, less sleep, and poorer academic performance among those who worked 20 or more hours in a week.

Beyond the aforementioned studies, little research exists to document the effect of work may have on the immediate health habits of college students. Personal habits formed during college years can often become life-long habits, so promoting positive habits seems incumbent upon higher education health professionals. With more than 17 million people currently enrolled in US colleges and universities (ACHA-NCHA, 2008), there exists a critical mass of people that can benefit both individually and collectively from positive, or improved, health habits. However, before strategies can be implemented that are designed to improve the health habits of millions of college students, it is prudent to first determine which habits are most concerning and what barriers exist that prevent students from optimizing their health. The latest ACHA/NCHA Report (2008) and the College Student Health Survey Report (2008) both emphasized similar areas of concern for college students, including increased stress levels, lack of regular physical activity, poor dietary habits, and increased body weight. In one of the first studies to look at healthy living barriers, Miller *et. al.* (2008) noted that time spent at work was strongly related to certain negative health behaviours. Given the paucity of literature on this important topic, more comprehensive research is needed to further explore the association of work and health related factors of college students. Therefore, the purpose of this study is to assess the relationship of employment status with lifestyle related health factors in college students.

Methods

Design and Sample

Data for this study was part of a larger data set of a biosocial study on the students of a Midwestern university. All students (N=841) enrolled in a university required general education course were asked to participate. Data for this study were available from a total of 564 students (334 male and 230 females) with a response rate of 67 per cent. All participants completed an online health survey and attended an anthropometric measurement session. The majority of the participants are either freshmen or sophomore (83 per cent of male and 90 per cent of female), the mean age was 19.3+2.1 years for males and 18.6+1.1 years for females, and the students were representative of the overall university student population, or more than 100 different academic majors. The study was conducted in accordance with the guideline set by Institutional Review Board of the concerned university.

Measuring Instrument

The online survey was a self-completed 20-item questionnaire where the participants were asked various questions related to demography and lifestyle. Question topics included living arrangement, employment status, physical activity, sedentary activity, homework, dietary habits, and sleep duration. The questionnaire was previously tested on similar sample populations in the same school for several years prior to this study.

The employment status of the participants was assessed by asking how many hours per week they work. In the demography section, participants were asked to report their age, year in school, and whether they are living on or off campus. The data on sleep was collected by asking the participants how many hours they sleep each night on average. To assess the level of moderate to vigorous physical activity (MVPA) of the participants, they were asked how many days in the previous week they engaged in strength or resistant training and aerobic physical activity or exercise other than casual walking. The participants were further asked how many fast food meals and how many servings of fruits and vegetables they ate in last 24 hours. The addiction habits of the participants were assessed by asking how many cigarettes they smoked and how many alcoholic beverages they drank in the past 7 days.

The data on sedentary behaviours were assessed by asking participants to report their screen time (time spent in front of a screen e.g. television, computer, video, etc.) and television viewing time in last 24 hours. Several studies have utilized 24 hour time diaries or recall to determine when sedentary behaviours occur over the course of a day and have shown acceptable recall and reliability (Juster 1986, Vandewater *et. al.* 2004, Vandewater *et. al.* 2006, Hager 2006). The data on academic activity were collected in terms of homework by asking the participants how much time was devoted for academics outside of school hours. The anthropometric measurement of height and weight were measured directly from each student. The subsequent BMI was calculated for each student in kg/m^2. Body fat percentage was calculated using the equations given by Durnin and Womersly (1974). Unlike earlier studies that included the students GPA, it was not used herein due to the large percent of freshman students.

Data Reduction

Data on the employment status of the participants were collected by asking how many hours they spent in a job each week during the academic year. Initially, it was decided to use the data as a continuous variable. However, after reviewing the responses, it was found that most responses were reported as multiples of 5 or 10. Therefore, the participants were categorized according to amount of time spent in employment as 'No work' (0 working hour) (M=174, F=105), 'Irregular' (1-19 working hours) (M=78, F=75), and 'Regular' (>20 working hours) (M=82, F=50).

Data on year in school was categorized into : freshmen, sophomore, and upper division (juniors and seniors). The data on living arrangement (on-campus vs. off-campus), physical activity (insufficient [less than 4 days of MVPA a week] vs. sufficient), smoking status (no vs. yes), and alcohol intake (no vs. yes) were categorized as dichotomous variables. Data on sleep duration was categorized into 'insufficient' (<7 hours sleep), 'sufficient' (7-8 hours sleep), and 'more than sufficient' (>8 hours sleep).

The daily fruit and vegetable intake data were categorized into two groups: '0-2 serving' and '>3 serving'. The screen time data were categorized into four groups: '<1 hour', '1 to <2 hour', 2 to <4 hour', and '4 hours or more'. Television viewing time was categorized as: '<30 minutes', '30 minutes to <1 hour', 2 to <3 hour', and '3 hours or more'. Duration of homework was categorized as: '<1 hour', '1 to <2 hour', 2 to <3 hour', and '3 hours or more'. BMI of the students were classified as: < 20 kg/m^2, 20 to <25 kg/m^2, 25 to <30 kg/m^2, and 30 kg/m^2 or higher.

Data Analysis

Distributions of the participants were cross-tabulated for work categories with demographic and categorical lifestyle variables to study the relationship between lifestyle variables and employment patterns among students. Chi-square tests were conducted to examine the possible relationship of employment status and the categorical lifestyle variables. Descriptive statistics and one-way analysis of variance were calculated for all the continuous variables to examine their association with work among college students. Further, a post hoc test (LSD) was calculated for the variable showing significant difference among the different employment status of the college students.

A multinomial logistic regression model was used for the association of employment status with the physical and behavioral traits. The employment status of the students was taken as a dependent variable in the logistic regression analyses considering the 'no work' group as a reference category. The odds ratio, confidence interval, and the significance level of the corresponding Wald statistic were calculated for all other employment status categories considering each physical (BMI and body fat percentage) and behavior trait as predictors.

All the analyses were done separately for each gender. The significance level for all analyses was set at 0.05. All statistical analyses were done using SPSS 15.0 software.

Results

The descriptive statistics of the participants across their employment status for different demographic, lifestyle, and anthropometric variables are presented in Table 18.1 separately for each gender. For males, the distribution of employment status shows that the majority of 18y. (66 per cent), 19y. (50 per cent), and lower division (freshmen and sophomores) students (55 per cent) reported not working at all. While the same holds true for 18y. (58 per cent) females, but lesser percentage

Table 1: Descriptive Statistics of the Participants across Their Employment Status for Demographic, Lifestyle and Anthropometric Variables

Categorical variables	Male					Female				
	N *n=174*	*No work* *n=78*	*Irregular* *n=82*	*Regular*	*Chi-square*	*N*	*No work* *n=105*	*Irregular* *n=75*	*Regular* *n=50*	*Chi-square*
Age (years)		per cent	per cent	per cent			per cent	per cent	per cent	
18	137	65.7	21.9	12.4	28.159*	149	57.7	32.9	9.4	52.395*
19	104	50.0	23.1	26.9	df=4	50	26.0	40.0	34.0	df=4
20 or more	93	34.4	25.8	39.8	p < 0.001	31	19.4	19.4	61.3	P < 0.001
School Year										
Freshmen	190	61.6	20.0	18.4	17.192*	162	56.2	32.7	11.1	15.143*
Sophomore	86	41.9	27.9	30.2	df=4	45	17.8	37.8	44.4	df=4
Upper division	58	36.2	27.6	36.2	p=0.002	23	26.1	21.7	52.2	P < 0.001
Living arrangement										
On-campus	207	78.7	66.2	21.7	55.848* (df=2)	172	56.4	33.1	10.5	57.182* (df=2)
Off-campus	127	21.3	29.1	26.0	p<0.001	58	13.8	31.0	55.2	p<0.001
Sleep		***per cent***	***per cent***	***per cent***			***per cent***	***per cent***	***per cent***	
< 7 hr/ night	71	42.3	31.0	26.8	6.854	46	23.9	37.0	39.1	17.530*
7-8 hr/ night	220	53.2	23.2	23.6	df=4	151	50.3	29.8	19.9	df=4
> 8 hr/ night	43	62.8	11.6	25.6	p=0.144	33	54.5	39.4	6.1	p=0.002
Physical activity										
Insufficient	169	47.3	24.9	27.8	3.120 (df=2)	138	44.2	29.7	26.1	3.970 (df=2)
Sufficient > = 4d/wk	164	56.7	22.0	21.3	p=0.210	91	47.3	37.4	15.4	p=0.137
Meal										
< 3 servings/ d	158	51.3	20.9	27.8	2.149 (df=2)	113	46.0	29.2	24.8	1.740 (df=2)
3 or more srv/d	176	52.8	25.6	21.6	p=0.341	117	45.3	35.9	18.8	p=0.419
Fast Food										
None	259	53.3	25.5	21.2	7.715 (df=2)	185	49.7	33.0	17.3	12.064* (df=2)
1 or more srv/ d	75	48.0	16.0	36.0	p=0.021	45	28.9	31.1	40.0	p=0.002
Fruit and vegetable										
0 to 2 srv/d	147	46.9	21.1	32.0	7.808 (df=2)	97	47.4	23.7	28.9	8.107* (df=2)
3 or more srv/ d	187	56.1	25.1	18.7	p=0.020	133	44.4	39.1	16.5	p=0.017
Smoking										
No	302	52.6	22.8	24.5	0.533 (df=2)	215	47.0	33.5	19.5	9.417* (df=2)
Yes	32	46.9	28.1	25.0	p=0.721	15	26.7	20.0	53.3	p=0.009
Alcohol intake										
No	187	52.4	25.7	21.9	2.176 (df=2)	158	48.7	32.3	19.0	2.825 (df=2)
Yes	147	51.7	20.4	27.9	p=0.337	72	38.9	33.3	27.8	p=0.244
Screen time										
< 1hr.	48	54.2	20.4	25.0	7.905	32	47.6	21.4	31.0	6.216
1hr. to < 2hr.	62	38.7	25.8	35.5	df=6	54	42.6	35.2	22.2	df=6
2hr. to < 4hr.	154	57.1	23.4	19.5	p=0.245	93	43.0	35.5	21.5	p=0.399
4 hr. or more	70	51.4	22.9	25.7		41	53.7	34.1	12.2	

Categorical variables

	Male					Female				
	N *n=174*	*No work* *n=78*	*Irregular* *n=82*	*Regular*	*Chi-square*	*N*	*No work* *n=105*	*Irregular* *n=75*	*Regular* *n=50*	*Chi-square*
Age (years)		per cent	per cent	per cent			per cent	per cent	per cent	
Alcohol intake										
No	187	52.4	25.7	21.9	2.176 (df=2)	158	48.7	32.3	19.0	2.825 (df=2)
Yes	147	51.7	20.4	27.9	p=0.337	72	38.9	33.3	27.8	p=0.244
Screen time										
< 1hr.	48	54.2	20.4	25.0	7.905	32	47.6	21.4	31.0	6.216
1hr. to < 2hr.	62	38.7	25.8	35.5	df=6	54	42.6	35.2	22.2	df=6
2hr. to < 4hr.	154	57.1	23.4	19.5	p=0.245	93	43.0	35.5	21.5	p=0.399
4 hr. or more	70	51.4	22.9	25.7		41	53.7	34.1	12.2	
TV viewing										
< 30 min.	94	53.2	25.5	21.3	3.584	105	47.6	33.3	19.0	4.137
30min to < 1hr.	70	50.0	18.6	31.4	df=6	39	48.7	30.8	20.5	df=6
1hr, to < 2hr.	92	50.0	23.9	26.1	p=0.733	49	34.7	38.8	26.5	p=0.658
2hr or more	78	55.1	24.4	20.5		37	51.4	24.3	24.3	
Homework										
< 1hr.	115	46.1	20.0	33.9	13.115*	52	44.2	25.0	30.8	3.969
1hr. to < 2hr.	96	53.1	30.2	16.7	df=6	57	47.4	35.1	17.5	df=6
2hr. to < 3hr.	62	58.1	16.1	25.8	p=0.041	48	43.8	35.4	20.8	p=0.681
3hr. or more	61	52.1	23.4	24.6		73	46.6	34.2	19.2	
BMI Categories										
< 20	35	42.9	25.7	31.4	4.254	35	51.4	31.4	17.1	1.987
20 to < 25	192	55.7	21.9	22.4	df=6	130	45.4	33.8	20.8	df=6
25 to < 30	75	46.7	24.0	29.3	p=0.642	44	40.9	26.3	27.3	p=0.921
30 or higher	32	53.1	28.1	18.8		19	47.4	32.5	26.3	

Continuous variable

	Male			Female		
	No work	*Irregular*	*Regular*	*No work*	*Irregular*	*Regular*
Screen time (min.)	153.25+104.43	149.79+105.07	145.30+108.31	137.05+97.18	139.40+89.70	115.34+94.47
TV time (min.)	70.48+71.59	67.18+69.48	66.56+69.15	48.95+62.54	46.40+60.25	49.50+49.61
Homework (min.)	97.06+79.80	88.68+71.16	78.54+86.77	122.74+95.56	126.20+90.48	109.30+95.56
Weight (kg)	78.88+14.98	79.11+17.02	77.34+12.79	64.74+14.13	64.61+11.96	66.72+11.76
Skinfold (mm)	13.99+7.30	13.13+6.42	14.56+6.91	22.93+7.73	23.09+7.12	25.56+6.72
BMI (kg/m^2)	24.26+4.31	24.35+4.76	24.02+3.88	23.24+4.02	23.45+3.96	24.36+4.13
Fat per cent	20.47+7.54*	21.11+7.11	23.90+7.56*	31.00+4.42*	31.24+4.07	33.01+3.93*

No work = 0 hr/wk, Irregular = 1-19 hrs/wk, Regular = 20 hrs and more/wk.

* $p < 0.05$ level indicating significant differences between/ among work categories within a gender.

(26 per cent) of 19y. old females reported not working. Among the lower division female student 48per cent reported a 'not working' status.

The majority of students living on-campus reported not working at all (males 78 per cent, females 57 per cent), while only 21 per cent of male and 14 per cent of female off-campus students reported not working. Of the off-campus students that do work, 37 per cent of males and 36per cent of females was working regularly i.e. working at least 20 hours a week.

Mean hours of sleep per night for males (7.33 hours) and females (7.39 hours) were quite similar. For males, hours for sleep was not affected by employment status but a significant association were found for females. Of the male students who reported sleeping less than 7 hours, 27 per cent worked 20 or more hours per week. Of the female students reporting sleeping less than 7 hours, 39 per cent of them worked 'regularly'. Of the male students reporting more than eight hours of sleep, 26 per cent worked regularly, and 6per cent of the female students in the same sleep duration worked regularly.

Regardless of gender, more than half of all working students reported an insufficient amount of MVPA. Non-working males were the only group to report more than 50 per cent performing sufficient weekly PA (moderate to vigorous activity for four or more days). All other work categories reported more than half of all students performing no weekly PA or less than sufficient weekly PA.

The female students who used to eat fast food daily, 71 per cent were working and 40 per cent were working regularly. This demonstrated a significant association between fast food consumption and working status in female students, however, there were no significant relationship in male students (52 per cent were working and 36 per cent were working regularly). A significant association was also noticed between work status and daily fruit and vegetable (FV) consumption in female students but not in male students, with a lower proportion of students consuming 3 or more servings daily of FV as work category increased.

The vast majority of all students did not use cigarettes (males 90.4 per cent, females 93.5 per cent). However, of the female students who reported smoking regularly, 53 per cent of them also worked regularly, which was significant. For males, working status had no effect on cigarette smoking. Although alcohol consumption was not significantly different for any work category in either gender, there was a trend towards a greater proportion of students consuming alcohol as the hours of work increased.

Results of the descriptive statistics for sedentary activities (screen time and television viewing time), homework, and certain anthropometric variables (body weight, BMI, and triceps skinfold), showed no significant association among the different employment categories for either gender. ANOVA and LSD post hoc test showed body fat percentage in both males and females to be significantly higher in the regularly working group compared to the non-workers.

The association of employment status with the physical and lifestyle variables in college students were assessed through calculating the multinomial logistic regression and the results were presented in Table 18.2 for each gender. A negative association of employment status and age was reported for both genders. An estimated odds ratio of 0.44 for 18 year old males implies that the odds of working 'irregular' over 'no work' was about 56per cent lower than for those males aged 20 or more years. Similarly, for 18-year-old females, the odds of working regularly over not working was about 95per cent less than it is for females 20 and older. A negative association was found for working > 20 hours a week for both genders living on-campus compared to off-campus students, and also for lower division students compared to upper division students.

Female students working >20 hours a week were 14.7 times more likely to report insufficient sleep compared to non-working females. Employment status did not show a significant effect on hours of sleep for male students. Though not significant, working students tend to be less likely to accumulate a sufficient amount of weekly PA compared to non-working students.

Meal frequency was not affected by work status for either gender. Regularly working males and females are less likely to report eating no fast food, indicating that students working 20 or more hours a week were more likely to eat fast food than non-working students were. Conversely, males and females that worked the most (>20 hours/wk) were more likely to report eating no fruit and vegetable (FV) compared to non-working students.

Regularly working females were significantly less likely to be a non-smoker compared to non-working females. Work status had no significant effect on cigarette smoking in males, or on alcohol consumption for either gender.

There was no significant association reported with work status and sedentary behaviors of the students of either gender. Although BMI was

Table 18.2: Multinomial Logistic Regression Analysis Examining Association of Employment Status Different Demographic and Lifestyle Variables in College Students

	Male			*Female*		
	No work	*Irregular*	*Regular*	*No work*	*Irregular*	*Regular*
Age group						
18 years	Ref.	0.444 (0.370-0.870)	0.163 (0.081-0.330)	Ref.	0.570 (0.174-1.863)	0.051 (0.017-0.151)
19 years	Ref.	0.615 (0.300-1.260)	0.466 (0.241-0.901)	Ref.	1.538 (0.407-5.815)	0.413 (0.128-1.328)
20+ years	Ref.	-	-			- -
Year in school						
Freshmen	Ref.	0.426 (0.202-0.899)	0.299 (0.147-0.610)	Ref.	0.699 (0.203-2.401)	0.099 (0.033-0.298)
Sophomore	Ref.	0.875 (0.381-2.008)	0.722 (0.329-1.588)	Ref.	2.550 (0.596-10.917)	1.250 (0.348-4.486)
Upper division	Ref.	-	-	Ref.	-	-
Living arrangement						
On-campus	Ref.	0.368 (0.207-0.656)	0.118 (0.065-0.215)	Ref.	0.261 (0.107-0.639)	0.046 (0.018-0.117)
Off-campus	Ref.	-	-	Ref.	-	-
Sleep						
<7 hr/night	Ref.	3.960 (1.316-11.914)	1.555 (0.628-3.848)	Ref.	2.140 (0.755-6.061)	14.727 (2.851-76.088)
7-8 hr/night	Ref.	2.354 (0.858-6.458)	1.091 (0.503-2.364)	Ref.	0.820 (0.367-1.830)	3.553 (0.776-16.256)
>8 hr/night	Ref.	-	-	Ref.	-	-
Physical activity						
Not sufficient		1.356 (0.793-2.318)	1.561 (0.919-2.652)		0.853 (0.467-1.548)	1.813 (0.873-3.763)
Sufficient >= 4d/wk		Ref.	Ref.		Ref.	Ref.
Meal						
<3 servings/d	Ref.	0.842 (0.491-1.443)	1.329 (0.785-2.251)	Ref.	0.801 (0.442-1.452)	1.297 (0.659-2.553)
3 or more srv/d	Ref.	-	-	Ref.	-	-
Fast Food						
None	Ref.	1.435 (0.701-2.936)	0.531 (0.295-9.57)		Ref.	0.616 (0.271-1.400)0.251 (0.111-0.570)
1 or more srv/ d	Ref.	Ref.	Ref.	Ref.	Ref.	Ref.
Fruit and vegetable						
None to 2 srv/d	Ref.	1.004 (0.582-1.732)	2.043 (1.200-3.481)	Ref.	0.567 (0.304-1.059)	1.632 (0.828-3.218)
3 - 5 or more srv/d	Ref.	-	-	Ref.	-	-
Smoking						
No	Ref.	1.509 (0.187-12.185)	0.873 (0.354-2.149)	Ref.	0.950 (0.102-8.893)	0.208 (0.059-0.728)
Yes	Ref.	-	-	Ref.	-	-
Alcohol intake						
No	Ref.	1.241 (0.719-2.141)	0.776 (0.458-1.313)	Ref.	0.773 (0.403-1.480)	0.545 (0.268-1.112)
Yes	Ref.	-	-	Ref.	-	-
Screen time						
<1hr.	Ref.	0.865 (0.339-2.210)	0.923 (0.380-2.243)	Ref.	0.707 (0.252-1.987)	2.860 (0.865-9.458)
1hr. to <2hr.	Ref.	1.500 (0.632-3.560)	1.833 (0.816-4.118)	Ref.	1.241 (0.525-3.207)	2.296 (0.694-7.590)
2hr. to <4hr.	Ref.	0.920 (0.455-1.863)	0.682 (0.338-1.375)	Ref.	1.241 (0.575-2.924)	2.200 (0.725-6.676)
4hr. or more	Ref.	-	-	Ref.	-	-
TV viewing						
<30 min.	Ref.	1.086 (0.525-2.247)	1.075 (0.496-2.330)	Ref.	1.478 (0.599-3.646)	0.844 (0.327-2.178)
30min. to <1hr.	Ref.	0.841 (0.365-1.937)	1.689 (0.772-3.698)	Ref.	1.333 (0.456-3.899)	0.889 (0.283-2.794)
1hr. to <2hr.	Ref.	1.082 (0.516-2.272)	1.402 (0.658-2.989)	Ref.	2.359 (0.844-6.597)	1.614 (0.552-4.719)
2hr. or more	Ref.	-	-	Ref.	-	-
Homework						
<1hr.	Ref.	0.922 (0.427-1.991)	2.274 (1.026-5.040)	Ref.	0.769 (0.327-1.806)	1.689 (0.693-4.120)
1hr. to <2hr.	Ref.	1.208 (0.571-2.555)	0.970 (0.401-2.342)	Ref.	1.007 (0.464-2.187)	1.899 (0.346-2.340)

	Male			Female		
	No work	Irregular	Regular	No work	Irregular	Regular
Screen time						
<1hr.	Ref.	0.865 (0.339-2.210)	0.923 (0.380-2.243)	Ref.	0.707 (0.252-1.987)	2.860 (0.865-9.458)
1hr. to <2hr.	Ref.	1.500 (0.632-3.560)	1.833 (0.816-4.118)	Ref.	1.241 (0.525-3.207)	2.296 (0.694-7.590)
2hr. to <4hr.	Ref.	0.920 (0.455-1.863)	0.682 (0.338-1.375)	Ref.	1.241 (0.575-2.924)	2.200 (0.725-6.676)
4hr. or more	Ref.	-	-	Ref.	-	-
TV viewing						
<30 min.	Ref.	1.086 (0.525-2.247)	1.075 (0.496-2.330)	Ref.	1.478 (0.599-3.646)	0.844 (0.327-2.178)
30min. to <1hr.	Ref.	0.841 (0.365-1.937)	1.689 (0.772-3.698)	Ref.	1.333 (0.456-3.899)	0.889 (0.283-2.794)
1hr. to <2hr.	Ref.	1.082 (0.516-2.272)	1.402 (0.658-2.989)	Ref.	2.359 (0.844-6.597)	1.614 (0.552-4.719)
2hr. or more	Ref.	-	-	Ref.	-	-
Homework						
<1hr.	Ref.	0.922 (0.427-1.991)	2.274 (1.026-5.040)	Ref.	0.769 (0.327-1.806)	1.689 (0.693-4.120)
1hr. to <2hr.	Ref.	1.208 (0.571-2.555)	0.970 (0.401-2.342)	Ref.	1.007 (0.464-2.187)	1.899 (0.346-2.340)
2hr. to <3hr.	Ref.	0.590 (0.236-1.479)	1.374 (0.559-3.377)	Ref.	1.101 (0.484-2.504)	1.156 (0.435-3.072)
3hr. or more	Ref.	-	-	Ref.	-	-
BMI category						
<20	Ref.	1.133 (0.357-3.600)	2.078 (0.618-6.989)	Ref.	1.100 (0.292-4.142)	0.600 (0.143-2.511)
20 to <25	Ref.	0.741 (0.307-1.793)	1.139 (0.421-3.082)	Ref.	1.342 (0.420-4.286)	0.824 (0.252-2.692)
25 to <30	Ref.	0.971 (0.362-2.609)	1.781 (0.609-5.206)	Ref.	1.400 (0.383-5.123)	1.200 (0.322-4.469)
30 or higher	Ref.	-	-	Ref.	-	-
BMI (kg/m^2)	Ref.	1.005 (0.945-1.068)	0.987 (0.927-1.050)	Ref.	1.014 (0.944-1.089)	1.068 (0.985-1.158)
Fat per cent	Ref.	1.012 (0.976-1.050)	1.062 (1.025-1.100)	Ref.	0.972 (0.876-1.08)	1.123 (1.033-1.221)
Skin fold (mm)	Ref.	0.980 (0.940-1.022)	1.011 (0.975-1.047)	Ref.	1.003 (0.962-1.046)	1.047 (1.001-1.096)
Homework (min.)	Ref.	0.999 (0.995-1.002)	0.997 (0.993-1.000)	Ref.	1.000 (0.997-1.003)	0.998 (0.995-1.002)
Screen time (min.)	Ref.	0.884 (0.744-1.050)	0.999 (0.997-1.002)	Ref.	0.883 (0.739-1.055)	1.086 (0.863-1.367)
TV time (min.)	Ref.	0.999 (0.996-1.003)	0.999 (0.995-1.003)	Ref.	0.999 (0.994-1.004)	1.000 (0.995-1.006)

No work = 0 hr/wk, Irregular = 1-19 hrs/wk, Regular = 20 hrs and more/wk.

The numbers in parenthesis showing 95 per cent CI for corresponding odds ratio.

Values in bold with p for corresponding wald statistics < 0.05.

not significantly associated with work status, body fat percent was. The significant odds ratio (1.062) for body fat among male regular working students indicated that for each one percent increase in body fat there was a 6per cent greater likelihood of being a regular worker than a non-worker. For females, there was a 12 per cent greater likelihood of being a regular worker with each one percent increase in body fat. Therefore, both male and female students who are regular workers were significantly more likely to have a higher level of body fat compared to non-workers.

The results of the stepwise multivariate logistic regression analysis considered the employment status of the students as the dependent variable, and all physical and behavior traits as independent variables, were presented in Table 18.3 (males) and Table 18.4 (females). The analysis reported that only residence status is significantly associated to the working status of male students. The p value for goodness of fit was not significant (0.441), indicating the data are consistent with the model assumption in this analyses. The model was capable of predicting 58 per cent of observed data for male students. For female students, age group, residence status, and sleep were found to be associated with their working status. The p value for goodness of fit was not significant (0.393), and the model was capable of predicting 58.3 per cent of observed data for female students.

Discussion

The results of this study consistently show an association of health risk factors with regular working hours (>20 hours per week) amongst college students. The associated health risks are insufficient sleep, insufficient physical activity, low consumption of fruits and vegetables, increased cigarette smoking and alcohol consumption, high BMI, high body fat, and less time for academic activity. These findings are corroborative to the findings of Adam and Colner (2008) and Miller *et. al.* (2008), however, there is a contrast with the result of Leslie *et. al.* (1999).

Interpreting the negative association between employment status and selected health behaviors should be done with caution, as it also appears that those who work, but less than regularly, are do not suffer the same negative health consequences. Unlike students working > 20 hours a week, those working less did not show any significant increase in health risks or physical characteristics. Moreover, the group working less than regularly (<20 hours/wk) showed no differences in most health and

Table 18.3 : Stepwise Logistic Regression Analysis Examining Association of Employment Status with Different Demographic, Anthropometric and Lifestyle Variables in Male College Students

	Odds-Ratio (CI)			*Goodness of fit test*	*Predicted Correct per cent*
	Irregular	Part-time	Regular		
Living arrangement					
On-campus	0.884 (0.272-2.872)	0.300* (0.161-0.558)	0.119* (0.066-0.216)	p = 0.441	58.0
Off-campus	Ref.	Ref.	Ref.		

Irregular = 1-9 hrs/wk, Part-time = 10-19 hrs/wk, Regular = 20 hrs and more/wk.

The numbers in parentheses showing 95 per cent CI for corresponding odds ratio.

* p for corresponding Wald statistics is < 0.05.

Table 18.4 : Stepwise Logistic Regression Analysis Examining Association of Employment Status with Different Demographic, Anthropometric and Lifestyle Variables in Female College Students

	Odds-Ratio (CI)			Goodness	Predicted
	Irregular	Part-time	Regular	of fit test	Correct percent
Age group					
18 years	0.751	1.150	0.153*		
	(0.114-4.956)	(0.252-5.249)	(0.042-0.561)		
19 years	1.000	2.688	0.627		
	(0.132-7.548)	(0.576-12.551)	(0.169-2.326)	p = 0.393	58.3
20+ years	Ref.	Ref.	Ref.		
Living arrangement					
On-campus	0.728	0.261*	0.126*		
	(0.144-3.673)	(0.086-0.791)	(0.042-0.373)		
Off-campus	Ref.	Ref.	Ref.		
Sleep					
< 7 hr/ night	1.549	2.197	16.807*		
	(0.359-6.689)	(0.643-7.503)	(2.613-108.088)		
7-8 hr/ night	0.637	0.872	3.949		
	(0.201-2.021)	(0.327-2.325)	(0.712-21.914)		
> 8 hr/ night	Ref.	Ref.	Ref.		

Irregular = 1-9 hrs/wk, Part-time = 10-19 hrs/wk, Regular = 20 hrs and more/wk.

The numbers in parentheses showing 95 per cent CI for corresponding odds ratio

* p for corresponding Wald statistics is < 0.05.

physical traits compared to the 'no work' group, and for some variables even faired slightly better.

Data presented herein showed contrasting viewpoints regarding the impact of work on health, i.e. there is no linear gradient between hours worked and negative health behaviors. Therefore, it may be best to consider the results within the context of the social cognitive theory, as Miller *et. al.* (2008) have recently done. Bandura's social cognitive model (Bandura, 1997) theorized a reciprocal relationship between the individual, the environment, and the behaviours. In this study, college students were concerned enough about the rising cost of academics and cost of living to engage in varying levels of employment. Those who worked altered their 'environment' compared to non-workers; and the more hours worked, the more the environment was altered. This change in environment then exerted a negative influence on the health and health habits of students, particularly those working >20 hours a week. The time constraints associated with regular work seem to encourage college students to eat fewer meals, eat more fast food, and not engage in sufficient levels of physical activity. This in turn creates an unhealthy environment that is difficult to move away from as long as the economic pressure, real or perceived, continues to exist. Conversely, students working < 20 hours a week do not appear to suffer the same negative health consequences, similar to research previously published by Miller *et. al.* (2008). As with many behavioural traits, it can be hypothesized that students working <20 hours a week are better able to balance all of their responsibilities, and can therefore prosper; students working more (>20 hr/wk) may be less likely to strike an optimal balance of work, school, and life, and therefore suffer.

The interplay of all the preconditions and contributing factors explaining the association of employment status with lifestyle among the college students can be understood from Figure 1. It is noted within this study that the majority of off-campus students engage in regular work hours and have generally worse health behaviours than on-campus students. Living off-campus may be a key precursor to unhealthy habits of college students, as there is an increased financial burden along with the freedom to use alcohol and tobacco, neither of which are allowed while living on-campus. This presents an interesting paradox, as the off-campus student is likely pressured to work, or work more, to support their current lifestyle, especially compared to the on-campus students. However, this increase in work, coupled with attending classes, presents a barrier to physical activity, adequate sleep, and preparing healthy meals.

In these multifarious ways, the increased burden of work inhibits healthy living and thus creates the negative cycle of health.

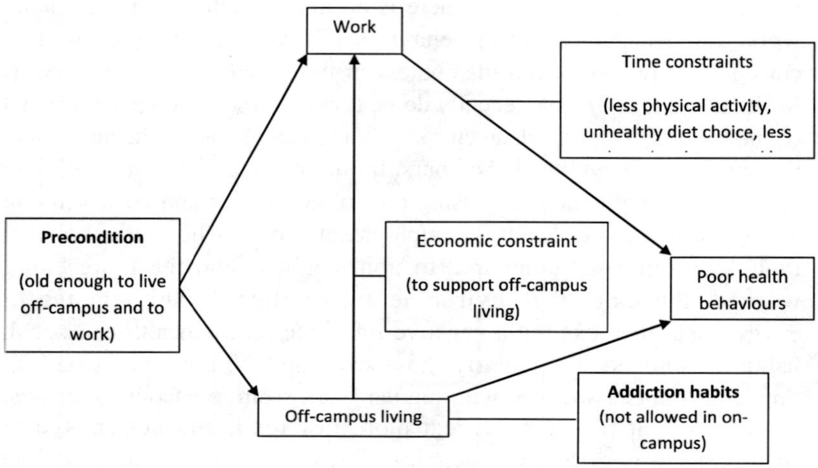

Fig. 18.1 : Schematic Diagram Explaining the Interplay of Contributing Factors for Association between Employment Status and Lifestyle among the College Students

This study is cross-sectional and implies an association rather than any cause-effect relationship. The sample of students was almost exclusively Caucasian and from the upper Midwest, limiting the generalise ability of the results. The study does not have data on socio-economic status of the individual participants, which may be a key deciding factor in the working status of students. The data were collected through an online self-reported survey, however, the questionnaire was pretested and care was taken for the validity of the data.

In spite of the limitations, this study makes a significant contribution regarding the present knowledge on working status and health behaviours in college students, an area that is currently limited in the published literature. While working during college has become almost a necessity due to family and individual finances, the amount of work should be carefully considered. Students that limit the amount of time spent at work also regularly engage in health behaviours, while those working excessively tend to compromise their health. Future studies on larger, more diverse populations will be needed to support these associations. However, the results of this study will be useful to the health educators, health administrators, and financial planners in formulating wellness plans for college students.

References

Adams, T.B. and Colner, W. (2008) The association of multiple risk factors with fruit and vegetable intake among a nationwide sample of college students. Journal of American College Health, 56(4) : 455-461.

ACHA/ NCHA. 2008. American College Health Association/ National College Health Assessment Spring 2007 Reference Group Data Report (Abridged), 56, 5 March - April 2008.

Astin, A. (1993) What matters in college? Four critical years revisited. San Francisco, CA : Jossey-Bass.

Bandura, A. (1997) Social Learning Theory. Englewood Cliffs, NJ : Prentice-Hall.

Pennington, D.C., Zvonkovic, A.M. and Wilson, S.L. (1989) Changes in college satisfaction across an academic term. Journal of College Student Development. 30(6) : 528-535.

College Student Health Survey Report. (2008) University of Minnesota, Boynton Health Services, Minneapolis, MN. 2007. Available at: http:// www.bhs.umn.edu/healthdata/

results/index.htm. Accessed July 15, 2008.

Durnin, J.V.G.A. and Womersly, J. (1974) Body fat assessed from total body density and its estimation from skinfold thickness: measurements on 481 men and women aged from 16 to 72 years. British Journal of Nutrition, 32(1): 77-97.

Ehrenberg, R. and Sherman, D. (1987) Employment while in college, academic achievement, and postcollege outcomes: a summary of results. Journal of Human Resources, 22(1) : 1-23.

Hager, R.L. (2006) Television viewing and physical activity in children. Journal of Adolescent Health, 39(5): 656-661.

Harding, E. and Harmon, L. (1999) Higher education students' off campus work patterns. Olympia, WA, Washington State Institute for Public Policy.

Healy, C.C., Oshea, D. and Crook, R.H. (1985) Relation of career attitudes to age and progress during college. Journal of Counseling Psychology, 32(2): 239-244.

Hood, A.B., Craig, A.F. and Ferguson, B.W. (1992) The impact of athletics, part-time employment, and other activities on academic achievement. Journal of College Student Development, 33(5): 447-453.

Juster, F.T. (1986) Response errors in the measurement of time use. Journal of American Statistical Association, 81(394): 390-402.

Leslie, E., Owen, N., Salmon, J.B., Bauman, A., Sallis, J.F. and Lo S.K. (1999) Insufficiently active Australian college students: perceived personal, social, and environmental influences. Preventive Medicine, 28(1) : 20-27.

Miller, K., Danner, F. and Staten, R. (2008) Relationship of work hours with selected health behaviors and academic progress among a college student cohort. Journal of American College Health, 56(6): 675-679.

National Center for Education Statistics. (2008) Mini-digest of Education Statistics 2006. Available at: http://nces.ed.gov/pubs2007/2007067.pdf. Accessed June 15, 2008.

Pascarella, E.T., Bohr, L., Nora, A., Desler, M. and Zusman, B. (1994) Impacts of on campus and off campus work on first year cognitive outcomes. Journal of College Student Development, 35(5) : 364-370.

Stern, D., and Nakata, Y. (1991) Paid employment among U.S. college students: trends, effects, and possible causes. Journal of Higher Education, 62(1) : 25-43.

Vandewater, E.A., Shim, M. and Caplovitz, A.G. (2004) Linking obesity and activity level with children's television and video game use. Journal of Adolescence, 27(1) : 71-85.

Vandewater, E.A., Bickham, D.S. and Lee, J.H. (2006) Time well spent? Relating television use to children's free-time activities. Pediatrics, 117(2) : e181-e191.

19

Conventional Health Care System in Selected Villages of Rural West Bengal : A Brief Glimpses

Abhijit Ghosal and Sovan Chakraborty

Introduction

Socio-cultural pattern of the community is one of the major factors towards the availability and use of different kinds of treatment. Health and disease are related to sociological and cultural resources of a community in a specific environment (Hasan, 1967). Local health traditions are mostly undocumented and oral. They are probably as old as the advent of humankind. These oral or folk medical traditions are extremely diverse, since they are rooted in natural resources located in so many different eco-systems. It has been estimated that about 8,000 medicinal plant species and more than 200 animal and mineral sources are used in treating health problems in India. These health traditions are dynamic, innovative and evolving and consist of various health practices based on local epistemologies and empirical experience. They are not restricted to any social or economic class.

Marriott (1955) had critically examined the socio-cultural problems involved in introducing more effective medical techniques to the conservative Indian village Kishangarhi. He took representative from different social strata and found out conflicts that were obstacles to the spread of western medicine. Prasad (1961) opinion that,

> "Our village society not yet completely emerged from the era of spirits, demons and theology influencing medicine. Worship of deities followed by fasting during disease and calamities. Conjuring and exorcism is sill practiced. Pilgrimages are made by a large number of people on the banks of the holy rivers as religious gathering under the divine tree to propitiate the Gods and the deities and to gain physical and spiritual health."

Khare (1963) focuses mainly on medical beliefs held by the residents of Indian villages and stresses the fact that these beliefs quite often link with the contrasting medical systems. Kakar (1977) has done several in depth studies of the socio-cultural aspect of health and illness in medium sized villages of Ludhiana district. Ghosh (1970) stated that diseases are though to be resulting from sins, crimes and disobedience of natural and religious laws. Religion has been held responsible for many differences and norms affecting the fundamental values and behavioral pattern in life including health behavior (Chaudhury, 1989). Every religion has three aspects: values, symbols and practices. Prescribed therapy to cure the diseases is the action of appeasing the Gods with prayers, vows, invocation, holy baths and sacrifices. The people believed in luck, charms, talisman, amulets, divine strings, divine rings, beads, horoscope, rites and rituals. Karuppaiyan (1986) in a research paper on Traditional medicine and folk societies asserted the roles of shaman as priest, magician and medicine man to heal the tribal people of Kerala. Shaman spits and beats the patients who suffer from hysteria. Shaman removes some hair from the patient head and nails them on a nearby tree-intrusion of spirits. He tries amulets, talisman on the arms and necks of the patients to protect them evil spirits that is sprit possession.

A folk medical system is any health system at variance with Western, scientific medicine, Ayurvedic, classical Chinese, etc. This is possible because folk health systems are open systems, accepting substantive input from and thus capable of functionally contributing to-economic, familial, ritual, moral, and other institutional sectors. Modern, scientific medicine, on the other hand, is a largely closed system, "based on precisely defined knowledge, technique, and procedures, all of which are discontinuous from ordinary social process" (Manning and Fabrega 1973). An open system is an adaptive system. It is capable of incorporating new environmental elements and thus "may change or elaborate its structure as a condition of survival or variability" (Buckley 1968).

Every culture has its particular explanation for ill health. Cultures provide people with ways of thinking, that are "simultaneously models of and models for reality" (Greetz, 1973). The traditional healer, as defined by the WHO (1976), is a person who is recognized by the community in which he lives as competent to provide health care by using vegetable, animal and mineral substances and certain other methods based on the social, cultural and religious background, as well as on the knowledge, attributes and beliefs that are prevalent in the community, regarding physical, mental and social well-being and the causation of disease and disability. Traditional or local medicine remains an important source of medical care in the developing countries even though it is not officially recognized by the government health care programs (Jaspan, 1969). It persists in urban as well as rural settings despite the availability of allopathic health services. Studies have shown, however, that its general persistence is decreasing its importance over generations, particularly among socially isolated nuclear families. In traditional medical systems worldwide, afflictions that beset body and mind can be explained in both naturalistic and super naturalistic terms (Kleinman, 1980). When a wound does not heal, when a sickness does not respond to treatment and when the normally expected and predictable does not happen, other explanations beyond the organic are sought (Scheper-Huges and Lock, 1987). Herbs were the first medicines used by pre historic men. They are therefore, part of every cultural tradition and have helped the development and growth of herbalist. Herbal medicine is a major component in all indigenous peoples' traditional medicine and a common element in ayurvedic, homeopathic, naturopathic, traditional oriental and Native American Indian medicine.

Area, Population, Materials and Methods

The present study was conducted in Matiary village of Nadia district of West Bengal. The village is situated at Matiary-Banpur Gram Panchayat in Krishnaganj C.D. Block of Nadia District. The distance from C.D. Block Office to the village is 26 kms. and from the district town is approximately 75 kms. Bangladesh International border was very near to the studied village. But the other side of the village was surrounded by the paddy field, International railway line and other villages. The village is connected by *moorum* (non-metallic) road with all season. Settlement pattern of the village is scattered type. The people of this village practice agriculture as well as they depend on daily labour work to run their livelihood smoothly. Different castes and classes were inhabited in the village. In the village Hindu people was form majority but Muslim, Scheduled Castes and Scheduled Tribes was also there. Total population of Matiary-Banpur Gram Panchayat was 7,253, among them 3,731 males and 3,522 females (Census of India, 2001).

The present study deals with the healing practices and traditional medical systems among the rural people of Matiary village of Krishnaganj C.D. Block in Nadia district. The major objective of the study was to understand the concept of health, disease and treatment as well as to examine the different magical and religious healing practices among the rural communities. It is important to observe the role and functioning of traditional medical practitioners in the community and collection of different types of methods of treatment.

To fulfill the methodology and objectives a purposive sampling was done for this study and a total 200 families was surveyed. Major emphasis was given into the case study methods. Village information and family structure collected from the villagers by using structured interview and observation methods. The data analysis was done by using SPSS

Table 19.1 : Age Structure of the Studied Population

Age Group (in years)	*Male*	*per cent*	*Female*	*per cent*	*Total*	*per cent*
0-4	39	4.23	28	3.04	67	7.27
5-9	45	4.89	44	4.78	89	9.66
10-14	62	6.73	50	5.43	112	12.16
15-19	59	6.41	43	4.67	102	11.07
20-24	44	4.78	39	4.23	83	9.01
25-29	34	3.69	38	4.13	72	7.82
30-34	33	3.58	40	4.34	73	7.93
35-39	41	4.45	48	5.21	89	9.66
40-44	38	4.13	30	3.26	68	7.38
45-49	30	3.26	29	3.15	59	6.41
50-54	22	2.39	14	1.52	36	3.91
55-59	22	2.39	10	1.09	32	3.47
60-64	10	1.09	8	0.87	18	1.95
65-69	9	0.98	5	0.54	14	1.52
70-74	1	0.11	3	0.33	4	0.43
75+	1	0.11	2	0.22	3	0.33
Total	490	53.20	431	46.80	921	100.00

statistical software and by case study. Below a brief structure was given regarding Age-Sex structure and educational status of the studied population.

Two hundred sample household had 921 members, of which 490 were males and 431 were females. The age structure of the studied villages (Table 19.1) indicates that 15.85 percent of males and 13.25 percent of females were less than 15 years of age. Of the total population 29.09 per cent were below 15 years of age. Similarly, it can be seen that 14.88 percent of males and 13.03 percent females were in between 15 - 30 years of age. The age structure is more or less stable from 15-40 years. The structure starts tapering after 50 years.

Educational Status

Education is considered as a key to the achievement of status and position in a society and it is one of the common factors which are behind the low health status. Literacy is a very good social indicator which shows the attitude of people towards modern medical practices and decision making. Table 19.2 reflects the educational status of the studied population and which indicate that 24.98 percent of the population is illiterate which shows their negligence towards education Literacy rate turns out to be 68.74 percent among them but most of the cases are of dropout. Female literacy rate (33.11per cent) which slightly lower than male literacy rate (41.91per cent).

Table 19.2 : Educational Status of the Studied Population

Educational Status	*Male*	*per cent*	*Female*	*per cent*	*Total*	*per cent*
Can Not Sign	103	11.18	124	13.46	227	24.65
Can Sign	1	0.11	2	0.22	3	0.33
Below Primary	10	1.09	5	0.54	15	1.63
Class 1 to 5	173	18.78	175	19.00	348	37.79
Class 6 to 10	134	14.55	89	9.66	223	24.21
Class 11-12	28	3.04	9	0.98	37	4.02
Graduation and Above	9	0.98	1	0.11	10	1.09
Not Applicable	32	3.47	26	2.82	58	6.30
Total	490	53.20	431	46.80	921	100.00

Health Facilities and Practices

Health is a dynamic concept which changes in accordance with the situation, whether it is created by social, economic, psychological or environmental forces. There are certain social indicators which manipulate health situation. Source of water, sanitation, drainage and overall hygienic condition are some of them.

Table 19.3: House Type

House Types (Material used for Houses)		*No. of Families (n= 200)*	
Roof	Asbestos	29	14.50
	Concrete	55	27.50
	Straw	76	38.00
	Tiles	40	20.00
Wall	Bamboo	68	34.00
	Concrete	79	39.50
	Mud	53	26.50
Floor	Concrete	89	44.50
	Mud	111	55.50
	Wood	0	0.00

In the present study, House types are one of the major factor which focuses on the socio-economic condition of the population. The habitation pattern is scattered. Majority of the houses were *kaccha;* built of mud and the roofs were thatched with straw or somewhere it was covered with asbestos but few houses were *pucca;* built by brick and cement. Some of the houses have walls made up bamboo covered with plastic sheets and the roofs were thatched with straw. There was lack of proper ventilation in these houses so, the rooms are remain dark and cool during day time. Very few houses have separate cattle shed.

For cooking purpose they used fuel as dry wood and leaves, crop residues, cow dung and others includes coal, gas, kerosene etc. In every house a cooking place is present but it was noticed that the majority of the cooking places were inside the house and rests were prepare food in outside their houses.

Sources of Water

The villagers depend on tube well and well for drinking water. But they were using pond water for general purpose, such as cooking, bathing, washing and agriculture. Pond water used for washing purpose. But some of them were aware that well water is not hygienic, for this reason they purify well water for drinking purpose. For purification they used cloths and bleaching powder but majority of the population were not involved purifying the water. As the water of those wells and ponds was unhygienic they were affecting by various types of diseases like, dysentery, cholera and various water borne diseases.

Table 19.4: Source of Drinking and Washing Water

Source	*No. of Families*			
	Drinking	*per cent*	*Washing*	*per cent*
Tube Well	124	62.00	111	55.50
Well	76	38.00	52	26.00
Pond	0	0.00	37	18.50
Total	200	100.00	200	100

Drainage and Sanitation

There is no drainage system in the villages. The rain water was stagnant in various holes and shallow low lands found here and there in the villages. In which mosquito lay eggs and for that reason the villagers frequently affected by malaria. The villagers have no permanent latrine in their houses. Most of them have gone in open field. Recently Gram Panchayat is giving sanitation facility to the villagers by constructing latrine. As they are traditionally using the free open field as latrine, they feel uncomfortable with the new latrine constructed by the Gram Panchayat. So, they are not availing the sanitary facilities granted by the Gram panchayat. They are took bath in village ponds and they rarely used soap and oil during bath. They clean their teeth with ash and *Neem* (*Azadirachta indica*) twigs. For this reason, various types of diseases like Tuberculosis, Malaria and Dysentery mostly affect the villagers. During the rainy season they are mostly affected with dysentery due to lack of the purified drinking water and sanitation facilities.

Pattern of Diseases

Disease and illness are two related terms, but there is difference between the two. It is argued that disease refers to an objective diagnosis of a disorder, while illness refers to the presence of a disease plus the individual's perception and response to it (Barren and Zarit, 1985). Some of the common diseases are enlisted in Table 19.5 which shows the disease pattern of the studied population.

Table 19.5 : Pattern of Disease

Type of Diseases	*Number*	*per cent*
Arthritis	5	1.87
Anemia	23	8.61
Asthma	4	1.50
Cough and Cold	43	16.10
Diarrhoea	22	8.24
Eye Problem	10	3.75
Fever	33	12.36
Headache	7	2.62
Jaundice	17	6.37
Malaria	19	7.12
Pneumonia	8	3.00
Reproductive Disease	16	5.99
Stomach Ache	10	3.75
Snake Bite	9	3.37
Skin Diseases	12	4.49
Tuberculosis	27	10.11
Typhoid	2	0.75
Total	267	100.00

A comprehensive list of the common diseases of the studied area has been given in the above table. Here the disease history of last one year has been considered in each family. It has been found that the common disease of the areas is cough and cold along with fever, tuberculosis and diarrhea. Diarrhea is caused due to the consumption of contaminated water and this incidence is common to the children living in poor living condition, unhygienic and crowded situation. Anemia is a common problem among the adult women. Skin diseases are caused by the pond water which is use for bathing by many people.

Health Units and Their Services

Every culture irrespective of simplicity or complexity has its own system of beliefs and practices regarding the concept of disease and health care practices. The Government has launched many health schemes but it is unable to fulfill the demand in every corner of the society. Besides, thousands of villages in India still do not have Primary Health Centres (PHCs). In the studied villages the concept of health and hygiene were mostly based on traditional belief and practices. Because of illiteracy, lack of health services and qualified medical practitioner, the sick and depressed ones seek the help from traditional medical practitioner and healer whoever is available in the region at the time of need.

Table 19.6 : Preference of Treatment

Types	*Number*	*Percentage*
Traditional	178	66.67
Modern	89	33.33
Total	267	100

The concept of family planning was present among them but due to low literacy rate and shyness of the people they have not used any modern preventive method. The women were more illiterate than male so they were believed more on prayers and offerings rather than any scientific method. Primary Health Centres and Sub Centres distributed free condoms but due to shyness and poor literacy rate they were not used it. The villagers have strong faith on traditional medicine men for curing gynecological problem and family planning. The new born baby was born in the hand of traditional birth attended or *Dai ma;* they were responsible to cut the naval cord of the new born baby with a sharp iron blade. The villagers have some rituals and traditions during pregnancy and delivery period not only for the mother and new born baby but also for the whole family and the relatives. During pregnancy period they are not allowed to go outside at night. The pregnant women tied a talisman to save herself and her upcoming baby from evil eyes. They also have some food taboos to avoid the bad effects of supernatural powers. After delivery the mother eats some herbal medicine as prescribe by the traditional medicine man if necessary. But in major complications they follow villages quack doctors or goes to the local hospitals.

Magico-religious Beliefs and Healing Practices

The people of the studied villages believed that diseases are caused by natural, spiritual and supernatural forces. Diseases are also attributed to the wrath of ancestral spirit, ghost intrusion, villages' deities, evil eyes and violating of some taboos. The spirit of all the dead members of the family are remembered and worshipped. The ancestors are given the offerings first before the food is taken by the survivors in the family. Villagers worship various village deities to cure specific diseases. Such as in case of chicken pox villagers worship *Devi Sitala*, for snake bites they worshipped *Devi Monosa*. The rural folk believe that the deities have strong power to harm the lives of the people. In order to obtain some worldly accomplishments and to enjoy pleasure they develop an affinity to them and unshakable faith in them. Each clan has its own deities or super natural entity and worshipped on special ritual occasion and even on festivals. These deities are considered as special patrons and protectors of the members of the clan.

Below few case studies of traditional medical practitioner including quacks and disease affected patients were given :

Case No 1

Gurupada Sarkar is traditional medicine man in the village Banpur. He is 52 years old. He has experienced in herbal medicines. He collects the medicinal plants from nearby fields and bushes as well as from nearby jungles. He also cultivates some medicinal plants in his court yards. He learnt this process of treatment from his father. He treats various diseases like dysentery, sexual problems, cough and cold, cholera, etc. He treated all types of patients including Hindu, Muslim, tribal, rich and poor from nearby and distant villages and even towns. The patient party had to promise in prior condition about the offerings they want to give to any temple or mosque after complete recovery. Now a day's he faced the problem about scarcity of medicinal plants, so there were some obstructions at the time of treatment particularly in case of serious cases. Because in past there were so many medicinal plants available in surrounding his house, but in these days there was scarcity of those plants due to lack of maintenance and that leads to make helpless situation at the time of treatment of serious patients. According to him the patient's category depends upon the seasonal variation. In the seasons of summer and rainy days there were large number of patients suffering from stomach problem and dysentery. The patients suffering from the attack of supernatural powers was lesser than the past. The treatment of a woman suffering from white exudation for a long time got remedy through his intensive treatment is considered as his best treatment during his long experience in this profession.

Case No 2

Asu Maity is a specialist in herbal medicine and soothsayer. He is 65 years old. He is proficient in establishing contact with supernatural beings through some ceremonies of divination as far as cure are concerned. He is always respected by the members of the village and looked upon as an image of high morals and ethics. He has taken fees from the patient but the amount varies from case to cases. He gathered this knowledge from his father. He is specialized in spirit possession. He cures diseases like *bhuta dhora* (spirit intrusion), soul loss, snake bite, dog bite and other poisonous bites. He gives talisman to the patients to tie it on neck or upper arm with red string. He also gives blow in air (*Jar fuk*), *jol pora, tel pora, nun pora* for different spirit intrusion cases. *Jol pora* is a cup of water with holy *mantras. Tel pora* is half cup of oil and *Nun pora* is one full tea spoon salt with holy *mantras* of different diseases like spirit intrusion, soul loss, due to malevolent spirits etc. Besides these he also practices ayurvedic and herbal medicines for curing diseases. He has a vast knowledge of different species of herbal plants. He cures patients of snake bite or scorpion bite by chanting *mantras* with some herbal plants. For snake bite he uses the roots of *Urena lobata* and applied on bite area as a poultice and one table spoon of paste is given orally. For dog bite he uses *Achyranthes aspera* plants. The root paste is applied over the bite area as a preventive medicine against hydrophobia. It is applied once, immediately after bite. He knows many more plants name and their uses but he is not disclosed the names because of the misuse of these plants. Due to deforestation traditional forest degraded day by day. So, valuable medicinal plants are not available in nearby locality.

Case No 3

To recover from general and casual diseases villagers' was to visit a quack. As the fees were very nominal so it was accessible to each of the villagers. Quack offered the necessary medicines to the patient's so it was an additional facility for the villagers and there was no question to go to any outside medicine shops. Radhamohan Dwary is a 72 years aged man was residing in the village Matiary. His family members were 8 including his sons, daughter-in-law and grandsons. He was a widower. Along with his medical practices he also managed the agricultural work. As per the requirement he also took help from his sons during the time of treatment. He claimed as a Registered Medical Practitioner. He was famous for the treatment in the field of hernia, female diseases and general diseases. But according to him patients of fever, malaria and typhoid was so high during those days. Clinical diagnosis was the main procedure of his treatment. He supplied major necessary medicines and he also performed minor surgical operations with the help of his assistant. As reported he had to check on average 20 to 25 patients of different diseases in a day. His practice time was 8.00 A.M. to 12.00 Noon in the morning and 5.00 P.M. to 8.00 P.M. in the evening. His remuneration was Rs 20 excluding the prices of medicines. But as he told in many cases villagers were not able to pay the said money. So he had to take the offerings as people can afford. He was experienced about thirty years in this profession but critical patients were referred to the hospital.

Case study of patients

Case No 4

During last four years Gangaram Ghosh aged 48 was affected by Diarrhoea. He was suffering from general symptoms of hysteria and did not know the reasons behind such happenings. Consulted a *Kabiraj* (medical practioner specialist in herbal medicine) resided in the village Banpur. The said healer prescribed herbal medicines for remedial purpose. The medicines were taken two times in a day and there were some taboos of taking non-vegetarian food. He had to pay Rs. 20/- in each time of his visit to *Kabiraj* including the cost of medicine. As his income was low so he borrowed money for continue of his treatment. But he did not feel any relief after taking medicine continuously for one year. Then he decided to visit district rural hospital but not able to mange any money for the said purpose. Then he again consulted with another traditional medicine man resided in Matiary village. After taking three months medicines he feels little bit cure.

Case No 5

As reported by his brother, Uttam Mudi age 51 years was mentally dis-balanced during last four years. He also informed that it was the malevolent action of a spirit of evil eye. First he consulted a traditional healer for his brother treatment. The said healer resided in the village Matiary (but he does not disclose his name). Talisman along with some herbal medicines was prescribed for the treatment along with remedies of spirit possession. Patient's family had to spend Rs. 60/- for the said purpose but there was no response after taking regular medicines and observing of different taboos. Then the said patient was treated by different traditional healer but there was also no satisfactory progress. As a remedial procedure a number of *yagya* occurred in the patient's house along with sacrifices of hen and goat. As a result of that different categories of talismans were given to the patient. A total Rs. 500/- was spent in each time for performing such arrangements.

Case No 6

Jaundice affected Chintamoni Soren realised that the said disease can attack any one due to natural cause. But she was not known about the specific reasons behind the disease. She visited the traditional healer for remedy. The patient and the healer were sure about the disease through yellow colour of urine, eyes and body. Further, reluctance of taking protein food was also an added symptom. A single dose of liquid herbal medicine was given to her. She had to follow some food restrictions for three months. Taking of high protein and fat food was prohibited. Patient had to give only Rs. 10/- to the healer for the medicine. She was cured within three months.

Case No 7

Rahim Sekh a 55 years old man attacked by Malaria and it suffered for two months. He or his family was not known the reasons behind the disease because it was first time in their family. After realising some bad symptoms he consulted a quack doctor at Banpur. He visited the doctor twice and had to purchase medicines following doctor's prescription. Blood test as advised by the quack doctor was the main diagnostic test for the detection of the disease. His family spent Rs. 1500/- for the whole treatment, which included doctor fees of Rs. 50/- in each visit, medicine cost, diagnostic cost and conveyance cost from village to district towns. To manage the said money all the domestic animals had to sell including some agricultural land.

Discussion

Though many advancements have taken place in modern health care system in the villages of the studied areas, but till today the villagers first contact their traditional healers before taking important health care decision. Reason for that was the non availability of doctors and medicines in nearby Sub Health Centres and Primary Health Centres. Traditional healing system is a simple divination process of a preliminary method of healing. At first the affected person was taking to the traditional medical practitioner. He smears the sacred mud on all over the body and keeps it on head. Until the manifest symptoms of the afflicted person subsided within the time prescribed by him, further probing would not be attempted. The elementary process of divination would cure those who have feared or the children having fever due to the attack of evil spirit. Hindus attach great importance to the holy water given by the priest of temple. They believed that the holy water has a supernatural power which has immense curative value. The holy water is generally administered to the different diseases. Such as in case of chicken pox, the Hindus sprinkling holy water which is taken from *Devi Sitala*, throughout houses and also smear the holy water throughout the body of the patient. Hindus and Muslim irrespective of their religious background have deep scented faith in the curative powers of the ceremony air blowing especially for cures children's illness. Children below the age of 5 years are taken to the Mosque early in the morning or evening. The pious Muslim (*Moulabi*) who came out from prayer, flow vital air on the children face and body. Any evil spirit or evil eye is cast away by this practice. Some even sprinkling holy water on the children's head and body and also give some water for drinking. The traditional medical practitioners were very much depending on herbal plants. Some herbal medicines are made from the powder of dried ginger; dried green litchis, dried green *bel (Aegle marmelos*) and tablets made from *kalmegh* (*Andrographis Paniculata*), *tulsi* (*Ocimum sanctum*), *basak* (*Adhatoda Vasica Nees)* are also used for various diseases. Some medicines are used in the form of country drugs (herbal leaves) to be prepared with vegetables and curry to be taken along with food. As most of the country drugs are bitter in taste, so the traditional medicine man advice the patients especially for children to mix drugs with ghee or honey. For fracture, head ache, body pain, muscle pain herbal extract mixed with oil, salt, turmeric is applied on affected region. Leaves are placed over broken limbs and bandaged.

Conclusion

According to villagers the diseases are caused by different reasons which are attributed to supernatural agencies such as sorcery, breach of taboos, object intrusion, spirit intrusion and loss of souls. Most of the rural people believe that intrusion of object or evil spirit into one's body may cause illness. They believe that wearing of dress or ornaments of dead persons may cause illness as the spirit related to objects may enter into their body. Many rural people believe that the intrusion of spirits which were not properly propitiated or for which necessary scarifies were not made. Measles, chickenpox, cholera, fever, paralysis, hysteria and other disease are believed to be caused by intrusion of sprits of forest, trees, rivers and the spirits of persons who died in accidents and during childbirth. They have believed in the existence of souls. The soul survives one's body and gives life into his body. Its loss or injury is believed to cause illness or death. The taboos are found regulating habits and customs related to health and hygiene.

To know the overall health status of a population it is very crucial to observe their day-to-day health consciousness and knowledge about health and hygiene. In the matter of hygiene the question of drinking water and sanitation are given the first priority. The availability of safe and adequate drinking water has a direct relation on the working conditions and health of the people and their capacity for optimum production. Water-borne disease and death, particularly of children every year, and the drudgery of women could be directly attributed to a lack of adequate potable water, inadequate sanitation and poor hygiene practices. Majority of the houses were mud built and villagers had the concept of using cow dung in their courtyard in every day. Further, it was used in the whole house at least once in a year. They were well known about the antiseptic quality of cow dung. The mud built floors are regularly polished by cow dung and for keeping it dust free they used water with mud.

The health situation of the population of a country like India can be improved with the amelioration of the health status of the downtrodden section of population. In India these can be achieved through the improvement of health scenario of rural people residing different parts of the country. It is stated that the present study is made to explain the concept of health, disease, medical system and medical belief and practices of rural West Bengal. Magico-religious activities performed to ward-off diseases, ghost attack, snake bite and related misfortunes. It can be said the blending action of magic and religion. In all the villages the said activities could be observed in different occasions and in different circumstances. The importance of magico-religious activities were decreasing among those villagers as they realised nothing could be achieved through that sort of practice as per health and disease is concerned. It was recorded that the use of different types of herbal ingredients, auspicious articles and special things in different rituals reflect the necessity of those in daily life for better health and protection. The studied population accustomed to use them not only in occasion but also for day-to-day survival. It also established that those people had a definite concept about good health and safe living and it was traditionally acquired from their ancestors. According to the studied villagers if cause of disease was supernatural then they were willing to avail the traditional way of treatment provided the availability and efficiency of the healer. So in a nutshell it can be said that the concept of health, disease and treatment is changing day-by-day and losing its traditional way due to impact of modern medical era. There has been a constant erosion of these traditions in the past two centuries. Besides the known reasons for erosion of cultural diversity, such as the western model of education, one of the largest contributors to the erosion of these local health traditions has been the acceptance of development models in which western medical systems are promoted. The current western education model fails to impress on the young generation the rationale and logic of the traditional practices, leading to their neglect. Modern medicine recognises the physical, biological and emotional aspects as the cause and treatment of diseases. In local health traditions, however, the communities consider that in addition to the physical, biological and emotional aspects, there is also a spiritual element in every organism. Consequently, many local diagnostic and healing practices include spiritual elements, such as prayers, offerings, and auspicious timing of the practice. It is common to find, however, that these spiritual practices are considered superstitious, as it is extremely difficult to explain the effect of the local health practices within the framework of mainstream medical science.

Bibliography

Buckley, W. (1968). Society as a Complex Adaptive System, In *Modern Systems Research for the Behavioral Scientist*. W. Buckley (Ed.), pp. 490-513. Aldine, Chicago.

Chaudhury, B. (1989). Social Science, Health and Culture : The Tribal Situation. *Social Action*, Vol. 39. No. 3, pp. 243-253.

Census of India (2001). *Census of India*. Office of the Registrar General, New Delhi.

Ghosh, A.K. (1970). Selection Intensity in the Kota of Nilgiri Hills, Madras. *Social Biology*, Vol. 17, pp. 224-225.

Greetz, C. (1973). *The Interpretation of Cultures*. Basic Books, New York.

Hasan, R.A. (1967). *The Cultural Frontiers of Health in Village India*. Manaktales, Bombay.

Jaspan, M.A. (1969). *Traditional Method Theory in South East Asia*. University of Hull, Hull.

Khare, R.S. (1963). Folk Medicine in a North Indian village. *Human Organisation*, Vol. 22, No. 1, pp. 36-40.

Kakar, D.N. (1977). *Folk and Modern Medicine (A North Indian Case Study)*. New Asian Publishers, Delhi.

Kleinman, A. (1980). *Patients and Healers in the Context of Culture: An Exploration of the Borderland Between Anthropology, Medicine and Psychiatry*. University California Press, Berkeley.

Karuppaiyan, V. (1986). Traditional Medicines in Folk Societies. *Bulletine of Traditional Culture*, pp. 49-60.

Manning, P.K. and H.F. Fabrega, (1973). The Experience of Self and Body : Health and Illness in the Ghipas Highlands. In *Phenomenological Sociology*. G. Psathas (Ed.), pp. 251-301. John Wiley, New York.

Marriott, M. (1955). Western Medicine in a Village of Northern India. In *Health, Culture and Community*. B.D. Paul (Ed.) Russell Sage Foundation, New York.

Prasad, B.G. (1961). Some Common Beliefs and Customs in Relation to Health and Disease in Uttar Pradesh. *Antiseptic*, Vol. 58. No. 3, pp. 225-238.

Scheper-Huges, N. and Lock, M. (1987). The Mindful Body : A Prolegomenon to Future Work, *Medical Anthropology Quarterly*, Vol. 1. No. 1, pp. 6-41.

WHO (1976). *The World Health Report*. World Health Organisation, Geneva.

20

Health, Poverty and Economic Development with Special Reference on Rural Odisha

Anjali Dash

INTRODUCTION

The role of health in influencing economic outcomes has been well understood at the micro level. Healthier workers are likely to be able to work longer, be generally more productive than their relatively less healthy counterparts, and consequently able to secure higher earnings than the latter, all else being the same; illness and disease shorten the working lives of people, thereby reducing their lifetime earnings. Better health also has a positive effect on the learning abilities of children, and leads to better educational outcomes (school completion rates, higher mean years of schooling, achievements) and increases the efficiency of human capital formation by individuals and households (Strauss and Thomas, 1998; Schultz, 1999). Health has a positive and statistically significant effect on the rate of growth of GDP per capita. Higher incomes potentially permit individuals (and societies) to afford better nutrition, better health care and, presumably, achieve better health.

Improvements in health result in improvements in national income, poverty could decline on account of both the standard 'trickle-down' effects and an increased financial capacity of nations to set up safety nets. There is a good deal of evidence suggesting that countries that experience a steep rise in growth rates of real GDP per capita also experience impressive declines in poverty (Barro and Sala-i-Martin, 2004). Improvements in health, when directed at the poor, can contribute more directly to poverty reduction and serve as an element of a 'pro-poor' growth strategy. The poor bear a disproportionately higher burden of illness, injury and disease than the rich. The poor suffer ill health due to a variety of causes, poor nutrition for instance, which reduces the ability to work and weakens their resistance to disease. With their body often being their main income-earning asset, sickness and disability have significant adverse implications in terms of loss of work and incomes, compounded by their inability to obtain adequate health care. Frequently, treatment expenditure and loss of earnings force poor families to exhaust their savings and assets, and take recourse to borrowing, leading to more poverty and poor health status. If health turns out to have significantly influenced India's economic performance; this may call for investing more public funds in health, given that health budgets have been severely resource-constrained in recent years.

Poverty is a measure of income that indicates inadequate command over material resources. The level of poverty in a country or region depends upon the level of income as well as its distribution. Any policies or programmes which alter the distribution of income would affect poverty. In a country or state with a large income inequality there would be a relatively large number of poor people or people with a low income (below a fixed poverty line), even if the country/state has a high per capita income. A higher rate of economic growth would reduce poverty if growth affects the distribution of income in ways that pulls up the bottom tail of the distribution. Countries that pursue a growth-oriented strategy firmly believe that growth will have its trickle-down effects that will help reduce poverty.

On the poverty-health link, some argue that poverty can cause poor health while others maintain that low income and poor health are caused by some common factor such as genetic endowments or education. Poverty can have an adverse impact on health because of malnutrition and also due to poor sanitation, unsafe drinking water supply, etc. Much of the disease burden in developing countries is due to the intake of an inadequate diet. Since expenditure on food forms a major portion of the budget of the poor, eradicating poverty could be instrumental in reducing malnutrition and the resulting ill health (Wagstaff, 2001).

Population with inadequate food intakes is to consider several related aspect of food: share of food in consumption expenditure and marginal propensity to spend more on food due to increase total expenditure and composition of food consumption. At very low level of per capita income, a household spend a very high proportion of its income and per haves, and even greater proportion of any increase in income on food. At such low level of per capita income, the average propensity to spend of food will be closed to unity. The marginal propensity will exceed the average and most of the food consumption will consists of the starchy staples. As income increases the average propensity to spend on food reaches a maximum equal to the marginal propensity at that level of income and then declines.

India is an agro base country where more than 60 per cent of the agricultural labour households are poor and account for the over 44 per cent of all poor households in rural India. The poor households self employed in agricultural occupations consist largely of small and marginal farmers, tenants and share croppers. Thus the phenomenon on rural poverty in India is primarily one of insufficient access to sustained and productive employment or insufficient access to land.

Trained in India

Gridding poverty is growing every day around the world. In spite of spending billions of rupees aimed at alleviation or reduction of global poverty, the problem has eluded solution. The socio-economic development programmes have, by and large accrued to the rich. In 1981 nearly 100 million people in the world were suffering for poverty, malnutrition, disease, despite that sapped their energy, reduce their work capacity and created despondency. Due to poverty infant mortality rate and malnutrition was high, life expectancy and literacy were far less than developed countries.

In India, rural poverty level was 57.33 per cent in 1971, 35.55 per cent in 1991 and in urban areas it was 45.89 per cent and 32.43 per cent respectively. After the economic reforms in 1991 the rural poverty rose. Poor are increasing year to year at greater pace during the economic reforms period. The poor are unable to pay for medicine when they are sick and are unable to afford even two meals a day. According to Prof. U.R Rao, "if the poor in India start eating one more food a day, the go down would be empty and India will have to import large quantity of food grains". He states emphatically that over 100 million people in the country go to bed each day with hungry stomachs. While food grains production has reduced a stagnant plateau, population continues to steadily increase which may result in a specter of millions dying of naked starvation in the coming decayed.

Several states, national and international projects aimed at directly attecting the poverty, of creating employment opportunity through industrialisation and Government sponsored welfare programmes have failed to realise the policy intents. Unless poverty is eliminated, no other socio-economic development could succeed. The poor counties spend less on health, education and other social infrastructures. Therefore illiteracy is more in the poor countries, malnutrition is excruciating, hygiene is not up to the desire level; population is more in under/ unemployed are swelling in number. A country with mass poverty can never succeed in its economic development too. Since economic reforms have turned anti-poor, suitable policy oriented towards the upliftment of the poor in real terms should be formulated.

Poverty encourages child and bonded labour and thereby compels children to work by ignoring education. So poverty caused literacy and malnutrition. All these prevent proper human development, there by resulting in the loss of precious human resources. Economic development can never be successful as long as mass poverty and illiteracy are not routed out.

In rural India, for ages, have no sanitation facilities. Over 95 per cent of rural societies leave their night soil in open areas since they do not have toilet facilities. Open air toilet cause environmental pollution create unhygienic atmosphere which cumulatively spread various kind of diseases. For overcome this problem community toilet should be built and properly maintained in all the villages are lacking proper roads and water drains due to which rain water gets logged in and around the locality, breading mosquitoes and other hazardous bacteria.

Odisha Context

Now we come to the case of Odisha Poverty and health situation and how it affects to economic development. Odisha is richly endowed with a variety of mineral deposits, and valuable forests and a long coastline, still it continue to be one of the poorest states in the country. As per the estimates made by Planning Commission in 2004-05, 39.9 per cent people come under Below Poverty Line categories which were 47.15 per cent in 1999-2000. In orders to tackle this problem, a number of poverty alleviation programmes are being implemented. Table 20.1

given below show the trend in population living Below Poverty Line in rural areas from 1977 to 2005 India vs. Odisha.

Table 20.1 : Percentage of Population Below Poverty Line in India and Odisha (Rural)

Years	*Odisha*	*India*
1977-1978	72.38	53.07
1983-1984	67.53	45.65
1987-1988	57.64	39.09
1993-1994	49.72	37.27
1999-2000	48.01	27.09
2004-2005	39.8	21.8

Source : Economic Survey of Odisha

In the above Table poverty trend in rural areas of Odisha reduced from 72.38 per cent in 1977-78 to 39.8 per cent in 2004-05 in comparison to all India level which reduced from 53.07 per cent to 21.8 per cent. But in urban areas of Odisha poverty has reduced from 50.92 per cent to 40.3 per cent, which rate in India reduced from 45.24 per cent to 21.7 per cent. The poverty trend in Odisha is declining but always this ratio is high in compare to national level.

Table 20.2 : Incident of Poverty in Odisha vise-a-vise Major States, 1977-78 to 2004-05

States	*1977-1978*	*1983*	*1987-1988*	*1993-1994*	*1999-2000*	*2004-2005*
Andhra Pradesh	39.31	28.91	25.86	22.19	15.77	11.10
Bihar	61.55	62.21	52.13	54.96	42.60	32.50
Gujrat	41.23	32.79	31.54	25.21	14.07	12.50
Haryana	29.55	21.37	16.54	25.05	8.74	9.90
Karnatak	48.78	38.24	37.53	33.16	20.04	17.40
Kerala	52.22	40.42	31.79	25.43	12.72	11.40
Madhya Pradesh	61.78	49.78	43.07	42.52	37.43	32.40
Maharashtra	55.88	43.44	40.41	36.86	25.02	25.20
Odisha	70.07	65.29	55.58	48.56	47.15	39.90
Punjab	19.27	16.18	13.20	11.77	6.16	5.20
Rajasthan	37.42	34.46	35.15	27.41	15.28	17.50
Tamil Nadu	54.79	51.66	43.39	35.03	21.12	17.80
Uttar Pradesh	49.79	47.07	41.45	40.85	31.15	25.50
West Bengal	60.52	54.85	44.72	35.66	27.02	20.60
ALL INDIA	**51.32**	**44.48**	**38.36**	**35.97**	**26.10**	**21.80**

Source: Economic Survey, Government of Odisha

Table 20.2 reports the percentage of population Below Poverty Line in Odisha as compare to other major States. It is observed from the above Table that though the incidence of poverty in Odisha is declining over the time, it is still highest among major States. As per the estimation made by Planning Commission, the percentage of population in Odisha Below Poverty Line in 2004-05 stood at 32.4 per cent. Further, the estimation also reflects that percentage of population Below Poverty Line in rural Odisha was lower than the urban Odisha.

Some special features of poverty in Odisha

As per National Sample Survey Organisation (NSSO) data, poverty group in Odisha:-belongs to Scheduled Castes/Scheduled Tribes households, are engaged as hired labourers, have households size 5-7, are landless or marginal farmers' with 0.5 Hector or less land.

Natural calamities

A disproportionately large proportion Scheduled Castes and Scheduled Tribes population in western and southern Odisha is very worsens position.

Rural poverty is the highest in Odisha because many of them depend on agricultural and forestry sector for their livelihood.

Odisha lack high quality infrastructure. A large number of rural poor, particularly in hilly and interior areas suffer from physical exclusion and are unable to access education, health and safe drinking water facilities. Optimal exploitation of its vast natural resources demands heavy investment in infrastructural development.

A number of Poverty Alleviation Programmes have been initiated to arrest the chronic and extreme poverty through employment generation and creation of durable and productivity assets with the support of institutional credit and provision of subsidies with a view to providing livelihood.

Self Employment Programmes

In order to improve the economic status of the rural poor, several anti poverty programmes like Integrated Rural Development Programme (IRDP), Development of Women and Children in Rural Areas (DAWCRA), Training for Rural Youth for Self Employment (TRYMES), Ganga Kalyan Yojana (GKY), Million Well Scheme (MWS), Swarnajayanti Gram Swarozgar Yojana (SGSY), Self Help Groups (SHGs), Sampoorana Grameen Rozgar Yojana (SGRY). Besides this National Rural Employment Guarantee Scheme (NREGS) is a scheme for rural people.

National Rural Employment Guarantee Scheme

The National Rural Employment Guarantee Scheme launched in 2005 for rural poor. This Scheme in the first phase, come into operation in 19 districts of the state w.e.f 2nd Feb 2006 and subsequently the scheme is in implementation in full swing in all the 30 districts at present. The salient features of the scheme are :

1. 100 days unskilled wage employment to a rural family in a financial year.
2. Equal wage for men and women.
3. Payment of wage on weekly basis but not later than 15 days.
4. Registration and providing job card in Gram Panchayat.

It does not matter how many programmes Government implemented to reduce poverty but it is a matter that how much that programmes are working. Many of the state failed this entire programme (Datar, 2007).In Odisha also this programme failed. Many of the villagers do not know that this scheme is for them.

Health Care Situation

In the case of health care services, access is a basic requirement and an important aspect. One can distinguish between two kinds of access: physical and economic. Physical access can be either population coverage-based or area coverage-based. Economic access refers to direct cost of accessing the services. In Odisha, the population covered per public health facility is good and the coverage is better than in nine other major states. However, the area coverage is very poor. The problem of physical access is compounded by two other factors: poor roads as well as transport connectivity. The economic access refers to a situation in which a majority of population will have adequate treatment at affordable prices given their income. It is thus not surprising to find that poor physical and economic access affect the utilisation of public health care facilities. Equitable access to health care requires that all citizens be able to secure an adequate level of care without excessive burdens. Discussions of a right to health care have frequently been premised on offering patients access to all beneficial care, to all care that others are receiving, or to all that they need or want. By creating impossible demands on society's resources for health care, such formulations have risked negating the entire notion of a moral obligation to secure care for those who lack it.

However, it is influenced by various factors like the degree of awareness about illness, the educational level and the accessibility, availability and affordability of health care services, drinking water facility and other factors like caste, sex and religions, choice and preference pattern. Demand is determined not completely by price and income but by occurrence and extent of illness. Some time moral hazard types of situation occur in the demand side. In rural areas who are underdeveloped majority of the people are too poor to afford payment. Poor quality of health services might be another major factor for low level of utilization of health services. Odisha is well known for her backwardness not only in terms of per capita income but also in human development indicate as well. Especially the health sector despite the intervention of Government and NGOs, the Infant Mortality Rate in the state remain at 69 per1000 in 2008, which is much higher than national level (53 per 1000). To reduce this IMR rate, mother and child health care National Rural Health Mission implemented where ASHA play an important role.

METHODOLOGY

The study is mainly based on both primary as well as secondary sources. Secondary sources like Economic Survey of Odisha, National Family Health Survey (NFHS)-3, District Level Health Survey (DLHS)-3, National Sample Survey Organisation (NSSO), various reference journal have used for the background of the study and primary level information has collected from a village, Brahmanipali situated in the District of Sonepur, Odisha. It has collected the responses of patients and other members of households belonging to different classes of households. The household were selected using a stratified random sampling procedure. Out of the 139 households with a population of 662 of the Brahmanipali village, 98 households were selected from the studied village. As per 2001 census 37 per cent are Scheduled Castes (SC), 26 per cent are Scheduled Tribes (ST). The village has two parts and the SCs reside outside the village and rest others reside in the main areas of the village. The average size of the sample household is 4.7. Of the total population, 337 (51 per cent) are male and 325 (49 per cent) are female. Of these 98 households, 33 per cent are SC, 42 per cent are ST and the rest are Other Backward Classes (OBC) and general. We have classified the households into four categories namely rich, middle, poor and very poor categories on the basis of annual income earned per household and assets. Of the total sample households 5 (5.3 per cent) belong to rich category, 24 (24.4 per cent) are middle category, 30 (30.6per cent) poor categories, and the rest 39 (39.7per cent) very poor categories. Most of the rich and middle categories have education 10th standard and above. By contrast the poor and very poor groups have low level of education.

RESULS AND DISCUSSION

Brahmanipali is a rural village of Odisha, where more than 40 per cent people living Below Poverty Line. Their main occupation is agriculture, daily wage labourer and some forest related activities. So the people mostly depend on Government health care facilities. But infrastructure in this village is very poor. Like tube well is the main source of drinking water. But the village has only two tube wells, one is located in the middle portion of the village and other one is situated where the Scheduled Castes (SC) households are inhabited. The SC do not uses the other tube well because of social barriers. The quality of water of these tube wells is not good due to lack of proper maintained.

They had to consume dirty water that comes from the tube well located in their locality. The surrounding of tube well is also very dirty as the used water get logged and absorbed into the nearby area of the tube well. In Odisha the coverage of safe pipe drinking water was hardly 9 per cent as per 2001 Census. Further hardly 3 households in the studied village have toilet. In Odisha 14.89 per cent of households have access to toilet. Majority of households use metal pot, earthen pot and cemented pot for storage drinking water. About 82 per cent of households use fire wood for cooking. Dwelling structure of the households may influence the health condition of the household members. The housing condition of the studied village is not satisfactory. Only 9 per cent of the households belong to rich and middle groups have *pacca* houses, and rests of the households have *kuchha* houses.

Morbidity Rate and Pattern of Morbidity

Morbidity measures the frequency of illnesses prevailing during the reference period. Table 20.3 depict prevalent rate of diseases (among both male and female) during the last 30 days from our reference period. This is compare with the NSSO data finding for Odisha in rural areas context relating to 52nd and 60th rounds surveys. According to 60th round survey of NSSO the overall prevalent rate of morbidity was 77 per cent in comparison with 88 per cent at all India level. But according to 52nd round survey of NSSO (with 15 days as reference period) it was 62 for Odisha and 55 for India.

Table 20.3 : Morbidity (prevalent) Rates of Diseases During last 30 Days in the Study Village

Different Economic Classes	*Male*	*Female*	*Total*
Rich	38	38	77
Middle	25	33	57
Poor	37	49	85
Very poor	34	48	82
Overall	33	44	76

Source : Field Survey.

The prevalent rate of diseases among the female in Odisha is relatively more as par the NSSO survey 2004. This is also similar in our survey, 33 per 1000 male population in comparison with 44 per 1000 population in case of female (Sen, 2002; Sunder and Sarma, 2002). The overall Morbidity Rate is high among the poor and very poor categories and this ratio is relatively higher among females compared to males. In middle class group also the Morbidity Rate among females is less in comparison with that of rich. The overall Morbidity Rate among the poor category is very high i.e. 85 in the studied village.

Table 20.3 depict that Morbidity prevalent Rate is high among females. This ratio is also high in poor category and low in middle category. Surprisingly, the reported Morbidity prevalence Rate among the Scheduled Tribes is considerably higher than that among the other social groups. Their low level of socio-economic condition, illiteracy and hygiene situation is responsible for high Morbidity Rate. It is observed that prevalence of illness increases with age.

Cost of Treatment

The high cost of health care has serious implication for the livelihood of the households in general and for poor households in particular. Households responding to medical need and spending a large share of annual income on health care may affect their other essential expenditure. The expenditure incurred for treatment of diseases has been estimated by us from the primary information collected from the study village. Due to the hospitalisation of a patient, a household has to spend a large amount of money which is beyond his capacity. In such a case he has to borrow from different sources because he cannot postpone such expenditure. In that situation the household has to spend a substantial part of its income for repaying the debt and it may end up in indebted situation. (Salveraj and Karan, 2009; Shing, 2010).

Table 20.4 : Percentage of Health Expenditure, Borrowing and without Interest Rate Borrowing

Different Economic Class	*Expenditure per HH (in Rs.)*	*Avg.cost per patient (in Rs.)*	*Percentage of Health expenditure out of total income*	*Percentage of expenditure out of total income*	*Percentage of Health expenditure out of total expen-diture*	*Percentage borrowing out of total health expen-diture*	*Percentage of health expenditure out of their own source*
Rich	41280	20640	14	57	25	24	76
Middle	11248	6297	14	71	28	45	55
Poor	4089	1961	20	85	24	95	5
Very Poor	1484	1033	15	87	17	95	5
Total	6702	3786	15	70	25	45	55

Source : Field Survey

The cost of medicine of overall patients constituted 23 per cent of the total health expenditure with high variation across classes of patients. It is interesting to know that in case of poor and very poor, this cost varied from 43 to 48 per cent in contrast to only 19 per cent in case of middle class and 8 per cent in case of rich group. Every group of patient has to buy medicine from outside, the hospital, where they seek for treatment either at private or Government hospital.

The average health expenditure per household where patients are found is given in Table 20.4. It was Rs. 6702 during the study period for overall households with large variance across different groups. Similarly the average cost per patient for the overall groups was Rs. 3786 with wide variation across the different classes, with Rs. 1033 for very poor and Rs. 1961 for poor category.

Health expenditure as a percentage of total income of different classes is given in the Table 20.4. Overall households it constituted 15 per cent of total income with wide variation across different classes.

Debt Position

Expenditure on medical care seems to have a negative impact on economic condition of the households. Borrowing or sale of assets is widely prevalent among the patients belongs to poor and very poor groups in the studied village. During the study year out of 98 households, 35 patient household had borrowed to meet their health expenditure. The main source of borrowing was money lender and the interest charges on such loans varied from 36 per cent to 120 per cent per annum. Most of the poor households have borrowed loan for financing health care expenditure on harsh terms and conditions. Indebtness situation is more in case of small and marginal farmers (Shing, 2010).

Conclusion and Policy Suggestions

India is a developing country where more than 40 per cent people living Below Poverty Line. They do not have adequate amount of food for a day. Thus their nutritional status become goes down. They do not have adequate energy to do work better. So majority of the poor have sought medicare from Government sector namely Primary Health Care Centre. The cost of health care in the Government sector is relatively cheaper in comparison with that of private sector. In contrast the majority of middle and rich groups have gone to private sector for treatment. It is observed patients of poor and very poor categories there was delay in seeking medical treatment. The reasons for this delay include lack of finance, lack of awareness and a subtle way of discrimination of girl child in the study village. Even this is also found in rural Odisha. An average of 15 per cent of the income of overall households utilised some variance across the classes in the study village. But borrowing for private sector constituted 45 per cent of health expenditure for overall households. By contrast, 95 per cent expenditure borrowed by poor households. Poor households had to borrow at exorbitant rate of interest transferring collaterals to the lenders, they would suffer income and assets loss and may fall in debt trap. In such a situation in rural Odisha there is urgent need for provision of Primary Health Care (doctors as well as para-medical medicare) and drinking water to reduce the morbidity, mortality rate and burden of diseases as well as proper implementation of Poverty Alleviation Programme. Even the gender significantly can be reduced drastically if there is effective access to Public Health Care at affordable price.

Policy Implication

A strong positive association is observed between initial per capita income and long-run economic growth in per capita income across the States. That is, States with a higher initial income have grown faster than States with a lower initial income. This has the effect of widening the gap between the rich and poor States.

There is also a strong association between per capita income and health status (LEB and IMR) of the population. The nexus between growth, poverty and health based on cross-sectional data of Indian States over a period of time point to the following :

States that have experienced higher levels of growth over the thirty year period witnessed a lower level of poverty, except Kerala and West Bengal.

Per capita income and the percentage of the population living Below the Poverty Line are negatively related; possibly the growth in income in the past three decades has the desirable trickle-down effect.

There is an inverse relationship between poverty and LEB.

Increasing investment in health is a required policy intervention for accelerating the economy's growth rate.

Growth-oriented policies would result in bringing about improvements in the health status of the population.

Policies promoting growth would also have the desirable effect of reducing poverty. Overall, there is a compelling reason for stepping up both public and private investment in health which would pay off in the long run.

Bibliography :

Agnihotri, B. (1999). Eliminating Severe Malnutrition in Odisha : Profile of a Campaign. *Economic and Political Weekly,* Vol. 34, No. 51, pp. 3616-3621.

Almas, A. (1999). Health Status of Tribals of Odisha. pp. 1. *Odisha Voluntary Health Association, Bhubaneswar.*

Ashtekar, S. (2008). National Rural Health Mission : A Stocktaking. *Economic and Political Weekly,* Vol. 43, No. 37.

Baru, R., A. Acharya, S. Acharya, A.K. Shiva Kumar and K. Nagaraj (2010). Inequities in Access to Health Services in India: Caste, Class and Region. *Economic and Political Weekly.* Vol. 45, No. 38.

Castro-Leal, Florencia, Julia Dayton, Lionel Demery and Kalpana Mehera (1999). Public Social Spending in Africa : Do the Poor benefits?. *The World Bank Research Observer.* Vol. 14, No. 1. pp. 49-72.

Das Gupta, Monica (2005). Public Health in India : An Overview, *Policy Research Working Paper Series.* pp. 3787, The World Bank.

Das Gupta, M. (2005). Explaining Asia's "Missing Women" : A New Look at the Data, *Population and Development Review*, Vol. 31, No. 3, pp. 529-535. The Population Council, Inc.

Dasgupta, R and I. Qadeer (2005). The National Rural Health Mission (NRHM) : A Critical Overview, *Indian Journal of Public Health*, Vol. XXXXIX, No 3.

Dash, A. (2009). Access to Health Care in Rural Odisha, M. Phil. Dissertation, Sambalpur University, Odisha.

Datar, C. (2007). Failure of NREGS in Maharashtra, *Economic and Political Weekly*, Vol. XLII., No. 34.

Donaldson, C. and K. Gerard (1992). Economics of Health Care Financing, *Mackmillen Press.*

Government of Odisha. *Report on District Level Health Survey – 2 and 3.* Family Planning and Welfare Department, Bhubaneswar.

Government of Odisha. *Report of Economic Survey of Odisha (2009-10)*, Bhubaneswar.

Haan, D.A. and A. Dubey (2005). Poverty, Disparities, or the Development of Underdevelopment in Odisha, *Economic and Political Weekly.*

Martha, C. Nussbaum and A. Sen. *The Quality of Life*, Oxford University Press.

Narayan, S.S. (2001). *Economic Policy and State Intervention,* Oxford University Press.

NFHS-2 (1992) and NFHS-3(2005) Odisha and India.

NSSO, 52nd and 60th Round.

Odisha Human Development Report (2004).

Pande, G.C., P.C. Pande and P.S. Bisht (2000). *Current Economic Issues Policies : 2000A.D.*

Selvaraj, S and A. Karan (2009). Deepening Health Insecurity in India : Evidence from National Sample Surveys since 1980s. *Economic and Political Weekly,* Vol. 44, No. 40, pp. 55-60.

Sharma, O.P. (2000). *Rural Health and Medical Care in India*, Manak Press.

Shing, N. (2010). Rural Health Care and Indebteness in Punjab. *Economic and Political Weekly,* Vol. 45, No 11.

Sinha, A. (2009). In Defence of the National Rural Health Mission, *Economic and Political Weekly,* Vol. 44, No. 40.

Zubkoff, M. (1977). *Health : A Victim or Cause of Inflation?* New York.

21

Age Variation in Obesity, Adiposity and Central Fat Distribution among the Bengalee Adult Males of Hridaypur, North 24 Parganas, West Bengal

Chandra Sekhar Roy, Ashish Mukhopadhyay and Mithu Bhadra

INTRODUCTION

Distribution of fat and the amount of fat in human body is very important to calculate the risk factor of various diseases. Abnormal fat distribution is strongly associated with various diseases. When excess body fat is accumulated in the body a condition developed which is known as obesity. Obesity is a worldwide public health problem; in last few decades, prevalence of obesity has increased at alarming rate all over the world not only in western hemisphere, but also in the developing countries (WHO, 1998). It arises when intake of the food is in excess of physical needs that means when the energy balance is not correct. Kopelman (2000) suggests that obesity is now so common in the world's population that it is beginning to replace under nutrition and infectious disease as the most significant contributor to ill health. The prevalence of obesity recently increased in Asia as well as western countries (Ohzeki *et. al.*, 1990).

Obesity has also been defined as a condition in which excess accumulation of fat in adipose tissue. In normal man percentage of body fat is 15-18 per cent. In normal individual 65-70 per cent of adipose tissue is fat and 15-30 per cent of total body weight constitutes with adipose tissue. Distribution of fat is very important in the study of obesity. Vague in 1956 was the first to point out that there may be two type of human obesity (android and gynoid), depending upon bodily distribution of fat. Furthermore he emphasized that individuals with android obesity (upper body obesity) had more risk of developing health problems than the gynoid (lower body obesity).

Body Mass Index (BMI) can be considered to provide the most useful for estimation of the prevalence generalized obesity within the population and the risk associated with it. It is highly correlated with body fat more than any other indices. In the present study BMI is used to understand the prevalence of obesity in different age groups and the variation within them. A graded classification of overweight and obesity using BMI value provide valuable information about increased body fatness. It allows meaningful comparison of weight status within and between populations. For meaningful comparisons between or within populations, WHO (2000) advised to use the single BMI cut-off points. A BMI of 30 or more is widely accepted as obese. It allows firm basis for evaluating intervention.

Obese individual with excess fat in the intra-abdominal depots are at particular risk of the adverse health consequences of obesity. Waist circumference is a good indicator of deep adipose tissue and it is related to fat mass and when it used in a ratio with hip circumference is also a good indicator of masculine distribution of adipose tissue. Waist circumference is a convenient and simple measurement that is unrelated to height, but correlates closely with BMI and Waist Hit Ratio (WHR) and is an approximate Index of intra abdominal fat mass and total body fat (Lean *et. al.*, 1996).

The Conicity Index (CI) implies that abdominal obesity is modeled as progression of a body from a cylindrical shape towards the shape of a double cone, i.e. two cones with a common base at Waist level. Unlike WHR, it takes into account the overall adiposity of the individual and is also independent of hip circumference. Theoretically, the predicted range of CI is between 1.00 (perfect cylindrical) and 1.73 (perfect double cone) (Valdez, 1991). Conicity Index has been reported to be associated with various CHD factors to a similar extent as WHR (Valdez *et. al.*, 1993).

Several studies from India have dealt with age changes in adiposity obesity and body fat distribution. A few studies have been conducted in the Bengalee population. A cross-sectional study of 279 older (50+ years) urban Bengalee Hindu Women was undertaken to find out the age variation in adiposity and central fat distribution by Bose and Das Chaudhuri (2000 a). Another study is age trends in anthropometric characteristic among elderly population of Bengalee Hindu men in Calcutta, India (Bose *et. al.*, 2000b). A study on age and sex variation in adiposity and central fat distribution was conducted by Gosh, Bose and Das Chaudhuri in 2001. Bhadra, Mukhopadhyay and Bose conducted a study on prevalence of overweight and obesity among adult Bengalee Hindu women of Kolkata, India in 2003. No study on obesity, adiposity, and central body fat distribution among adult men aged between 20 to 50 years has been reported from the Bengalee population. Aim of the present study is to find out age variation in adiposity, obesity and central fat distribution among the adult Bengalee Hindu men aged between 20-50 years and also the prevalence of obesity and overweight among them.

MATERIALS AND METHODS

Present study was conducted among adult Bengalee Hindu males residing at Hridaypur area within the Barasat Municipality under the jurisdiction of Kolkata Metropolitan Development Authority (KMDA) in the district of North 24 Parganas, West Bengal. The study population of present investigation consisted of 300 males aged 20 to 50 years. The mean age of the population is 36.82 (SD 9.25) years.

Requisite information on socio-demographic profile was collected by interview schedule method. A total four anthropometric measurements were taken for each subject. These anthropometric measurements include height, weight and two Circumferences — minimum Waist Circumference and maximum Hip Circumference. Body Mass Index (BMI), Conicity Index (CI) and Waist-Hip Ratio (WHR) were calculated using the measurements mentioned above. Body Mass Index and Waist Hip Ratio were computed using standard equations (WHO, 2000) or equations of WHO (2000).

All the anthropometric measurements were done by investigator using standard anthropometric technique (Lohman *et. al.*, 1988). Height was measured to the nearest 0.1 cm.. using Martin's anthropometer and the body weight of the subject was recorded to nearest 0.5 kg.. on weighing scale. Both for height and weight, the subjects were requested to remove their shoes and wearing minimum cloth. Circumference measurements were made to the nearest 0.1 cm.., using a steel tape. Minimum Waist Circumference was measured at the smallest Circumference of the torso, which is the level of natural Waist. Maximum Hip Circumference measurement was made horizontally at the level of maximum extension of the buttocks.

From the four anthropometric measurements– height, weight, minimum Waist Circumference and maximum Hip Circumference, Body Mass Index (BMI), Conicity Index (CI) and Waist-Hip Ratio (WHR) were calculated. BMI is the Ratio between body weight in kg.. and square of height in meter, expressed as BMI= weight/height (kg../m.^{2}). CI is the Index for measuring the central adiposity. It was derived from the equation proposed by Valdez *et. al.* (1993), where the Waist Circumference or abdominal girth is in meter, weight in kg.., and height in meter. The value 0.109 is a constant that result from conversion of units of volume and Mass into units of length. CI = Waist Circumference in m./ 0.109 "(weight in kg../height in m.). WHR it is the Ratio of minimum Waist Circumference and the maximum Hip Circumference. It is the indicator of abdominal adiposity. WHR = Waist Circumference (cm..) /Hip Circumference (cm..).

Data were collected on a pre-designated pro-forma and finally these data were transferred into a tabular form. The descriptive statistics like mean, standard deviation, were calculated using the specific statistical formulae. Variation within the age group individuals and between age group individuals of adiposity, obesity and central body fat distribution was examined using analysis of variance (ANOVA).

RESULTS AND DISCUSSION

Table 21.1: Anthropometric Characteristics of Study Population (n=300)

Variables	*Mean*	*SD*
Height (cm..)	165.09	6.77
Weight (kg..)	63.21	12.32
Body Mass Index (Kg../m.^{2})	23.11	3.87
Minimum Waist Circumference (cm..)	81.95	10.47
Maximum Hip Circumference (cm..)	90.75	8.26
Waist Hip Ratio	0.90	0.08
Conicity Index	1.22	0.09

The mean and standard deviation (SD) of seven anthropometric variables, Height, Weight, Minimum Waist Circumference, Maximum Hip Circumference, Body Mass Index, Waist-Hip Ratio and Conicity Index of study population consisting of 300 Bengalee adult males are presented in the Table 21.1. The mean weight of the study population was 165.09 ± 6.77 cm.. and the mean weight was 63.2 ± 12.32 kg.. In case of Waist Circumference and Hip Circumference means were found to be 81.95 ± 10.47 cm.. and 90.75 ± 8.26 cm.. respectively. Whereas mean Waist-Hip Ratio, derived from Waist and Hip Circumferences, was calculated and found to be 0.90 ± 0.06. Using the measurements height and weight an Index derived, known as body Mass Index. BMI, which is a good indicator of obesity, and the mean BMI was 23.11 ± 3.87 kg../m.^{2} in the study. The mean value of Conicity Index of Bengalee adult male of present study was 1.22 ± 0.09 kg../m.^{2}.

Table 21.2: Anthropometric Characters and Derived Indices by Age Group of Study Population

Variables	*Age Group*					
	Group-I 20-29years		*Group-II 30-39 years*		*Group-III 40+ years*	
	n=89		*n=88*		*n=123*	
	Mean	*SD*	*Mean*	*SD*	*Mean*	*SD*
Height (cm..)	166.40	6.82	165.00	6.57	164.13	6.77
Weight (kg..)	61.55	11.65	63.80	13.20	64.00	12.10
Body Mass Index (Kg../m.^{2})	22.15	3.48	23.27	4.02	23.69	3.93
Minimum Waist Circumference (cm..)	78.87	10.04	81.20	10.50	84.70	10.09
Maximum Hip Circumference (cm..)	89.25	8.25	90.70	8.16	91.80	8.23
Waist-Hip Ratio	0.88	0.06	0.89	0.06	0.93	0.01
Conicity Index	1.19	0.09	1.20	0.08	1.25	0.10

In the present study of 300 male individuals aged between 20 to 50 years were classified in to three age groups, Group I (20-29 years), Group II (30-39 years) and Group III (40 years and above). The mean height of the subject of the Group I was 166.40 ± 6.82 cm.. whereas in Group II and Group III it were 165.0 ± 6.57 cm.. and 164.13 ± 6.77 cm.. respectively. The mean weight of the Group I was 61.55 ± 11.65 kg.., in Group II it was 63.80 ± 13.20 kg.. and in case of Group III mean weight was 64.00 ± 12.10 kg.. A gradual increase in mean weight was observed among the individuals of Group I to Group III. Whereas mean height of the individuals of Group I was greater than the Group II and Group III. Using the two measurements height and weight, BMI an Index was calculated. The individual of Group I had mean BMI of 22.15 ± 3.84 kg../m.^{2} and in Group II and Group III the mean values were 23.27 ± 4.02 and 23.69 ± 3.93 respectively. Here an increase in mean BMI was observed gradually from individuals of Group I to Group III. This indicated a gradual increase in fat accumulation from Group I to Group III.

Waist Circumference, which is an indicator of deep adipose tissue and it is related to fat Mass. Mean Minimum Waist Circumference of Group I was 78.87 ± 10.04 cm.., in Group II it was 81.20 ± 10.50 cm.., and in Group III it was 91.80 ± 8.23 cm... Mean Waist Circumference, which is an indicator of central obesity, was increased with the increasing age from age Group I to age Group III gradually. Maximum Hip Circumference of Group II had the mean value of 89.25 ± 8.25 cm.., and among the individuals of Group II the mean value was 90.70 ± 8.16 cm.. and Group III had the mean 91.80 ± 8.23 cm...

Waist Circumference when used in a Ratio with Hip Circumference, Waist-Hip Ratio, is a good indicator of central body fat distribution. High Waist-Hip indicates central obesity. Mean Waist-Hip Ratio of Group I was 0.88 ± 0.06, Group II showed the mean of 0.89 ± 0.06, and Group III showed a little higher mean than the previous two age groups (0.93 ± 0.01). This result suggests that abdominal fat deposition was increased gradually from Group I tom Group III as age progresses.

Conicity Index is another measure of central adiposity. The Conicity Index was derived from the measurements Waist Circumference, weight and height. The mean Conicity Index of Group I was 1.19 ± 0.09, in-Group II it was 1.20 ± 0.08, and finally in Group III the mean was 1.25 ± 0.10. Group III had the higher mean than the Group I and Group II. This indicates that the deviation from the Circumference of an imaginary cylindrical shape to a double cone shape.

Table 21.3 represents the analysis of variance of the anthropometric variables. Analysis of variance (ANOVA) was performed to test the age variation in the level of adiposity, obesity and central body fat distribution among the Bengalee adult men aged 20 to 50 years. The result reveals that there was no significant difference in mean height ($p>0.05$) of male adult individuals belonging to three different age groups mentioned earlier. This is because all the subjects under study belonged to the Bengalee

Table 21.3: Analysis of Variance (ANOVA) of Anthropometric Variables

Anthropometric Variables	***Square of Variance***	*df*	*Sum square*	*Mean sum of square*	***F Ratio***	***Remarks***
Height (cm.)	Between the age groups	2	131.870	65.935	1.44	Not significant (p>0.05)
	Within the age group	297	13560.587	45.659		
	Total	299	13692.457			
Weight (kg.)	Between the age groups	2	399.839	199.920	1.32	Not significant (p>0.05)
	Within the age group	297	44981.072	151.451		
	Total	299	45380.912			
Waist Circumference (WC (cm.))	Between the age groups	2	1783.407	891.704	6.07	Significant (p< 0.05)
	Within the age group	297	43597.504	146.793		
	Total	299	45380.912			
Hip Circumference (HC (cm.))	Between the age groups	2	398.718	199.359	2.96	Not significant (p>0.05)
	Within the age group	297	20004.146	67.354		
	Total	299	20402.864			
Waist Hip Circumference (WHR)	Between the age groups	2	0.099	0.050	7.55	Significant (p < 0.05)
	Within the age group	297	1.949	0.007		
	Total	299	2.048			
Body Mass Index	Between the age groups	2	109.335	54.667	3.72	Significant

Anthropometric Variables	***Square of Variance***	*df*	*Sum square*	*Mean sum of square*	***F Ratio***	***Remarks***
	Within the age group	297	4366.428	14.702		
	Total	299	4475.763			
Conicity Index (CI)	Between the age groups	2	0.289	0.144	18.48	Significant ($p<0.05$)
	Within the age group	297	2.318	0.008		
	Total	299	2.607			

adult population. After 18 years of age growth in height is generally ceased so there is no further increase in height. Among aged persons after attainment of 55 years or above the height may decrease due to the effect of aging. A slight increase of mean weight was observed among males belonging to three age groups. But the result of ANOVA indicates that there was no age group variation in weight ($p>0.05$). That means age had no influence on body weight in the present study. HC (Hip Circumference) also showed similar result. WC (Waist Circumference), WHR (Waist-Hip Ratio), BMI (Body Mass Index), showed significant value of F test ($p < 0.05$) among the males belonging to the three age groups under study. It is established and also mentioned earlier that the BMI gives general obesity–adiposity of an individuals where as WC, WHR, and CI provide the condition of central obesity of an individual. In the present study significant values of F-test ($p < 0.05$) in case of above three measurements among the Bengalee adult males of three suggested that aging had some effect on these variables. The significant positive correlations of age with these variables were studied in the Bengalee population (Gosh *et. al.*, 2001, Gosh, 2002).

Table 21.4: Prevalence of Underweight and Obesity by Age Group Categories

Categories	*Age Group* Group I (20-29 years)		Group II (30-39 years)		Group III (40+ years)	
	Number of Individuals	*per cent*	*Number of Individuals*	*per cent*	*Number Individuals*	*Percent*
Underweight	17	19.10	13	14.77	13	10.57
Normal	49	55.06	45	51.14	65	52.85
Over weight	21	23.60	27	30.68	40	32.52
Obese-I	2	2.25	2	2.27	4	3.25
Obese-II	0	0.00	1	1.14	1	0.81
Obese-III	0	0.00	0	0.00	0	0.00
TOTAL	89	100.00	88	100.00	123	100.00

The frequency of underweight and overweight and obese individual is presented in the Table 21.4. The frequency of underweight ($BMI< 18.5$) was gradually decreasing with the increase of age. Group I had highest frequency of underweight individuals (19.10 per cent) and in Group III it is lowest (10.57). The frequency of obese individuals in different age groups were slightly different from each other. Obese III

(BMI>40.00) was not found among studied population. Obese II (BMI > 35.00) was also not found in age Group I.

The percentage of overweight was quite higher in the studied samples (29.33 per cent). The number of overweight individuals were more in Group III (30.52 per cent) and but it was low in Group I (23.60 per cent). In Group II the percentage was (30.68 per cent) closer to the percentage of Group III. This indicates that the amount of excess fat deposition in the body increased with increasing age. The overall prevalence of obesity in the studied population was 3.33 per cent. The percentages of obese individuals were similar among the three age groups; however, Group III had slightly higher percentage (4.07 per cent). The most important fact that derived from the result was that the percentage of overweight among the studied Bengalee population was at an alarming stage. It may be noted that the estimation was based on indirect technique, i.e. Anthropometry and international classification of adult overweight and obesity (WHO, 2000) cut-off points were utilized.

Table 21.5: Obesity Based on Waist Circumference in Study Population

Age Group	*Sample size*	*Normal*	*Centrally obese*
Group I (20-29 years)	89	48 (53.93)	41 (46.07)
Group II (30-39 years)	88	43 (48.86)	45 (51.14)
Group III (40+ years)	123	33 (26.83)	90 (73.17)
All age combine	300	124 (41.33)	176 (58.67)

Percentages are presented in parentheses

Table 21.5 and Table 21.6 show the presence of centrally obese individual in respect of Waist Circumference and Waist-Hip Ratio. Table 21.5 presents the prevalence of obesity and based on Waist Circumference among the males under study. The overall percentage of centrally obese individuals was 58.67. More than 50 per cent of the population was centrally obese in respect of Waist Circumference. The distribution of centrally obese persons among the three age groups show that the Group III had the highest percentage (73.17 per cent) and Group I had the lowest percentage (46.07 per cent) and the Group I just crossed the 50 per cent, the percentage was 51.14 per cent. It may be suggested from the result that the excess fat deposition in the abdominal area was increased with the increasing age.

Age Group	*Sample size*	*Normal*	*Centrally obese*
Group I (20-29 years)	89	55 (61.80)	34 (38.20)
Group II (30-39 years)	88	44 (50.00)	44 (50.00)
Group III (40+ years)	123	43 (34.96)	80 (65.04)
All age combine	300	142 (47.33)	158 (52.67)

In Table 21.6 reveals the occurrence of centrally obese persons among the studied population on the basis of Waist-Hip Ratio. The cut-off point of the Waist-Hip Ratio was adopted as recommended by JNC for WHR>0.95 (male). The overall percentage of centrally obese persons in respect of Waist-Hip Ratio was 52.67 per cent. But the distribution shows the higher percentage of centrally obese persons in age Group III (65.04 per cent); relatively low percentage (38.20 per cent) was observed in age Group I and the half of the total sample size of Group II was centrally obese in respect of WHR in the present study.

Considering the variables of Waist Circumference and Waist-Hip Ratio it was found that more than half of the surveyed population of Bengalee adult male of Kolkata was centrally obese. But in case of Waist Circumference the percentage was higher (58.67 per cent) than the Waist-Hip Ratio (52.67 per cent). In both cases, it is noted that the occurrence of obesity was increased through increasing age. Three age groups also showed the difference in the percentage of centrally obese individuals. On the other hand the percentage of obese individual on based on BMI was 3.33. It may be concluded that the prevalence of central obesity measured as Waist Circumference (58.67 per cent) and Waist-Hip Ratio (52.67 per cent) was higher than the generalized obesity. The result also pointed to the fact that in all the three age groups the occurrence of central obesity was higher than the as compared with generalized obesity among the Bengalee adult males.

Bibliography

Bhadra, M. and Mukhophadhyay, A. (2003) Obesity : A critical health problem of new millennium. *Journal of Anthropological Survey of India.* 52: 67-75.

Bhadra, M., Mukhophadhyay, A. and Bose, K. (2005) Overweight and obesity among adult Bengalee Hindu women of Kolkata, India *Human Ecology*, 13: 69-74

Bose, K. (2002) Age trends in adiposity and central body fat distribution among adult white men resident in Peterborough, East Anglia, England. *Colligium Antropologicum.* 26(1): 179-86

Bose, K. and Das Chaudhuri, A.B. (2000) *A Review of Studies on Central Body Fat Distribution among Indians.* Salmoli Publication, Calcutta

Bose, K. and Das Chaudhuri, A.B. 2000a Age variation adiposity and body fat composition among older Bengalee Hindu women of Calcutta, India. *Anthropogischer Anzeiger.* 61: 311-321.

Bose, K. and Mascie -Taylor, C.G.N. (1998) Conicity Index and Waist-Hip Ratio and their relationsHip with total cholesterol and blood pressure in middle-aged European and migrant Pakistani men. *Annals of Human Biology*, 25(1) : 11-16

Gosh, A., Bose, K. and Das Chaudhuri, A.B. (2000) A Comparison of anthropometric characteristics between normotensive and hypertensive individuals among a population of Bengalee Hindu elderly men in Calcutta, India. *Journal of Royal Society for the Promotion of Health*, 120(2): 100-106.

Gosh, A., Bose, K. and Das Chaudhuri, A.B. (2001) Age and sex variation in adiposity and central fat distribution among elderly Bengalee Hindus of Calcutta, India. *Annals of Human Biology*, 28(6): 616-623.

Gosh, A., Bose, K., Chakravarti, S., Das Chaudhuri, A.B., Chottopadhyay, J.and Dasgupta, S. (2004) Central obesity and coronary risk factors. *The Journal of The Royal Society for the Promotion of Health,* 24(2): 86-90.

Henneberg, M. and Veitch, D. (2002) Is obesity is as measured by body Mass Index and Waist Circumference in adult Australian women just as a result of the life style? *Human Ecology*, Special Issue No.13. New Delhi Kamal Raj.

Khongsdier, R. (2001) Body Mass Index of adult males in 12 populations of Northeast India. *Annals of Human Biology*, 28(4): 374-383

Kopelman, P.G. (2000) Obesity as a medical problem. *Nature*, 404: 635-643

Lean, M.E.J., Han, T.S. and Deurenberg, P. (1996) Predicting body composition from simple anthropometric measurements. *American Journal of Clinical Nutrition*, 63:4-14

Lohman, T.G., Roche, A.F. and Martorell, R. (1998) *Antropometric Standardisation Reference Manual.* Chicago: Human Kinetics Book.

Musaiger, A.O. and AL-Mannai, M.A. (2001) Weight, height, body Mass Index and prevalence of obesity among the adult population in Bahrain. *Annals of Human Biology, 28*(3): 346-350

Vague, J. (1956) The degree of masculine differentiation of obesity: A factor determining predispositions to diabetes, atherosclerosis, gout and uric calculous disease. *American Journal of Clinical Nutrition*, 4:20-34.

Valdez, R. (1991) A simple model-based Index of abdominal adiposity. *Journal of Clinical Epidemiology,* 44: 955-956

Valdez, R., Seidell, J.C., Ahy, Y.I. and Weiss, K.M. (1993) Anew Index of abdominal adiposity as an indicator of risk for cardiovascular disease. A cross population study. *International Journal of Obesity*, 17:77-82.

World Health Organization (2000). Obesity, preventing, and managing the global epidemic. *Report of the WHO Consultation Technical Report Series*, No.894., Geneva: World Health Organization.

22

Nutritional Assessment of Adult Male Munda and Oraon Tribals of Paschim Medinipur, West Bengal, India

Kaushik Bose, Bigitendriya Debsharma, Subal Das

Introduction

This chapter reports an anthropological research undertaken on adult male Munda and Oraon, tribals of Paschim Medinipur. India probably has the largest number of tribal communities in the World (Topal & Samal, 2001). The vast majority of the tribal populations reside in rural areas of the country. An anthropometric assessment of health and nutritional status of the community with respect to Body Mass Index (BMI) and Mid Upper Arm Circumference (MUAC) records the state of health of the population that lives under poor economic conditions. In general, tribal populations of India are recognized as socially and economically vulnerable (Collins, *et. al.,* 2000).

Ferro-Luzzi and James, 1996 have proposed MUAC cut-off points for use in screening acute adult under-nutrition. They base these on extrapolation from more normally nourished populations in developing countries, without reference to data from acutely undernourished adults during famine. Although there is some evidence that the undernourished category may be associated with increased morbidity in chronically undernourished populations (Duffield, 1998), we doubt whether the criteria proposed are appropriate for screening acutely undernourished adults. The MUAC has been recommended as a useful measure in diagnosis of malnutrition among adults in developing countries (James *et.al.,* 1994). MUAC is an appropriate indicator for the assessment of acute adult under-nutrition. The indicator is useful for both screening acute adult under-nutrition and for estimating prevalence of under-nutrition at a population level.

Objective of present study was to evaluate the nutritional status, based on MUAC and BMI of adult Munda and Oraon of Paschim Medinipur District, West Bengal. We also compared our findings with available previous studies which have evaluated nutritional status of various populations based on BMI and MUAC.

Materials and Methods :

Study Sample :

This cross sectional study was conducted among 210 (106 Munda and 104 Oraon) adult male age ranges from 18 to 75 years were measured from both tribal communities. The total population of West Bengal at 2001 Census has been 80,176,197. Of these 4,406,794 persons were Scheduled Tribes (STs) constitute 5.5 per cent of the total population of the State. The State has registered 15.7 per cent decadal growth of ST population in 1991-2001 (D.C.O., 2005). There are total thirty eight (38) notified STs in the State. Oraon comprises 14 per cent and Munda, 7.8 per cent of the total Scheduled Tribes population of West Bengal.

Study Area :

This study was carried out as part of a dissertation work being undertaken by the author (BD). The study area comprised of two villages namely Muradanga and Taldanga; situated approximately 130 kms. from Kolkata, the provincial capital of West Bengal.

Measurements :

Internationally accepted standard protocol was followed (Lohman *et.al.,* 1998) for anthropometric measurements. Anthropometric variables include height, weight and mid upper arm circumferences. The information on ethnicity and age were obtained from all subjects in prepared questionnaire.

The BMI was computed using the following standard equation :

BMI = Weight (kg.) / height (m.^{2}).

Nutritional status was evaluated using internationally accepted BMI guidelines (WHO, 1995). The following cut-off points were used :

CED BMI <18.5

Normal: BMI = 18.5-24.9

Overweight: BMI e" 25.0

CED was further divided into CED III, CED II and CED I as BMI < 16.0, 16.0-16.9 and 17.0-18.4 kg./m.2, respectively.

We followed the World Health Organization's classification (1995) of the public health problem of low BMI, based on adult populations worldwide. This classification categorises prevalence according to percentage of a population with BMI< 18.5.

Low (5-9 per cent): warning sign, monitoring required.

Medium (10-19 per cent): poor situation.

High (20-39 per cent): serious situation.

Very high (e" 40 per cent): critical situation.

MUAC (cm.) = Mid-Upper Arm Circumference

Males and females were classified as undernourished if they had MUAC values of < 23.0 cm. and < 22.0 cm., respectively.

Student's t-test was performed to test for sex differences in mean MUAC and BMI. Age-group differences in CED based on MUAC and BMI were determined by ANOVA test (F test). All statistical analyses were undertaken using the SPSS Statistical Package. Statistical significance was set at $p < 0.05$.

Result

Age-group specific number, Mean, Standard Deviation and prevalence of CED distribution for the Body Mass Index (BMI) and Mid-Upper Arm Circumference (MUAC) of Munda and Oraon adults are presented in Tables 1 and 2. Mean MUAC were 23.05 cm. (Munda) and 23.61 cm. (Oraon). Of these, 35.8 per cent Munda and 29.6 per cent Oraon had an arm circumference measurement that was less than standard cut-off value for men (23 cm.). Similarly, 35.8 per cent Munda and 36.5 per cent Oraon had BMI less than 18.50- 24.99 kg./m.^{2} (normal range). Examination of the arm circumference and BMI means and prevalence of CED calculated for Munda and Oraon of four different age groups revealed an apparent effect of age on this parameter among them. The mean MUAC was greatest for Munda (24.36 cm.) aged 31 to 40 years and least for Munda (21.60 cm.) aged > 50 years in the oldest age group and the BMI mean was greatest for Munda (20.75 kg./m.^{2}) aged 31 to 40 years and least for Munda (18.19 kg./m.^{2}) aged > 50 years in the oldest age group. While the arm circumference mean was greatest for Oraon (23.98 cm.) aged 18 to 30 years and least for Oraon (22.62 cm.) in the oldest age group and the BMI mean was greatest for Oraon (19.84 kg./m.^{2}) aged 18 to 30 years and least for Oraon (18.15 kg./m.^{2}) in the oldest age group respectively.

Table 22.1 : Estimated Prevalence of Under-nutrition Based on BMI and MUAC Among Adult Male Munda of Paschim Medinipur District, West Bengal

Age Group (in years)	*Sample Size*	*BMI (kg./m.^{2})*		*MUAC (cm.)*		*BMI (kg./m.^{2})*	*MUAC (cm.)*
		x	*s.d.*	*x*	*s.d.*	*CED (per cent)*	*CED (per cent)*
18-30	45	19.25	1.71	23.27	1.68	37.8	26.7
31-40	16	20.75	2.67	24.36	1.94	6.2	18.8
41-50	22	19.73	2.26	23.18	2.40	40.9	40.9
> 50	23	18.19	2.24	21.60	2.41	47.8	60.9
Total	106	F= 4.941; P= 0.003		F= 6.219; P= 0.001			

Table 22.2 : Estimated Prevalence of Under-nutrition Based on BMI and MUAC Among Adult Male Oraon of Paschim Medinipur District, West Bengal

Age Group (in years)	*No.*	*BMI (kg./m.^{2})*		*MUAC (cm.)*		*BMI (kg./m.^{2})*	*MUAC (cm.)*
		x	*s.d.*	*x*	*s.d.*	*CED (per cent)*	*CED (per cent)*
18-30	54	19.84	2.12	23.98	1.97	29.6	22.2
31-40	21	19.31	2.17	23.79	2.21	42.9	28.6
41-50	14	19.58	2.35	23.0	1.57	21.4	28.6
> 50	15	18.15	3.16	22.62	1.58	66.7	60.0
Total	104	F= 2.090; P= 0.106		F= 2.502; P= 0.064			

Prevalence of CED among Munda (Table 22.1) based on MUAC and BMI clearly revealed that with the advancement of age, prevalence of CED also inclined (except 31 - 40 years) gradually and the prevalence of CED increase was maximum (20.0 per cent, based on MUAC) for >50 years age group and 6.9 per cent (based on BMI) for > 50 years. Similarly prevalence of CED among Oraon based on MUAC and BMI showed gradual incline in CED from 18-30 years to > 50 years (except 41 - 50 years) then suddenly incline of 31.4 per cent (based on MUAC) for > 50 years of age group and 45.3 per cent (based on BMI) at the same age group. There were no significant ethnic differences existed both in MUAC and BMI. There is clear age group difference observed among Munda for mean MUAC (F = 6.219***, df = 3) and BMI (F = 4.941**, df = 3). No significant age group difference existed among Oraon for mean MUAC. Thus, it is clear from the Tables that Munda and Oraon adults of Midnapore, West Bengal are in very serious to critical situation for all age groups (except 31 - 40 years Munda) and the oldest among them are experiencing the most critical situation with respect to their health and nutritional status.

Discussion and Conclusion

WHO (1995) states that conventional BMI cutoffs for defining CED may not be appropriate for older people 70 years and over, because of age-related changes in body composition. In the absence of alternatives, we used the conventional values, but feel strongly that research is needed on this subject.

Mid Upper Arm Circumference (MUAC) has recently emerged in the literature as a potential screening tool for poor nutritional status (James *et.al.,* 1994) analyzed its usefulness in adults, and calculated cut-off equivalent to Body Mass Index (BMI) and cut-off for Chronic Energy Deficiency (CED), using a range of data sets from developing countries. MUAC is an appropriate indicator for the assessment of acute adult under-nutrition. This indicator is useful for both screening acute adult under-nutrition and for estimating prevalence of under-nutrition at a population level (Collins *et.al.,* 2000). The assessment of adult nutritional status using MUAC requires no equipment apart from a tape measure. As the index is the actual measurement itself, mathematical manipulation of the measurement obtained is not necessary. The ease with which MUAC can be assessed makes it suitable for nutritional screening during the height of an emergency where time and skilled personnel are at a premium (Collins *et.al.,* 2000).

Figure 1 compares the prevalence of CED based on BMI among the different ethnic groups with the present study. It is clear from this figure that Mundas (35.8 per cent) and Oraons (36.5 per cent) of the Midnapore were experiencing serious nutritional stress. Highest prevalence of undernutrition was observed among the Santals (55.0 per cent) of Bankura district (Ghosh and Malik, 2007) and lowest among them was Dhimals (27.0 per cent) of Naxalbari, West Bengal (Datta *et.al.,* 2007).

Figure 2 compares the prevalence of CED based on MUAC among the different studied ethnic groups. It is clear from this figure that Kora Mudis (51.2 per cent) of the Paschim Midnapore (Besai *et.al.,* 2008) have highest prevalence of CED followed by Slum dwellers (43.5 per cent) of Paschim Medinipur (Bose *et.al.,* 2007), Mundas (35.8 per cent) present study, Santals (33.7 per cent) of Orrisa (Bose *et.al.,* 2006), Telegas (32.7 per cent) of Paschim Medinipur (Banik, 2007) and Oraons (29.8 per cent) present study using MUAC.

The MUAC measurement reflects adult nutritional status as defined by BMI (Collins, 1996). The measurement of MUAC has been used as a useful screening method for the assessment of nutritional status in different ethnic groups (Olukoya, 1990; James *et.al.,* 1994). Since it is the most reproducible and simplest measurement to perform, its use has been recommended in nutritional studies (Harries, 1984).

Measuring MUAC has several advantages; the measurement can be taken quickly and at little cost. It requires neither sophisticated equipment nor anything but the most basic literacy level to carry out (Rodrigues, 1994). However, although an MUAC value < 23 cm. have been recommended for use to define undernutrition (James *et. al.,* 1994) this value may not be the most appropriate cut-off point in all ethnic groups. A recent study from Nigeria (Khadivzadeh, 2000) reported that a MUAC cut-off point of 23 cm. was optimal for the north of the country, while a 24 cm. cut-off point was more appropriate for the South. A similar cut-off point of 24 cm. was also obtained in a recent study from South India (Rodrigues, 1994). Thus, there is a need for more studies using MUAC in different ethnic groups of India so that they provide ethnic specific cut-off points of MUAC to facilitate better public health planning and implementation.

It may be wise to add here that the uniqueness of our study is the paucity of data on the prevalence of undernutrition, based on MUAC, from India. We conclude that, Munda and Oraon tribals of Paschim Medinipur distirct, West Bengal, were experiencing serious to critical nutritional stress. Appropriate nutriti-onal intervention programs should be imple-mented among these ethnic groups.

References

Bisai, S., Bose, K., Katun, A., Ganguli, S., Das, P., Dikshit, S., Pradhan, S. and Mishra, T. 2008. Nutritional stress in Kora Mudis of two districts in West Bengal. India: A comparative statement, in S.K. Basu and S.D. Banik (eds.), Enviroment Pollution. Protection and Policy Issues. New Delhi : APH Publication Corporation. pp 379-389.

Bose, K., Chakraborty F., Mitra K. and Bisai S. 2006. Nutritional status of adult Santal men in Keonjhar district, Orissa, India. Food and Nutrition Bulletin. 27(4), pp. 353-6.

Clinical Nutrition, 2(3-4), pp.193-6.

Collins S. 1996. Using middle arm circumference to assess severe adult malnutrition during famine. The Journal of the American Medical Association. 276(5):pp.391-395.

Collins, S., Duffield, A. and Myatt, M. 2000. Assessment of nutritional status in emergency-affected populations, ACC/SCN, Geneva, Switzerland. Ferro-Luzzi A and James W.P. 1996. Adult malnutrition: simple assessment techniques for use in emergencies. British Journal of Nutrition 75(1), pp.3-10.

Datta B. S., Bose, K., Bisai, S., Bhattacharya, M., Das, S., Jana, A., Purkait, P., (2007). "Chronic energy deficiency among adult Dhimals of Naxalbari, West Bengal: Comparison with other tribes of Eastern India." Food and Nutrition Bulletin, 28(3), 348-352.

Datta Banik, S. 2007. Age-Sex and Diurnal Variation of Blood Pressure in Different Nutritional States Among the Adult Telegas of Kharagpur in West Bengal, India. Collegium Antropologicum. 31(3): pp. 717-722.

Directorate of Census Operations, West Bengal, 2005; Primary Census Abstract, West Bengal , Vol.-II.

Duffield A. (1998) Anthropometry, morbidity and mortality in rural savannah. PhD dissertation, London School of Hygiene and Tropical Medicine, London.

Ghosh. S. & Malik, L.S. (2007). "Sex Differences in Body Size and Shape among Santhals of West Bcngal". The Anthropologist, 9 (2), 143-149.

Harries, A.D., A. J. Laura., R. V. Heatley., R. G. Newcombe. and J. Rhodes 1984. Precision of anthropometric measurements: the value of mid-arm circumference.

James, W.P.T. Mascie-Taylor C.G.N. Norgan NG, Bristrian, B.R. Shetty, P. and Ferro-Luzzi, A. 1994. The value of arm circumference measurements in assessing chronic energy deficiency in Third World adults. European Journal Clinical Nutrition 48(12) pp. 883-894.

Kaushik Bose, Samiran Bisai, Priyanka Das, Swapan Dikshit and Sampa Pradhan. Journal Human Ecology, 22(2): 171-176 (2007). Relationship of

Income with Anthropometric Indicators of Chronic Energy Deficiency among Adult Female Slum Dwellers of Midnapore Town

Khadivzadeh, T. 2000. Mid upper arm and calf circumferences as indicators of nutritional status in women of reproductive age. East Mediterranean Health Journal, 8:4-5, pp.612-8.

Lohman TG, Roche AF, Martorell R (1988) Anthropometric Standardisation Reference Manual. Human Kinetics Books, Chicago.

Olukoya, A.A. 1990. Identification of underweight women by measurement of arm circumference. International Journal of Gynecology and Obstetrics, 31(3), pp.231-235.

Rodrigues, V.C. Rao, R.S. and Lena A. (1994) Utility of arm circumference as a screening instrument to identify women at nutritional risk. Tropical doctor, 24(4), pp.164–166.

Topal, Y.P.S. and Samal P.K. 2001. Causes for variation in social and economic conditions among tribes of Indian Central Himalaya: A comparative study. Man in India 81(1-2), pp. 87-102.

World Health Organization (1995) Physical status: the use and interpretation of anthropometry. Technical Report Series no. 854. World Health Organization, Geneva.

23

Poverty and Reproductive Mother-Child Health: An Emerging Problem in the Unorganised Occupational Sector

Somenath Bhattacharjee

Origin of Food Production

Struggle for existence is the key factor to survive in the world. Human being is a social animal. He is the only primate who has the ability to make tools, technological devices and to communicate ideas to conduct the natural systems for own beneficiaries. This is true from the dates back. The first evidence of ancestors of modern human being could be traced out way back to the period of lower Palaeolithic stage at 1,000,000 B.C. Further in response to the change of environment man relied upon extra bodily equipment of his own making and in this context they invented fire, constructed his own dwellings, prepared garments to cover his nudity along with the quest for better and more protective tools. Ultimately he emerged to be the ruler of material world and got assimilated with new cultural dimension. On the other hand civilisation is a phase of culture which is related to the outward behaviour of man and which is mechanical and external. By civilisation MacIver points towards the whole mechanism or apparatus which man uses in his endeavour to control the condition of life. These changes or applications were not static but it had reached a number of new features. With the changing dimension of time and gradual alternation of surrounding environment and climatic condition, the livelihood of human being has passed on through different successive stages and it created new feature of human civilization. In this context the most developed and most advanced form of human civilissation is the stage of urbanisation and industrialisation.

Towards the end of Upper Palaeolithic, people seemed to have got food from hunting migratory herds of large animals. Beginning about 14,000 years ago people in some regions began to depend less on big game hunting and more on relatively stationary food resources such as fish, shellfish, small game and wild plants (Ember & Ember, 2002). About 10,000 years ago, at the end of the Pleistocene, the last ice age sheet retreated, sea levels rose, winds shifted and environments changed (Lavenda, 1998). Animals and plants responded to these transformations, as did the human being for their food. Perhaps the most striking feature of this period of human history is the domestication of plants and animals in seven different areas of the world between 10,000 to 4,000 years ago (Smith, 1995). The activities that led to domestication in the deliberate attempts of foraging peoples to increase both the economic contribution and the reliability of one or more of the wild species they depended on for survival , and thus reduce risk and uncertainty (Smith,1995). Human beings and plants however did not domesticated overnight. This relationship varied in several important ways. David Harris classified these into four major food yielding systems 1) Wild-plant-food procurement, 2) wild-plant-food production, 3) cultivation and 4) agriculture. On the other hand animal domestication is for the mutual benefit.

Most archaeologists have thought that the Fertile Crescent the arc of land stretching up from Israel and the Jordan valley through southern Turkey and then downward to the slope of Zagros mountain in Iran was one of the earliest centres of plant and animal domestication. In Alikosh of South Western Iran until about 5500 B.C agriculture and herding become increasingly important; in Catal Hayuk of Turkey the lentil, wheat, peas and burley were produced in surplus; in Meso America tomato, cotton, maize, beans and squashes were in plentiful quantity. In North America the dogs and turkeys were the main domesticated animals. In the central Andes of the new world animals were a significant part of economy used for wool, meat and transportation. The people of Southern China also reared water buffalo, pigs and dogs. There is a definite evidence of cultivated rice in Thailand after 4,000 B.C. The early farming villages were egalitarian societies. Things began to change about 5,000 years ago in South Western Asia and shortly thereafter in Egypt, Indus Valley, China, Meso America and the Andes. These six regions of the globe were the first to invent essentially independently a new way of organising society called as social stratification which was based on the assumption that different groups in the society were entitled to different amount of wealth, power and prestige. To get from egalitarian forms of social organisation to social stratification involves the evolution of social complexity. Social stratification was made possible when domestication of plants and animals produced amount of food that exceeded the basic subsistence needs of the population. This surplus production permitted some members of society to stop producing food altogether and to specialise in various occupations or in new social roles. Occupational specialisation permitted the production of a wide range of goods, yet it also created a wide gulf between most of societies members and a new social class of rulers who successfully claimed the lions share of this new wealth as their due one (Lavenda,1998). Thus the unequal distribution of wealth and unparallel status of livelihood is not a recent phenomenon, rather it occurred from a prolonged period when the human being were able to produce from the land and was able to control the authority of the resources in their own confinement. The ancient civilisations of the world flourished in different times in different regions and ultimately led to the development of an urban society surrounded by fertile agriculture and villages. At first Mesopotamian civilisation flourished in the river deltas of the Tigris and Euphrates in 5,000 BC. The second is the Egyptian civilisation in the valley of river Nile in 3,000 BC. Third, the Indus civilisation in the valley of Indus river in 2,500 BC, the fourth major civilisation in China in the valley of Hwang Ho river in 1500 BC (Khan, 2006).

Under this way of progress, the consequences of industrial revolution were used to denote the phenomenon of broad changes that occurred during the latter part of the 18th century in Europe. An industrial society uses sophisticated technology based on machinery powered by advanced fuels to produce material goods. A primary feature of industrial societies in comparison to non-industrial societies is that most productive labour involves factory and office work rather than agricultural or foraging activities. This pattern has produced new forms of economic organisation and social class arrangements. In terms of political organization, industrial societies became the first well-developed nation–states, political communities that have clearly defined territorial borders dividing them from one another. The overall consequences of the industrial revolution are often referred to as modernisation. The economic, social, political and religious changes related to modern industrial and technological change (Scupin, 2000). In this consequence urbanisation is the most talked about phenomenon in this century, developing mostly on the basis of industrialisation and other means of communication with outside world throughout the globe. Mainly it has two distinct points of differences one is the wealth and conveniences related with the daily livelihood of the rich urban dwellers and the other one is the hard struggle for a large section of people, known as urban poor.

Urban Poverty, Hunger and Maternal Health

According to the global reports of urbanisation world (UNCHS, 1996) two main features are noted during last two decades—a) growth in urban poverty, b) limited achievement in improving the housing conditions (Chaudhuri, 2003). Besides these urban developments almost all of the urban centres however confronted with massive problems of providing employment, housing, transport and drainage. The rapid increase in the urban population has serious implications on the basic services and infrastructure like water, sanitation, houses, food, electricity, education, health etc. More than 1/4th of the urban dwellers are reported to be surviving at the subsistence level where the basic amenities of life are acutely lacking. Urban sprawl is widespread and is characterised with vicious cycle of poverty, unemployment and social disorganisation (Nagpaul, 1996). Mostly these people are engaged with a number of uncleaned occupations related with sanitation, sewage, drainage, menials, rag pickings and collection of household garbage. On the other hand they are also related with construction works as well as collection and supply of raw materials for the perspective of urban development. Thus these downtrodden sections of people are working as a scavenger to remove the waste products from the urban provinces to keep the habitation clean and healthy, but they are facing all sorts of negligence and deprivation form their urban dwelling counterparts. Urban poor occupy the lowest rugs of the social hierarchy and deprive of basic services and amenities. They occupy the marginal positions in the socio- cultural system of the communities. They are the supplier of raw materials and they are the carrier of goods and products related with the flourishment of trade and commerce for the development of urban capital market but they are facing all sorts of economic deprivation and all sorts of constraints in their daily life. They are regarded as the urban poor in comparison to the so called elite and wealthy section of the urban dwellers.

According to Gillin and Gillin, "Poverty is that condition in which a person either because of inadequate income or unwise expenditure, does not maintain a scale of living high enough to provide for his physical and mental efficiency and to enable him and his natural dependents to function usually according to the standards of society of which he is a member" (Sharma, 2004, cf. Gillin and Gillin). Goddard mentioned that, "Poverty is insufficient supply of those things which are requisite for an individual to maintain himself and those dependent upon him in health and vigour" (Sharma, 2004, cf. Gillin and Gillin). According to World Bank Report in 2002, poverty is synonymous with poor quality of life, food insecurity, under nutrition, illiteracy, low level of income, deprivations in various forms and low human resource base development. Customarily, poverty is defined on the basis of per capita income. Planning Commission of India adopted the balanced diet criteria recommended by the Nutrition Advisory Committee of the Indian Council of Medical Research, the initial poverty line per capita per month of Rs 35 at 1961-62 price index was further modified to Rs 20 per capita per month at the same price index. In 1981 the Planning Commission appointed a task force which presented a norm of 2,400 kilocalories/2,100 kilocalories per person per day in the rural/ urban areas using 1973-1974 NSSO data and fixing the poverty line at Rs 49.09 Rs 56.64 per capita per month at 1973-1974 price index for rural/ urban areas; where in 2002, BPL census for the Tenth Plan mentioned per capita per month income up to Rs 540 for indicating the same.

World Development Report 2000-2001 states that nearly half of the world's poor live in South Asia, a region that accounts for roughly 30 per cent of World's Population. In the perspective of urban poverty in India 22 per cent of Indian urban population live in slums against 32 per cent of the World's urban slum dwellers (Census 2001). The survey done by The National Sample Survey Organisation (NSSO) in the Ministry of Statistics and Programme Implementation, Government of India during July 2002-December 2002 has released the report that about fifty two thousand slums were located in the urban areas of the country and about 8 million urban households lived in these slums. According to the reports of Planning Commission of India in 2006-2007, 15 per cent or about 49.5 million urban dwellers are living below poverty line. With 285.3 million urban population in 2001, India has shown a level of urbanisation of 27.8 per cent. Nearly 37.8 per cent of the total urban population of India is concentrated in million plus cities with 27 per cent of them living in slums. Incidences of poverty and its manifestation in its various forms are becoming a common feature for Indian cities, out of every five persons, one is Below Poverty Line (Economic Survey: 2001-2002). The following tables are highlighting their livelihood status and insecurity of food, nutrition and shelter in comparison to their higher elite counterparts. The urban poor are lacking the common minimum facilities of livelihood, food and shelter or they can accumulate the common minimum necessities in utter constraints.

Hunger is both a cause and an effect of poverty. It holds back economic growth and limits progress in reducing poverty. The United Nations Millennium Development goals have set their first goal to eradicate extreme poverty and hunger to halve between 1990 and 2015. Still hunger continues to be a global tragedy. About 852 million people are still chronically or acutely malnourished. The negative economic impact of hunger is dramatic, with annual losses of at least 6–10 per cent in forgone GDP due to losses in labor productivity. Economic growth alone is insufficient for eliminating hunger because so many hungry people live in deep “poverty traps”, beyond the reach of markets. Poor and hungry people often face social and political exclusion, unable to demand their rights. They have little access to education, health services, and safe drinking water.

People go hungry despite an abundant world food supply, because they cannot obtain food of sufficient quantity or quality to meet their nutritional requirements. There are many reasons for this to be so. In analyses by the task force and other researchers, the following factors emerged as strongly correlated with high levels of underweight preschool children in developing countries: poverty, low food production, mothers’ lack of education, poor water, sanitation and health facilities and climatic shocks. Research has found that women’s education was associated with 43 per cent of the reduction in child malnutrition between 1970 and 1995, followed by increases in agricultural production (26 per cent), and improvements in the health environment (19 per cent) and in women’s status relative to men (12 per cent). Adequate nutrition begins at the household level, where gender discrimination, traditional practices, and inadequate nutrition awareness can limit the food intake of women and children. For example, the best nourishment for small children is exclusive breastfeeding for the first six months, then breastfeeding plus complementary foods through their first two years. Yet women may not be able to produce breast milk of sufficient quality and quantity when they themselves are malnourished. In some parts of the world, intra household inequalities may result in women and girls eating last, finishing what remains after the men and boys have eaten.

Though India has made an appreciable progress in improving the overall health status of its population but it is far from satisfaction. The pace of decline of infant and child mortality on one hand and maternal mortality on the other hand has been quite low. The health problems of mothers and newborns arise as a result of synergistic effects of malnutrition, poverty, illiteracy, unhygienic living conditions, infections and unregulated fertility. At the same time, poor infrastructure and ineffective public health services is also responsible for low inadequate obstetric care. The national average of MMR is 254 per 100,000 live births (SRS-2004-2006), which in itself is very high compared to the international scenario like Sweden (5), USA (24), Brazil (58) and even in neighbouring countries like Bangladesh (340), Pakistan (260), Sri Lanka (39) and Thailand (48).

The persistence of hunger and abject poverty in India and other parts of the world is due in large measure to the subjugation, marginalisation and disempowerment of women. Women suffer from hunger and poverty in greater numbers and to a great degree then men. At the same time, it is women who bear the primary responsibility for actions needed to end hunger: education, nutrition, health and family income.

Looking through the lens of hunger and poverty, there are seven major areas of discrimination against women in India. India has exceptionally high rates of child malnutrition, because tradition in India requires that women eat last and least throughout their lives, even when pregnant and lactating. Malnourished women give birth to malnourished children, perpetuating the cycle. Females receive less health care than males. Many women die in childbirth of easily prevented complications. Working conditions and environmental pollution further impairs women's health. Families are far less likely to educate girls than boys, and far more likely to pull them out of school, either to help out at home or from fear of violence.

Women work longer hours and their work is more arduous than men's, yet their work is unrecognised. Men report that "women, like children, eat and do nothing". Technological progress in agriculture has had a negative impact on women. In women's primary employment sector—agriculture—extension services overlook women. In recent years, there has been an alarming rise in atrocities against women in India, in terms of rapes, assaults and dowry-related murders. Fear of violence suppresses the aspirations of all women. Female infanticide and sex-selective abortions are additional forms of violence that reflect the devaluing of females in Indian society. While women are guaranteed equality under the constitution, legal protection has little effect in the face of prevailing patriarchal traditions. Women lack power to decide who they will marry, and are often married off as children. Legal loopholes are used to deny women inheritance rights.

India has a long history of activism for women's welfare and rights, which has increasingly focused on women's economic rights. A range of Government Programs have been launched to increase economic opportunity for women, although there appear to be no existing programs to address the cultural and traditional discrimination against women that leads to her abject conditions.

The greatest tragedy facing humanity today is the persistence of chronic hunger—an intolerable phenomenon that takes the lives of 24,000 of us every day. For fully one-fifth of humanity, life is a daily struggle to survive in conditions of relentless poverty. Day after day, the lives of one billion individuals are cut short or terribly diminished by chronic, persistent hunger. Day after day, one billion people are denied the opportunities they need to lead healthy and productive lives. People living with chronic hunger exist in conditions of severe poverty. What they lack is the chance to change their situation, to develop their own self-sufficiency. The most potent confirmation of this fact can be seen in the lives of women. They, along with their children, are the main victims of hunger, and they are also most lacking in opportunities to end their own and their families' hunger.

Traditionally, women bear primary responsibility for the well-being of their families. Yet they are systematically denied access to the resources they need to fulfill their responsibility, which includes education, health care services, job training, and access and freedom to use family planning services. In order to gain a shared understanding of the condition of the status of women in India and its impact on the persistence of hunger, this document surveys papers done by leading scholars in Indian development issues. It is organised in a framework of seven issues that characterise the plight of resource-poor women, with a focus on rural women, in India: malnutrition, poor health, lack of education, overwork, lack of skills, mistreatment and powerlessness.

A Study on the Stone Crushers

Studied Area and the People

The present study has been done on an occupational group, who are related with the stone based occupation on Balasan river bed. The studied people inhabited in the Balasan Colony located beside the Balasan river. It was under the Atharokhai Gram Panchayat, within the Matigara C.D. Block of Darjeeling District in West Bengal. The inhabitants of the said colony were diversified in caste, community and ethnic groups. Among them the study was done on 200 Rajbanshi families. Meanwhile it is to be mentioned here that the Rajbanshis are considered as the largest Scheduled Caste group of North Bengal. Meanwhile, most of the studied families were earlier inhabited in Bangladesh and they were settled agriculturists. However, due to severe political unrest in there during 1971 and several other problems in latter, those people were forced to migrate by leaving their established settlement, settled occupation, stable livelihood and a number of personal belongings. They were almost roofless and resourceless in condition and in this circumstance; they came to various parts of North Bengal. The Balasan river in its tide from the high altitude of the Himalayas carried out stone, sand, boulders as a natural flow of raw materials to the plains. The people of Balasan Colony, who were mostly engaged with the stone-based occupation, collected the stone, sand, boulders and broke the stone into different shapes and sizes. From the Balasan river those were supplied to urban Siliguri and other adjacent urban centres of North Bengal and Bihar, for urban construction, river embankment and several other purposes.

It is to be mentioned here that the studied area was located at the sub- Himalayan foot-hills and it was an area of plentiful natural resources like stones, sand and boulders. Moreover it is a region of heavy showers. As a result, the Balasan river had waist deep water throughout the entire year and the concerned level raised a lot during the rainy season. Moreover due to continuous influx of natural resources like stone, sand the river bed was quite dusty as well as it was very much moist in condition. Thus, it could be predicted that the studied people had to conduct their prime occupational pursuit in a moist, dusty and polluted atmosphere. In this consequence, the concerned people might have a probability to become quite vulnerable to a number of occupational injuries and other diseases related with their working atmosphere as well as daily livelihood circumstances. Further, their socio-economic condition would be considered with prime importance as it was related with working environment and their daily livelihood condition as a whole. Their cultural aspects would be an important parameter to analyse the impact of their working and surrounding environment on their daily livelihood condition in totality.

Objective of the Study

The present study had the prime objective to:

1. To know about the economic condition of the studied people.
2. To know about the issues related with their food and nutrition.
3. To know about the multifarious aspects associated with their reproductive mother child health situation.

Methodology Applied

The present study has been done among the 200 families in this colony having 1012 populations, with 507 males and 505 females; and the sex ratio is 997.

The entire study had been done through intensive field work. In this regard Preliminary Census schedule was applied on the families to collect data about their period of migration, cause of migration, occupational change, present occupational pursuit, demographic aspects, concept of health, disease and treatment and their daily food habit. Further, interviews were taken from the key informants to know about their early settlements, their previous socio- cultural practices and concerned changes of those issues due to migration. Information was also taken about the formation of the colony and the factors related with the stone crushing occupation. Thereafter, case studies were taken on the people regarding their suffering from different diseases. It also emphasised about their way of treatment and several hindrances related with the treatment. The data collected through field work was analysed in detail to know about the various factors related with the socio-economic condition of the stone crushers, and particularly to analyse in depth that, how their working atmosphere and occupation has a deep co-relation with their health situation.

Occupation and Income

Balasan river flows downward from Himalayas with natural resources like sand, stone, boulders. The colony members supplied those raw materials for urban constructions in adjacent areas. The stone based economy was the prime source of income for most of the families of Balasan Colony. Excluding the children, 94.82 per cent male and 87.16 per cent female were either primarily or secondarily involved with the stone crushing work. The main interesting feature was that, their daily requirements had forced most of the women to give prime importance to their work despite their household activities. It is to be mentioned here that the females and the children who were primarily engaged in household work and education respectively, were simultaneously involved in the stone crushing work secondarily either in the stone field or in their houses to fulfill their familial requirements. The most interesting thing was that due to their struggle for survival only 20.44 per cent female were able to give prime importance to their family. The said work was conducted in any climatic condition and the concerned people went to the river bed early in the morning and did their work throughout the entire day. The occupation was totally free from any kind of gender biasness and the people were very hard working to earn their livelihood. To provide the financial support the entire family worked as a production unit. They had to work in a dusty polluted, unhygienic stone field over day long in more or less every season. Most of them had to work for more than 8 hours.The female who were mostly involved in the household work, also did the stone crushing work for 3-4 hours in a day. They worked under '*sardars*' (team leaders) and could get their payment once in a week (on Tuesday) according to their quantity or amount of work. Those people who were engaged with loading the stones and sand to the truck were also paid weekly by the *sardars*. The people who were engaged with loading could hardly load three trucks per day and they worked in a group of 3-4 member, and each of them could earn Rs 20 to Rs 25 by loading per truck. It is to be noted that most of them could load the trucks hardly 4-5 days in a week. Considering their monthly income 26 families could earn below Rs. 1000/- per month, 154 families earned between Rs 1,001 to Rs. 2,000 and the rest of the families earn above Rs 2,000 per month. Despite their hard working schedule the stone crushers were not at all paid proper remuneration. Their average family member was 5 in number and with this poor level of income any how they could manage their needs. In their earlier settlement the studied people were mostly depended on the agricultural crops and fishes of their own land, village ponds and nearby rivers but now this scenario had changed completely. Now they mostly had to depend on market based products. Thus poverty and misery had become an integral part of their daily life.

Quality of Food and Nutrition

The people living at the Balasan Colony are mainly engaged with the stone based economy. The people are so busy in their working schedule that they have the mere chance to go for a properly balanced nutritious diet. They earn a very low amount of money from this source of occupation. So, with this little amount of money it is impossible for the people to maintain a good healthy diet regularly. They totally depend upon rice, pulses and vegetables daily. For them to eat egg or fish or meat is next to impossible daily. They buy these sort of nutritious foods sometime once a week or so. If we consider the case of children and pregnant women they can't got milk or fruits at all for the proper nutrition. So two facts are quite clear they have a very little chance to take food at regular interval in a healthy surrounding and whenever they take food it is not at all reaching to the nutritious value as required for a normal human being to maintain health and mind free from any kind of physical disorder.

It is to be mentioned here that the kitchen garden is absent here. Kitchen garden is a very good source of vitamin. It is very cheap source for poor. But this leaking of kitchen garden is leading them towards acute malnutrition.

The following table gives us more details:

Table 23.1: Distribution of Family on the Basis of Daily Feeding Schedule

Feeding Schedule	*Yes*		*No*		*Total Number of Family*
	Number of Family	*Percentage*	*Number of Family*	*Percentage*	
Break Fast	140	70 per cent	60	30 per cent	200 (100 per cent)
Lunch and Dinner	200	100 per cent	Nil	Nil	200 (100 per cent)
Tiffin only	40	20 per cent	160	80 per cent	200 (100 per cent)
Break Fast And Tiffin	40	20 per cent	160	80 per cent	100 (100 per cent)

From Table 23.1 it is quite clear that the entire household mainly depends on lunch and dinner. Only 20 per cent families take both breakfast and tiffin regularly while, 80 per cent families are not able to take their tiffin.

From Table 23.2 it is quite clear that all their quantity of food intake lies in a very low nutritious level. Only 7 per cent families once in a week take fish and 5per cent families once in a week take meat. But taking milk and fruits in a week is simply beyond imagination to them.

So, the food intake of the hard working people of Balasan Colony does not give them the proper calorie of energy, which they should need regularly to cope up with the heavy daily labour. Further, with the help of Anthropometrics measurement the Body Mass Index of 100 students (between age group of 5-14 years) was taken. Their Body Mass Index proves severe malnutrition among them due to poor quantity of daily food intake.

Table 23.2: Distribution of Family on the Basis of Type of Food Taken.

Type of Food	Consuming Schedule						Total Number of Family
	Daily		Weekly Once		Occasionally		
	Number of Family	Per-centage	Number of Family	Percentage	Number of Family	Perce-ntage	
Rice, Pulse and Vegetables	200	100	-	-	-	-	200 (100)
Egg	Nil	-	20	10	180	90	200 (100)
Soya Bean	Nil	-	40	20	160	80	200 (100)
Fish	Nil	-	14	7	186	93	200 (100)
Meat	Nil	-	10	5	190	95	200 (100)
Milk	Nil	-	Nil	-	200	100	200 (100)
Fruit	Nil	-	Nil	-	200	100	200 (100)

	Weight (kgs.)
Body Mass Index=	< 19 = Under weight 19-25 = Normal weight 25-30 = Mildly over weight

Table 23.3: Distribution of Individuals on the Feature of Body Mass Index

Total Individual	*Body Mass Index*				
	< 19	19 To 25	25 To 30	30 To 40	> 40
100 (100 per cent)	83 (83 per cent)	17 (17 per cent)	Nil	Nil	Nil

It is clearly revealed that only in 17 per cent cases the concerned children have achieved the status of adequate growth and nutrition, while in most of the cases they were acutely malnourished.

Reproductive Mother-Child Health Issues

The female folk of the Balasan Colony are married quite at an early age and so their sexual relations and child bearing features also states from quite an early age. The overall economic crisis and imbalance diet has created a severe problem on the health feature of women. Some time they are forcefully engaged into sexual relations by the male and this rather bring some unwanted pregnancies too. Most of the studied women 75.75 per cent bear the child within the age of 15 to 19 years which quite an immature physical stage of a girl to conceive a child. Beside this 15.90 per cent bear child within 14 year of age, showing a more distress condition. So, it is quite clear that the women bear child from an early stage. Under the condition of severe malnutrition due to some sexual forces of husband women often have to bear children beyond their physical capacity. These forceful pregnancies create a weakness among their bodies.

Most of the women 28.26 per cent have 3 children each. 10.14 per cent have 4 children, 6.52 per cent have 5 children and 2.89 per cent have 6 children each of them. So, in such a nutritive background this very hazardous for every woman to bear the children and this tell upon their health. Giving a pregnant woman proper nutritious diet is simply imaginary to the people. They give the same food as usual they intake. The giving of animal proteins, milk or fruits to the pregnant women is simply impossible to them. Thus, the pregnant mother was unable to get proper nutritious nourishment and on the other hand simultaneously the child in the womb too is malnourished. As a result the babies born with a very low body weight of 2 kg. as informed by Health Centres Personnel.

The following table gives more details-:

Table 23.4: Distribution of Families on the basis of Diet Given to a Pregnant Women Daily

Total Number of Families	*Nutritional Quantity*									
	Rice, Pulse and Vegetable		*Fish / Egg / Meat*		*Milk*		*Fruit*		*Medicine*	
	Daily	*Weekly*	*Daily*	*Weekly*	*Daily*	*Weekly*	*Daily*	*Weekly*	*Daily*	*Weekly*
200 (100 per cent)	200 (100 per cent)	-	-	60 (30 per cent)	-	22 (11 per cent)		14 (7 per cent)	-	38 (19 per cent)

From Table 23.4 it is clear that during pregnancy 100 per cent dependence is on vegetarian diet only. 30 per cent families one day in a week try to afford the expense of animal protein given the pregnant women. 11 per cent give milk weekly and 7 per cent give fruits weekly to the pregnant women. The medicinal cares as directed by Colony Health Centre officials or doctors are given in 19 per cent families and that is also in a week only.

The families are not so much interested to give their pregnant women folk proper medical care during their pregnancy period. They take their women to Primary Health Centre and get some basic instructions. They some time took the women to the Medical College for proper medical check up. But there is the malpractice for not to continue the medicines or relevant guides throughout the entire pregnancy period. But there is also a tendency to take pregnant women to the Healers of the colony who does not give any kind of proper guidance to them. Table 23.5 shows the distribution of ever pregnant women on the basis of medical check up during pregnancy of Women.

Table 23.5: Distribution of Ever Pregnant Women on the Basis of Medical Check up During Pregnancy of Women

Total Number of Ever Pregnant Women	*Medical Check Up During Pregnancy Period (Number and Percentage)*			
	No Check Up	*To Quack*	*At Medical College Or Rural Public Health Centre*	*To Traditional Healers*
132 (100 per cent)	51(38.63 per cent)	10 (7.57 per cent)	66 (50 per cent)	5 (3.78 per cent)

From Table 23.5 it is quite clear that a good number of people 38.63 per cent are not at all interested to medical check up of the pregnant women. 50 per cent individuals take the pregnant women either to medical college or at the rural Public Health Centre for check up. But there is the practice of 7.57 per cent and 3.78 per cent people to take the pregnant women to quack doctors and healers respectively for check up. Their ignorance and negligence does not provide the birth of the child in a proper hygienic condition and scientific manner. They usually make the child birth activity at their own house under the supervision of local *Dai* (midwife). But when woman suffers from the foetal loss then it makes them alert and in latter pregnancy stages they go to the Medical College for childbirth. The following table gives more details about the place of delivery of ever pregnant women.

Table 23.6: Distribution of Ever Pregnant Women on the Basis of Their delivery Place

Total Number of Ever Pregnant Women	*Delivery Place (Number and Percentage)*			
	At Medical College	*At House*	*Both at House and Medical College*	*Role of Dai*
132 (100 per cent)	30 (20.55 per cent)	80 (60.15 per cent)	22 (17.29 per cent)	94 (70.67 per cent)

From Table 23.6 it is clear that 60.13 per cent deliveries are taken place at house and 22.55 per cent are at Medical College. But when the women suffered from any kind of child loss then it made him to give delivery at Medical College. So in these cases 17.29 per cent the childbirth occurs both at their house and medical college. But it is obvious that whenever the child birth takes place at the house, the majority of cases 70.67 per cent are attended by *Dais*, it is noteworthy to say that the *Dais* are not properly trained. After pregnancy it is very essential for a proper nutritious food and medical care for newly become mother. But the distress economical condition of the people of Belasan Colony does not provoke them to do so. They give the mother as usual vegetarian feeding and they think it less important to give any kind of further medical check up. After taking a rest of a week or two, the woman directly goes to the work field and start their stone work again. This plays a very adverse role to their health feature naturally.

It was evident that, consumption of high caloric food comes to a very minimum level. 15 per cent household's women, fruits weekly by 5 per cent and milk weekly by 10per cent women, weekly take animal protein. 20 per cent household gives the medical care to their women. The mothers due to their lack of basic amenities have been provoked to go their work field regularly. The poverty makes the mothers a very little time to make proper nourishment of their child. The newborn babies are simply unable to survive without their mothers touch. So the mothers take their child with them to river belt. The mother starts to stone crash and her child is laid down beside on a cloth under the umbrella. The mother gives their child breast-feeding at regular interval. It is rather impossible for women to make herself clean before taking over child for breast-feeding. This causes a lot of physical abnormalities among the child. When the child gradually grows up they also take their meal with their parents at the river belt. The dusty environment easily contaminates a lot of germs to their meal and this cause a lot of physical abnormalities to them physically. This is not a feature of one day but it is going on year after year and so their physical disorder is also a yearlong phenomenon. The overworking of the women being during pregnancy caused a very adverse effect to the baby at the womb. The overworking when reaches at maximum level then the pregnant women suffer from severe injury. Then they generally go to medical college where the doctors check up the pregnant woman and decide whether the baby in the womb is living or died. Generally all the foetal loss takes place within the six months of pregnancies. The following Table 23.7 gives more details about the foetal loss during pregnancy period.

Table 23.7: Distribution of Cases of Foetal Loss During Pregnancy Period

Total Number of Foetal Loss	*Cases of Foetal Loss During Pregnancy Period (Number and Percentage)*			
	3-4 Months	*4-5 Months*	*5-6 Months*	*More Than 6 Months*
22(100 per cent)	5 (22.73 per cent)	10(45.45 per cent)	7 (31.82 per cent)	Nil

From Table 23.7 it is clear that most cases of foetal loss occur during 4-5 months which is 45.45 per cent. During 5-6 months 31.82 per cent foetal loss occurs and the least number 22.73 per cent cases occur during the period of 3-4 months. After giving the birth of the child the mother and the whole family neither give the child proper nourishment nor they can give any proper care. So, the child gradually grows up with utter negligence. The unscientific water contaminated by the child results in a lot of abdominal and intestinal disorders and this sometimes become severe. Keeping the child in the polluted and hot climate openly at the Balasan River Belt lead to fever and cough-cold for the child. All these kinds of severe diseases sometimes tell upon the lines of their child.

Table 23.8: Distribution of Ever Pregnant Women Who Have Lost Their Child

Total Number of Mother Who Have Loosed Their Child	*Number of Child Death Suffered by Mothers (Number and Percentage)*		
	1	*2*	*3*
45 (100 per cent)	29 (64.44 per cent)	10 (22.22 per cent)	6 (13.33 per cent)

Table 23.8 clearly indicates that the most number of women 64.44 per cent have loosed their 1 child, 22.22 per cent have loosed 2 children and 13.33 per cent have loosed 3 children. So these are the poor condition of the women who become pregnant and suffer a number of problems before and after pregnancy. Giving birth to a child is a very joyful thing in a family but here the pregnancies give some kind of sorrowing things both for women and the new comer.

General Observation

Human being is facing a continuous struggle for their survival. In this context, accumulation of food is a prime matter of concern. In most of the cases, human being can accumulate a fold of rice in exchange of his hard manual labour. The studied people of Balasan Colony were the worst sufferer of displacement and occupational alternation. After their resettlement, stone crushing occupation was the only scope of income for them. They got involved in the said work and were associated with hard manual labour. However, irrespective of their rigorous effort, they had a very poor level of income. With this mere earning, it was much difficult for them to earn the common minimum livelihood and requisite amount of nutritious food for their family members. Again, they had a very little scope to provide adequate food and nutrition for the reproductive mothers and newly born children. Meanwhile, even during the period of pregnancy, the womenfolk had work for long duration in the stone field to earn the bread for their families. It might be a major factor for the high rate of infant mortality in the studied area. Ultimately, poverty and malnutrition was deeply associated with and it had created an acute adverse impact on the reproductive mother and child health issues among the stone crushers.

References

Biswas, S.K. and S. Bhattacharjee, The Stone Crushing Women of Balasan River Bed: An Appeal from Humanitarian Perspectives (141-157) in A.Bhuimali(ed) South Asian Journal of Human Rights, Vol. 1, No. 1 – 2, 2005.

Biswas, S.K. and S. Bhattacharjee, 2006.Effect Of Land Alienation: A Study Between A Scheduled Caste and A Primitive Tribal Group (89-114), in Swapna H. Samel(ed) Rights of Dalits, Serials Publications, New Delhi.

Biswas, S.K. and S. Bhattacharjee, 2007. *Health Situation Among the Stone Crushers of Balasan River Bed in Siliguri,West Bengal, India* (182-202), in B. Chaudhuri and S. Chaudhuri (eds) IUAES INTER CONGRESS on Mega urbanisation, Multiethnic society, Human Rights and Development *(Vol-5) Health Environment Development and Other Essays : Anthropological Perspectives*, Inter India Publication, New Delhi.

Biswas, S.K. and S. Bhattacharjee, 2007. *Disadvantaged Migrant People on Balasan River Bed* (101-116), in Anil Bhuimali (ed) "Development of Scheduled Caste" Serials Publications, New Delhi.

Biswas, S.K. and S. Bhattacharjee, 2008. *Misery of Displacement A Study of the Rajbansis of Tarijot Colony (217-230)*, in Voice of Dalit, Vol 1, No.2 (July- December), MD Publications, New Delhi.

Census, 2001. Government of India, New Delhi.

Chaudhuri, S. 2003. *The Urban Poor: Struggle For Existence*, in Journal of Indian Anthropological Society, Vol. 38 (355-361) Calcutta.

Chaudhuri, S. 1987. *Beggars of Kalighat Calcutta*, Anthropological survey of India, Calcutta.

Chirot, D. 1986. Social Change in the Modern Age, San Diego.

Chronicle India, 2007. Chronicle Books, Noida.

Dasgupta, B(ed). 1988. Urban Migration and Rural Change: A Study of West Bengal, A. Mukherjee & Co, Calcutta.

Dhadave, M.S. 1989. *Sociology of Slum*, Archives Books, New Delhi.

Dube, S.C.1990. *Indian Society*, National Book Trust, India.

Ember, C, M. Ember, P.N. Peregrine, 2002. *Anthropology*, Pearson Education Asia.

Gill, R. 1997. Issues and Perspectives of Urban Poverty: The Indian Experience, in Urban India, Vol.xvii, No. 1&2.

Jhingan, M.L, B.K.Bhatt, J.N Desai, 2003. *Demography*, Vrinda Publications, New Delhi.

Khan, S.A. The Earliest Urban Civilization in India, In *Man in India*, January-June 2006, Vol. 86 No. 1&2 (121-131).

Majumdar, P.S, I. Majumdar, 1978. *Rural Migrants in An Urban Setting*. Hindustan Publishing Corporation, Delhi.

Nagpaul, H. 1996.Modernization and Urbanization in India: Problems and Issues, Rawat Publication, Jaipur.

Sandhu, R.S.2000.*Housing Problem in Urban India* in Social Change, March-June, Vol30, No. 1&2.

Schultz, E.A, R.H.Lavenda, 1998. *Anthropology*, Mayfield Publishing Company, California.

Scupin, R. 2000. *Cultural Anthropology: A Global Perspective*, Prentice Hall, New Jersey.

Sharma, R.K.2004. *Urban Sociology*, Atlantic Publisher, New Delhi.

Singh, S. *Urban Poverty and Gender In India*, in NagarLok, January-March, 2004. Vol. xxxvi

No.1-8, Indian institute of Public Administration, New Delhi.

Singh, S.D, K.P. Pothen, 1982. *Slum Children In India*, Deep and Deep Publications, New Delhi.

Sivaramakrishnan, K.C, A. Kundu, B.N Singh, 2005. Oxford Handbook of Urbanization in India, Oxford University Press.

Smith, B.D.1995. The Emergence of Agriculture, Scientific American Liabrary, New York.

Planning Commission of India, 2002. *Tenth Five Year Plan, 2002-2007(Vol-II)*, Government of India, New Delhi.

The World Bank, 2002. India: Urban Sector Strategy, Energy and Infrastructure Unit, South Asia Regional Office.

UNCHS,1996. An Urbanizing World, Global Report on Human Settlement, Oxford University press, Oxford.

Wahwa, K. 2000. *How do We Tackle Slums*? in The economic Times, April 11, New Delhi.

World Development Report, 2000-2001. *Attacking Poverty*, Oxford University Press, New York.

World Economic and Social Survey, 2004. *International Migration* United Nations Academic Foundation, New Delhi.

Part IV: Vulnerable and Essentials of Our Populations

24

Role of Tribal Women in Indigenous Health Care System in Two Districts of West Bengal

Sudip Bhui

Introduction

In the second decade of Twenty first century women makes their glorious contribution in our Nation building. Health care sector is essential to each and every communities as well as social groups of entire society. Indigenous health care system even in today provides to its client some sort of reliance and to its researchers becomes a golden treasury. Women play a crucial role in this age-old tradition, though these facts could not get importance in policies, programs and research themes.

Rath and Acharya (2007) stated that Tribal medicine- men play a pivotal role in Man-plant- Animal- Spirit to understand causation and cure of diseases. Kapoor (2006) make an interrelated typology among supernatural agencies, food habit and effect of environment. Kingston and others (2009) examine the effectiveness of medicinal plants in treatment of skin diseases and also emphasis on the preservation of these plants. Rajpramukh (2006) in their study in Eastern Ghat meet the healers with the supernatural affiliation and collect the data on diagnosis of disease. Basu(1993) express the limitation of integrated study on Tribal women in complete domain health care system.

Now, we may go through some glimpses about the women in Indigenous health care system. The field experiences come from two villages namely Kamlasole (Nayagram C.D. Block) and Darda (Balarampur C.D. Block) of Paschim Medinipur district and Purulia district. The fields belong to a lateritic, forest covered area, inhabited majorly by tribal brethren.

Socio-cultural Perspectives

The women of tribal society are consider main pillar in economic life as well as socio-cultural cohesion, interactions and to make continue traditional heritage. Though, they less empowered with literary world and advance science-technological skills, but their day to day contribution have been uprising present and forthcoming generations to get a rhythm with globalisation. They have greater contribution in child rearing, taking care of the elders, kitchen gardens, agricultural activities, forest collections etc. Generalized part of the world view also is carried on by the women folk. Their personal beliefs, ideology influence and construct the thinking pattern of children, adolescents and adults through domestic interactions.

Problems in Participation

The patriarchal mode of society makes a passive status of women in governance of village communities as well as in health care sector. Some superstitions like witchcraft, sorcery, and ill-spirits are blamed when women start treatment with enchanting spellings and etc. Members of society cannot rely on them in purpose of treatments and women healers do not avail broader network of society. Collection of medicinal herbs from remote forest or grasslands is not possible for lack of security in proper moments. The owners of these skills, generally male members do not desire to transfer knowledge to females. In connection of busy schedule of domestic works they get the minimum time to acquire and practice this tradition.

Prospects

Problems of physical and mental health on its onset are detected in family and generally by women members of this family. They provide preliminary domestic measures in these conditions. They also make care and give the food items following the taboos of food what are complimentary with treatment. The patients get emotional support as well support from religious affiliations from their mother, sisters or other female members of households. Through their services in kitchen gardens medicinal herbs. Sometime they plant necessary herbs and plantains with medicinal values. One old women of Kamlasole village gave service herbal healing by hawking in several villages, she also help local doctors, Non Government Organisation (N.G.O.) workers with her enormous knowledge. In Darda village, three women practice treatment in headache, skin diseases, arthritis etc.

Conclusion

We have to unearth a vast area in women enterprises in Indigenous Health Care System to enrich our nation in health care sector, especially in the third world countries like India. Women may be involved in prepare, nurture, preserve and dissemination of knowledge in gardens of medicinal herbs. Through the Self Help Group, they can involve themselves in preservation of ex-situ medicinal herbs as well as provide healing services. Workshops, seminars etc are also organised to cater the knowledge and in search of better health care. Policy level contributions and launching programs are much more crucial to make success in this venture.

Bibliography

Basu, S.K. (1993): Health Status of Tribal Women in India. *Social Change*, 23(4) Dec

Kapoor A K (2006) Ecology, Disease pattern and Indigenous Healing aspects in *Himalayan Communities , in Indigenous Health Care and Ethno-medicine* ed. By A N Sharma (*et.al.*), Sarup and Sons , New Delhi

Kingston C and other (2009) Indigenous knowledge of using medicinal plants in treating skin diseases in Kanyakumari district, Southern India, *Indian Journal of Traditional Knowledge*, Vol-8(2), Apr

Raj Pramukh K.E. and P.D.S. Palkumar (2006) Indigenous Knowledge: Implications in *Tribal Health and Disease, Stud.* Tribes Tribals, 4(1): 1-6, Kamla-Raj enterprises, Haryana.

Rath S S (2004) Indian Tribe and their urgent and emerging health status *An overview in Tribal Health and Medicine*, ed. By. A K Kalla and P C Joshi .Concept Publishing, New Delhi.

25

Functional Disability of the Elderly Santal People

Mohan Chandra Dolai and FalguniChakrabarty

Introduction

India is a land of most rapidly ageing populations (aged 60 and above) in the developing world. This phenomenon is marked by a series of social, cultural and epidemiological implications due to the greater prevalence of morbidity and functional disability in this age group. Functional status is an individual's ability to live independently and to relate to their environment or to perform normal daily activities required to meet basic needs, fulfill usual roles and maintain health and well-being. Functional status subsumes related concepts of interest: functional capacity and functional performance. While functional capacity represents an Individual's maximum capacity to perform daily activities in the physical, psychological, social and spiritual domain of life, functional performance refers to the activities people actually do during the course of their daily lives. A maximal exercise test measures physical functional capacity, while a self-report of activities of daily living measures functional performance.

Functional status can be influenced by biological or physiological impairment and socio-economic factors, symptoms, mood and other factors. It is also likely to be influenced by health perceptions. For example, a person whom most judge to be well but who views himself as ill may have a low level of functional performance in relation to his capacity.

Loss of functional disability is associated with increased risk of institutionalisation and fallsand, it was considered an independent risk factor for mortality. Numerous studies have shown an association between aging and higher risks of functional dependence, as well as a high prevalence of functional disability or limited functional ability in the older adult population. These studies highlight that the added years of life should be accompanied by quality of life and should be free from the high cost of dependence. The decline in functional status may also be associated with a num-ber of multidimensional factors that interact to determine this status in older adults. Early detection of these factors can help prevent functional dependence in this group.

Functional ability is a key indicator of elderly to stay at home. For progressive chronic diseases like heart failure and chronic obstructive pulmonary disease, it is particularly important to understand functional ability as functional status losses are inevitable. Slowing the decline, then, is the goal for most patients with these diseases and the health care workers caring for them.

Functional status has been used to describe motor function, ability to perform ADL (Activities of Daily Living) and the ability to perform Instrumental Activities of Daily Living (IADL) (Knight, 2000). As people grow old they may experience that their health deteriorates and that being old often involves functional decline (Bank, 1995). Decline functional status is measured by an individual's loss of independence in Activities of Daily Living (ADL) and Instrumental Activities of Daily Living (IADL) over a period of time.

What is Functional Disability?

A functional concept of disability, defines a disability as any long-term limitation in activity resulting from a condition or health problem. This is the World Health Organization (WHO) definition and is the recommended international standard for data collection on disability. The use of this standard ensures that the results are comparable with those from other countries.People who indicated that they experienced difficulty in performing any of the activities, such as difficulty walking up and down a flight of stairs or difficulty hearing what is said in a normal conversation with one other person, were considered to have a disability.

Objectives of the Present Study

The main purpose of this study is to assessing the functional disability of the elderly Santal people living in their home assessed by two different functional scales such ADL and IADL. The study also aims to understand the prevalence and self reported health status of tribal elderly living in a social environment. The relevance and importance of assessing functional disability of tribal elderly was also within the objectives of this study.

Materials and Methods:

A uni-ethnic village resided by the Santal tribe was purposively selected for the present study. The village is named Dhadkidih and located within Ghatsila Police Station in the district of Singhbhum in Jharkhand State, India. In the village there are only 56 elderly (aged 60 and above as per Indian context) Santal populations across both the sexes. All aged people who are permanently staying in their own house were considered for the present study. A structured questionnaire schedule was used to collect data on social milieu and demographical aspects of the respondents. Functional status of the respondents were assessed by using the Barthel Index (BI) of Activities of Daily Living (using bowel, bladder, bathing, feeding, dressing, grooming, transferring, toilet use, mobility and stairs use) and the Lawton Instrumental Activities of Daily Living (telephone or mobile use, shopping, food preparation, housekeeping, laundry, transferring, own medication and handling finance). Other standard anthropological methods like participation observation, case studies were also followed. The data were computed by using SPSS v 16.0.

Results:

Table 25.1 shows the socio-demographic characteristics of the respondents. The mean age of the respondents was 71.61 years old and the median age was 72 years. As per distribution of the sex of the respondents female (55.36per cent) predominated over male (44.64per cent). It is evident from the Table1 that in case of the age group 80 and above there is more female elderly (19.35per cent) compared to their male counterpart (12.00 per cent). Among the studied population 28.57per cent were widow, 14.29per cent were widower and 57.14per cent were married. Out of total male population 68per cent were married where as out of total female population 48.39per cent were married.

In case of educational status of the respondents it is found that there are only 07.14 per cent persons who received primary education and remaining population were unlettered. Table 25.1 shows that among the females (96.86per cent) were illiterate where as in case of male 88.00 per cent were unlettered out of total male respondents.

Table 25.1: Socio-demographic Characteristics of the Respondents

Charecteristics	*Male*		*Female*		*Total*	
	Number	*Percentage*	*Number*	*Percentage*	*Number*	*Percentage*
Population	25	44.64	31	55.36	56	100.00
Age Group(in year)						
60 – 69	12	48.00	13	41.94	25	44.64
70 – 79	10	40.00	12	38.71	22	39.29
80 – 89	03	12.00	06	19.35	09	16.07
Marital Status						
Married	17	68.00	15	48.39	32	57.14
Widow	00	00.00	16	51.61	16	28.57
Widower	08	32.00	00	00.00	08	14.29
Education						
No Education	22	88.00	30	96.77	52	92.86
Primary	03	12.00	01	03.23	04	07.14
Family type						
Joint	24	96.00	26	83.87	50	89.28
Nuclear	01	04.00	02	06.45	03	05.36
Broken	00	00.00	03	09.68	03	05.36
Occupation						
Unskilled labour	02	08.00	01	03.23	03	05.36
Agriculture	18	72.00	02	06.45	20	35.71
Household chores	00	00.00	15	48.39	15	26.79
Traditional healer	01	04.00	00	00.00	01	01.79
No Occupatio n	04	16.00	13	41.94	17	30.35
Living Status						
With spouse	01	04.00	04	12.90	05	08.93
With sons	08	32.00	12	38.71	20	35.71
With spouse and sons	16	64.00	10	32.26	26	46.43
Alone	00	00.00	05	16.13	05	08.93

It is evident from the above table most of the respondents live in joint family. There are only 05.36per cent female who are living in broken family. However, 46.43per cent respondents are living with their spouses and sons.Among the total respondents 35.71per cent are without spouse and they are living with their sons. Only 08.93per cent female respondents have solitary living.

Among the total respondents 35.71per cent are engaged in agricultural activities in their own land and out of the total female respondent 26.79per cent participate in household chores. The household chores are always the activity of the females in the village. Out of the total respondents more female (41.94per cent) are without any occupation compared to their male counterpart (16.0per cent).

Table 25.2: Age group wise Functional Level of Studied Sample

	Functional level	*Age group (in years)*		
		60-69 (per cent)	*70-79 (per cent)*	*80+ (per cent)*
ADL	Totally dependent	0.00	0.00	33.33
	Very dependent	0.00	4.55	44.44
	Partially dependent	4.00	9.09	0.00
	Needs help to do	4.00	40.90	11.12
	Independent	92.00	45.46	11.11
IADL	Dependent	4.00	13.64	66.67
	Low function	0.00	27.27	33.33
	High function	64.00	54.55	0.00
	Independent	32.00	4.55	0.00

According to Barthel Index (BI) 22 respondents (39.29 per cent) were functionally dependent on at least one of the Activities of Daily Living. The categorisation of dependency levels has been presented under Table 25.2. Among the respondents belonging at the age group 60 to 69, 92.00 per cent were functionally independent. However, among the respondents belonging at the age group 70 to 79it is found that there were 45.46per cent 'independent', 40.90 per cent have 'need help to do', 09.09per cent 'partially dependent' and 04.55per cent 'very dependent' as per Barthel Index. Among the respondents at the age group 80 and above 33.33per cent were 'totally dependent', 44.44per cent were 'very dependent' and 11.12per cent were in 'need help to do' as per BI.

According to Lawton Instrumental Activities of Daily Living (IADL) out of the total number of respondents 47 (83.93per cent) were dependent on at least one activity. Functional level of 64.0per cent population was high and 32.0per cent were totally independent but only 04.0per cent were dependent on IADL and they are belonging at the age group 60 to 69. Among the populations within the age group 70 to 79 there were 54.55per cent people who were 'functionally high' followed by 27.27per cent people under the category of 'low functional level' and 13.64per cent people under 'totally dependent' category and only 04.55per cent were under 'independent' category. The functional level of the population aged 80 and above is lower compared to the population belonging at the age ranging from 60 to 79 since at the age group 80 and above 66.67per cent were 'totally dependent' and 33.37per cent belonging to the category of 'low function'.

From the Table 25.2 it is also revealed that as the age of the population go on, the dependency rate of ADL and IADL increases. Dependency rate is higher in case of female because they live longer than their male counterpart. It is also revealed that the studied population is more dependent on IADL (83.93per cent) than ADL (39.29per cent).

Table 25.3: Types of Functional Dependency

ADL (No. of dependent = 22)			*IADL (No. of dependent = 47)*		
Dependence on	*No*	*Percent of dependency*	*Dependence on*	*No*	*Percent of dependency*
Bowel	11	50.0	Telephone use	05	10.64
Bladder	16	72.73	Shopping	07	14.89
Bathing	11	50.0	Food preparation	31	65.96
Feeding	04	18.18	Housekeeping	23	48.94
Dressing	07	31.82	Laundry	07	14.89
Grooming	05	22.73	Mode of transportation	25	53.19
Transferring	06	27.27	Own medication	04	08.51
Toilet use	12	54.55	Handle finance	35	74.47
Mobility	05	22.73	Stairs	**	

* Some respondents were dependent in more than one activity.
**In the study area all the houses were single storey mud house without stairs.

It is revealed from Table 25.3 that out of total population 39.29per cent shows some kind of dependence on Activities of Daily Living (ADL) assessed by Barthel Index (BI) which encompasses question assessment on bowl and bladder continence, ability to bathing, feeding, dressing, grooming, transferring (e.g. from bed to chair etc.), ability to use toilet, mobility and ability to climb stairs. The most common type of functional dependence were bladder continence (72.73per cent) followed by toilet use (54.55per cent), bowel continence (50.0per cent), bathing (50.0per cent), dressing (31.82per cent), problem of transferring (27.27per cent), grooming (22.73per cent), mobility (22.73per cent) and 18.18per cent with feeding.

It is evident from Table 25.3 that among the respondent dependency ratio on Instrumental Activities of Daily Living (IADL) based on M.P. Lawton is greater than the Activities of Daily Living (ADL).Like ADL, Lawton Index encompasses eight questions such as telephone use, shopping, food preparation, housekeeping, laundry, transportation, own medication and handling finance. The most common dependence on IADL were in handling finance (74.47per cent) followed by preparing food (65.96per cent), transferring (53.19per cent), housekeeping (48.94per cent) and least dependency with shopping (14.89per cent), laundry (14.89per cent), telephone use (10.64per cent) and own medication (08.51per cent).

Table 25.4: Mean sd and t-test of ADL and IADL of Studied Sample

Variable	*Number*		*Male*		*Female*		*t-value*	*P*
	Male	*Female*	*Mean*	*Sd*	*Mean*	*Sd*		
ADL	25	31	4.4800	0.91833	4.0000	1.39044	1.483	0.144
IADL	25	31	2.7600	0.83066	2.9032	.97826	-0.582	0.563

From Table 25.4 it is evident that the mean value of male is greater than female in case of ADL and in the case of IADL mean value of female is greater than male. It also depicts that the t-value is found to be non significant in case of difference in mean values of both ADL and IADL, between males and females.

Table 25.5: Age group wise mean (sd) and ANOVA of ADL and IADL among the Studied Sample

Variable	*Age group (years)*			*F*	*Sig.*
	60-69 (n=25)	*70-79 (n=22)*	*80+ (n=9)*		
ADL	4.880 (0.44)	4.272 (0.83)	2.222 (1.39)	35.939	0.000
IADL	3.400 (0.50)	2.772 (0.75)	1.444 (0.52)	33.600	0.000

It is clear from the Table that the mean of ADL in the age group of 60-69 is greater than other two age groups (70-79; 80 and above). Further, the mean of IADL in the age group of 60-69 is also greater than other two age groups. For both the parameters, the mean differences are found to be significant (F=35.939 and 33.600 for ADL and IADL, respectively).It indicates that mean score of ADL and IADL is highly significant.

Table 25.6: Correlation co-efficient of ADL and IADL

	ADL	*IADL*
ADL Pearson Correlation N	1	.672** 56
IADLPearson Correlation N	.672** 56	1

Note:** Correlation in significant at the 0.01 level.

There is the correlation between ADL and IADL and the association between ADL and IADL is positively significant (r=0.672).

Discussion

It is revealed from the study that there are high percentages of elderly people i.e. 10.20per cent within the studied village and the figure is greater than the national level (7.5per cent as per 2001 census) since it is found that the total population of the village under study is 549 and out of them 56 were aged (age 60 and above). Among the elderly population (aged 60 and above) of the village there are more number of elderly females that their male counterpart and in terms of longevity female also ascend over male and these two features are very much in tune with the global scenario.On the aspects of marital status of the respondents we find more married couple than both the widow and widower. Maximum of the elderly respondents live with their spouse and married son and thus live in joint family. Most of the widow and widower reside with sons and only 08.93per cent of the widow lives a lonely. Approximate 75per cent of the elderly males are engaged in agricultural activities and 50per cent of the females perform only the household chores. It is noticed that there are more economically inactive elderly female than their male counterpart in the village since there are more longevity among the females and it is well established that here is a relation between age and occupation and physical activities of man decrease with the aging process.

We found that 92per cent of the elderly people (aged 60 and above) under study belong to age group 60-69 and are independent on ADL.

However, it is evident that percentage of independency decreases with the increase of age. It is also found that respondents at the age 80 and above were functionally 'very dependent' followed by 'totally dependent' category compared to the elderly segment below the age of 80. Among the respondents in the age ranging from 70 to 79 it is found that 45.46per cent of them need help from someone to do such kind of day to day essential activities. It may be said that functionally they were independent when this segment was in the age ranging from 60-69 years and they may be 'fully dependent' at the age of 80 and above. Similarly, all of these findings are applicable to IADL; however, dependency of IADLs is higher than ADLs because this is more skilled job and requires more complex expertise.Concerning the functional capacity based on the result of this study 39.29per cent population are dependent on ADL and the percentage increasing to 83.93per cent for IADL.

In the area of ADL, the study depicted that continence (both bowel and bladder) was the activity with higher dependence. On other hand in case of IADL, handling finance were the most dependent ones.

Conclusion

On the basis of the preceding sections of the present article it may be stated that the functional decline is common among the elderly population under study. The risk factors for functional decline are age as well as presence of ailments rather than socio-economic status. Compared to their male counterpart, declined functional level, development of the disability and dependence found more among the female elderly owing to their greater longevity and widowhood. Prevention of functional decline of the elderly people need priority and such prevention may be possible by way of detecting the functional decline at first stage followed by rehabilitation and/or quality care in the home.There are negative effects of decline of functional status on health and the concept of "Active Ageing" fully demolishes by decline of functional status. The authors suggest that the current study may be extended further over a large number of elderly populations across different ethnic groups so that same may be used for future policy planning, execution and service enhancement purposes.

Bibliography

Bank, S.P. (1995).Before the last leaves fall: Sibling connections among the elderly.*Journal of Geriatric Psychiatry*, 28, 183-195.

Beland, F., Zunzunegui, M.V. (1999).Predictors of functional status in older people living at home.*Age and Ageing*. 28, 153-159.

Biswas, S.K. Ageing in Contemporary India. 8th Indian Anthropological Society Occasional Papers.

Chan, K.M., Pang, W.S., Ee, C.H., Ding, Y.Y., Choo P. (1999). Functional Status of the Elderly in Singapore.*Singapore Medical Journal*, 40 (10).

Fillenbaum, G.G. (1988). Activities of daily living. The Encyclopedia of Ageing, 2,7-9.

Heikkinen, R. L., (1998). The role of physical activity in healthy ageing.*World Health Organization- Ageing and HelthProgramme.*

Hoffman, T., McKenna, K., Cooke, D. & Tooth, L,. (2003). Outcomes after stroke: Basic and instrumental activities of daily living, community reintegration and generic health status. *Australian Occupational Therapy Journal*, 225-233.

Jagger, C., Spiers,N.A.,Clarke, M. (1993). Factors associated with decline in function, institutionalization and mortality in the elderly. Age and Ageing, 22, 190-197.

Knight, M M. (2000).Cognitive ability and functional status.*Journal of Advanced Nursing,* 31 (6), 1459-1469.

Kua, E.H. (1991). The Functional Status of Elderly Chinese 75 Years and Older.*Singapore Medical Journal.* 32, 221-224.

Lawton, M.P., Brody, E.M., (1969). Assessment of older people: Self-maintaining and instrumental activities of daily living. *Gerontologist* 9, 179-186.

Lawton M.P. (1988).Scales to measure competence in everyday activities.*Psychopharmacology Bulletin* 24, 609-614.

Million-Calenti, J.C., Tubio, J., Pita-Fernandez, S., Gonzalez-Abraldes, I., Lorenzo, T., Fernandez-Arruty, T., Maseda, A. (2010). Prevalence of functional disability in activities of daily living (ADL), instrumental activities of daily living (IADL) and associated factors, as predictors of morbidity and mortality. *Archives of Gerontology and Geriatrics,* 50, 306-310.

Zeng, Y., Vaupel, J.W., Xiao, Zhenyu., Zhang, C., Liu, Y. (2002). Sociodemographic and Health Profiles of the Oldest Old in China.*Population and development review.* 28 (2), 251-273.

26

Socio-Economic Problem and Assessment of Nutritional Status of Elderly Male of Chakdah Municipal Town, West Bengal

Bigitendriya Debsharma

Introduction

Nowadays, India has been suffering from great nutritional problem. More than half the World's undernourished populations live in India (Krishnaswami, 2000). World Health Organization (1995) has recommended that anthropometry could be used to assess the nutritional and health status of adults. Low Body Mass Index (BMI) and high levels of undernutrition (based on BMI) are major public health problem especially among rural underprivileged adults of developing countries (WHO, 1995). Although adult nutritional status can be evaluated in many ways, the BMI is most widely used because its use is simple, inexpensive, safe and suitable for large scale surveys (Lohman *et. al.*, 1988; Ferro-Luzzi et al., 1992; James et al., 1994; Lee and Nieman, 2003). Thus, BMI is the most established anthropometric indicator used for assessment of adult nutrition status (Lee and Nieman, 2003).

This chapter reports an anthropological research undertaken on elderly males of Chakdah Municipal Town of Nadia District of West

Bengal. Advances in medical technology, better nutrition and healthcare have extended the human life span in 20th century. The 21st century must therefore live with the consequences of that far-reaching achievement. One million people cross the 60 year mark every month, and of them 80 per cent are in the developing World. The age of 60 or 65 years, roughly equivalent to retirement ages in most developed countries is said to be the beginning of old age. The United Nations generally uses 60+ years to refer to the older population.

According to 2001 Census total population of India is 102,86,10,328 of which 60+ population is 7,66,22,321 (7.44 per cent of the total population). The numbers of urban and rural elderly in India are 1,91,77,607 and 5,74,44,714 respectively.

In case of West Bengal, as per 2001 Census the total population is 8, 01, 76,197 of which the number of 60+ years population is 57,00,099 (7.11 per cent of the total population of West Bengal). Among the total elderly persons of West Bengal 33.21 per cent live in urban areas and 66.79 per cent are rural inhabitants.

An anthropometric assessment of health and nutritional status inhabitants of the community with respect to Body Mass Index (BMI) and Mid Upper Arm Circumference (MUAC) records the state of health of the population that lives under poor economic conditions. In general, the elderly peoples of India are recognised as socially and economically vulnerable.

Ferro-Luzzi (1990) and James *et.al.* (1994) have proposed MUAC cut-off points for use in screening acute adult undernutrition. They base these on extrapolation from more normally nourished populations in developing countries, without reference to data from acutely undernourished adults during famine. Although there is some evidence that the undernourished category may be associated with increased morbidity in chronically undernourished populations, we doubt whether the criteria proposed are appropriate for screening acutely undernourished adults. The MUAC has been recommended as a useful measure in diagnosis of malnutrition among adults in developing countries. MUAC is an appropriate indicator for the assessment of acute adult under-nutrition. The indicator is useful for both screening acute adult under-nutrition and for estimating prevalence of under-nutrition at a population level.

Some Brief Notes

Nutrition

Nutrition is the provision, to cells and organisms, of the materials necessary to support life. Many common health problems can be prevented or alleviated with a healthy diet. A poor diet can have an injurious impact on health, causing deficiency diseases such as scurvy and kwashiorkor; health-threatening conditions like obesity and metabolic syndrome; and such common chronic systemic diseases as cardiovascular disease, diabetes, and osteoporosis. In general, people can survive for two to eight weeks without food, depending on stored body fat and muscle mass. Survival without water is usually limited to three or four days. Lack of food remains a serious problem, with about 36 million people dying every year from causes directly or indirectly related to hunger. However global food distribution is not equal, and obesity among some human populations has increased to almost epidemic proportions, leading to health complications and increased mortality in some developed, and a few developing countries.

Malnutrition

Malnutrition means bad nutrition. The term applies equally to overnutrition as to undernutrition, but it tends to be used more for the latter than the former. It has been estimated that the proportion of the World's population exhibiting overnutrition now matches that showing undernutrition.

Assessment of Nutritional Status

The assessment of the nutritional of an individual or group involves the collection of information: on diet, biochemical indices, anthropometry, clinical signs, morbidity and mortality statistics. The value and place of this disparate group of measurement can best be understood by considering the process of becoming malnourished.

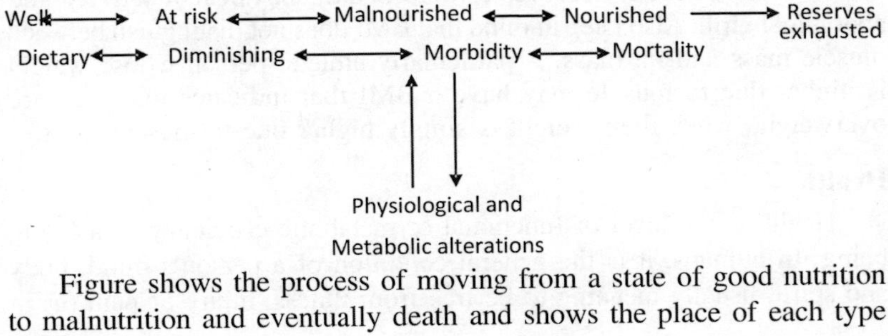

Figure shows the process of moving from a state of good nutrition to malnutrition and eventually death and shows the place of each type of measurement.

Body Mass Index (BMI)

Body Mass Index is defined as the individual's body mass divided by the square of his or her height. The formulae universally used in medicine produce a unit of measure of kg/m^2. The BMI for human body fat based on an individual's weight and height. BMI does not actually measure the percentage of body fat.

BMI provided a simple numeric measure of a person's "thickness" or "thinness", allowing health professionals to discuss over- and under-weight problems more objectively with their patients. For a given height, BMI is proportional to mass. However, for a given mass, BMI is inversely proportional to the square of the height. So, if all body dimensions double and mass scales naturally with the cube of the height, then BMI doubles instead of remaining the same. This result in taller people having a reported BMI that is uncharacteristically high compared to their actual body fat levels.

Interpreting your BMI

If your BMI is below 18.5, you are considered underweight. Consider speaking to your doctor about ways that you can add healthy calories to your diet. If your BMI is 18.5 - 24.9, you are considered to be a normal weight. Keep following a healthy diet and exercise plan to maintain your weight and health. If your BMI is 25.0 - 29.9, you are considered overweight. It is very important to consider making some lifestyle changes that incorporate better nutrition and activity choices. Speak to your doctor or a nutritionist for some ideas if necessary. Finally, if your BMI is above 30, you are considered obese. Obesity has been linked to a number of serious health complications, so it is imperative to make some changes now. Please discuss any diet and exercise plan with either your doctor or a nutritionist.

Limitations of BMI

While the BMI tool is fairly reliable, it is only one tool that physicians use in evaluating a person's health status. It is important to take other measures like blood pressure, cardiac health, physical inactivity and abdominal girth. Also keep in mind that BMI does not distinguish between muscle mass and fat mass. A particularly athletic person whose weight is higher due to muscle may have a BMI that indicates that they are overweight, when their weight is simply higher due to muscle mass.

Health

Health is the level of functional or metabolic efficiency of a living being. In humans, it is the general condition of a person's mind, body and spirit, usually meaning to be free from illness, injury or pain (as in "good health" or "healthy"). World Health Organization's (WHO's) definition of "health"- The most famous modern definition of health was created during a Preamble to the Constitution of the World Health Organization as adopted by the International Health Conference, New York, 19-22 June, 1946; signed on 22 July 1946 by the representatives of 61 States and entered into force on 7 April 1948. Health is a state of complete physical, mental and social well-being and not merely the absence of disease or infirmity.

The maintenance and promotion of health is achieved through different combination of physical, mental, and social well-being, together sometimes referred to as the *"health triangle"*. The WHO's 1986 *Ottawa Charter for Health Promotion* further stated that health is not just a state, but also "a resource for everyday life, not the objective of living. Health is a positive concept emphasising social and personal resources, as well as physical capacities."

Chronic Energy Deficiency (CED)

CED is defined as a "steady state" where an individual is in energy balance, i.e. the energy intake equals the energy expenditure, despite the low body weight and low body energy stores. Thus, by never growing to a normal size or having experienced one or more stages of energy deficiency, the individual has arrived at a reduced body weight with possibly limited physical activity, which have allowed the energy demands of a lower Basal Metabolic Rate (BMR) and reduced amounts of activity to balance the lower intake.

If a simple, objective, and reliable definition of CED is based on anthropometry, it is important to evaluate the range of weight-height indices suitable for this purpose. While different types of indices may be used, the Body Mass Index (BMI) may be ideal.

In broad terms, the body is composed of: active tissue mass, (lean body mass or fat free mass) and fat mass which is the body's principal energy store:

$$\text{Body Weight} = \text{fat free mass} + \text{fat mass}$$

The steady state will change when either energy supply is reduced or demands for energy output increase and this change is not counterbalanced on the other side of the equation. In response to this change, there is a fall in body weight but not essential energy output. Monitoring of individuals has shown that body weight does change as soon as energy imbalance occurs (Ferro-Luzzi, 1990).

CED as Diagnosed by Anthropometry

One of the simplest ways of diagnosing CED in adults would be to resort to the use of an uncomplicated, reliable and easily obtainable anthropometric measure such as height, body weight or some combined index of weight and height. Recent reports have advocated that height may be particularly useful as an index of socio-economic conditions in developing societies because populations which are poorly fed and subject to repeated infections rarely grow well in either childhood or adolescence and fail to achieve an adult stature which is commensurate with their full genetic potential (Gopalan, 1987).

Objectives :

1. To evaluate the nutritional status, based on MUAC and BMI of elderly males of Chakdah Municipal Town of Nadia District, West Bengal.
2. To find out the Socio-economic problem of the elderly population of proposed study area.

Materials and Methods

Study Sample

The present cross sectional study was conducted among 250 elderly males age 60 years and above were measured from 22 wards of the Chakdah Municipal Town. Random sampling method was used to sampling the population. Data on socio-economic background of the individual respondent, food habits, last two years disease, their living condition and day-to-day activities have been collected with the help of household census survey, interview technique aided by structured questionnaires.

Study Area

The Chakdah Municipal Town is selected as study area which consisted with 22 wards, near the Chakdah railway station; approximately 95 km. far from Kolkata, the provincial capital of West Bengal. Chakdah today is totally service sector oriented economy along with business as an un-organised informal sector. Total population of Chakdah Municipality is 86,965 according to 2001 Census.

Economic Profile of the Study Area

An important feature of the Chakdah's economic fabric is the Chakdah *Haat* traditionally known as the Mrityunjoy Singher *haat* which functions every Friday. The typical *haat* feature of temporary stalls is absent as majority of the sales counters are permanent shops. Thus transactions also happen on other days against a user charge paid to the Municipality. Products primarily evolve around handloom and textile based items. *Sarees* comprise indigenous products as well as *sarees* from the well known producing hubs in Phulia. The turnover of the *haat* is good as it serves as major trading centre for Kolkata as well as adjoining areas.

People in the region work in neighbouring areas and in Kolkata. Industries are almost nonexistent except a few small-scale industries mainly plastic factories. Chakdah was once a prominent centre of jute industry but over the years jute industries have faced a dwindling fate. Chakdah was also an important centre of indigo cultivation. The debris of indigo factories are still found in and around Municipality. In 1789, a disastrous flood washed away all the factories along the Sukhsagar. It ended the indigo cultivation in Chakdah. In the Chakdah Municipality small businesses are growing at a fast pace within the Municipal area and constitutes a major economic base of the Municipality. There are just seven small scale industries in the Municipal region.

Measurements

Internationally accepted standard protocol was followed for anthropometric measurements. Anthropometric variables include height, weight and mid upper arm circumferences. The information on ethnicity and age were obtained from all subjects in prepared questionnaire.

Methods for Taking Measurements

The technique of the various measurement, were collected on this purpose are as follows:

Height (HT) :

It measure the vertical distance from floor to the top most point (vertex) of the head. The subjects head is straight (FH Plane) at the time of measurement. Height was recorded to the nearest 0.1cm.

Instrument used : Anthropometer.

Weight (WT) :

It is defined as the composite measure of the total body size. Weight was recorded to the nearest 0.5 kg.

Instrument used : Weighing machine.

Mid-Upper Arm Circumference (MUAC) :

This circumference is measured in the mid-line of the arm, a point midway between the lateral projection of the acromion process of the scapula and the inferior margin of the olecranon process of the ulna. The level of measurement is determined by measuring a distance between the two points, using a tape, with the elbow flexed to 90° with the palm facing superiorly. It was recorded to the nearest 0.1cm.

Instrument used : Non stretchable fiber tape.

The BMI was computed using the following standard equation :

BMI = Weight (kg.)/height (m.^{2}).

Nutritional status was evaluated using internationally accepted BMI guidelines. The following cut-off points were used:

CED BMI < 18.5

Normal: BMI = 18.5-24.9

Overweight: BMI ≥ 25.0

CED was further divided into CED III, CED II and CED I as BMI < 16.0, 16.0-16.9 and 17.0-18.4 kg./m.^{2}, respectively.

We followed the World Health Organization's classification (1995) of the public health problem of low BMI, based on adult populations worldwide. This classification categorises prevalence according to percentage of a population with BMI< 18.5.

Low (5-9per cent): warning sign, monitoring required.

Medium (10-19per cent): poor situation.

High (20-39per cent): serious situation.

Very high (≥ 40per cent): critical situation.

MUAC (cm) = Mid-Upper Arm Circumference

MUAC value < 23: Undernutrition

Brief Literature Review :

First gerontological researches in India were started by Prof. P.V. Ramamurti in the early 1960s. The major aim of his research was to find out the specific psychological problems faced by the elderly people after their retirement.

In the late 1960s Prof. H. D. Marulassidiah started his research work among the old peoples of Makunti village (district Dharwar, Karnataka). The major emphasis of his research was to understand the influence of urbanisation on older person.

In the early 1970s a group of social scientist from Tata Institute of Social Sciences (TISS) conducted research on the pensioner of Bombay. Their major aim was to understand the problems of pensioner of greater Bombay.

In terms of range of issues addressed by the researchers on elderly population of India are largely centred on middle class, educated and service sector populations. The major aspects which are covered by these researchers may be tentatively projected under the various subheadings like: exploration into the economic crises of the elderly people; family environments and care of the elderly people; extra familial rehabilitation and conditions of the institutionalised elderly people; abuses perpetrated on old-age persons; leisure and recreation of the older people; issues related to socio-psychological adjustment; health related issues of the elderly people.

Most of the above mention studies are addressed to a single issue of the elderly rather than encompassing the multiple issues. However, study of Dandekar (1996) is a notable exception to it. Her study in Maharastra covers number of aspects of the elderly at a time. But she again did not deal with urban and rural elderly separately. Khan's studies (1997) in the city of New Delhi entitled 'Elderly in Metropolis' only dealt with demographic and socio-economic aspects of the elderly. He did not focus anything about the health aspects of the elderly of New Delhi. Without these Health and Nutrition related research papers were reviewed to prepare this article.

Result

Age-group specific number, Mean, Standard Deviation for the Body Mass Index (BMI) and Mid-Upper Arm Circumference (MUAC) of Elderly Males are presented in Tables 1 and 2 showing that nutritional status based on BMI that is 87.2 per cent Elderly peoples are undernourished and 12.7per cent are Normal as well as nutritional status based on MUAC that is 84.8 per cent belongs to under nutrition and 16.2 per cent only in normal situation out of 250 Elderly males. Mean BMI of different age groups were calculated 21.24, 21.9 and 21.46 where F=0.586 and P=0.558. Mean MUAC were 22.26 cm., 22.09cm. and 22.33 cm., Standard Deviation (SD) were 0.96, 0.95 and 0.79 where F=1.156, P

Table 26.1 : Mean and SD of BMI, MUAC, Height and Weight in Different Age Groups of Elderly Males

Age Group (in years)	*Total No.*	*BMI(Kg./m.^{2})*		*MUAC (Cm.)*		*HT (Cm.)*		*WT (Kg.)*	
		Mean	*SD*	*Mean*	*SD*	*Mean*	*SD*	*Mean*	*SD*
60-65	117	21.24	1.63	22.26	0.96	1.5995	3.86	54.28	3.65
66-70	63	21.19	1.53	22.09	0.95	1.6062	3.47	54.61	3.39
71-80	70	21.46	1.50	22.33	0.79	1.5940	3.64	54.47	3.30
Total	250	F=0.586; P=0.558		F=1.156; P=0.316		F=1.811; P=0.166		F=0.201; P=0.818	

Table 26.2. Prevalence of Under Nutrition Based on BMI and MUAC among Elderly Males

Variable	*Total No.*	*Nutritional Status*	
		Under Nutrition (per cent)	*Normal (per cent)*
BMI	250	218 (87.3)	32 (12.7)
MUAC	250	212 (83.8)	38 (16.2)

=0.316. Mean Height, Weight and SD were calculated in different age groups. The Mean BMI and MUAC showing the Elderly males in different age groups are undernourished but there showing no significant differences.

Discussion and Conclusion

The present study is on the nutritional status of Elderly male that is consider as 60 aged people, that time the elderly people gradually loose their working strength and muscle power, so they have to need regular diet intake nutritious food for proper nutritional status. WHO states that conventional BMI cutoffs for defining CED may not be appropriate for older people 70 years and over, because of age-related changes in body composition . In the absence of alternatives, we used the conventional values, but feel strongly that research is needed on this subject.

Mid-Upper Arm Circumference (MUAC) has recently emerged in the literature as a potential screening tool for poor nutritional status analysed its usefulness in adults, and calculated cutoffs equivalent to Body Mass Index (BMI) and cutoffs for Chronic Energy Deficiency (CED), using a range of data sets from developing countries. MUAC is an appropriate indicator for the assessment of acute adult undernutrition. This indicator is useful for both screening acute adult undernutrition and for estimating prevalence of undernutrition at a population level. The assessment of adult nutritional status using MUAC requires no equipment apart from a tape measure. As the index is the actual measurement itself, mathematical manipulation of the measurement obtained is not necessary. The ease with which MUAC can be assessed makes it suitable for nutritional screening during the height of an emergency where time and skilled personnel are at a premium· The MUAC measurement reflects adult nutritional status as defined by BMI.· The measurement of MUAC has been used as a useful screening method for the assessment of nutritional status in different ethnic groups (Olukoya, 1990) Since it is the most reproducible and simplest measurement to perform, its use has been recommended in nutritional studies (Harries, 1984).

Measuring MUAC has several advantages; the measurement can be taken quickly and at little cost. It requires neither sophisticated equipment nor anything but the most basic literacy level to carry out. However, although an MUAC value < 23 cm. have been recommended for use to define undernutrition (James, 1994), this value may not be the most appropriate cut-off point in all ethnic groups. A recent study from Nigeria reported that a MUAC cut-off point of 23 cm. was optimal for the north of the country, while a 24 cm. cut-off point was more appropriate for the South. A similar cut-off point of 24 cm. was also obtained in a recent study from South India (Rodrigwes. 1994). Thus, there is a need for more studies using MUAC in different ethnic groups of India so that they provide ethnic-specific cut-off points of MUAC to facilitate better public health planning and implementation.

Bibliography

Desai, K.G., ed. (1982). *Ageing in India*. Bombay: Tata Institute of Social Sciences.Dandekar, Kumudini; (1996). *The Elderly in India*, Sage Publication, India Pvt. Ltd.

Ferro-Luzzi, A. (Ed.). (1990). Biology of adaptation to seasonal cycling of energy intake. *Eur. J. Clin. Nut.* 44 (Suppl. 1):1125.

Ferro-Luzzi, A., W. P. James, Lee and Nieman, (2003), *British Journal of Nutrition*, 75 (1996) 3.-

Gopalan, C. (1987). Heights of population - an index of their nutrition and socio-economic development. *Bull. Nutr. Found. Ind.* 8: 1-5.

Harries, A.D., A. J. Laura., R. V. Heatley., R. G. Newcombe., J. Rhodes, *Clinical Nutrition,* 2, (1984) 193.

James WPT, Mascie-Taylor CGN, Norgan NG, Bristrian BR, Shetty P, Ferro-Luzzi A (1994) The value of arm circumference measurements in assessing chronic energy deficiency in Third World adults. *European Journal Clinical Nutrition*. 48:883–894.

Khan,M.Z. 1997. *Elderly in Metripolis*. Inter India publications, New Delhi.

Krishnaswami, K. (2000). Country profile: India. nutritional disorders-old and changing. *The Lancet* 351, 1268 – 1269.

Lee, R.D. & Nieman, D.C. (2003). *Nutritional Assessment.* New York: McGraw Hill.

Lohman TG, Roche AF, Martorell R (1988) *Anthropometric Standardization Reference Manual*. Human Kinetics Books, Chicago.

Olukoya, A. A. *Internet Journal of Gynecology and Obstetrics*, 31 (1990) 231.

Rodrigues, V. C., R. S. Rao., A. Lena, *Tropical Doctor* 24 (1994) 164.

Technical Report Series no. 854. World Health Organization, Geneva.

WHO 1986 *Ottawa Charter for Health Promotion* further stated that health is not just a state, but also "a resource for everyday life, not the objective of living. Health is a positive concept emphasizing social and personal resources, as well as physical capacities."

World Health Organization (1995) *Physical status: the use and interpretation of anthropometry.*

World Health Organization (1995) Physical status: the use and interpretation of anthropometry. Technical Report Series no. 854. World Health Organization, Geneva.

World Health Organization as adopted by the International Health Conference, New York, 19-22 June, 1946; signed on 22 July 1946 by the representatives of 61 States (Official Records of the World Health Organization, No. 2, p.100) and entered into force on 7 April 1948.

27

Child Workers : A Great Hindrance on the Way to Development

Biswanath Gan

The term child labour is, at times, used as synonym for employed child or working child. But a working child is one who subjects himself or herself to work, unpaid or free, instead of being at the school at a tender and formative stage of his or her life. The Operation Research Group (ORG) in India defines a working child as "….a child failing within 5-14 age bracket and who is at remunerative work, may be paid or unpaid and busy at any hour of the day within or outside the family…." (Panigrahi, 1997). There is no commonly accepted definition of child labour. Definitions are varied and unclear. Considering this fact, the following characteristics may be considered as the distinguishing marks of the child labour:

Violates a nation's minimum age laws.

Threatens children's physical, mental, or emotional well-being.

Involves intolerable abuse, such as child slavery, child trafficking, debt bondage, forced labour, or illicit activities.

Prevents children from going to school.

Uses children to undermine labour standards

In Encyclopedia of Social Sciences, child labour is defined as "when the business of wage earning or if participation itself or family support conflicts directly or indirectly with the business of growth and education, the result is child labour". Child labour is a serious problem and it is present in many of the developing and advanced countries of the world too. The child labour is a complex matter and it is deeply rooted in the socio-economic fabric of the society that it may not be wise to rely on one single approach to dealing with it. However, child labour is present in all parts of the world and no doubt it is the violation of human rights. According to ILO estimates, some 250 million children between the ages of five and 14 work in developing countries alone. About half, or some 120 million work full time, while the rest combine work and schooling. In some cases as many as 68 per cent of these children are engaged in hazardous work. According to Census of India, 2001, there were 1.26 crore working children in the 5-14 age groups as compared to 1.13 crore in 1991. The state wise distribution shows that the largest number of working children were found in Uttar Pradesh (19,27,997), followed by Andhra Pradesh (13,63,339), Rajasthan (12,62,570), Bihar (11,17,500), Madhya Pradesh (10,65,259) and West Bengal (8,57,087). Child labour is a serious complex problem not only in India but all over the world. Child labour is certainly a socio-economic phenomenon and in this context the poverty, unemployment, illiteracy, social discrimination and demographic expansion are generally considered as the most important causal factors for large scale employment of children. The well stated fact is that the child labour is necessitated by the financial requirement of the parents. In this connection, Biswas (2006) mentioned that a large number of children worked in stone crushing sector at Balasan River basin of Darjeeling district, West Bengal, of whom many were undocumented migrants and the main reason for the involvement of children into this work was their serious economic setback. In this context, Gan (2012) mentioned that those children were suffering from various ill health and so many factors like hard physical labour for prolong hours in a day, hazardous working condition, poor quality and unhygienic food habit, poor standard of personal hygiene, absence of Primary Health Centre, improper care of diseases and ailments, dependency of traditional medicine men and local quacks, lack of health consciousness and awareness, poverty and so on were responsible for it. Again, Biswas and Gan (2012) observed that the daylong working involvement, financial constraint deprived the children of all their fundamental needs and rights like food, dress, shelter, opportunity of education etc. However, poverty is the main cause of child labour. Indeed, it was seen that those poor families had an average around five members' family and due to this fact it was very difficult for them to live on the earning of only one family member. Therefore, most of the children of those families were bound to involve in this work to support their family income. Poverty, illiteracy as well as lack of educational facilities among the poorer section of the society are the prime cause for children to start working early. These ignorant people do not think twice about engaging their children in manual labour, since they are not aware of the harmful physical and mental trauma it can inflict on the child. Being poor, they cannot afford a decent education for the children, nor do they understand the importance of primary education in children's lives. Child work can badly hinder children's development. All human rights apply to all boys and girls. While societies may vary in their ideas on childhood and child development, one thing that all can agree on is the importance of the well being of children. It is well recognised everywhere that children need special care and protection for healthy development because of their need and vulnerability (Tiwari, 2004). The number of child labour is increasing rapidly in India and the situation is becoming out of control for Government of India to uproot it from the very roots. Child labour is a great hindrance in child's development as well as in nation's development too. Children are considered as an extremely valuable asset for society. They can play an important role in the development of any nation. But it is true that many of the children work in different places and it is evident that the children worked in various sectors like tea shop, hotel, motel, restaurant, garage, mines, agriculture, manufacturing sectors such as brassware, match factory and fireworks, diamond cutting, gem polishing, glassware, carpet making, etc. as a child worker/labour. Therefore, the issue of child labour and its impact on their development is a matter of grave concern. However, in this context many of the children worked in stone field at Balasan River basin under Matigara C.D. Block, Darjeeling district of West Bengal either with their family or separately. To conduct this study, 50 families were selected. There were 90 children found in the 5 to 14 years age group. Among them, 75 children were engaged in stone based work. Anthropological methods like observation, case study, interview, census schedule etc. were used to collect the data.

The studied people came from various places and mostly from Bangladesh. They came here in resourceless condition. Even, they were facing many problems in their daily life related to maintain their daily livelihood, education, nationality and so on. In this regard, the children of most of the said families had to do work in stone field to assist their family income rather than given the importance of education and other enjoyment.

The information was collected during 2010 to 2011.

Case 1: Sujay Barman is a ten years aged boy belonged to Rajbanshi community lived in Purba Rangia village located on Balasan River basin adjacent to Siliguri town in the district of Darjeeling, West Bengal. They migrated here around eight years ago i.e. 2004 from Bangladesh primarily due to utter financial constraint. His father was died of physical illness in 2006. He was the bread earner and stone crusher by profession. After his death the rest family members including Sujay, his mother and elder sister altogether shared the burden of economic responsibility followed by the same occupation. The stone based occupation was the only source of income and their total family income is Rs. 1700/- per month. Sujay got involved with stone crushing activity only. He told that it was very hard and hazardous job but nevertheless he had to do it as his contribution to the family income was very essential. He got involved in this job nearly three years ago, when he was only seven years aged. He was not so interested to continue this job rather would like more to quit it if he got any other better opportunity. But who will offer him better job? A tear rolled down his face when he said they are poor so they can't hope for something better and nobody will come forward to extend their helping hands. Sujay worked hard for the whole day in inhuman working condition. Due to heavy work load he could hardly manage the time to study at home, play games and also for other recreational purposes. Sujay stopped going school because he could not manage adequate time for studies. He had to work hard for the whole day even sometimes he went out from the classes to join with his mother in the stone field. His regular school attendance was a seldom happening factor. He hardly got adequate rest. He could manage a fold of rice only if he worked. So, if he took rest, the family income would be decreased. Ultimately the heavy work load had seriously told upon his health, education and other development.

Case 2: Swapna Barman, thirteen years old girl belonged to Rajbanshi community. She was born in Bangladesh. They migrated here around seven years ago i.e. 2005 from Bangladesh mainly due to land alienation, poverty and socio-religious factors. After migration they were settled down at the studied village, Purba Rangia. In her family she has father, mother, two younger sisters and a brother who is junior to her. Both of her parents got involved in stone based job as prime earning source. But their earnings simply failed to ensure a minimum security for living. Under this circumstance, finding no other alternatives they sent their children to work. Therefore, Swapna had to involve in this work at a very early age to assist her family financially. Swapna did both stone crushing and sand gathering works and earned nearly Rs. 500/- per month. However, the total family income is nearly Rs. 2600/- per month. She was not satisfied with this job as it was very much labourious and hazardous job. Nevertheless she had no other option but continue it because she had a fear of scolding or often beating too by her parents. She told that her working involvement adversely affected her studies. Swapna was studying in class IV. She could not go to school every day because she had to help her mother. She had to do work almost throughout the week. She worked from morning to evening. She used to get up very early in the morning and then performed necessary domestic work. Generally she used to go to working place around 9.00 a.m. after having meal. At the noon she came back home and took lunch and very after she took rice meal to the working field for other family members and returned home at around 5.00 p.m. Her school attendance was a seldom happening factor due to involvement in work for the whole day. She disclosed a truth that she had to drop out of school because she could not continue both work and schooling simultaneously. Indeed, due to insufficient family income she could not continue her studies. She seemed to realise the reality that without proper educational attainment she will not be able to get a job. Who would offer it? So, she had to continue this job. Moreover, her parents rebuked her and often beat her soundly if she was absent in work. Swapna could manage the time hardly for playing games with peer group as she had to perform domestic chores too besides stone based job. She burst into tears while talking about her pathetic state as she was often rebuked or even beaten up soundly by her parents if she raised her eyes from work for a moment too.

Case 3: Hriday Singha aged thirteen years, a boy belonged to Rajbanshi community. He was born in Bangladesh. In his family he has father, mother, sister and an elder brother. They lived in the studied village. They migrated here in the year 2000 due to socio-religious and financial problems. After migration stone based work was the only way of making their living. Both his parents got involved in stone based economy to earn their living. But their little earnings could not feed them to fill. Therefore, for the sake of mere subsistence they forced their children to involve in this work. Hriday had been working for last six years. He involved stone crushing activity and often help his parents in stone collection activity. Their total family income is approximately Rs. 2700/ - per month. Apart from this, he has to help his parents in domestic chores such as carrying water, cleaning house, shopping and so on. Often he goes to market for shopping. Hriday reported that his father is a hard hearted man who reproached him always and even sometimes beat him soundly if he was absent in work. He could play only when his father goes to market but indeed it is a seldom happening factor. Both his parents usually scolded him if he do not help in household chores. He had dropped out of school when he was in class IV. His only remorse was that he always used to try to attend the class regularly. But it was hardly possible due to daylong involvement in work. Even his parents do not allow him to go to school regularly rather they used to like more to send him to the stone field. He told that he was scolded bitterly or even, often he was beaten up by his parents if he was absent in work. His daily working schedule was generally started like this- he used to get up at around 6.30 a.m. After morning fresh and having rice meal he went to stone field. During lunch he took pup rice etc. he has to work often up to evening. He generally used to comeback home at the evening when the work is over for the day. Even sometimes he used to go out from the class to join in work in the stone field. This prolong working schedule did not let him continue his studies.

Case 4: Sabitri Barman was a twelve years old girl, belonged to Rajbanshi community. She was born in Bangladesh. They came here in 2006 from Bangladesh due to poverty, socio-religious insecurity and so on. Sabitri has three younger sisters. After migration they finally settled down here. After migration both her parents got involved in stone based occupation. But feed to the fill was simply beyond their capacity. To get a financial support parents motivated their children to do this work. Sabitri has been working for four years. She do both stone crushing and stone collection jobs. She contributed her earnings to the family. Sabitri said that she has to continue this work against her will as her parents are quite satisfied with her earnings. They never loved her. They scolded her and sometimes beat her if she do not do the work. She had dropped out of school when she was in class-III. Her parents could not bear the expense of education like fees of private tuition, books; even she was not provided the minimum educational requirements. Due to day long involvement in work she could not attend the class. Besides these, there were so many obstacle factors to continue her studies. But nevertheless, she never got the positive response a bit from her parents for continuing her studies. Apart from this, Sabitri had to assist her mother in domestic chores like washing clothes, sweeping floor, cleaning the house and utensils, carrying water, going to shop and so on. Hence, the domestic work was just like heaping of sorrow upon sorrow to her which adversely affected her education. Again, the family environment, the intra-familial and inter-familial conflict etc. were not in favour of her study at home. Apart from involvement in work, there are many obstacle factors for her poor educational status.

Among the studied 50 families there were 90 children of 5 to 14 years age group, of whom more than 84 per cent children were involved in stone based work. They had to do the various types of stone based works like collection of sands, pebbles/stones even boulders too from the river. Apart from this, many of the children also had to do the household works along with the stone based work. They woke up early in the morning and after morning refreshment many were bound to go to the stone field otherwise, they had to remain in empty stomach. The economic situation of most of the studied families was varied from Rs. 1500/- to Rs. 3000/- per month, which was very difficult for maintaining their daily livelihoods for their average five members' families. To run the families they had no option but involvement of the children in the said work. They were interested to continue their education but overall situation did not permit them to do the same. In many cases dropouts were reported. Parents could not bear the expense of education including fees of tuition, books and other necessary requirements. It was seen many could not attend school regularly due to their working involvement as it was necessary to assist their family income. Even, if they were absent in this work, in many cases they were scolded and beaten by their parents. Generally they could not participate in games and failed to share their joys and sorrows. They did not get the required food as well as nutrition and even in many cases they had to remain in empty stomach. It was reported that many were sick but the parents were not in a position to bear the cost of proper treatment. Even, in many cases they were debarred from their parental love and affection. Moreover, their health, education and physical and psychological grown up were affected seriously.

However, day long working involvement harms children's social and educational development. Due to prolong working hours child labourers were deprived of school education, social interaction, personal development and leisure and recreation. Apart from these, children face many physical hazards and ill health. Therefore, child labour deprives children of their education, social, mental as well as physical development and their childhood is stolen. Childhood is an important period of life as it shapes adulthood and it is a serious moment for safe and healthy human development. But child labour has a deep adverse effect on a child's future here.

Observation and Recommendation

Child labour is a major problem in present world especially in poor and developing countries. It is a great hindrance for any development. Children are working in different sectors instead of education and other development. Due to various reasons and particularly for their survival this involvement is necessary. They do not get the necessary facilities to lead a normal life. The child labour, poverty, illiteracy, poor health etc. are very much related with each other. Besides poverty, deprivation of fundamental needs like education, lack of awareness and poor implementation of child labour laws also responsible for involvement of children into work. The child labour (prohibition and regulation) act 1986 was passed to eradicate all types of child labour from society but ultimately nothing significant came out. Various policies and programs were taken by the Government of India but indeed, it is very difficult for them to eliminate such social evil from very Indian roots. We all know that right to life is a fundamental right but why few enjoy it? So, we need to join our hands together to eliminate child labour from society. Apart from this, Government as well as Non Government Organizations should take necessary steps to solve this serious problem. Hope with all the efforts one day our country, India will definitely get rid of this social evil and will be able to provide a tension free life to the children.

Findings from this study show that, the development of children is seriously being hampered due to their day long working involvement. But a child requires play, recreation, physical, mental and cultural activities for their development and socialisation as well. Therefore, some special recommendations in order to their better life chances are given below :

Reduce poverty by increasing employment opportunities to the people.

Increase education opportunities by providing free and quality education to every child.

Implementation of child labour laws properly.

Increase public awareness about fundamental rights of children.

Launch necessary child care programmes.

Bibliography

Biswas, S. K. (2006), Child Worker, Poverty and Hunger: A Study among the Stone Crushers of Balasan River Bed, *Indian Journal of Human Rights and Justice* 2 (1 and 2): 25-37.

Biswas, S. K. and B. Gan (2012), Child Abuse in An Unorganised Sector: A case Study, In A. K. Census of India 2001, Paper 1 of 2001, *Provisional Populations Totals: India,* Office of the Registrar General, India.

Child Labour Public Education Project, http://www.continuetolearn.uiowa.edu/labourctr /child_ labour/about/what_is_child_labour.html, retrieved on 10.8.2012, at 6 pm.)

Gan, B. (2012), Child Worker and its Effect on Health: A Study on Stone Crushing Sector, In S. Biswas (eds.) *Human Health: A Bio-cultural Synthesis*, New Delhi: Concept Publishing Company PVT. LTD.

ILO to consider sweeping universal ban on worst forms of child labour, http://www.ilo.org/glob al/about-the-ilo/newsroom/news/WCMS_007930/lang—en/index.htm, retrieved on 21 .9 .20 12, at 9 pm.

Kale, S., *Causes and Effects of Child labour*, http://www.buzzle.com/articles/causes-and-effects-of-child-labour.html, retrieved on 23.7.2012, at 3.25 pm.

Naidu, M.C. and K. Dasaratha Ramaiah (2006), Child Labour in India - An Overview, *J. Soc. Sci.*, 13(3): 199-204.

Panigrahi, D.K. (1997), 'Child labour in India: A point of view', *Social Change,* 27 (3-4): 50-56.

Tiwari, J. (2004), Child Abuse and Human Rights; Vol. 2, Delhi: Isha Books.

Unit II: Children's Rights, http://www.globaled.uconn.edu/GlobalEdI/ProjectAwareness /unit2.htm, retrieved on 12.8.2012, at 11 pm.

28

Governance and Women Empowerment through Participation

Bidisha Banerjee

Introduction

In the era of globalisation, whether one likes or not, it can be stated with some degree to conviction that women fall into the poor section of the society in terms of their access to benefits from the process. Nobody is surprised or even too upset by this fact as it is taken for granted that globalisation will cause such hazards in the economy. Like any accident in a bus women and children are highlighted as the killed or severely injured passengers, in any way situation women die or become the refugee. Similarly there is nothing surprising that women will be worst affected in the local economy is destroyed, if local food production is taken away, if the security of livelihood is lacking. The rural development discourse has therefore shifted to the discourse of poverty alleviation.

The women in Indian society, despite pious promises enshrined in Indian Constitution to impart social, political and economic justice, equality of status and opportunity, freedom of thought and expression and also of doing away of any kind of discrimination on the basis of sex, continue to reel under awesome poverty and oppression. Therefore social justice to women will necessarily means giving them not only gender equality but also rightful place in the society. The Indian women at times immoratalised as goddess, never found their rightfall place in society or even in family. They are treated as were tools to bear the burdens of the family restricted to the role of bearing children and fulfilling duties of a wife or a mother only. A society, where women i.e.; the half of the population, enjoy a low status, cannot be said egalitarian. The low status of women in Indian society is primarily due to the fact that they have no control over material and social resources. Further it is compounded by lack of participation opportunities in the decision making process of the family.

Objectives :

The objective of this study are following :

(i) To study the different programmes through which women can participate.

(ii) To study the present scenario of India as well as West Bengal in respect of political empowerment of women.

(iii) To study the present situation of India as well as West Bengal in respect of economical empowerment of women.

Governance

Governance is said to be the process where by public institutions conduct public affairs, manage public resources and guarantee the realisation of human rights. The concept of governance is not new. It is as old as human civilisation. It simply means the process of decision making and the process by which decisions are implemented. Governance can be used in several context such as corporate governance, international governance, national governance and local governance. Since governance is the process of decision making and the process by which decisions are implemented, an analysis of governance focuses on the formal and informal actors involved in decision making and implementing the decisions made.

The true taste of governance is the degree to which it delivers on the promise of human rights, civil, cultural, economic, political and social rights. The key question is : Are the institutions of governance effectively guaranteeing the right to health, adequate housing, sufficient food, quality education, fair justice and personal security ? Clarifying the concept of good governance, the Commission on Human Rights identified its key attributes as

1) transparency
2) responsibility
3) accountability and
4) participation

Thus the concept includes elements of both democracy and public administration participation is common to both.

Participation

Women's participation in rural development has been sought to be achieved through the organisations of women at the grass root level. The Community Development Programme accorded an important role to the organisation of women, who constitute nearly half of our population, so that the enthusasiatic participation in rural development was effectively ensured. As a result organisations of women known as *Mahila Mandals* came to be established in a phased manner in different states. Most of its branches carry our independent activities and projects on their own. The broad objectives of these *Mandals*, as outlined in several documents were:

i) to help women to participate in development programmes.
ii) to provide opportunities for discussing their needs and problems and share responsibilities with other according to their interests and abilities.
iii) to act as an agency for planning, developing and executing programmes for women.
iv) to help them understand their role and responsibilities.
iv) to foster group efforts in the implementation of activities.
v) to develop different kinds of activities for the common good and
vi) to develop leadership among women.

Women must learn participative skills in democracy because unless they themselves share responsibilities and participate in fulfilling them, they do not strengthen in democratic structure of their society. In any developmental and welfare activity people's participation is a very essential component. For the optimum utilisation of the local institutions, its essence lies in the proper coordination of individual and social efforts.

Different Programmes through which Women can Participate

The centrally and state sponsored schemes launched by the Government of India and in all States and Union Territories are implemented by the DRDA'S though the Block Development Officers, as per guideline prescribed by the Government of India The programmes that the DRDA deals with at present are as follows :-

Swarnajayanti Gram Swarojgar Yojana (SGSY) :

As national policy, the SGSY programme was launched in the state during the year 1999 – 2000 with the objective of bringing every assisted poor family above the poverty line within a period of three years through the implementation of micro-enterprises. The scheme emphases on cluster and group approach. The programme covering various aspects of self-employment such as organisation of the poor into Self-Help Groups (SHG), training, credit, technology, infrastructure and marketing. It is envisaged that 50 per cent of the groups formed in each block should be exclusively for women who will account for the least 40 per cent of the *swarozgaris*. Under the scheme women are encouraged in the practice of thrift and credit, which enables them to become self-reliant. Through assistance in the form of revolutionary Fund, Bank Credit and Subsidy, the *Yojana* seeks to integrate women in the economy by providing increasing opportunities of self employment. While women were demanding for mainstreaming and entering macro economy the micro-credit has brought them back into the micro-credit for micro-trade, with a high interest rate which even the being industrialists are not paying.

The logic of SHG's as space for engagement, negotiation and struggle, goes beyond credit and addresses a wide range of development issues, including the role of social mobilisation in women's empowerment. Since more often than not SHG's are promoted and nurtured by external agencies, the process of organising, capacity building and supporting the groups in the formative stages assumes critical importance. Social intermediation is seen as a process of building both social capital and institutional capital for preparing these groups to engage in financial and social mediation. There is a growing dimension on the potential of microcredit to change gender relations or challenge existing social hierarchies.

Indra Awaas Yojana (IAY)

Indira Awaas Yojana (IAY) programme was introduced with the objective of providing dwelling houses to the rural poors. This is a centrally sponsored programmes where funding is shared between the Centre and State on 75 : 25 basis. Under the scheme, priority is extended to widow and unmarried women. It has been laid down that IAY houses are to be allotted in the name of women members of the household or alternatively in the joint names of husband and wife.

Sampoorna Grameen Rozgar Yojana (SGRY)

Following the merger of the erstwhile JGSY and EAS, the Ministry of Rural Development announced and launching of the SGRY with effect from October 2002. This is funded on 75 : 25 ratios between the Centre and State. The objective of the programme is to generate employment to the rural labourer by providing food grains as wages per man day. The department has been implementing this scheme with emphasis on agricultural related activities to supplement the production and economic activities of the rural people specially the women.

National Rural Employment Guarantee Scheme (NREGS)

This is a centrally sponsored employment generation scheme, implemented in consonance with the enforcement of the section IV of NREGA 2005. The scheme is funded on the basis of 90 : 10 between the Centre and the State. The objectives of this scheme are:

(i) To provide 100 days of guaranteed employment in a financial year to every household in the rural areas.

(ii) To create durable assets in rural areas and

(iii) To strengthen the livelihood security to the rural household.

One important consequence of NREGA has been the increase in the wage level for women,. In an already tight supply situation NREGA entered the arena offering work to all who are willing to work. Women workers did not abandon agricultural employment altogether. The women are willing to take up such work early in the morning and late the afternoon. The overall impact of a revamped NREGA on women's employment led to dramatic result. Since agricultural production had to go on, there arose a condition where both types of work have to be sequenced.

Economic Empowerment

While discussing women's economic empowerment it is essential to remember that a part of the work that women do is paid and a part unpaid. The proportion of unpaid work done by women is very high compared to that the paid work. An inquiry into women's work has also been essential for assessing women's empowerment. According to the UNDP guidelines, women's economic participation is an important element of the Gender Empowerment Measure (GEM). GEM examines whether women and men are able to actively participate in economic and political life and take part in decision making. In West Bengal work participation of went hand-in hand with social and political participation of women, especially in rural areas. This has been possible due to a decentralised planning programme implemented through a three tier panchayet system which has involved women in economic, social and political processes simultaneously at the grassroot level. Economic participation has been categorised an administrative and other work, where work appears as a main category.

The proportion of main and marginal workers in the total workforce calculated for both female and male workers in the rural and urban areas provide proof of the extent of marginalisation of female labour. It is available in the census data.

Table 28.1 : Marginalization of Female Labour from 1981 ˘ 2001 (Worker population ratio)

Category	*Census years*		
	1981	*1991*	*2001*
Male (Main)	48.71	50.50	47.32
Male (Marginal)	1.51	0.86	6.91
Female (Main)	5.81	8.07	8.86
Female (Marginal)	2.26	3.60	9.22

Source: Census of India

If we look at the Table 28.1 we can see there is an increase in marginalisation of female labour force and it is still continuing. We can now see the state among the 15 major states in the country according to female work participation rate and the change in this rate between 1991 and 2001.

From the above Table 28.2 it is clear that a few states like Haryana improved their status significantly with respect to female work participation between 1991 and 2001, in West Bengal it remained under 20 per cent.

The overall picture that emerges is different with respect to different sectors of female employment. There has been increase in the number of earning middle class females over the last few years but it is not sufficient, So more attention is needed.

Table 28.2 : Female Work Participation Role at the National Level and 15 Major States of the Country between Census 1991 and 2001

Country/States	*Census Years*	
	1991	*2001*
India	22.25	25.68
Himachal Pradesh	34.82	43.69
Andhra Pradesh	34.32	34.93
Rajasthan	27.40	33.48
Maddhya Pradesh	32.68	33.10
Maharashtra	33.11	32.59
Karnataka	20.39	31.88
Tamil Nadu	29.9	31.32
Gujrat	25.96	28.03
Haryana	10.76	27.31
Odisha	20.79	24.62
Tripura	13.76	21.02
Assam	21.61	20.80
Bihar	14.86	18.84
Punjab	4.40	18.68
West Bengal	11.25	18.08

Political Empowerment

To ensure people participation, the 73rd and 74th amendments to the Constitution of India brought about a three tier representative Government at the district level and below. The most striking point with regard to these amendments is one third reservation of elected officers for women and Sc's/ST's in proportion to their population. Adequate representation of women and weaker secctions will certainly bring qualitative change in the functioning of panchayats. For the socio-economic advancement and empowerment of women gender specific interventions are warranted for several reasons including development of the nation is hampered if half its problems lag behind whether in political participation or in socio-economic empowerment. Since the status of a group or individual in society is determined mainly by the extent of power they yield in public life, political power can certainly be expected to pave the way for the emancipation and higher status of women. In this context the National Women Commission noted that the greatest event for women's empowerment in India since Independence is, undoubtedly, the amendments to the Constitution reserving one third seats for women in Panchayats and Nagarpalikas, thereby empowering women to participation in the political process at the grass root level.

The National Women Commission also held consultations with women's organisations expert and State Governments and planned to organise and develop training modules for elected Panchayat members. It is proposed to pursue this furthers in the coming days. Having witnessed the encouraging presence of women in panchayats and urban civic bodies, it is our turn now to look at women's participation at the state and national level.

Table 28.3 : Representation of Women Members from First to Thirteenth Lok Sabha

Lok Sabha	*Total Seats*	*No. of Women Contested*	*No. of Women Elected*	*Percentage of Women Elected*	*No. of Women Elected from West Bengal*
First (1952-57)	499	Data Not Available	22	4.4	1
Second (1957-62)	500	45	27	5.4	2
Third (1962-67)	503	70	34	6.7	2
Fourth (1967-71)	523	67	31	5.9	2
Fifth (1971-76)	521	86	22	4.2	2
Sixth (1977-80)	544	70	19	3.4	2
Seventh(1980-84)	544	142	28	5.1	2
Eight (1985-90)	544	162	44	8.1	5
Ninth (1990-91)	517	198	27	5.2	2
Tenth (1991-96)	544	325	39	7.18	3
Eleventh (1996)	544	599	40*	7.18	4
Twelfth (1998)	544	271	44*	8.8	5
Thirteenth (1999)	542	NA	48	8.86	5

Source : Press Information Bureau, Government of India.
Note: *One member nominated by the President of India.

Table 28.3 shows that the number of women Members of Parliament from the state had gone up to 5 but plummeted in the two subsequent Lok Sabhas. This is also all-Indian trend during the same period.

Conclusion :

A society that denies awakening and enlightenment to women, who constitute half its member is like a building without a foundation. It is bound to founder. Without philosophical or mental revolution among the women there cannot be any social change. There must be a fundamental change on a national level. We are soaring in the skies of scientific advancement.

It has been observed that women who are elected are not always treated with due respect. Many elected women complained that their suggestions were not considered seriously nor were they consulted while decisions were being made. Some felt their views were ignored only because they are women. At times they were pressurised by their husbands to approve their decisions made by the male dominated Panchayats. It has also been noticed that reservation played a vital role in quantitative participation of women but in a patriarchal social structure a number of complementary intervention are to be needed.

Rural Development in the initial period built infrastructure. Now it is in the lives of the people, particularly women, as have to engage themselves in activities which in many ways do not benefit them directly.

Bibliography

Bagchi, J. (2005) *The Changing Status of Women in West Bengal 1970 – 2000 The challenge Ahead*

Behera, M.C. (2006) *Globalising Rural Development Competing Paradigms and Emerging Realities*

Chakravarty, U. (2011). Binging Gender into History : Women, Property and Reproduction. *Economic and Political Weekly*

Ghatak, M. (2002) Recent Reforms in the Panchayat System in West Bengal Towards Greater Participatory Governance *Economic and Political Weekly*

Purohit, B.R. and S. Joshi *Social Justice in India*

Sharma, B.M. and R. Singh (2004) *Good Governance, Globalisation and Civil Society*

Sharma, K. (2011) Small Loans Big Dreams : Women and Microcredit in a Globalising Economy. *Economic and Political Weekly*

Sing, K. (2010) *Rural Development In India : Retrospect and Prospects*

Tandon, R.K. (1998) *Women In Modern India*

29

Malnutrition among Young Adult Male Gond Tribals of Sirki Village, Chhattisgarh

Shatruhan Singh Shyam, Huidrom Suraj Singh and Subal Das

The ethnicity based cross-sectional study was carried out in Sirki village of Korba District in Chhattisgarh in October 2012 to assess the prevalence of undernutrition among the young adults. Undernutrition was evaluated using World Health Organization (WHO) Body Mass Index (BMI) and MUAC cut-off points respectively. A total of 200 males aged 19 to 33 years were measured for weight, height and Mid-Upper Arm Circumference (MUAC). The overall prevalence of undernutrition using BMI and MUAC were 21.5per cent and 53.5 per cent. According to WHO classification (1995) of the public health problem of low BMI, based on adult populations worldwide, the young males of this tribe were in serious condition. Nutritional intervention is needed for them to overcome with this situation.

Tribals are the most vulnerable section of our country with respect to health and nutritional status (Das & Bose, 2012). Tribal comprises 8.1 per cent (Census of India, 2011) of the total population of the country. More than 675 (approx) tribals resides in India. Chhattisgarh is notable for the high proportion of Scheduled Tribes. Out of the total population of Chhattisgarh, Tribals constitute at least 32.5 per cent, which is highly significant figure. The tribes of Chhattisgarh are mostly a primitive ethnic group who faithfully follow all traditional customs and their archetypal age-old ritual. The oldest and most populous tribe of Chhattisgarh is the Gonds. The Gonds Tribals, who are also recognised as the Koytorias are widely dispersed throughout the state. The unique and one of a kind *Ghotul* marriage tradition of the Gonds is renowned all across the world. Present research dealt with the study of prevalence of under-nutrition among studied Gond males.

The ethnic based cross-sectional descriptive study was conducted in the village of Sirki of Pali Block of Korba District in Chhattisgarh to evaluate the nutritional status of young adult males. A total of 200 males were selected purposefully from the said village. Data were collected on a pre-designed and pre-tested schedule by house to house visit by one of the author (SSS). Weight, height and MUAC were measured using the standard methodology (Lohman et al., 1988). Under-nutrition was evaluated using BMI (< 18.5 kg/m^2) and MUAC (d" 23.0 cm) of the WHO standard.

The mean age in years of Gond males were (26.14 ± 4.17). Table 29.1 shows the (mean ± standard deviation, minimum & maximum and prevalence of CED and malnutrition based on BMI and MUAC) of used anthropometric variables of the adult males belonging to Gond community. The rates of under-nutrition (CED; BMI d" 18.5 kg/m^2) in male Gonds were observed to be high (21.5 per cent) (Serious situation) and using MUAC were found to have very high (53.8 per cent) (Critical situation). Conclusion drawn from present study was that the male Gonds of Sirki village was experiencing high to very high rate of under-nutrition using above mentioned indicators. Nutrition implementation program should be given to them for overcome the said situation. Moreover, the prevalence of under-nutrition in this study is less than most of the studied tribal population in India and more than few of them (4). Adults (young ones) at the age range of 19-33 years are very crucial with respect to their reproductive life because at this stage they begin their parenthood and if they were undernourished the future generation will obvious lag behind with respect to their health perspectives and with their reference median population values.

Table 29.1 : Descriptive Statistics and Nutritional Status of the Male Gond Tribals (N=200)

Variable	*Mean*	*Std. Deviation*	*Minimum*	*Maximum*
AGE (years)	26.14	4.17	19	34
Weight (kg.)	56.64	8.01	29	78
Height (cm.)	167.38	5.58	139.80	177.20
MUAC (cm.)	23.76	3.10	17.00	32.00
BMI (kg./m.^{2})	20.17	2.56	12.93	28.83
(BMI < 18.5; kg./m^2)			(MUAC $\leq$ 23.0 cm)	
Normal	CED*	Overweight	Under-nutrition	Normal
72.5 per cent	21.5 per cent	6.0 per cent	53.8 per cent	46.2 per cent

References

Das, S., and Bose, K. (2012). Age and sex variations in body mass index and chronic energy deficiency among adult Santals of Purulia district, West Bengal. India. *In New Trends in Body Mass Index Research edited by Alard Vermeulen and Edme De Smet (Eds.).* NOVA Publishers Inc, pp-81-96; 2012.

Census of India 2011. Instruction Manual for Houselisting and Housing Census. http://censusindia.gov.in/2011-Documents/Houselistingper cent20English.pdf

Tribes of Chhattisgarh. http://www.indianetzone.com/50/tribes_chhattisgarh.htm.2010.

Lohman T. G., Roche A. F. and Martorell, R. (1988). Anthropometric Standardisation Reference Manual. Human Kinetics Books, Chicago.

Index

J

K

L